THE DECLINE OF THE CALIFORNIOS

THE DECLINE OF THE

Californios

A SOCIAL HISTORY OF THE SPANISH-SPEAKING CALIFORNIANS, 1846-1890

by *Leonard Pitt*

UPDATED WITH A NEW FOREWORD
BY RAMÓN A. GUTIÉRREZ

UNIVERSITY OF CALIFORNIA PRESS
BERKELEY, LOS ANGELES, LONDON

UNIVERSITY OF CALIFORNIA PRESS

BERKELEY AND LOS ANGELES, CALIFORNIA

UNIVERSITY OF CALIFORNIA PRESS, LTD.

LONDON, ENGLAND

ISBN: 0-520-21958-9 (PBK. : ALK. PAPER)

LIBRARY OF CONGRESS CATALOG CARD NUMBER: 66-13564

PRINTED IN THE UNITED STATES OF AMERICA

08 07 06 05 04 03 02 01 00

9 8 7 6 5 4 3 2

THE PAPER USED IN THIS PUBLICATION MEETS THE MINIMUM
REQUIREMENTS OF ANSI / NISO Z39.48-1992 (R 1997)
(PERMANENCE OF PAPER). ∞

TO DALE

Contents

And Ahab spake unto Naboth, saying, Give me thy vineyard that I may have it for a garden of herbs because it is near unto my house: and I will give thee for it a better vineyard than it; or, if it seem good to thee the worth of it in money.

And Naboth said to Ahab, The Lord forbid it me, that I should give the inheritance of my fathers unto thee.

I Kings 21

Foreword

by Ramón A. Gutiérrez

Thirty-two years have passed since the 1966 publication of Leonard Pitt's path-breaking work, *The Decline of the Californios: A Social History of the Spanish-Speaking Californians, 1846–1890.* Over the course of these years, thousands of readers have been profoundly influenced by this all-time best-selling book of California history. Some have turned to *The Decline of the Californios* seeking answers for problems that ethnic Mexicans have faced in California since 1848. Others have fingered the book's pages, savored its delicious prose, become thoroughly engrossed in its gripping narrative, reading with sheer delight this historical work of art. An updated edition of the book is testament to its enduring scholarly legacy, to the importance of the questions Pitt posed, which are as significant today as they were over three decades ago.

Pitt began working on *The Decline of the Californios* during the early 1950s as a history doctoral student at the University of California, Los Angeles. Of Jewish Polish immigrant stock, freshly transplanted from New York City, in Los Angeles Pitt became intensely interested in the condition of California's "Spanish-speaking population." At UCLA Pitt studied with John W. Caughey, who had himself been a student of Hubert Howe Bancroft, the famous historian of the American West whose collections established the Bancroft Library at the University of California, Berkeley. This intellectual tie to Bancroft later proved important; as Pitt scoured the archives seeking sources with which to chronicle the Californios' decline, he relied extensively on the transcribed interviews—the Californio narratives, as they are called—that Bancroft and his assistants collected at the end of the nineteenth century.

The Decline of the Californios began fortuitously. As Pitt recalls, "I met Professor Paul Taylor at Berkeley. He was the person who urged me to write a history of the Spanish-speaking people of California as my dissertation. Carey McWilliams's 1949 book, *North From Mexico: The Spanish-Speaking People of the United States*, so inspired me that I tried to model my own book after his."[1] Today few would dispute that Pitt matched and even superseded McWilliams's work, writing one of the most moving histories of California, one that is deeply empathic toward its subjects yet brutally honest about Anglo prejudice and past discrimination toward ethnic Mexicans.

In *The Decline of the Californios*, Pitt told with great pathos and power the story of the displacement of California's ethnic Mexican ranching elite, primarily in Southern California. Beginning his history with early Anglo-American contacts in the 1820s, Pitt chronicled the social and cultural conflicts that followed the Bear Flag Rebellion, the War between the United States and Mexico, the Gold Rush, and the demographic onslaught of the mid–nineteenth century. By studying the Californios, Pitt sought to understand the process of submerging "'alien' cultures into the American melting pot." At the time, Pitt thought that the Californios represented "an instance of the worldwide defeat of the relatively static, traditionalist societies by societies that were oriented to technology and the idea of progress."[2]

Since its appearance, *The Decline of the Californios* has been greeted largely with fame and acclaim, spawning historical monographs by several generations of younger scholars but also provoking caustic critique. Pitt wrote a history of the state's Spanish-speakers from 1846 to 1890, but by focusing on language as the principle marker of oppositional identity, he overlooked other equally important stratifying marks, particularly those of class, race, gender, generation, and place. To fully comprehend the differences between elite Californio ranchers and lowlier town dwellers, or *pobladores*, today one must read *The Decline of the Californios* alongside Albert Camarillo's *Chicanos in a Changing Society: From Mexican Pueblos to American Barrios in Santa Barbara and Southern California, 1848–1930*, Richard Griswold del Castillo's *The Los Angeles Barrio, 1850–1890: A Social History*, and Ricardo Romo's *East Los Angeles: The History of a Barrio*.[3] All of these monographs were written by Chicano-identified historians who claimed "insider" knowledge of the ethnic Mexican cultures they studied. Logically they found complexity, discovering ethnic, racial, generational, and class variations where Pitt saw only a homogenized Californio identity.

In the themes he articulated while writing *The Decline of the Cali-*

fornios in the early 1960s, Pitt gave scant attention to larger structural forces such as imperialism, state violence, economic expansionism, and the power of ideology, such as Manifest Destiny. However, by 1966, when *The Decline of the Californios* first appeared, the Watts Riots of 1965 had occurred; the war in Vietnam was rapidly escalating; and César Chávez had, in 1965, brought attention to the plight of Mexican agricultural workers by leading a pilgrimage from the fields of Delano to the state's capitol in Sacramento. In this climate of social unrest and egalitarian possibilities the Chicano political identity movement began, seeking to understand the past, critically assess the present, and imagine a future of different possibilities.

The *Decline of the Californios* was pulled into the vortex of these political events both wittingly and unwittingly. The first generation of Chicano historians who self-consciously set out to write critical histories of the displacement of their ancestral group—historians such as Albert Camarillo, Richard Griswold del Castillo, and Ricardo Romo—were all profoundly influenced by Pitt's framing of the issues. Pitt had written the first history from the point of view of the Californios who had lost all of their wealth, power, and position. Each of these historians complicated, illuminated, and expanded the story Pitt told, but, in addition, they also paid greater attention to the burning issues of the day: imperialism, racism, and political empowerment.

Readers eager to know of the racial injustices of the past greeted *The Decline of the Californios* with applause. But the acclaim was far from uniform. Some critics deemed the work racist and politically duplicitous. Raymond V. Padilla's searing "A Critique of Pittian History" blasted Pitt for perpetuating a romantic fiction of the Californio past, for depicting the Californios as static and tradition-bound, decimated because of their own inability to change in the face of a "progressive" Anglo-American culture. While Watts stood in ashes, Pitt clung to hollow notions of historical objectivity that were ill-suited to the deathly struggles of the day, Padilla complained. What was necessary, thought Padilla, was a Chicano-inspired rendering of the past, written by and for Chicanos, not Anglo-written histories that simply legitimated and rationalized Chicano subordination.[4]

Pitt never explicitly responded to Padilla's critique, or to any other, in print. But that he was influenced by the political mobilization of Chicanos in California and by some of the criticism that greeted his work, there is no doubt. In 1970, when the third printing of *The Decline of the Cali-*

fornios was released, this edition included in the concluding chapter a greatly extended footnote—note 20a—which stated, among other things: "[T]he Californios were the victims of an imperial conquest.... The United States, which had long coveted California for its trade potential and strategic location, finally provoked a war to bring about the desired ownership."[5] Why was the footnote added? "Rudy Acuña, my friend and colleague for many years at the California State University at Northridge, convinced me that I had to add it," Pitt explained. Acuña, a Chicano historian and long-time Los Angeles political activist, recalled that he persuaded Pitt to add the footnote to acknowledge the role that the United States government played in the War with Mexico, and to demonstrate solidarity with the movements of oppressed peoples at home and in the Third World.[6] Like Carey McWilliams who had inspired him, Pitt had set out to write a pro-Californio account. That some Chicano activists in the late 1960s read his tome as anti-Chicano was clearly disturbing to Pitt, given his own social and political sympathies.[7]

Today, with over three decades of new critical historical scholarship on California, most of the criticism of *The Decline of the Californios* is easy to understand. Much of the romanticism about Mexican California and the narrative of quick and utter demise of the Californios under American rule, which so centrally infused Pitt's account, was a product of the historical sources he used. Hubert H. Bancroft and his assistants collected the Californio narratives, which Pitt exploited so well in his work. However, at the end of the nineteenth century, not all the Californios were asked, or, for that matter, were willing to talk to Bancroft's assistants about what life had been like before and after the American conquest. The partiality of the views recorded in Bancroft's Californio narratives, the social context in which they were gathered, and the inordinately large role they have played in the writing of California's past ever since is only now beginning to be understood. In *My History, Not Yours: The Formation of Mexican American Autobiography*, Genaro M. Padilla has studied the oppositional discourses and strategies of textual resistance to conquest embedded in these narratives.[8] Rosaura Sánchez, in her *Telling Identities: The Californio Testimonios*, likewise examines Bancroft's narratives both as literary texts and as artifacts that can be used to understand the ways in which space structures identity.[9]

Chicano historian Douglas Monroy, in *Thrown Among Strangers: The Making of Mexican Culture in Frontier California*, has brought a com-

FOREWORD xi

plexity to our understanding of Mexican California by looking at Indian-white relations, by disentangling class fractions and frictions among the Californios, and particularly by exploring those forces that generated gender inequality and sexual exploitation.[10] Though she takes a longer historical sweep, Lisbeth Haas, in *Conquests and Historical Identities in California, 1769–1936*, writes a relational history of social groups under colonial and neocolonial rule, and by so doing illuminates the oppositional role that culture can play in the structuring of geography, memory, and identity.[11] And any student interested in knowing how the Californios were shaped and how they in turn shaped their environment,[12] how continental ideologies ruminated in Alta California,[13] and how complex a balance of power existed between local indigenous chieftains and the elite Californio ranching class[14] should survey the essays gathered in *Contested Eden: California Before The Gold Rush*, edited by myself and Richard J. Orsi. None of these themes were central to Pitt's project.

Pitt's *The Decline of the Californios* was a product of its time—but a time that it has not outlived. Pitt was concerned about the late-nineteenth century assimilation of the Californios at the very moment, in 1965, that massive numbers of Mexican immigrants were beginning to enter the United States. He took the subject position of the Californios he chronicled. He wrote a relational history of social groups before it was widely accepted that groups could not easily be studied in isolation of one another. He was profoundly concerned about bigotry, prejudice, and discrimination—issues still ever potent in California. And he told this history with passion, verve, and tireless archival density and research. These are some of the elements that account for the continued importance of Pitt's *The Decline of the Californios*.

San Diego
September 1998

NOTES

1. Personal telephone interview with Leonard Pitt, August 16, 1998.
2. Leonard Pitt, *The Decline of the Californios: A Social History of the Spanish-Speaking Californians, 1846–1890* (Berkeley and Los Angeles: University of California Press, 1966), p. viii.
3. Albert Camarillo, *Chicanos in a Changing Society: From Mexican Pueblos to American Barrios in Santa Barbara and Southern California, 1848–1930* (Cambridge: Harvard University Press, 1979); Richard Griswold del Castillo, *The Los Angeles Barrio, 1850–1890: A*

Social History (Berkeley and Los Angeles: University of California Press, 1979); Ricardo Romo, *East Los Angeles: The History of a Barrio* (Austin: University of Texas Press, 1983).

4. Raymond V. Padilla, "A Critique of Pittian History," *El Grito: A Journal of Contemporary Mexican-American Thought* 6, no. 1 (Fall 1972), pp. 3–41.

5. Pitt, *The Decline of the Californios*, p. 296.

6. Personal telephone interview with Rudy Acuña, August 21, 1998.

7. Pitt has asked that footnote 20a not be included in this edition.

8. Genaro M. Padilla, *My History, Not Yours: The Formation of Mexican American Autobiography* (Madison: University of Wisconsin Press, 1993).

9. Rosaura Sánchez, *Telling Identities: The Californio Testimonios* (Minneapolis: University of Minnesota Press, 1995).

10. Douglas Monroy, *Thrown Among Strangers: The Making of Mexican Culture in Frontier California* (Berkeley and Los Angeles: University of California Press, 1990).

11. Lisbeth Haas, *Conquests and Historical Identities in California, 1769–1936* (Berkeley and Los Angeles: University of California Press, 1995).

12. M. Kat Anderson, Michael G. Barbour, and Valerie Whitworth, "A World of Balance and Plenty: Land, Plants, Animals, and Humans in a Pre-European California," in *Contested Eden: California before the Gold Rush*, eds. Ramón A. Gutiérrez and Richard J. Orsi (Berkeley and Los Angeles: University of California Press, 1998), pp. 12–47.

13. Michael J. González, " 'The Child of the Wilderness Weeps for the Father of Our Country': The Indian and the Politics of Church and State in Provincial California," in *Contested Eden*, pp. 147–72.

14. Steven W. Hackel, "Land, Labor, and Production: The Colonial Economy of Spanish and Mexican California," in *Contested Eden*, pp. 111–46

Preface

"If one is to sympathize with the [old] Californians," Bernard De Voto asserted, "it must be only a nostalgic sympathy, a respect for things past." A statement of this kind, authoritative but condescending, can dampen one's enthusiasm for pursuing a study of the Californians; "nostalgic sympathy" may suffice to sustain antiquarians but not professed scholars. Yet in one sense De Voto's point is well taken: even in their heyday, the Spanish and Mexican Californians were numerically too small and culturally too backward to contribute to mankind much that was new or original. In the crowning phase of their evolution, the Yankees beat them badly and all but swept them into the dustbin of history.

Despite my initial doubts, however, the longer I worked on this project—a study of the Californians after De Voto's "year of decision, 1846"—the more I became convinced that it touched at least tangentially some large and consequential themes of history. Lost causes have a way of illuminating winning ones. Thus, the desperate effort of the vanquished to maintain their birthright even in defeat seemed to explain the central meaning of Manifest Destiny, which provided the initial stimulus in the Yankee's westward drive (an event De Voto has described with unsurpassed brilliance). That the 400,000 victors in this historic confrontation never ceased explaining away the mere 10,000 vanquished, as if nagged by pangs of conscience, itself seemed a phenomenon worthy of study. Viewed from this perspective, sympathy is misplaced if bestowed on the Californians only, for it is owing to the bemused Yankees nearly as much as to their victims.

The present study is, by its very definition, state history. Perhaps it is also a contribution to local history—that of southern California—and to American social history. There is little point in trying to pin the right

xiii

label on it, for each reader is free to accept it or not, as he pleases. But I conceive of this work primarily as a phase of the ethnic history of California and of the United States. It is part and parcel of the story of immigration and nativism, of the confrontation of Anglo-Saxons with persons of other cultures, of the submergence of those "alien" cultures into the American melting pot. One curious twist, though, is that in California the dominant Yankees are for once cast in the role of immigrants, while the "foreigners" are native-born. Even more broadly considered, I see this study as an instance of the worldwide defeat of the relatively static, traditionalist societies by societies that were oriented to technology and the ideal of progress. Although that struggle occurred widely in the course of European expansionism, the fascinating thing is that it occurred only rarely on American soil. For, prior to the Mexican War the United States had not actually defeated and absorbed an entire culture, except that of the Indians. It is this that gives the fate of the Californians a special poignancy and meaning.

Like every local or state historian who tries to see the largest possible implications for his work, I, too, have attempted to see the "macrocosm in the microcosm." If this conception of my work sounds too grandiose, it is balanced by the very mundane and practical aspect of this investigation: the role of California's contemporary Spanish-speaking minority is at once enormously important and enormously misunderstood, and thus in need of elucidation. Hence, what follows may at the very least be taken as an effort to go back to first instances in order to shed light on a contemporary social issue.

My approach has been not only to dig into the materials much more deeply than previous authors but, wherever possible, to let the subjects speak for themselves—a method that has, I hope, added value to this book. I show, in essence, that the current predicament of the Spanish-speaking has far deeper and older roots than might appear to those who reckon time from the Mexican Revolution of 1910, or from World War I and the mass migration northward which followed. No doubt, the twentieth-century influx from Mexico of Spanish-speaking is the most important, but long before it came, the dominant group had carved out the channels into which it would flow. Encrustations of prejudicial laws, traditions, and attitudes are older and stronger than one who dates events from but one generation ago might suppose.

The terminology used in this work poses some problems. The central concern here is with the native-born Californians, or *Californios*, and to a lesser extent with Mexican immigrants. The term that covers both groups without offending either and at the same time does not smack of jargon is "Spanish-speaking." Although it was never used conversationally in the nineteenth century and is slightly cumbersome, it nevertheless focuses on the lowest common denominator of the Spanish-Mexican heritage—language—and for that reason seems most applicable. (Carey McWilliams first used it to good advantage in his *North from Mexico: The Spanish-Speaking People of the United States.*) This and other specialized terms appearing frequently in my work are explained in the glossary of ethnic terms at the end of the book.

The sources, too, presented a variety of problems. For one thing, many of the data that had to be culled from the available materials were submerged in a veritable quagmire of sentimentality and myth. For another, subjectivity apart, the accuracy of some personal reminiscences may be questioned because California's Spanish-speaking were largely illiterate, and because some of them who did write, or who were able to dictate their personal memoirs, often did so late in life and from memory. Moreover, the bulk of extant data was provided by the articulate few, who do not necessarily represent the mass of their countrymen, or—even worse—was provided by Americans, who were largely biased. Finally, the available records on some old-line California communities in the north were so sketchy that I was compelled to dispense with the idea of writing a geographically comprehensive account. Instead, this work dwells primarily on southern California, despite the unfortunate imbalance that results.

Fortunately, the work of many previous writers has simplified my work. Monographs, books, and articles written by California specialists from Hubert Howe Bancroft onward, and also the contributions of antiquarians, have guided the direction of my research. Carey McWilliams' *North from Mexico* deserves special mention, for although it was constructed largely from secondary works, it provides innumerable insights and seminal ideas for the specialized researcher. (It is still the best general survey work in the field.) The accessibility of data at the Huntington Library, the Bancroft Library, and other repositories of course made this work possible in the first place, and the cooperation of the librarians at these institutions made it a true pleasure. Dr. Jackson Mayer's personal collection of material on southern California also was of great assistance.

I am grateful to the Henry E. Huntington Library and Art Gallery for permission to reproduce the photographs used as illustrations in this volume.

I am greatly indebted to Professor John W. Caughey for guiding my graduate studies in this subject at the University of California, Los Angeles, and to Professor Aubry C. Land who, as chairman of the Department of History at the University of Maryland, made funds available to complete the research and writing. The Huntington Library has my thanks for a summer grant-in-aid. My former colleague at Maryland, Frank Otto Gatell, provided unrelenting but welcome and necessary stylistic criticism. The Reverend Francis Weber, O.F.M., of Queen of Angels Seminary read the manuscript in part, and Andrew Rolle of Occidental College read it in its entirety and supplied valuable criticisms of its content, which I have tried to incorporate into the text. Miss Ruth Mueller of the University of California Press gave the manuscript a most meticulous final reading. Miss Marcia Buehler and Mrs. Sharon Smith did much of the typing, and Mrs. Martha Barcus did the index, for which I am thankful. Finally I owe a debt of gratitude to my wife, Dale, above all for her forbearance.

L. P.

San Fernando Valley State College
Northridge, California

Halcyon Days:
Mexican California,
1826-1845

CALIFORNIANS caught an early glimpse of the modern era on November 20, 1818, when the Argentine pirate and patriot, Hippolyte de Bouchard, seized Monterey to imbue it with the "spirit of liberty." His hopes were soon dashed, however, when the men of Monterey neither rallied to his noble banner nor fought him, but instead preferred to stay at home with their panicking womenfolk and children. "Liberator" Bouchard, understandably discouraged, sacked the town and sailed away at the first opportunity.[1] Ten years more would elapse before California would feel ready for "liberation" and for the ideas that shattered Spanish power and inaugurated social revolution throughout Latin America.

The school of thought that celebrates the Spanish era as California's golden age marks its decline with Bouchard's raid, or, more properly, with the arrival of Mexican Governor José María Echeandía in 1826. This school argues that the saintly piety of the mission fathers and the heroism of the *conquistadores* gave way to the cruelty, materialism, and bathos of the Mexican *políticos*. *Liberalismo* became the villain, an ideology whose effect George Tays likened to that of a "malignant

---

[1] Mariano G. Vallejo, "Recuerdos históricos y personales tocante a la Alta California: ... 1769–1849," 1875, MS, Bancroft Library (Berkeley, Calif.), II, 83–97; Peter Corney, *Voyages in the Northern Pacific* (Honolulu, 1896), pp. 119–138.

malarial epidemic." [2] Another school regards the Mexican era as the "true Arcadia," the culmination of the promise inherent in the Spanish beginnings.[3] In considering the decline of Hispanic California it is, however, more relevant to assess the Californians' own response to Mexicanization and gauge its future implications, rather than to bemoan or celebrate it. The problem, in other words, is to delineate the leading tendencies of the era 1826 to 1846 and to learn how they conditioned the Californians for their final ordeal, the confrontation with *Americanos.*

In 1826, California's Spanish heritage was still in strong evidence.[4] Only one generation separated California from the pioneer stage, a fact still obvious in the crudity and sparseness of settlement. Stretched along a 500-mile coastline, the "rationals," the *gente de razón,* numbered about 8,000 and in Monterey, the capital, 300. From the beginning, California had been little more than an outpost of empire, a remote frontier. Since the province lay at the farthest reaches of New Spain, itself a Spanish colony, California's colonial status was twice removed. This geographic and political isolation bred provincialism. An essentially medieval and clerical society, California had twenty-one Franciscan missions which subordinated all and sundry to their will. Neither the military officers at the *presidios,* nor the civilians in the *pueblos* and *ranchos,* could rival the power of the padres in their heyday.

The Spanish heritage, however, compared with the Mexican, creaked with decrepitude. Thus, liberalismo kept filtering into the province despite a wall of conservatism. Mariano Vallejo, ten years old during Bouchard's raid, gradually caught the drift of world history and acknowledged of those "liberators" that "patriotism was their incentive and liberty their god." [5] The idealism of youth made a rebel of Vallejo,

[2] George Tays, "Revolutionary California: The Political History of California during the Mexican Period, 1820–1848" (rev. ed.; unpublished Ph.D. dissertation, University of California, Berkeley, 1934), p. iv.

[3] See, for example, Gertrude Atherton, *The Splendid Idle Forties* (New York, 1902).

[4] This chapter leans most heavily on Hubert Howe Bancroft, *History of California* (I–IV, San Francisco, 1884–1890), still the most useful account of pre-Yankee days; see also his *California Pastoral, 1796–1848* (San Francisco, 1888); Irving Berdine Richman, *California under Spain and Mexico, 1535–1847* . . . (Boston, 1911); and Nellie Van de Grift Sanchez, *Spanish Arcadia* (Los Angeles, 1929), a "social" history.

[5] "Historia," quoted in Tays, *op. cit.,* p. 83.

but he was forced to bide his time because his elders remained "all very much attached" to king and pope and "prayed at the break of dawn, at noon, at sunset, and at bedtime." His young nephew, Juan Bautista Alvarado, and their cousin, José Castro, also became rebels. These three young "conspirators" formed a secret junta for the study of politics and history and had absorbed a good dose of *radicalismo* by 1826, when Governor José María Echeandía arrived and became the chief resident apostle of the new ideology. In 1831, young Mariano boarded a Mexican vessel and took home a small library of banned books. As ill luck would have it, his sweetheart reported the "sin" to a priest, who promptly caught the youths red-handed with a forbidden work (*Telemachus*) and commanded them to yield the books, go to confession, and do penance. Much to the horror of their relatives, especially their mothers and sisters, the trio refused and were unofficially "ex-communicated." [6]

This circle of Monterey youths was experiencing nothing more than the awakening typical of the Creoles of Mexico and, indeed, of all Latin America. Because they lived on the farthest perimeters of revolution, they caught only partial glimpses and heard merely fugitive rumors of the main movements many months, and even years, later. Nevertheless, the message came through: They began to yearn vaguely for education, the reduction of clerical power, freedom of expression, liberation of bondsmen, the end of colonial status, and self-government. However belatedly, the Enlightenment was overturning the old order. Castro, Vallejo, and Alvarado soon had accomplices in every community—Carlos and José Antonio Carrillo of Santa Barbara; Juan Bandini, a Peruvian resident of San Diego; the brothers Pio and Andrés Pico at Los Angeles; Santiago Arguëllo; and Pablo de Portilla —until eventually most of the younger generation and some of their elders professed the liberal heresy proudly.

The first mutation caused by the spread of *liberalismo* was in the religious realm. The temporal authority of the clerics continued to annoy the younger men as they matured. As a grown man, Don Mariano flatly refused to pay a tithe to finance the "impracticable" schemes of the first bishop of California, Bishop García Diego, although he never rejected Catholicism itself and single-handedly patronized the village

⁶ Quoted in *ibid.*, p. 64.

chapel at Sonoma. Outright resistance among the communicants everywhere except in Santa Barbara left the Bishop virtually penniless and paralyzed.[7] At the same time, the new generation deliberately rejected Spanish forms of piety. Domestic devotions fell off among the male part of the population until, by the end of the Mexican régime, Sunday Mass had become an affair for women, children, and neophyte Indians; men participated in the livelier religious fiestas, but as nominal Catholics only. Doubtless, the decline of Catholicism represented an unfortunate disintegration of a unitary way of life. Yet, liberalism was a satisfactory surrogate for religion, and religious change probably prepared the Californians for a future life in a pluralistic society.

Politically, California remained wrapped in its cocoon until 1831. It then began to stir out, goaded by Yankees and Mexicans made restive by a willful Mexican governor, Manuel Victoria, whose credo was "love of order, respect for authority and constant consecration to duty."[8] Although vague at first and always beclouded by petty interests, rebel aspirations hardened during a score of rebellions in the next fifteen years. Among the more important episodes was the unsuccessful assault of the Sonoran *vaqueros* of Los Nietos (near Los Angeles) against Governor José Figueroa in 1834; the attack on Governor Mariano Chico in 1835, which ousted him; and, most important, the uprising of the "federalists" Alvarado and Castro against the "centralist" governor, Nicolás Gutiérrez, in 1836, which secured the province virtual self-government. Thereafter, the Californians had many fallings-out among themselves until José Castro was about to battle Pio Pico in 1846, when the sudden intrusion of Captain John C. Frémont's "topographical engineers" ended that squall. By then, however, the Californians had realized their most important aspirations: autonomy within the Mexican Republic, separation of the military and civilian branches of government, and secularization of the missions.

Republicanism created new offices and expanded old ones, and thus gave the local gentry a practical knowledge of self-government. The numerous ceremonial positions aside, many offices carried an authority that nurtured in the incumbents a degree of sophistication. In a short

---

[7] Mariano Guadalupe Vallejo, "Documentos para la historia de California," 1874, MS, Bancroft Library, XI, 347–350; Bancroft, *History of California*, IV, 373.

[8] Tays, *op. cit.*, p. 147.

time hundreds of Californians served as governors, delegates to the Mexican Congress and the provincial junta, prefects, alcaldes, *juezes del campó* (judges of the plain), and representatives in the town councils and thus passed through a political or an administrative apprenticeship. Most observers questioned whether many *Californios* ever graduated to the rank of "journeyman"; Mexican Governor Chico asserted that all but a few Californians were "intimidated by energy and . . . bluster." [9] Yet, even as apprentices they were not as bumbling as the Mexicans and Yankees made them out to be; Chico discovered this when they turned on him and sent him packing from the province.

As preparation for service in gringo government, however, the old politics proved only partly useful. Its stock-in-trade was intrigue, not debate; rebellion, not compromise; élite leadership, not mass support; and, of course, the flaming *pronunciamiento*. When everything else failed, men reached for their guns. Such tactics conformed badly with the Anglo-Saxon scheme of things.

Because the Californians mixed serious ideological goals with naïve methods, their politics assumed a tragicomic air. Like the tribes of the Stone Age ever preparing for war but rarely fighting, the Californios cultivated a state of perpetual excitement which culminated in anticlimactic decrees or minor skirmishes; three casualties in one of these fights would represent a major tragedy. Some of the rebels themselves complained of speeches that rang too gloriously, of *políticos* who were too soft-hearted, of "great struggles" that were more like comic-opera episodes. Governor Carlos Carrillo, the first native-born governor, knew that his own family laughingly compared him to Sancho Panza.[10]

By Anglo-Saxon standards, California government came to be judged invidiously. Weighed properly by Latin-American standards, however, in the perspective of the movement for independence in the Spanish Empire, it fares much better. Viewed that way, correctly, California demonstrates an impressive unanimity on fundamental principles. After about 1835, scarcely a single active royalist remained in the

[9] Mariano Chico, Confidential Report, Aug. 30, 1836, quoted in Tays, *op. cit.*, p. 306.
[10] Tays, *op. cit.*, p. 457.

6   HALCYON DAYS

realm, nor a major civilian opponent of secularization of the missions. The "religious question," which then wracked all of Latin America, yielded to acclimation in California. That province demonstrated, further, a talent for leadership. Local leaders had to manufacture civil government from the whole cloth, with little formal preparation, and had to work in a province of vast distances without steady finances, military support, and genuine respect from the mother country. Yet, they accomplished their main goals. Best of all, they shed less blood and destroyed less property in the process than any comparable group of Latin Americans.

The new era produced yet another innovation: an ambivalence toward Mexico and things Mexican. Though freely mimicking Mexico's new ideology, the Californios struggling for autonomy learned to despise the bearers of that ideology—governors, soldiers, and colonists from *la otra banda* (the other shore). Since, among the upstanding citizens of Mexico, "to speak of California was like mentioning the end of the world,"[11] the government had to empty the jails of Sinaloa and Sonora to encourage colonization and military occupation of the northern part of the province. As a sort of Siberian work camp, California acquired hosts of petty thieves and political prisoners—18 in 1825, 200 in 1829, 130 in 1830, and so on. Those convicts usually arrived in a state of wretchedness exceeded only by that of the Indians. Bands of these so-called *cholos* (scoundrels) would brawl drunkenly on the public streets and commit theft and other assorted misdeeds—even homicide —while the political prisoners among them organized rebellions. This state of affairs greatly distressed the more genteel settlers.[12]

Second-generation Californians, although often themselves the children of cholos, nevertheless greeted the newcomers dismally, in many cases making no distinction between the outright felons and the dedicated colonists. In 1834, the Hijar-Padrés Colony, a group of respectable Mexican artisans, teachers, and tradesmen, had to flee northern

[11] Agustín Janssens, *The Life and Adventures of Don Agustín Janssens: 1834–1856*, ed. by William H. Ellison and Francis Price (San Marino, Calif., 1953), p. 11.
[12] Angustias de la Guerra Ord, *Occurrences in Hispanic California* (Washington, 1956), pp. 54–55.

California, while the *nativos* hounded them with cries of "Death to Mexico!" and "Kill the Mexicans!" [13]

Resisting the "degraded" influences of Mexico made men conscious of their California birth. In response to the new identity, the local nomenclature changed, until the native-born ceased calling themselves *Españoles* or *Mexicanos* and began to insist on the name *Californios*. The province was, however, vast, and the Californios felt the strongest ties to an immediate locale. This led to another innovation in the Mexican period, a north-south regional consciousness; it, too, proved divisive. Regionalism polarized around Monterey, Los Angeles, and Santa Barbara, although the latter town, often caught in a cross fire remained indifferent and confused. After the capital had been moved from Monterey to Los Angeles in 1835, each passing year intensified the rivalry until, in 1845, *abajeños* (southerners) and *arribeños* (northerners) were ready for open warfare. No matter what Alvarado or Castro wanted for Monterey, Pio Pico and others spitefully demanded the opposite for Los Angeles; when northerners spoke of stronger ties with Mexico, southerners espoused greater independence, and vice versa. The best that could come of this rivalry was a division of power and a truce. In 1846, Monterey's Castro seized control of the military headquarters and customhouse and gave the *Angeleño* Pico the governorship. North-south rivalries were further complicated by family feuds and personal ambitions, which later led to failures of communication and a lack of unity among the nativos—an inability to reach across space to make common cause against the superior gringo enemy. The final gift of political apprenticeship, then, was confusion and bickering.

Unquestionably, the chief reform of the Mexican era was secularization of the missions. Beginning in earnest after 1831, reaching full flood by 1839, and completed by 1845, secularization cut the last cord still linking California to its Spanish "mother." It upset class relations, altered ideology, and shifted the ownership of enormous wealth. It totally destroyed a fiefdom that in its heyday had included twenty-one

[13] Janssens, *op. cit.*, p. 55.

mission establishments, 15,000 Indian wards, great herds of livestock, millions of acres of land, and proceeds from a lucrative foreign trade. That revolutionary social and economic transformation was California's most important event before the discovery of gold; indeed, nothing in the experience of the Californios compares with it, except possibly the dissolution of the ranchos in the 1880's.[14]

That secularization came bloodlessly is a credit to both the padres and the civil officials. Authorized by the Mexican Constitution of 1824, it was set in motion late in Echeandía's régime by his decree of 1831 but made little headway until 1836. Even liberals conceded that the California Indians "do not possess the qualifications" for freedom and needed protection "against themselves," [15] a thought probably shared by the governor when he made a tentative promise of citizenship to the Indians and rather gingerly asked the friars to limit their floggings to fifteen lashes weekly and to allow married couples immediate freedom. Another governor sought to ease the friars out of their mission establishments and onto the frontier for new labors among the heathens, but he was unsuccessful. The most onerous burdens the government managed to impose on the missionaries were a mild civil tax and ideological sniping, both of which the Franciscans could handle with ease.

The Franciscans held nearly absolute sway over their communicants and threatened to resign en masse, should the government take more strenuous measures. A missionary strike would have brought a crippling work stoppage throughout the province. Fortunately, this threat never came to pass, since the friars settled for token resistance by refusing to swear allegiance to the Mexican constitution and by sermonizing against the republicans. They castigated the "radicals" who went among the Indians "preaching and dogmatizing that there was no hell." [16] Father Narciso Durán, head of the mission system, easily parried every thrust of the civil officials who were, in his words, "but yesterday savages" and are skilled at no greater art than horsemanship, yet presume to "teach the way to civilize men." [17] The fact that the Franciscans tried to prevent the *emancipados* from becoming slaves or

[14] Bancroft, *History of California*, IV, 61–63.
[15] Captain Portilla, quoted in Tays, *op. cit.*, p. 847.
[16] Alfred Robinson, *Life in California during a Residence of Several Years in That Territory* (San Francisco, 1891), pp. 152–156.
[17] Bancroft, *History of California*, III, 310.

savages and yet bowed graciously to the inevitability of secularization partly accounts for the absence of the bloodletting provoked elsewhere in Mexico by religious strife.

When the Californians took over the helm of provincial government in 1836, matters moved more swiftly. Doubtless, high ideals impelled them; but, whether a ranchero professed liberalismo and signed his letters "For God and Liberty!" or had no political persuasion at all, he knew that secularization might bring him wealth—he stood to gain whatever the padres and the Indians lost. The program thus proceeded apace in Alvarado's governorship, from 1836 to 1842. He sold or leased the mission lands and assets to private individuals for the supposed benefit of the creditors, of the government (which would collect a tax in the transaction), of the Indians (who would obtain land grants), and of the missionaries (who would be guaranteed subsistence).

The new owners and lessees began a rapid slaughter of mission livestock. By 1839, an investigation by Alvarado showed that two-thirds of the cattle had been butchered, three-quarters of the sheep, and half of the horses, for which the Franciscans and neophytes had received practically none of their rightful compensation. The governor, a better rebel than administrator, was guilty of favoritism and laxness, although not of lining his own pockets. To maintain the treasury, he issued drafts on mission property to government creditors, without recognizing the dwindling rate of mission inventories. His later attempt to reverse this policy and to salvage some property for the former mission inhabitants failed with the premature end of his term of office. By 1845, the original herds of 150,000 had dwindled to 50,000.

In the eyes of the gente de razón, Indian liberation had succeeded famously, but for the Indians themselves it was a painful experience. The neophytes were torn tragically between a secure, authoritarian existence and a free but anarchic one. Those who had spent their lives in the shadow of the Cross often rejected the proffered liberty, not out of fear of the padres' wrath but of the uncertainties of the outer world. Although examples of neophyte self-leadership were rare, Pacifico, an untypically forward young Indian of Mission San Buenaventura, demanded in 1828 that the 150 neophytes receive immediate release and land allotments. At best, however, the emancipados gained an illusory freedom. By 1829, the number of mission Indians had fallen from

15,000 to 4,500; by 1847 virtually all the remaining ones had gone free and either melted into the lower class of the pueblos, took up residence on the ranchos, went back to their *rancherías* (villages), or disappeared behind the pale. There, from 1836 to 1839, the "civilized" Indians stirred up their "wild" brethren so much that, in San Diego, for example, entire ranchos had to be abandoned. Even by the 1850's the neophytes remained a demoralized class, alternately a prey to disease, liquor, violence, submission, and exploitation.[18]

Mexican Governor Manuel Micheltorena, in 1843, gave the Franciscans a respite by calling a moratorium on secularization, an act that was of little use to the friars for lack of morale and of material support. California Governor Pico, who succeeded Micheltorena, returned to Alvarado's policy and, in fact, extended it by liquidating the missions altogether. For this some writers have maligned him, yet he evidently acted in good faith—perhaps even wisdom—since the remaining institutions were too small, too encumbered with debts, and too expensive for efficient operation. Through a controlled liquidation, Pico hoped to guarantee to the Indians some small measure of communal property, to the state a small tax, and to the friars subsistence. The final sale and lease of mission property came in May, 1845.[19]

The dethronement of the padres elevated the rancheros and introduced a new social order based on their authority. More than eight hundred of them shared in the carving up of 8 million prime acres. So swift was the division that, between 1841 and 1844, thirty new ranchos appeared in the Los Angeles district alone. Land in parcels up to 11 leagues could be had practically for the asking by those with the right connections or with a record of civil or military service. Some families obtained several great adjoining parcels and thus prevailed over 300,000 acres or more. By 1846, according to a list compiled by Thomas Oliver Larkin, forty-six men of substance, influence, or political power ruled California. They were largely self-made men, the *arriviste* corps of the recent past who had inherited little wealth from their fathers and mostly were landowners.[20]

---

[18] *Ibid.*, IV, 43–65; Ord, *op. cit.*, p. 25.

[19] Bancroft, *History of California*, IV, 369–371, 546–554; Fray Zephyrin Engelhardt, *The Missions and Missionaries of California* (Santa Barbara, Calif., 1929), I, 654 ff.

[20] Thomas Oliver Larkin, "Notes on the Personal Character of the Principal

The widespread distribution of land in Mexican California shaped a social structure notably different from that which evolved in the opposite end of the "Spanish borderland," New Mexico. In the province centering on Santa Fe, far fewer land grants were distributed relative to the size of the population. That society remained more rigid and more dependent upon the semifeudal bond between the *patrón* and his peons. New Mexican villages held the bulk of the population and became strong enough to resist disintegration even in the twentieth century. In California, village life tended to be eclipsed by rancho life. The availability of ranchland even to underlings, combined with the presence of an Indian laboring class to work that land, prevented the creation of a peon class among the gente de razón of California. Without peons, the patrón system lacked adequate grounding and developed only sketchily in California, whereas in New Mexico it had a powerful and lasting effect and merged with the American political and economic structure.[21]

The one institution that developed as strongly in California as in New Mexico was the family—a phenomenon that tends to underscore Margaret Mead's assertion that "to be Spanish American is to belong to a *familia*." [22] In California, the most important type of family was that of the ranchero. All lines of dependency radiated outward from his *casa* and embraced his children, his in-laws, other relatives, orphans, a bevy of Indian servants, sometimes also the residents of the nearest village. As Robert Glass Cleland puts it, the ranchero "provided a home for a host of poor relations, entertained strangers, as well as friends, . . . and begat as many sons and daughters as the Hebrew patriarchs of old." [23]

The ranchero, in effect, had inherited the esteem enjoyed by the patrón but not the peons customarily accompanying it. Ideally, his authority ran so deep that he could even legally flog his married children who already had their own offspring. In the more traditional households of Santa Barbara, youngsters solemnly kneeled and kissed papa's

Men," in George P. Hammond, ed., *The Larkin Papers, 1845–1846,* IV (Berkeley and Los Angeles, 1953), 322 ff.
[21] Florence R. Kluckhohn, Florence Rockwood, and Fred Strodtbeck, *Variations in Value Orientations* (Evanston, Ill., 1961), pp. 177–185.
[22] *Cultural Patterns and Technical Change* (New York, 1955), p. 153.
[23] *The Cattle on a Thousand Hills: Southern California, 1850–1880* (San Marino, Calif., 1951), p. 43.

hand before filing off to bed at night, and no son, not even one in his sixties, dared smoke, sit, or wear his hat in his father's presence without asking permission. Vallejo generalized: "In the breast of the old time Californians love of family was stronger than selfish and vile interest." Speaking of the Montereños who had clung to their casas instead of fighting off Bouchard, he estimated that "had they been Yankees it is likely that they would have acted differently." [24] Family feeling and respect for age thus produced powerful sentiments whose weakening the Californians would later find especially painful.

The entire economy depended on the production of cattle for the hide and tallow trade. Most rancheros also grazed sheep and horses, or raised grain crops or wine grapes. With the exception of soap, wine, and cloth, however, they rarely made finished products. The Yankees remonstrated with them about the neglect of other resources such as timber and fish, but the Californios showed no visible remorse; their rejoinder was that nobody starved in California, and that many enjoyed luxurious living. The gradual increase in shipping reduced California's long-standing economic isolation. As the traders from the United States and Britain took away larders of tallow and bales of dried skins, they introduced the finished products of the industrial revolution and some of the frills of more highly developed societies: furniture, dry goods, clothing, agricultural implements, salt, fireworks, and lumber. These imports reduced the crudities of frontier living and gave the gentry reason to regard themselves as enjoying the well-earned rewards of service to king or state—grandees without a court, aristocrats in a republic.

An orientation toward the present, not the past or the future, permeated the value system of the Californios. The "old mañana habit," to use Don Eugenio Plummer's term, [25] implied a satisfaction with what one had today. Men did not prepare for the future, as such. They did do hard work when it was necessary and did take pride in it, but more in anticipation of the fun that came right at the end of it, rather than for any anticipated distant need. Owing to a happy combination of good climate, ample land, and cheap Indian labor, the rancho order

---

[24] Quoted in Tays, *op. cit.*, p. 74.
[25] John Preston Buschlen, *Señor Plummer: The Life and Laughter of an Old Californian* (Los Angeles, 1942), p. 194.

worked smoothly on the basis of this value system. Once these tions worsened, however, the Californios had neither the necessary psychological nor the economic reserves to fall back upon. The future, in short, would come as a shock to them, and the Anglo-Saxon's preoccupation with labor, profit, and savings for the future always remained something of a mystery to them.

Bernard De Voto remarks on another aspect of the Californios' old value system, namely, that the standard of manners in California always exceeded the standard of living.[26] Thus, the rancheros, who had behaved like aristocrats even while poor, eased into affluence naturally, as if living up to a preestablished level of life—say, that of Spain in the eighteenth century.

The Californios exemplified the tendency of Latin Americans to make pleasure the chief end of work. Most of their enjoyments were formalized and communal. Saint's days and other religious holidays took a great deal of advance planning, but in most communities few days passed without either a spontaneous *baile* (dance), a fandango, an evening of singing and guitar playing, a cockfight, a round of bullfighting and bear baiting, or a horse race as part of the daily routine. On these occasions the celebrants consumed heroic amounts of food and drink, clearly indulging in conspicuous consumption. As to "recreations," the Californios' attitude could not possibly have been more opposite to that of the Americanos.

Whatever the failings of their civilization, the Californians took delight and pride in it. It gave them land, wealth, regal fun, family pride, a stake in government, and a sense of aristocratic refinement that was rare in the more isolated reaches of Latin America. Although whatever they possessed by 1846 had come to them but recently, they had held it long enough to cherish it, should anyone threaten to seize it. As Alvarado explained to incredulous Americans who wondered why the Californians defended themselves so well, "we who from our youth had been reared in the school of adversity . . . loved our country most dearly because we had only been able by immense sacrifice to maintain it at the level of contemporary civilization." [27]

---

[26] *The Year of Decision, 1846* (Boston, 1961), p. 113.
[27] Juan Bautista Alvarado, "History of California," 1876, trans. from Spanish, MS, Bancroft Library, V, 220–221.

"I myself, as a trader prefer everything as it is," Thomas Oliver Larkin confided to a friend on April 27, 1846; "the times and the country are well enough for me." A decade later he still confessed a yearning for "the times prior to July 1846 and all their honest pleasures, and the fleshpots of those days. Halcyon days they were. We shall not see their likes again." [28] Coming from Larkin, a levelheaded Yankee never given to flights of fancy, the phrase "halcyon days" amounts to the highest possible compliment for Mexican California.

Nonetheless, Larkin here expressed what definitely was a minority opinion: those aspects of California life which pleased him the most would have revolted a majority of his countrymen. With rare exceptions, they were not content merely to describe or to criticize California but wished to stand in moral judgment over it. If they occasionally conceded some favorable points—California's gorgeous scenery, the rancheros' splendid horsemanship, the punctuality with which their debts were paid, the openhanded hospitality, the Yankees made sure to recite a longer catalogue of the venial and cardinal sins practiced in the province.

The eyewitness accounts of Americans in California provide a rare example of culture conflict: they express both collectively and individually a deep-seated clash of values between the Anglo-American and the Latin-American culture. This clash involved elements such as the Protestant's condescension toward Catholicism; the Puritan's dedication to work, now familiarly known as the "Protestant Ethic"; The republican's loathing of aristocracy; the Yankee's belief in Manifest Destiny; and the Anglo-Saxon's generalized fear of racial mixture. In few places where Yankees embraced a non–Anglo-Saxon people—in Louisiana, New Mexico, Texas, Hawaii—did they document their fears so well as in California. At the same time, the travel accounts of no other area made as much of an impact on the popular mind; the fortyniners had devoured descriptions of California before rushing for the gold mines. Thus, the seeds of culture conflict were carried away from California and back again, over great distances.

"Judgmental" is the word for the Anglo-Saxon spirit in California in

---

[28] To Abel Stearns, quoted in John A. Hawgood, "The Pattern of Yankee Infiltration in Mexican Alta California, 1821–1846," *Pacific Historical Review*, XXVII (1958), 37.

that period, and examples of it are legion. Among the more influential published accounts were those by trappers James Ohio Pattie, who arrived in 1827, and James Clyman, who came in 1846; naval Lieutenant Charles Wilkes and lawyer Thomas Jefferson Farnham, who visited in 1841; and the resident trader, Alfred Robinson, whose widedly read *Life in California* appeared in 1846. Richard Henry Dana, Jr.'s, *Two Years before the Mast* (1840), probably the most popular book ever written about California, is of course also prime evidence. A volume published in 1847 by a responsible Englishman, Sir George Simpson, suggests that Anglo-Saxons generally had similar attitudes.

Every aspect of life in California came up for their scrutiny. What the Californians regarded as a high degree of family unity, those observers interpreted as parental neglect. The men, Robinson explained coolly, are "generally indolent, and addicted to many vices, caring little for the welfare of their children, who like themselves, grow up unworthy members of society." [29] The women, Dana added, "have but little virtue . . . the jealousy of their husbands is extreme, and the revenge deadly and almost certain." [30] (Robinson, married to a Californian, took offense at this remark, but in defending California's womanhood, damned its manhood all the more.) The political activity the Californians so relished, the Americans regarded as absurd. Clyman saw "every [political] change for the worse," [31] since no matter which faction seized power, the government ignored the time-honored safeguards of a republic, including the distinctions among the branches of government, a free press, public schools, and equal protection of the law. In addition, the courts, in Simpson's judgment, were "rotten to the core." [32] Although the rancheros congratulated themselves on having liberated the Indians, the Yankees saw the natives as still in thralldom; thus Pattie found their condition inside the missions to be no better than Clyman considered it to be outside. Indians, Clyman asserted, are "kept in a state of Slavery having or Receiving no compensation for

[29] *Op. cit.*, pp. 83, 84.
[30] Richard Henry Dana, Jr., *Two Years before the Mast: A Personal Narrative of Life at Sea* (Boston, 1895), p. 162.
[31] Charles Camp, ed., *James Clyman: American Frontiersman, 1792–1881, . . . His Own Reminiscences and Diaries* (San Francisco, 1928), p. 187.
[32] George Simpson, *Narrative of a Voyage to California Ports in 1841–42* (San Francisco, 1930), p. 75.

their labour except a scanty allowance of subsistence. . . ." [33] The Californios' material abundance, which they cherished as the fruit of their hard labor, observers reported as ill-gotten gains, stolen from the missions, maintained by servile labor, and augmented by a too-bounteous Nature. The Californians, in Clyman's eyes, were "a proud indolent people doing nothing but ride after herds from place to place without any apparent object." [34] "Nature doing everything, man doing nothing" was Simpson's summation of the economy.[35]

The nativos valued their military prowess, but Clyman certified it as "weak, imbecile and poorly organized and still less respected" (a stereotype that would recoil against the Yankee soldiers in 1847). The *National Intelligencer*, in April of 1846, told the gringo nation that "the Spanish portion of the inhabitants are a thieving, cowardly, dancing, lewd people, and generally indolent and faithless"—this, of a people who pictured themselves as Spanish noblemen. What more elegant and refined dances could there be in the entire world than their own, the Californians wondered? But Lieutenant Wilkes thought that "the coarse and lascivious dances which meet the plaudits of the lookers-on show the degraded tone of manners that exist." Neither could the Californios imagine hospitality more generous than theirs; yet, the Lieutenant, who had been a recipient of it, warned that the reputation for hospitality was unfounded, since the hosts insidiously bilked their guests through the beggary of their servants. The gentry presumed that they got along famously with the sea traders, yet Dana typified that class as leeches "fattening upon . . . [the Californians'] extravagance, grinding them into their poverty." [36] California's European roots were a source of pride to her people, but Farnham dwelt on "the Indian character" of the lower class, "the dull suspicious countenance, the small twinkling piercing eye, the laxness and filth of a free brute, using freedom as a mere means of animal enjoyment . . . dancing and vomiting as occasion and inclination appears to require." [37]

[33] James Ohio Pattie, *The Personal Narrative . . . during Journeyings of Six Years . . .* , in Reuben Gold Thwaites, ed., *Early Western Travels, 1748–1846* (Cleveland, 1905), XVIII, 306–307; Camp, *op. cit.*, p. 186.
[34] Camp, *loc. cit.*
[35] Simpson, *op. cit.*, p. 29.
[36] Dana, *op. cit.*, p. 223.
[37] Thomas Jefferson Farnham, *Travels in the Californias and Scenes in the Pacific Ocean* (New York, 1844), pp. 356–357.

Individual Californians look particularly grim in Anglo-Saxon accounts. The best that Alfred Robinson could say of his own father-in-law, José Antonio de la Guerra y Noriega, was that he seemed "amusing in his character." The *sole* recipient of Robinson's unstinting praise was the obscure tradesman Tiburcio Tapia, a former soldier who "by honorable and industrious labor had amassed so much of this world's goods as to make him one of the wealthiest inhabitants of the place." [38] In Farnham's account, José Castro stalks about like the villain of a morality play, "with a lean body, dark face, black mustachios, pointed nose, flabby cheeks, uneasy eyes, and hands and heart so foul as to . . . require a Spanish cloak . . . to cover them" [39] Dana depicts Juan Bandini as "the best representation of a decayed gentleman I have ever seen." When Dana encountered "Bandina" on shipboard, he described the don, lately returned from Mexico, in the following words:

. . . accomplished, poor, and proud, and without any office or occupation, to lead the life of most young men of the better families—dissolute and extravagant when the means are at hand; ambitious at heart and impotent in act; often pinched for bread; keeping up an appearance of style, when their poverty is known to each half-naked Indian boy. . . . he had a slight and elegant figure, moved gracefully, danced and waltzed beautifully, . . . he was polite to everyone, spoke to sailors, and gave four reals—I dare say the last he had in his pocket—to the steward who waited upon him.[40]

Dana managed to confound every one of the important details about "Bandina," except his dancing prowess: the don *did* have a legitimate occupation, that of ranchero; *did* have modest resources, if not wealth; and *did* have a sufficiently modern outlook to favor American annexation a decade later.

By the combined testimony of leading Yankees, then, California was not a place of real men sustained by traditions, institutions, and aspirations. Instead, it became an imaginary construct of two-dimensional characters moving about a pleasant landscape, "without any apparent object" in life. Some of these witnesses actually knew better (Robinson is an example) but allowed ulterior motives, such as the desire to convince American readers that California desperately wanted annexation,

[38] Robinson, *op. cit.*, p. 74.
[39] Farnham, *op. cit.*, pp. 67–68.
[40] Dana, *op. cit.*, pp. 223–224.

to get the better of them; other writers simply fell back on literary stereotypes. As a parting shot at Bandini, Dana remarks that the don "reminded me much of some of the characters of *Gil Blas*," an allusion to Le Sage's eighteenth-century picaresque novel, which was much discussed among Boston's literatteurs in the very months when *Two Years before the Mast* was being composed.[41]

Only rarely did the gringo witnesses rise above Hispanophobia. Larkin's illuminating correspondence, written for private eyes rather than for a contemporary reading public or for posterity, falls in that catagory; so does the published diary of Walter Colton (1850), although for special reasons. Written during the war years, that account nevertheless transcends the idea of Manifest Destiny; if anything, it errs in the opposite direction, toward Hispanophilia. The diary's author was a curious amalgam of a literary Romanticist and a philosophical puritan. He was a devotee of Byron, Percival, and Shelley, but also a Congregational minister, a product of Yale Theological Seminary and a militant advocate of temperance and Sabbatarianism. In 1847 the Reverend Colton alighted from a navy man-o'-war to serve as alcalde of Monterey. To him the Californians were indolent but also joyous, poor in body but happy in spirit, innocent instead of decadent, uncorrupted by too great an abundance of civilization, and blessed by a closeness to nature. They were morally childlike, generous, brotherly, and socially graceful. This he determined from close observance of daily affairs, fiestas, *meriendas*, and weddings. Happily, the Californians did not worship the false idol of gold—at least not until the Yankees taught them how to. Neither, for better or for worse, did they understand the true meaning of "profit": not even the most generous offer would part them from possessions they cherished or enjoyed. Thus, despite an air of moral superiority and rousseauean idealization, Colton came to a generally warm understanding of California.[42]

No matter what the Yankees felt or wrote about California, the fact is that in practice some adjusted to it comfortably, on its own terms. Those who did so were, by and large, the representatives of the "mari-

[41] Stanley Thomas Williams, *The Spanish Background of American Literature* (New Haven, 1955), I, 119.
[42] Walter Colton, *Three Years in California* . . . , ed. by Marguerita Wilbur (Stanford, 1949), *passim*.

time interest": [43] the supercargos, the retired sailing captains, and the resident shipping agents who catered to a monied class hungry for imported goods. They made profits as traders, smugglers, and dabblers in ranchland. John R. Cooper, Abel Stearns, William G. Dana (Richard Henry Dana, Jr.'s, uncle), John Warner, and others swore allegiance to the Mexican Republic, adopted Catholicism, married local women, and obtained legal land grants. Their property, their working knowledge of Spanish, and their understanding of the local manners earned them full acceptance into the élite. Others, like Thomas Oliver Larkin, enjoyed similar social success without submerging their religious and national identity or marrying locally. These seafarers exemplify the type whom Professor George I. Sánchez has looked for in vain in recent decades, the "Mexicanized gringo." [44]

Of an entirely different sort were the American farmers and fur trappers who came overland in the 1840's—the "pioneering interest." Most of these men settled in the Sacramento River valley, enjoying the hospitality of John Sutter's Fort or of Mariano Vallejo's casa. They hunted, planted and tended a few crops, or operated a whiskey distillery, but they remained cool toward the Californians; they did not marry local women, and never broke into "society."

Even while laughing at domestic politics, however, the pioneers could hardly resist getting into the thick of things, especially when asked to take some potshots at a Mexican governor. James Ohio Pattie and his trappers joined the cabal of Mexican convict Joaquín Solís, hoping to topple Governor Echeandía in 1831. First they cheered Solís, then went over to the other side and gave a huzzah for "Echedio." [45] The pioneers' most ambitious fling at politics occurred in 1836, when the backwoodsman Isaac Graham and forty *rifleros* enlisted with Alvarado to overthrow Governor Gutiériez on the promise of a land donation, a prize usually reserved for citizens. They contributed greatly to Alvarado's success, but retreated to their cabins grumbling about cowardice and betrayal when he accepted autonomy within the Mexican Republic instead of pressing for complete independence. They re-

[43] Hawgood, *op. cit.*, p. 31, following a thesis of Professor Norman F. Graebner's.
[44] Cited in Carey McWilliams, *North from Mexico: The Spanish-Speaking People of the United States* (Philadelphia, 1949), pp. 289–304.
[45] Pattie. *op. cit.*, pp. 292–294.

mained apostate, particularly because they never were given the land they had been promised.[46]

Americans again took a hand in provincial politics in 1841. Governor Alvarado and Commandante Castro, acting on sketchy rumors of a forthcoming Texas-type of coup, arrested sixty *extranjeros,* including former ally Graham, and sent them to Mexico as "enemies of the state." To everyone's surprise, the Supreme Government not only released the prisoners but indemnified them for the indignity they had suffered.

The man most responsible for this reversal was the American lawyer Farnham, a chance visitor in Monterey, who made it his patriotic business to sail to San Blas and get the prisoners released. Then, to publicize the "sufferings of Americans in California," he dispatched a series of letters to the American press and later published his inflammatory *Early Days of California.* As the first work to expound the pioneers' cause in California, the book was of some moment: it portrays Graham as another Davy Crockett. Like Davy at the Alamo, Isaac at Monterey was a "stout, sturdy backwoodsman, of a stamp which exists only on the frontiers of the American states. . . . [who] had nearly stepped in blood knee deep, among the carcasses of the hated Mexicans" and in 1836 nearly "crushed every mote of Mexican life" in California.[47]

Imaginary heroics aside, Yankee military forces could have defeated California almost at will, as an American flotilla proved in October, 1842. Acting on misinformation that war had broken out with Mexico, Commodore Thomas ap Catesby Jones captured Monterey by landing a few boatloads of marines. When he discovered that peace still prevailed, he good-naturedly hoisted back the Mexican standard, apologized, and then attended a fiesta in an attempt to dispel all hard feelings.

At first, neither the maritime nor the pioneering Americans pictured themselves as bearers of culture or as agents of national destiny. By 1836, however, both interests foresaw a confrontation with Mexico in which they would have a central role, and both tried to engineer the change. But, whereas the first sought limited goals and "legitimate" methods, the second favored aggression. The pioneering interest,

[46] Bancroft, *History of California,* IV, 2–42.
[47] Farnham, *op. cit.,* pp. 63–68.

represented by Lansford W. Hastings, Benjamin Ide, and others, took inspiration from the Texas Republic and plotted a coup d'état—to them the most admirable method of assuring Yankee annexation. Although never in close contact with official Washington, they foresaw eventual help from that quarter. They bided their time while their numbers grew.

Despite Farnham's effort to drum up a case for American martyrdom, the gringos had none of the really plausible claims to California such as their countrymen had acquired to Oregon and Texas. Americans could not seriously profess tenure by right of invitation, treaty, superior numbers, or long-term occupancy. For this very reason, Washington officialdom was trying to win California by negotiation—to be sure, a less glamorous means than rebellion, but serviceable. President James K. Polk wanted California badly enough to risk war for it, but he preferred the path of least resistance: if possible, he wanted to stay on friendly terms with the Californians and buy the province in the Mexican capital, but he was prepared for a military take-over if all else failed.

To his man in Monterey, Thomas Oliver Larkin, Polk entrusted the crucial work of shirt-sleeve diplomacy. From his casa near the "capitol," United States Consul Larkin kept prodding the Californians to cast off Mexican government in name as well as in deed. As a long-standing friend (he had arrived in 1832) and as the government's leading moneylender, he had their ear. After 1843, he strove for two objectives: first, an independent republic managed by Californians, Yankees, and Europeans; second, an American military protectorate—an arrangement just shy of annexation but sufficiently strong to keep Britain and France at arm's length. He promised to all Californians the benefits of free trade, representative government, public education, and agricultural progress, and to their government leaders, posts in the new government. Eventually he felt that he had them "eating out of his hand" and was reasonably confident that no blood need be shed in converting California into a Yankee territory. Unhappily, hot-blooded pioneers were toying with opposite ideas, which were to overthrow the "Larkin Plan." [48]

[48] Hawgood, *op. cit.*, p. 31.

Doubtless, the Californios had as myopic a view of the Yankees as the Yankees had of them—and based it on as much misinformation, prejudice, and cultural mythology. If so, however, they did not write treatises about it and in daily life showed more restraint than the Yankees displayed toward them. Their response to Larkin's diplomacy amply demontrates this. Professor Hawgood estimates that, barring the outbreak of war, "California would have become part of the United States in the long run, but of her own free will, at her own initiative and in her own good time, including that of her citizens of Spanish descent—who tended to move rather slowly—and might have passed through the transitional cushioning phase of being an independent republic, as had Texas before her." [49]

Mexico's dalliance with the Californians had much to do with their ambivalence and restraint toward Yankees. On the one hand, Mexico wanted to retain her "Siberian" department, extend its political freedom, and exploit its resources; on the other, she found herself always incapacitated by war and rebellion and unable to spare the minimum arms. A mere two hundred soldiers—real soldiers instead of convicts—and a monthly subsidy of 8,000 pesos could have done wonders; without such aid, the province was miserably defended. Monterey's only man-o'-war was so decrepit that it could not tack against the wind; and the presidio powder magazine ran so low that the commandante had to borrow explosives from a visiting frigate to fire a salute. As for the suggestion that Mexico sell California outright, Santa Anna, having lost Texas, could do no such thing and keep either his office or his head. In 1844, after two years of aimless groping, Manuel Micheltorena, the last Mexican governor, went home and left California to the vagaries of the future. The Supreme Government made a mental note to send help if, and when, conditions permitted, but in the meantime gave California the status of an international outlander. The two remaining principals, the Californians and the Americans, now eyed each other nervously.

Until 1846, courtesy had characterized the behavior of the Californios toward the Yankees. Except for a few lapses, local officials had not harrassed the gringos, although Mexican regulations demanded stern

[49] *Loc. cit.*

treatment of "foreigners." Moreover, if the rancheros had a low opinion of "leather-jackets" such as Graham, they liked the American seafarers well enough to accept them as sons-in-law and friends. No Yankee, not even the most loathsome, was *ever* turned away from a Californio's door while in a moment of need. Mariano Vallejo's reception of Americans (whom he hoped to use as a counterweight to his political enemies in the south) was lavish and unstinting.

Curiously, many California women seem to have been more favorably disposed toward the Yankees than were their men. (The product of the Yankee's superior romantic prowess! Farnham snapped.) The words of a wartime folk song bear out this alleged receptivity of California women to Yankees:

> Already the senoritas
> Speak English with finesse.
> "Kiss me! say the Yankees,
> The girls all answer "Yes!" [50]

At least the *señoras* of Santa Barbara felt quite pleased at the prospect of the American conquest in 1846. Mrs. Ord attests that they merely hoped that it would come about quickly and painlessly; perhaps Yankee rule would put an end to all the political confusion.

The Californians admired certain Yankee ideals, at least in the abstract, and generally thought more highly of the Yankee government than they did of Yankee citizens. Some, who had toyed with the idea of voluntary association with the United States—Juan Bandini and Mariano Vallejo, to name but two—had already voiced admiration of the American Constitution: that document seemed to have solved the problem of federalism in a marvelous manner. In fact, it was to be the Yankees' eternal misfortune in California to be measured against their nation's high principles; the fleshly representatives of the United States usually came out second best. For the creative economic energy of the Yankees, Californians had both admiration and criticism. Juan Bautista Alvarado, for one, agreed that the American maxim "Time is Money!" had worked some miracles in the world. It had "filled the East Indies with wooden nutmegs," as the saying went, and promised to do a great

[50] Works Projects Administration, Writers Program, *Los Angeles: A Guide to the City and Its Environs* (New York, 1941), p. 112.

deal for a backward place such as California. Yet it promised cold materialism, too, which no true Californian could endorse.[51]

Californians kept their tempers even as they grew conscious of the aggressive designs of the United States. Commodore Jones's mistaken seizure of Monterey in 1842, although ending innocently enough in a fiesta, was seen as a clear portent of evil things to come. Also, the local rifleros were suspected to be "on the *qui vive*." "Let us try to avoid a repetition of what happened in Texas" was the burden of many dispatches to Mexico City.[52] The Americans made the Californians as apprehensive by their presence as did the Mexicans by their absence.

Meantime, the Californians were so hopelessly embroiled among themselves that the spring of 1846 found the province in a particularly jittery state. The northerners recently had fought the southerners to a standstill over control of the treasury, which they both meanwhile had drained dry; José Castro and Pio Pico were about to resume the struggle and were lining up troops and horses for that purpose; and Indian depredations were increasing. Grasping at diplomatic straws, the northerners sought out the French consul with a request for a French protectorate, while the Angeleños, never to be outdone by the Montereños, went to the British consul with a similar entreaty. Both the British and the French officials dismissed the proposals as irrelevant, however.

With a possible Yankee take-over in the offing, the Californios were unsure whether to salute their hard-won autonomy in the Mexican Republic or bemoan their abandonment by the mother country. Nevertheless, an intangible allegiance on their part to Mexico remained strong to the bitter end—stronger even than Larkin imagined. Some of them feared that if they took a "neutral" stance during the war but should happen to remain Mexican subjects at war's end, they would open themselves to Mexico's thunderous wrath. To the very last, some of the more timorous Californians trembled at the thought that a Mexican army might march over the southern hills and deal as roughly with them as with the Yankees. Nor was the Californios' loyalty to Mexico based exclusively on fear; genuine Mexican patriotism among them never disappeared completely. As Alvarado explained, although Mex-

---

[51] *Op. cit.*, V, 220–221.
[52] Tays, *op. cit.* p. 597.

ico was the "bane of our existence" and although the United States offered a "brilliant future," Californians remained, in their heart of hearts, Mexicans: they could not in good conscience abandon the mother country in time of need.[53] Thus, a vague and contradictory patriotism prevailed, which eventually drove the Californians to abandon their neutrality and to fight under the Mexican flag, not as independents.

In summarizing the confusion of the spring of the last year of the Mexican era, Angustios de la Guerra Ord evokes the image of a huddle of bleating sheep: "Now," she sighs in response to Frémont's foray in March, "now it rains on the sheepfold." [54]

[53] *Op. cit.*, V, 220–221.
[54] Ord, *op. cit.*, p. 58.

II

Rain in a Sheepfold:
War and Annexation,
1846-1848

POPULAR accounts have long ascribed to the Mexican War in California much greater importance and far more virtue than it deserves. Local historians who glorify John C. Frémont and the pathetic Bear Flag Rebellion have, however, chosen to ignore the findings of every serious student of the war era, from Josiah Royce and Hubert Howe Bancroft to Bernard De Voto. Put briefly, those scholars have found that the United States connived rather cynically to acquire California, provoked the native Californians into a dirty fight, and bungled a simple job of conquest.[1]

The Californios' own view of the conflict generally supports the more scholarly view, for to them the war seemed less a military disaster than a grave affront to their honor. Not the fighting, but the treaty that ended the war and the subsequent gold rush consummated the conquest, in their way of thinking. Moreover, the Californios took pride in their wartime resistance—and with good cause, since they won the only memorable battle of that war. They also found tentative satisfaction in the way the struggle ended and in the tone of the military occu-

---

[1] This chapter leans heavily on Hubert Howe Bancroft, *History of California* (San Francisco, 1886), V, 1846 to 1848; George Tays, "Revolutionary California: The Political History of California from 1820 to 1848" (rev. ed.; Ph.D. dissertation, University of California, Berkeley, 1934); Bernard De Voto, *The Year of Decision, 1846* (2d ed.; Boston, 1961); and Otis A. Singletary, *The Mexican War* (Chicago, 1960).

pation: once the fighting had stopped, the United States military turned out to be the most amiable of gringos.

At dawn on June 6, 1846, a party of American riflemen awakened General Mariano Vallejo at his home in Sonoma. They announced the establishment of a new "Yankee Republic" and put him under arrest. Precisely why he was their chief hostage even they were uncertain, since everybody knew Vallejo as the Americanos' best friend; but if there was no Mexican army to seize, a general would have to do. Always affable toward strangers, Mariano Vallejo offered them a bottle of wine to drink while they were drafting their articles of capitulation; meanwhile, he retired to put on more respectable attire. When Don Mariano returned, the Americans took him, his brother Salvador, and his son-in-law Jacob Leese to Fort Sutter and turned them over to Frémont, who was in charge there. Thus began the Bear Flag Rebellion and the Mexican War, which toppled the old régime.

With elaborate boorishness Frémont's men kept the prisoners incommunicado for months, arrested their visitors, denied them even a walk in the open air, and stooped to stealing their personal effects. Behind bars, Salvador Vallejo harangued his brother for lavishing land and money on every passing gringo and extracted from him a belated promise to mend his ways. For the rest of their lives, neither man would forget the unjustice done him. Later, when retelling these events to sympathetic strangers, Salvador would bristle as he recalled seeing the soldiers "lazily stretched upon the clay floor . . . holding in their hands greasy patches of cards in lieu of bibles." Occasionally one of them had ambled forward saying, "Let me see if my Greasers are safe." At this point in his narrative, Don Salvador would rise to trot out an old document verifying that his father was a bona fide *don*. Then he would curse the "mulatto" "Pike County blackguard" who dared use the word "greaser" in addressing two men of the "purest blood of Europe!" [2]

[2] [José Manuel] Salvador Vallejo, "Notas históricas sobre California," 1874, MS, Bancroft Library (Berkeley, Calif.), pp. 21–22, 118–119, 132. Mariano Guadalupe Vallejo indicated that he never reconciled himself to the Bear Flag Rebellion, in "Recuerdos históricos y personales tocante a la Alta California: ... 1769–1849 ... ," 1875, MS, Bancroft Library, V, 117.

Convinced that their mission was to "make FREEMEN" of Spaniards, the rebels proposed to "liberate" California from despots, mock-republicans, and "criminals" like Governor Pico and Commandante Castro, who had robbed the missions and "shamefully oppressed the laboring people." Neither had the local Americans escaped oppression, for, although they had been invited to settle in California with promises of land and republican government, they had not received either and now stood in danger of eviction. The rebels charged that Castro intended to transport them to the desert and sure death. And who, if not the government, had inspired the Indians to burn the settlers' wheat? Furthermore, the rebels feared that unless they acted swiftly a British fleet, doubtless already under sail, would seize California from under the nose of the United States.

By "the favor of heaven . . . and by the principle of self-preservation; by the love of truth; and by the hatred of tyranny," they would submit neither to the "Spaniards" nor to the British and would instead create an independent republic based on civil and religious liberty and dedicated to the encouragement of "industry, virtue and literature." [3]

This bill of particulars mystified the Californians; aware of their own numerous shortcomings, they yet saw none that would serve as provocation for a Yankee rebellion. They already *were* civilized men, and well on their road to freedom; only their would-be liberators were crude and uncivilized. The Yankees knew that the Indian arsonists were acting on their own hook and that Castro was rounding up horses not to attack Americans but to fight Pio Pico, his own countryman. If the frontiersmen had suffered, it was mainly from neglect. Moreover, the Yankees were uninvited guests in the first place and had earned no valid claims on the government (except perhaps in rare cases such as that of Isaac Graham, who never did get the land promised him). Pio Pico's sale of mission property was none of the Yankees' affair. The government never drafted the Yankees into the army nor required them to pay taxes or join the Church. Moreover, if they disliked Mexican regulations, so did the Californians.

A feeling of betrayal underscored the Californians' hostility toward

---

[3] William Brown Ide, "Proclamation to the People of California," [June, 1846], MS, HM 4116, Huntington Library (San Marino, Calif.).

the *osos* (bears). In talks with Consul Larkin and in all their ruminations about how the end of the Mexican régime might come about, they had assumed that any fight would be against regulars—men worthy of themselves. Yet, as they watched the rebel columns come down from Sonoma they saw mainly *"leperos," "*grimy adventurers," "exiles from civilization." The bear emblem itself symbolized bestiality, for even though it was a bear so badly drawn that it resembled a hog, the bear remained Nature's pirate, a thief who thrived on the cattle that sustained the very lifeblood of civilization. And if the grim looks of the Americans and the Jolly Roger they bore as a standard were not proof enough of barbarism, one could see it in the ragtag of the procession—there marched some of Micheltorena's leftover cholos. Facts such as these shattered the credibility of Larkin's initial promises of "liberation" from Mexican "tyranny." [4]

The Californians explained the rebellion as plain, unadulterated rapine. They properly sensed the provocative rebel strategy, even if they failed to understand its motivation. With the breakdown of diplomacy and the beginning of war in Mexico, the time had come for the Yankees in California to "play the Texas game." [5] Unhappily for them, they lacked both the sure touch and the concrete grievances of the Texans; try as they might to conjure up another "Texas Republic," they failed. Without substantive grievances, and with their own government pursuing a policy of diplomacy, the rebels' success depended upon how far they could goad the Californians into action. If the Californians took the bait and retaliated against Vallejo's capture, they would validate the rebel cause and the United States government might respect the "republic" as a *fait accompli*. The flaw in this strategy was that it could degenerate into mere pillage, which Washington would spurn. And, indeed, when the Californians failed to respond actively, provocations increased. The dilemma of the Americans' position was voiced by Benjamin Ide, the rebel chieftain, in an exhortation to his men: "We must be conquerors . . . [or] we are robbers." [6] This the Californios sensed.

[4] Juan Bautista Alvarado, "Historia de California," 1876, MS, Brancroft Library, V, 186–187, 204; Salvador Vallejo, *op. cit.*, p. 597.
[5] Alfred Robinson, 1845, quoted in Tays, *op. cit.*, p. 597.
[6] Simon Ide, *A Biographical Sketch of the Life of William B. Ide* (n.p., 1880), pp. 123–128.

The announcement of Don Mariano's arrest did not have the anticipated effect; instead, it brought bitter smiles to many faces throughout California. After all, he who had consorted with devilish frontiersmen deserved all that he got. As other provocations ensued, however, the Californians grew alarmed. The rebels confiscated cattle and horses and looted homes as the communities north of the Carquinez Strait trembled under a reign of terror. At Rancho Nipomo, two leatherjackets enslaved a band of Indians, overworked and starved them, shot at the men for target practice, and raped the women. But the incident that evoked the most universal and lasting anger occurred that same June, along the shores of Suisun Bay. A patrol of rebels, led by their new leader, Frémont, was scouting the shoreline when it encountered three Californians landing in a rowboat: the aged ranchero José de los Reyes Berreyesa and his twin nephews, Francisco and Ramón de Haro. Although unarmed, the three Californios were mistaken for soldiers and shot peremptorily. Ramón was killed as soon as he reached the shore. Francisco then threw himself down upon his brother's body. Next, a command rang out: "Kill the other son of a bitch!" It was obeyed immediately. The old man asked bitterly: "Is it possible that you kill these young men for no reason at all? It is better that you kill me who am old too!" An American rebel coolly obliged.[7]

This was the story pieced together from eyewitness accounts by one of the dead Berreyesa's sons and another of his nephews, who shortly undertook an odyssey to recover the bodies. In Sonoma they accosted a man wearing the victim's clothing, but could not get him to part with the booty. The rotting corpses had been buried by Indians. Since Californians always maintained that the Berreyesa party was on a private mission, they classed the annihilation as pure barbarism. News of the incident electrified the provincials as nothing had before. "It was a night of deep meditation," writes Manuel J. Castro. "Until then, we *Californios* did not know whether we would have to struggle against savage hordes organized under the Bear Flag . . . or against civilized soldiers."[8]

In most wars such incidents are easily forgotten and, indeed, Ameri-

[7] Antonio Berreyesa, "Relación ... ," 1877, MS, Bancroft Library, pp. 8–11.
[8] "Relación sobre acontecimientos de la Alta California," 1876, MS, Bancroft Library, p. 194.

cans marked it lightly—Frémont simply reported that some of Castro's men were "killed on the beach" [9]—but the Californians engraved it indelibly in their folk memory. Other participants later suggested revenge as a motive. Supposedly, the guerrilla soldier Bernardo García had previously captured two Bear Flaggers named Cowie and Fowler, tortured and murdered them, and mutilated their bodies—a tale some Californios considered pure fabrication. They told many versions of the Berreyesa shootings, not always consistent with the facts; in the leading one, they had Frémont himself giving the cold-blooded execution orders, simply to avoid taking prisoners. They did not like Frémont any better when the Haro twins' father died a brooding death and an uncle of theirs, wracked by grief, followed old Haro to the grave. While the gringos canonized Frémont as a hero of the conquest, the lordly Berreyesas were dogged by one Yankee injustice after another until they were completely decimated.

Shocked by the osos and gravely disappointed by Frémont, the Californians felt pleasantly relieved early in July by an improvement in gringo policy. The arrival in Monterey of Commodore John Drake Sloat one month to the day after the rebellion altered the picture completely. As soon as Larkin rowed out and boarded the flagship and informed him of what had transpired to the north, Sloat began dispelling the darkling revolution as effectively as a breeze clears the summer fog in Monterey Harbor. "Old, sick and irresolute and a long way from Washington," the Commodore nevertheless knew better than to sanction Frémont's projected conquest of the south.[10] Sloat's "conquest" ran so smoothly that the sole casualty was a woman who, kneeling in church, suffered a bruised leg in the rush for the door at the announcement of his landing. He made the rounds of the town, posting a proclamation ending the republic and announcing California's absorption into the Union. Whereas the rebels had granted no privileges to the Californians, Sloat professed "full confidence in the honor and integrity of the inhabitants" of the province. He promised all who elected the path of peace the same rights and privileges of all citizens of the United States, including the right to choose their own magistrates.

[9] To Thomas Hart Benton, July 25, 1846, quoted in John Charles Frémont, *Memoirs of My Life* (Chicago and New York, 1887), p. 546
[10] De Voto, *op. cit.*, p. 280.

Hereafter, the American forces would purchase provisions at fair rates and with immediate compensation; the Church could rest secure in its possessions and customs; American goods would enter duty free and the value of California exports and real estate would soar. In all, Sloat concluded, "the country cannot but improve more rapidly than any other on the continent." [11]

This extinction of the Bear Flag Rebellion so intrigued the Californians hiding in the hills that all but the top officers returned to the capital; they even treated the fleet to a fiesta. "Though a quasi war exists," the naval chaplain, Walter Colton, wrote on July 28, "all the amenities and courtesies of life are preserved; your person, life and liberty, are as sacred at the hearth of the Californian as they would be at your own fireside. . . . He may fight you on the field, but in his family, you may dance with his daughters and he will wake the waltzing string" of his fiddle in your behalf.[12]

Thus, by the end of July, 1846, the Californians had tasted in rapid succession both the worst and the best of Manifest Destiny and now again were in for the worst. Sloat, for all his good wishes for the Californians, wanted no part of the Frémont-Larkin contest and felt relieved when Commodore Robert Field Stockton came to replace him a few weeks later. Even at best, Stockton was a gruff sea dog and no diplomat. (His quest for the Know-Nothing presidential nomination in 1856 may reveal something about his attitude toward Catholic "foreigners.") He neglected to salute the ladies and wore his sidearms when he sat; thus, to a people steeped in social proprieties he seemed the "true pirate chief." [13] Sloat issued a new proclamation rescinding the old one, in which he branded Castro a usurper who had sullied the name of an American (Frémont) and therefore deserved chastisement. The proclamation licensed the American forces to advance into the interior, instead of lingering on shipboard, and to shoot conspirators. This begat a counterproclamation, in which the Californios decreed death to any American who confiscated property. To prevent reprisals,

---

[11] John Drake Sloat, "Proclamation to the Inhabitants of California," [July 6, 1846], MS, FAC 101, Huntington Library.

[12] *Three Years in California* . . . , ed. by Marguerita Wilbur (Stanford, 1949), pp. 17–18.

[13] The Frenchman, Louis Gasquet, quoted in Tays, *op. cit.*, pp. 538–539.

Pico and usurper Castro left for Mexico, thus deflating Stockton's proclamation, but the invasion continued nevertheless.[14]

Although Stockton formally disbanded the "one-town, one-month republic," he cloaked its army in the respectable title "California Batallion of Volunteers," put Frémont in charge, and ordered it south to "pacify" the rest of the province. As perhaps both Frémont and he had intended, the new program provoked guerrilla warfare in parts of California which, by and large, had already surrendered. Wherever the naval squadron or the volunteer brigade landed, trouble erupted,[15] with the important difference that the abajeños fought back more successfully than their countrymen up north.

In August of 1846, an American martinet, Captain Archibald Gillespie, provoked the trouble in Los Angeles which was to prolong the outcome of the war by several months. He put a curfew on the town, closed the stores, and outlawed even the most innocuous social gatherings. One resident American observed that Gillespie enjoyed "humiliating the most respectable men." Fearful of conspiracy, Gillespie searched several houses, confiscated arms, and did everything in his power to intimidate the occupants. In response, Servulio Varela, a young Mexican dabbler in rebellions, took a score of drinking companions to Gillespie's quarters and taunted him with drum rolls and shouts of "¡Viva Méjico!" In a panic, Gillespie fired his rifle into the darkness and sent the intruders scurrying into the hills, where they were joined by hundreds of others, including professional soldiers. They chose José María Flores, a former Mexican officer, to drive the occupation force from the town.[16]

Flores soon accomplished his mission. His guerrillas managed to find an old four-pounder which could take an explosive charge and heave cobblestones and scraps of metal. That relic and lances made of laurel staves and barrel hoops made up their entire armory. The advantage of experienced leadership and of an aroused populace of 6,000 rooting for them made up for many shortcomings. Employing bluster and trickery, Flores and his men overwhelmed Gillespie's eighty dragoons and

[14] Colton, op. cit., p. 20; Alvarado, op. cit., p. 236 ff.
[15] In southern California, however, some Californios, as for instance José Jesús Pico and Juan Bandini, did come to like Frémont.
[16] De Voto, op. cit., pp. 367–371.

forced the captain to sign surrender terms. On October 4 the guerrillas lined the streets and gloated while Gillespie's dejected men marched out of town, toward San Pedro. Flores' band next cleared out remaining pockets of Yankee resistance at Chino and Santa Barbara, and finally deployed southeast of Los Angeles to stand off the army coming from New Mexico and the marines from San Diego. The Angeleños thus delayed the inevitable for four months.

The guerrillas' resistance culminated in action at the hamlet of San Pascual, the proudest moment of the war and one of the few skirmishes north of the Rio Grande worthy to be called a battle. The key to victory lay in a mistake by General Stephen W. Kearny and a show of courage by the Californios. On the best advice of scout Kit Carson, who thought all "Spaniards" cowardly, Kearny had left Santa Fe, New Mexico, with only 125 men. General Andrés Pico, brother of the exiled governor, was waiting for Kearny at San Pascual, where the road crossed the hilly approaches to San Diego. Pico's men, though greatly outnumbered, had long lances and fresh horses. The battle, "a vicious melee of cavalry sabres and clubbed muskets against lances," [17] lasted but five minutes. In it eighteen Americans died and as many were wounded, including Kearny, who was lanced twice and put out of action for several weeks; the Californians suffered no losses. After San Pascual, the Yankees spoke less of "Mexican cowardice" and more of "Californian valor," a reversal of folk history the Californios greatly appreciated.[18]

The Californios felt gratified that they had succumbed neither to "Spanish cowardice" nor to blind fury, as the gringos had expected them to, but had fought well against great odds—a fleet of warships and marines, infantry and cavalry, and a powerful and cocky nation. In their worst days they would look back and remember having taught the Yankee not to class them as cowards, but as brave men and good soldiers.

[17] Antonio F. Coronel, "Cosas de California ... particularmente ... en ... los años de 1846 y 1847 ... ," 1877, MS, C-D 61, Bancroft Library, pp. 78, 80; White, "California Back to 1828," quoted in Bancroft, Reference Notes, spring binder no. 9, MS, Bancroft Library.

[18] Mariano Vallejo liked to quote Kit Carson as having once said that the strength of the Californians lay "in running away"; see "Recuerdos históricos ... 1796–1849," 1875, MS, Bancroft Library, V, 172.

On January 13, 1847, Andrés Pico gleefully signed the Treaty of Cahuenga in which the unpredictable Frémont suddenly gave the Californians the equality he had earlier denied them. Pico and the other Californians were no better able at close range to follow Frémont's tricky thoughts than the scholar who studies him at a distance. In their eyes, he was less than an unalloyed hero—an officer and a gentleman, and yet a leader of thieves; a man of bloodshed, but also a generous peacemaker. Rumor mills explained his recent pandering to the Californios as an attempt to claim the governorship with their backing. Whatever the truth of the matter, they were pleased to observe that he halted the fighting on a high note.

The first two phases of American annexation, rebellion and military conquest, have greatly appealed to the popular imagination. The final stage, military government, by comparison seems inconsequential—an irritating interruption in the inevitable progress from Spanish-American to Anglo-Saxon control. And yet, the Californians saw the occupation favorably: to them it represented the last stage of the old order, and its worst feature was that it ended too soon.

By January, 1847, war had irrevocably separated California from Mexico and liquidated the native California government. Only certain diehards disputed these results, such as the men who stole a gun from a United States warship standing off Santa Barbara and buried it in the beach for a future day of deliverance. Most Californians simply returned home, preferring the quietude of rancho life. Since Alvarado had declined to become either interim governor or secretary of state, the United States Army formed a government without him.[19] Unfortunately, Californios who spurned such gestures lost the opportunity to speak for their people later on. Pio Pico's return from Mexico started in a Los Angeles saloon a back-room conspiracy of Yankee-haters lasting all of one day. An army investigation made light of the episode, dismissing the former governor as "an amiable, kind hearted man who has ever been the tool of knaves."[20] Pico, too, slipped back into the fold as a mere ranchero. As for the soldiers of the rank, Colton noted that

[19] Tays, op. cit., p. 808.
[20] J. D. Stevenson to Governor Richard B. Mason, July, 1848, in California and New Mexico, U.S. 31st Cong., 1st sess., H. Ex. Doc. 17 (Washington, 1850), pp. 599–600.

"they are very poor, having received no pay since our flag was raised. . . . They are entitled to our sympathy." [21]

The war had caused undeniable economic hardships. Cattle and horses had been killed, stolen, and scattered; crop fields had gone to weed; vineyards had been turned into forage by occupying Bear Flag troops. The resumption of ranching would have to await the return of vaqueros, shepherds, and domestics who had drifted away and of the reopening of the sea trade. The Indians, capitalizing on the white man's preoccupations, had grown more daring in their forays and could be suppressed only by the concerted efforts of Yankees and Californios. Mariano Vallejo left jail with his spirits shaken and his health threatened, only to discover that the rebels had destroyed crops, buildings, fences, and stock worth well over $100,000 and inflicted on his brother Salvador half that amount of damage. In estimating his defeat, Mariano also wrote off as a total loss the $60,000 owed him by Mexico for his military service.[22]

Some *ricos* had serious difficulties paying off prewar financial obligations. Alvarado laments that no sooner had he returned home than moneylenders Henry Mellus and Thomas Larkin arrived with an ultimatum. These "would-be friends" took Alvarado for a bankrupt debtor and demanded that, so as to liquify his assets and pay off his creditors, he convey his Rancho Mariposa to Captain Frémont. Alvarado had acquired Mariposa in the eleventh hour of the old régime, in the hope of holding on to it until its value rose; in the end, he had to sell it cheaply to Frémont. (Unknown to anybody just then, Mariposa had about $10 million in gold secreted in its bowels.)

These tangible material losses apart, the old ruling classes still preserved all that was dear in the way of religion, property, and social amenities; if they were politically alienated, socially they still reigned supreme. In most places daily life resumed where it had left off in antebellum days, and one hopeful note sounded for all who owned land—property values were rising steadily. One Montereño boasted that the worth of his ranchos had increased by $40,000, through the

[21] Colton, *op. cit.*, p. 175.
[22] Myrtle M. McKittrick, *Vallejo: Son of California* (Portland, Ore., 1944), pp. 275–276.

mere change of flags.[23] This promise of economic progress stilled a great many of the more strident critics of the new régime. Meanwhile, the aggrieved Mariano Vallejo had rallied enough composure to shave his whiskers according to the latest Yankee tonsorial fashion and go to San Francisco to march in the victory parade in Portsmouth Square. Most comforting of all to the Californios, the new army was attempting to preserve the status quo instead of wrecking it. General Kearny, Colonel Richard B. Mason, and General Bennet Riley, who served successively as military governors from February, 1847, until April, 1849, treated the Californians with kid gloves and at the same time kept those Yankees who might have harmed them firmly in check. In fact, in their zeal to retain the status quo, these American army officers created a government that in some ways seemed more Mexican than the one they had inherited from the Mexican governors.[24]

Kearny, in particular, endeared himself to the native Californians when he court-marshaled Frémont for claiming the title of military governor. This greatly amused the Californios, who remembered their own infernal bickering over the governorship a few years earlier. In the course of the legal contest, moreover, Kearny accused Frémont of "most cruelly and shamefully" abusing the native Californians who, had they not resisted the Bear Flaggers, "would have been unworthy the name of men." The general also promised immediate cash payments for the "unauthorized" confiscations of the Bear Flaggers.[25] Here was the curious spectacle of the conquering commander himself assuming the role of apologist for the Californios—his vanquished foes.

In view of the fact that for decades the native Californians had heard of the gringo's hatred of Catholicism, the army's deference to Church interests surprised them pleasantly. The army commanders officially discouraged civil marriages, diligently rousted poachers from mission property, and kept their own men completely in check. Apart

[23] Alvarado, op. cit., V, 250–251; Colton, op. cit., p. 52.
[24] Theodore Grivas, Military Government in California, 1846–1850, with a Chapter on the Prior Use in Louisiana, Florida, and New Mexico (Glendale, Calif., 1963), p. 154.
[25] Kearny to R. Jones, March 15, May 13, 1847, in California and New Mexico, pp. 284, 304.

from a curate who complained that the soldiers were flirting with the señoritas too near his church, no one had any serious dispute with the army over religious policy.[26]

Governor Mason artfully ingratiated himself with the gentry. He invariably paid his respects to the leading citizens and enjoyed their hospitality while touring his command, a great honor for the Californios. He listened carefully to their claims for war damages and, whenever he employed their services (as, for example, in fighting Indians), he paid for them promptly. If he had to punish, as he did in the case of the Santa Barbarans who stole the naval gun, he did so without rancor.

Best of all, Mason kept the army out of civil affairs, except for its help in preserving the new form of government and in assisting the local magistrates in keeping the peace. In the old communities, he enforced the Mexican legal code and ruled either "through channels" or not at all. His only innovations, the jury trial and the election of town officials, actually supplemented rather than negated previous governmental usage. The alcalde remained the mainstay of local government, combining in his person such duties as in the United States would be shared by mayor, municipal judge, jury, lawyer, notary public, and marshal.

Captain Henry W. Halleck, the American army's secretary of state, the man who oversaw the daily functioning of the occupation government, knew some Spanish and soon learned how to cater to the gentry. In naming men to public office, Halleck first called upon the former holder of an office to see if he was willing to serve. If rebuked, Secretary Halleck then encouraged other members of the old élite—both Anglo-American and Latin-American—to assume office. He seemed to want to balance the gringos and Californios on the government roster, as when he named both Sutter and Mariano Vallejo subagents for Indian affairs for the Sacramento frontier. Although he distributed the spoils of office to friends of the American cause whenever possible, both he and the other army officers understood local society well enough to know the limits of favoritism. In Santa Barbara, for example,

---

[26] Kearny, himself a Catholic, hardly needed orders to respect the Church, but see his instructions from Washington, in *ibid.*, p. 236 ff.; Curate to Prefect, in Clodomiro Soberanes, "Documentos para la historia de California," 1874, MS, Bancroft Library, p. 193.

they could have solicited support for a friend of the invading army to serve as alcalde, but, recognizing the pervasive importance of the Carrillos and the de la Guerras, installed them instead, despite their wartime hostility to the United States forces.

The roster of the military administration thus had a cosmopolitan character: of the 157 men installed in office from 1847 to 1849, 74 were born in the United States or Britain, 5 in continental Europe, and 48 in California and Mexico. They were a medley of Spanish-speaking rancheros, Yankee traders, Bear Flaggers from the Sacramento River valley, mustered-out army officers, pioneers of 1846 and 1847, and Europeans who had supported the Americans in the war. The Californios kept dropping out and being replaced by Yankees, who by 1849 were in the majority. The decrease in the number of "native sons" in government was partly offset, however, by the increase in the number of their gringo sons-in-law who entered the government each month.[27] Although the military government was something less than a perfect copy of California's social complexion, it was composed largely of natural leaders acceptable to the native Californians and, in principle at least, dedicated to working out an accommodation with them. The army, in fact, was the last important Yankee institution that could boast any such distinction.

Army policy could have succeeded if the garrisons had been strong enough to impose discipline uniformly on both sides, if official cordiality had had time to filter down to the ranks, and if the gold rush had not come so swiftly on the heels of conquest. The policy of the military actually did succeed in certain places where the army garrison commanded respect, where the gentry accepted defeat gracefully, and, above all, where the right man filled the job of alcalde.

Monterey was fortunate in its alcalde, Walter Colton. The Congregationalist preacher and Romanticist poet managed to get on well partly because he found positive virtues in the old legal practices. A courtroom operating without lawyers pleased him, for, with his

[27] Data on U.S. Army administration are from official correspondence scattered throughout *California and New Mexico*. Other Spanish names among officeholders of that time are: Angel, Armijo, Ávila, Buelna, Castro, Charhaunea, de Haro, Ezquer, Fernandez, Guirado, Guerrero, Lebrija, Lugo, Lopez, Larios, Lenano, Marron, Noe, Noriega, Ocampo, Ortega, Osio, Ruiz, Sanchez, Salazar, Sepúlveda and Suñol.

Testament handy, he needed no attorney to remind him of precedents. Californians displayed their confidence by going to him with the myriad petty affairs an alcalde supervised, from arbitrating money matters to chastising a fickle lover. He swiftly introduced the jury trial and new definitions for horse theft and other capital crimes, but he also diligently explained their meaning to the Spanish Americans and meted out lenient punishments for prisoners genuinely confused by the new system. He saw the befuddlement of the neophyte Indians, for example, who were seized for horse stealing. Believing that horses were so abundant as to be a species of public property, and knowing that exchanging horses without the other party's permission was common practice in old California, the Indians could not comprehend the Yankee's strict new notion of horse theft. Colton gave them not only light sentences but also a plug of tobacco and some clothing for their trouble.

Alcalde Colton also tried to elevate public morality by stamping out public gambling and drinking and "Sabbath breaking." Although he drove the drinkers and gamblers into the woods, he found Sabbatarianism difficult to enforce among a people who enjoyed life without regard to the calendar. When he politely refused to officiate as alcalde on the Lord's Day, the Californians graciously apologized for interfering with his "recreations. . . . such is the moral obtuseness which perversion of the Sabbath induces." [28] Ultimately he gave up his campaign for the purification of Sunday as something "wholly unintelligible" in Monterey, yet he did so philosophically and without anger, for he liked the Californians and, in a patronizing manner, respected their culture.

In communities other than Monterey, where the army lacked authority, the old-timers refused to accept defeat, and the officeholders had none of Colton's touch, military government was a practical failure.

San Jose, beyond effective reach of the army garrison at Monterey, lacked the basis of discipline. The old ruling clans, the Pachecos in particular, never really ceased fighting the gringos. Then, too, the flow of transient gold seekers dissipated the powers of local government and broke down all sense of order. By mid-July, 1848, Mexicans and Yan-

[28] *The Californian* (Monterey), Aug. 15, 1846; Colton, *op. cit.*, pp. 107–108.

kees heading for the Sierra brawled in town nightly. Drovers herded cattle directly through the main streets, butchering animals for sale as they went; the noise, the dust, and the stench were unbearable. And the Indians, seeing new opportunities to obtain stock, created additional havoc by their periodic forays on the ranchos.

Three gringos in succession—a long-time Yankee resident with a California wife, a respected Briton, and a Yankee immigrant of 1846—all tried their hand at the office of alcalde of San Jose with equally poor results. The first of the three, optimistically established in *ayuntamiento* (municipal government) and a jury, both comprised six Californians and six Americans. When he put Spanish Americans on trial, however, no matter what the charge, the "native element of the jury . . . failed to convict." Disappointed, this Yankee resigned.[29] His British successor first was plagued by Indian marauders and then by white cattle thieves masquerading as Indians, but he could not induce the local citizens to put aside their differences and hunt down the badmen. The Briton's replacement, the Yankee immigrant, had to work with the obstreperous Dolores Pacheco, who had seen fit to come back as second alcalde of San Jose. The Yankee knew that Salvio Pacheco had committed a felony and that failure to punish him would turn the law into a sham, at the same time, Don Salvio was now protected by his kinsman, Don Dolores. Realizing that any American who punished a Pacheco was risking his own life, this Yankee alcalde also resigned, advising Governor Mason to install in the office an army officer and back him with thirty or forty dragoons if a disaster was to be avoided. (Since Mason barely had thirty dragoons left in the entire command, one can imagine how he regarded this request.) [30]

The most telling problem of army administration was encountered by those few native-born officials who dared exercise authority against Americans. Americans saw the advantage of letting Californios control Californios, but they would give the native-born no license to govern

[29] H. S. Foote, *Pen Pictures from the Garden of the World, or, Santa Clara County, California* (Chicago, 1888), p. 82.
[30] J. S. Ruckel to Governor Mason (private correspondence), Dec. 28, 1847, unbound document, pp. 132–133, cited in Bancroft, Reference Notes, spring binder, "Crime, Criminals and Administration of Justice," MS, Bancroft Library; Charles White to Governor Mason, April 17, July 16, 1848, unbound documents, pp. 76–77, 122, in *ibid*. This news of chaos was deleted from *California and New Mexico*.

Yankees. This difficulty was faced in the San Jose–Santa Clara district by prefects (i.e., marshals) Felix Buelna and Antonio Pico who, in September of 1849, tried to overcome a "deplorable state of order" by using their broad powers to keep the *Norteamericanos* in line. To this end they posted a decree curtailing the carrying of arms, the sale of liquor, public dances, and the herding and killing of cattle on town streets. But, when Pico arrested one drunken gringo for gross insult, the prisoner's friends simply broke into the jail and released him. Pico never could recapture him.[31]

José Fernandez, Pacheco's replacement as second alcalde of San Jose, saw another hazard of working with Yankees. He generously left to his associate all business involving gringos and governed Spanish Americans only, a division of power made necessary by his own ignorance of English and the first alcalde's ignorance of Spanish. But, Don José complains, this arrangement allowed the first alcalde to manipulate the sale of pueblo lands and grow wealthy, while he, Fernandez, actually lost money while in office. "I lost my shirt," he explains, wistfully adding that if he could return to those days he would test out a few Yankee tricks that he had since learned.[32] The constant refrain of the Yankees and Californians, then, was that each was obstructing the other's efforts to maintain true law and order. Meanwhile, such law and order as had begun to emerge, rapidly broke down.[33]

At one point in 1849, the entire army of occupation consisted of only the governor and his cook, the other men having gone permanently absent without leave. No longer able to repress fellow countrymen itching for civil government, the army sanctioned a constitutional convention. This move in the direction of democracy unfortunately released the Californios to the flood tide of gringo hostility. Nevertheless, Governor Riley saw to it that the convention met in the old capital, Monte-

[31] Pio Pico, "Documentos para la historia de California. Archivo de la familia Pico," 1877, MS, Bancroft Library, I, 175. 183–184, 191, 352.
[32] José Fernandez, "Cosas de California" [1817–1850], MS, 1874, Bancroft Library, pp. 170–171.
[33] Monterey went through a mob scene shortly after Colton departed; see *California Star and Californian* (Monterey), Dec. 9, 1848. In Los Angeles the old settlers rebelled by refusing to vote for installation of a second alcalde; see Mason to S. C. Foster, Aug. 26, 1848, in *California and New Mexico*, pp. 659–660; Henry Halleck to Foster, June 22, 1849, in *ibid.*, p. 690.

rey, at Colton Hall, built by the alcalde and his Spanish-speaking convict laborers, which nicely topped off the army's efforts to maintain a sense of historical continuity in public affairs. Fortunately, although the gold rush threatened an immediate political upheaval, the Californios were in a position to participate in it and thus soften its impact. Of the forty-eight delegates elected to the convention in 1849, eight were Californios—a generous representation, considering that the number of Californios did not exceed 13,000 in a total population of 100,000.

The "native delegation" entered Colton Hall proudly decked out in traditional garb and sat at one table. Delegate José A. Carrillo had been in the thick of things for three decades, first as a plotter of rebellions, then as a soldier, and finally as a signatory to the Treaty of Cahuenga. Mariano Vallejo was suited for the job by intelligence, training, and wealth, as was his nephew Pablo de la Guerra, scion of an influential Santa Barbara family and a public official since 1838. José M. Covarrubias (often known to his friends as Miguel), although born in France, was part of Santa Barbara's social élite and had served as alcalde and as secretary to Pio Pico. The other four native delegates were less experienced. The Spanish-born shipping agent, Miguel de Pedrorena, owed his place largely to his support of the United States Navy during the war. (Commodore Stockton, ordinarily hostile toward Californios, had made him customs collector of San Diego.) Don Antonio Pico of San Jose also had supported the Americans; although never more than an alcalde, he was literate, popular, and influential. While Jacinto Rodriguez had served the militia and local government of Monterey and San Francisco, he possessed little experience in public matters. The absolute greenhorn among the native delegates was the wealthy rancher Manuel Dominguez of Los Angeles, a mestizo. Although not a político, "the Indian member" of the convention was significant by his very presence: his face could remind the gringo delegates of their responsibility toward the thousands of non-Caucasians in the state.

Elected unanimously, the Californio delegates had the esteem not merely of "their own kind" but of Yankees, too. Yet they faced obvious dangers: they lacked the "muscle power" they might have had from the company of old-line políticos such as Juan Bandini, Juan Alvarado, and Pio Pico, who—unfortunately—had dropped by the wayside about

1847. Also, considering the looseness of the provisions of the Treaty of Guadalupe Hidalgo, they had reason to feel anxious about their land titles and civil rights. The miners, moreover, promised to impose on the landed class a heavy tax.

The Californio delegates did, however, come into the chamber armed against trouble. For one thing, gringo delegates Abel Stearns, Hugo Reid, Stephen Foster, and William Hartnell shared many of their needs and aspirations. Those allies could understand the more intricate parliamentary maneuvers and could augment the Californios' voting strength on key issues. More important, if the Yankees hurled insults or grew surly, the Californios could threaten to bolt the chamber and give the convention a black eye in the federal Congress. This represented a considerable threat to a majority of delegates, who regarded congressional approval of the state constitution as the consummate goal of the proceedings. By reserving this trump card, the native Californios "did wield a sort of power in the democratic process . . . and by compromise secured some protection for themselves." [34]

In matters of protocol and symbolism, the convention dealt gingerly with the Californios. At the installation of Robert Semple, the former Bear Flag officer, as chairman, Mariano Vallejo, who had been a prisoner of the Bear Flaggers, was asked to accompany Semple to the chair. (Delegate John Sutter took the other arm.) A Mexican priest, Padre Antonio Ramirez, alternated with a Protestant minister in delivering the daily invocation. When the problem of choosing a state seal arose, delegate Vallejo seriously proposed an emblem showing a vaquero lassoing a bear. The chamber rang with laughter at this unconscious jibe at the Bear Flaggers, but rejected the proposal by one vote. Plainly, the majority was unprepared to show *quite* that much deference to Californios.

In their own modest way, the Californios helped mold key sections of the Constitution of 1849, including provisions on voting qualifications, taxation, state boundaries, and publication of state laws. They participated in committee work and, on sixteen issues that touched

[34] J. Ross Browne, *Report of the Debates in the Convention of California . . . September and October, 1849* (Washington, 1850), *passim;* and Donald E. Hargis, "Native Californians in the Constitutional Convention of 1849," Historical Society of Southern California *Quarterly,* XXVI (March, 1954), 3–13.

home, they commented to the chamber at large (de la Guerra and Vallejo through an interpreter, because of their limited English). The Californios spoke to the point and without flourish, except for Carrillo, who occasionally displayed his famous sharp tongue, as when he excoriated the most prominent figure in the chamber, William Gwin of Tennessee, for calling him a "foreigner." The more temperate de la Guerra could handle open debate without invective.

Contrary to expectation, the Californios did not always act as a bloc: in thirty-five important roll calls, they broke ranks seventeen times. The chief exception occurred when a gringo proposed limiting the suffrage to white males only and the Californios, to a man, joined in opposition.[35] De la Guerra arose to argue that many Californios were dark-skinned, and that to disfranchise them would be tantamount to denying them a part of their citizenship as granted by the Treaty of Guadalupe Hidalgo. But his most telling argument needed no words, since the convention could not logically allow mestizo Manuel Dominguez to sign the constitution and yet bar "half-breeds" from the franchise. After some grumbling by the hard-core chauvinists, the convention granted to the legislature the privilege of enfranchising certain Indians.

Other voting issues show disagreement among the Californio delegates. Carrillo was the only one among them to vote for admission of free Negroes into the province, probably on the advice that such a vote would speed territorial admission. On the question of statehood and boundaries, the southern delegates, irrespective of ethnic background, came instructed to vote for creation of a state in the north and a territory in the south. They hoped to control their own destinies in a thinly populated territory devoted mainly to pastoral pursuits, whose boundaries would exclude the vast concentrations of gringos to the north. The northern delegates, including Vallejo, on the other hand, had instructions to create a large state but no territory. The big-boundary faction argued that, ever since the 1819 treaty between the United States and Spain, California had included Nevada and most of Arizona and Utah. They also reasoned that the wider the boundaries, the longer the territorial status, and the cheaper the cost of government to the

[35] Hargis, *op. cit.*, p. 5.

propertied class. Finally, the Californians did win boundaries large enough to please them, although the victory proved a Pyrrhic one when the province became a state in record time.

Taxation vexed the Californios particularly, because most of the Yankees wanted to tax land heavily, but not gold or other forms of wealth. As a safeguard against tax excesses, the ranchers demanded local election of assessors. When opponents of this proposal intimated that the gentry would seize those offices and commit abuses, de la Guerra delivered a "fiery speech" defending the honor of his class. Local selection of assessors finally did pass. Other issues that arose were Carrillo's and de la Guerra's idea that the ranching counties should, in view of their small population yet large contribution to the treasury, be apportioned more seats in the legislature, but this suggestion was easily beaten down; so was Carrillo's proposal to make Santa Barbara the state capital. In a clear-cut victory, however, Don Pablo won unanimous adoption of a measure compelling the legislature to print all its laws in Spanish.

The Californios gave every indication of feeling reasonably satisfied with the Constitution of 1849, despite their several uphill fights. They never had to bolt the chamber, they voted with the majority in thirty-seven roll calls and dissented in only nine, and on the bright and cheery morning of October 12, they willingly signed their names to the document and joined in the "state-making" celebration. All of Monterey was turned into a fiesta as the cannons tolled a salute to the thirty-first state. "All [delegates] were in a happy and satisfied mood," according to Bayard Taylor who was there himself, "and none [more] so than the native members. Pedrorena declared that this was the most fortunate day in the history of California. Even Carillo [sic], in the beginning one of our most zealous opponents, displayed a genuine zeal for the Constitution, which he helped to frame under the laws of our Republic." [36]

The constitution was the only major document of state the Californios ever helped to shape. Even as the guns boomed, however, the locus of power had already shifted away from their capital, Monterey. Northeastward, in the Sierra, in the hurly-burly of the mines, the

---

[36] *Eldorado, or, Adventures in the Path of Empire* (New York, 1949), pp. 125–126.

gringos knew little and cared less about either the army's attempt to spare the Californios undue agony in their transformation, the convention's polite genuflections to the "Spaniards," or the efforts of the rancheros to retain influence in the new framework of government. The gringo newcomers, in fact, were beginning to impose on the Californians precisely the kind of absolute defeat the military had found so abhorrent and had tried so hard to forestall.

III

"Greasers" in the Diggings: Californians and Sonorans under Attack

WHY did the Spaniards and Mexicans fail to discover gold before 1848? What would have happened to them had they done so? These are two of the "iffiest" questions in all of California history.

The Mexicans had, in fact, discovered minor deposits of gold in southern California more than a decade prior to the historic Coloma discovery, but they did miss the big find in the Sierra. The causes of their oversight include a fear of Indian attack in the interior and a decision to hug the coast for protection; no population pressure ever drove them inward. The Spanish tradition of looking for signs of *oro* among the Indians, as in Hernán Cortés' conquest of the Aztecs, also played a role, although a negative one, for the California Indians did not manipulate gold. Another cause may have been that the contentment of rancho life after 1834 had sapped the rancheros' energy necessary to explore new territory. Or perhaps the trouble was, simply, bad luck: Captain Gabriel Moraga's forty-six expeditions before 1820 had brought him near, if not directly atop, the Mother Lode, yet no gleam caught his eye. The Spanish Americans generally did not want for daring as explorers or for skill as miners; centuries of experience in both had equipped them ideally for the fateful discovery they somehow failed to make.

As to what might have been their history had they chanced upon the Sierra gold, the possibilities are numerous. They range from the attainment of genuine cultural maturity and political independence to an even more crushing defeat than the one they received after 1849. Perhaps California would have become one of the most populous and heavily defended places in the Spanish Empire or in the Mexican Republic. The Californios might have had genuine Mexican military support in a war with the Yankees, and thus also a better treaty settlement. Conquest by a European power would not have been entirely out of the question either. The answer, of course, depends upon *when* one supposes the gold to have been discovered: the earlier the better for the Californios, from the standpoint of the growth of Yankee expansionism in the 1840's. One suspects, however, that Manifest Destiny somehow was bound to triumph along the Pacific Coast and eventually convert California into a Yankee province.

The Californios themselves scarcely ever engaged in such ruminations, for they were not a people to pine over lost opportunities and were faced with realities that gave them enough food for thought. The discovery of gold in 1848 made an enormous impact on them—the greatest in their brief experience: it brought them riches, for one thing; it threw them together with other Latin Americans, for another; and, most important, it opened them to full-scale Yankee penetration and conquest.

As news of the discovery spread in 1848, Californios speedily converged on the Sierra from all directions and, in a sense, made up for lost time. The experience of the Angeleños was typical. With Don Antonio Coronel taking on the function of patrón, the thirty Californios, Sonorans, and Indian servants had good luck from the outset. They immediately enticed some mountain tribesmen to accept baubles in exchange for gold nuggets and, after spying out the Indians' trove and plying them with more trinkets, they obtained their digging labor into the bargain. In one day Antonio himself ended up with 45 ounces of gold; Dolores Sepúlveda found a 12-ounce nugget; and Señor Valdez discovered a boulder buried only 3 feet down which had once blocked the flow of an ancient alluvial stream and produced a towelful of nuggets in a short time. He sold his claim to Lorenzo Soto, who took out a whopping 52 pounds of gold in eight days and then sold it to Señor

Machado, who also became rich. Even a Sonoran servant became fabulously wealthy overnight.[1]

In all, about 1,300 native Californians mined gold in 1848, the year of the bonanzas. If they had missed the opportunity to discover Sierra gold in the past, they did not do so now; nearness to the placers gave them the head start on the thousands of prospectors still getting their wits together for the voyage halfway around the world. The Californios had additional advantages in knowing precisely where and how to find gold and in gladly pooling their resources and dividing their labor. As a result, the organized Californians, though less numerous than the 4,000 individualistic Yankees in the mines that year, probably extracted as much gold as they. Coronel, a struggling Mexican schoolteacher, had pocketed enough gold to become a prominent landowner, viticulturist, and community leader. He and many other Californios resolved to make a second expedition the next year. They dismissed the news that a few Californios had been harried from their claims by fist-swinging Oregon Yankees, who refused to acknowledge that the Treaty of Guadalupe Hidalgo granted some Mexicans full citizenship: in 1848 "everything ended peacefully." [2]

In the year that followed, the story changed drastically. Coronel's return trip to the mines began badly, with a near-fatal brawl in a Sonoma saloon. One day he and *compadre* Juan Padilla were waiting for the wet January weather to clear, when a former Bear Flagger began to bully Padilla for having served as Bernardo García's henchman in the wartime atrocity against Cowie and Fowler. Padilla insisted that the charge was a lie, and the American replied with an assault. After a severe beating, Padilla lay in an upstairs room, hovering near death for several weeks, while below his accuser continued to threaten his life. Only Coronel's good reputation and the intercession of friendly Americans restrained the former Bear Flagger.

After nursing his friend back to life, Coronel returned to the Sierra. He fell in among Chileans, Mexicans, and Germans doing well at dry diggings until confronted with posters declaring that foreigners had no

---

[1] Antonio F. Coronel, "Cosas de California ... ," 1877, MS, Bancroft Library, pp. 140–186.

[2] Agustín Janssens, *The Life and Adventures in California of Don Agustín Janssens: 1834–1856*, ed. by William H. Ellison and Francis Price (San Marino, Calif., 1953), pp. 136–137.

right to be there and must leave the mines at once; resistance would be met by force. Although this threat never materialized, excitement mounted. In a nearby camp, a Mexican gambler's tent had been raided, and some Yankees accused five foreigners of stealing 5 pounds of gold. Coronel's associates doubted the accusation against at least one apparently honorable man and raised 5 pounds of gold to offer as ransom. Coronel conferred with a Yankee delegation and gave them the gold. The delegates then retired to consider the offer but never reemerged from the drunken and agitated crowd, which by then numbered into the hundreds. The money did no good; all five prisoners were convicted and flogged at once, and two of them, a Frenchman and a Chilean, were charged with a previous murder and robbery. Guilty or not, the pair scarcely understood enough of the proceedings to reply to the accusations. When Coronel next saw them they were standing in a cart, lashed together back to back and pinned with a note warning away defenders such as might come from Coronel's camp. A horse then jolted the cart from under the men, and California had witnessed its first lynching. That incident resulted, Coronel thought, from a declining gold supply and the Yankees' increasing jealousy of successful Spanish Americans.

As quickly as possible Don Antonio led his group away from the newly named "Hangtown," and resettled in the remote northern mines. But even there a hundred gringos appeared with the gruff announcement that the entire riverbed belonged exclusively to Americans who would tolerate no foreigners. Furious, some of Coronel's people who had reached the limit of their endurance planned armed resistance, even at the cost of their lives, but Coronel held back and sadly announced, "For me gold mining is finished." [3]

By July many other Californios had cause to echo Coronel's words. As the only true native-born citizens they did have a legitimate place in the mines, yet they knew no way to convince 100,000 hostile strangers of this truth. Fisticuffs or hand combat simply was not the Californians' style. Consequently, one of them carried into the field of combat a safe-conduct pass, signed by the army's secretary of state, which certified him as a bona fide citizen deserving of every right and privilege, of

[3] *Op. cit.*, pp. 125–140; Leonard Pitt, "The Beginnings of Nativism in California," *Pacific Historical Review*, XXX (Feb., 1961), 23–38.

every lawful aid and protection.[4] What good the pass did is not recorded, but the attacks mounted. For most Californios, the best answer was to go home and stay there: "Don't go to the mines on any account," one *paisano* advised another.[5] Out of pride, which prevented them from being converted into aliens by Yankee rogues and upstarts, few Californians ventured back into the maelstrom after 1849.

Musing over the gold rush from a safe distance, the Californians once more concluded that outsiders were, by and large, despicable. Mariano Vallejo said of the forty-niners without sparing any nationality, "The good ones were few and the wicked many." Hugo Reid ticked off the list of troublemakers:

. . . vagabonds from every quarter of the globe. Scoundrels from nowhere, rascals from Oregon, pickpockets from New York, accomplished gentlemen from Europe, interlopers from Lima and Chile, Mexican thieves, gamblers of no particular spot, and assassins manufactured in Hell for the expressed purpose of converting highways and biways into theatres of blood; then, last but not least, Judge Lynch with his thousand arms, thousand sightless eyes, and five-hundred lying tongues.[6]

The Californians now simply reverted to their customary circular logic, which held that evil came from outsiders, that outsiders were mostly evil, and that evil mothered evil. In no other way could they explain the ugly behavior of so many people, especially Americanos.

After a century of slow population growth, during which the arrival of twenty-five cholos or fifty Americans seemed a momentous occasion, suddenly and without warning California faced one of the swiftest, largest, and most varied folk migrations of all time. More newcomers now arrived each day in California than had formerly come in a decade. Briefly told, the story of the Californians in the gold rush is their encounter with 100,000 newcomers in the single year of 1849—80,000 Yankees, 8,000 Mexicans, 5,000 South Americans, and several thousand miscellaneous Europeans—and with numbers that swelled to a quarter

---

[4] Signed Oct. 26, 1849, by Captain Henry W. Halleck; see *California and New Mexico*, 31st Cong., 1st sess., H. Ex. Doc. 17 (Washington, 1850), pp. 869–870.
[5] Hugo Reid to Abel Stearns, April 22, 1849, quoted in Susana Bryant Dakin, *A Scotch Paisano: Hugo Reid's Life in California, 1832–1852* . . . (Berkeley, 1939), pp. 164–169.
[6] *Loc. cit.*

million by 1852.[7] Even assuming the goodwill of every last one of these strangers, they outnumbered the Californians ten and fifteen times over and reduced them to feelings of insignificance.

It is the destiny of ethnic groups in the United States to be thrown together with people of "their own kind" whom they neither know nor particularly like—perhaps even despise. This was the lot of the Californios in 1849, with the massive migration of Latin Americans. It was bad enough that by 1850 the Mexican cholos outnumbered the 15,000 Californios; even worse, angry Yankees simply refused to recognize any real distinctions between Latin Americans. Whether from California, Chile, Peru, or Mexico, whether residents of twenty years' standing or immigrants of one week, all the Spanish-speaking were lumped together as "interlopers" and "greasers." In this molding, the Californians, who had always kept aloof from cholos and earlier had won some grudging respect from the Yankees, lost most heavily. Their reputation as a people more heroic, handsome, and civilized than other "Spaniards" now dissolved. Their proximity to the greasers between 1849 and 1852 put them in actual jeopardy of their lives. In essence then, the Latin-American immigrants were a sort of catalyst whose presence caused the sudden and permanent dissolution of the social elements.

The biggest waves of Latin Americans came from Chile and northern Mexico. The Chileans excelled in baking and bricklaying and other skills and thus found themselves in especially great demand in California. They settled down at the foot of San Francisco's Telegraph Hill, in a place called "Little Chile," or went into the mines to dig, until expelled by the Yankees.[8]

Even more prominent and numerous were the northern Mexicans. Distinguishable from other Latin Americans by their billowy white pantaloons, broad sandals, and sombreros, the "Sonoranians" or "Sonorans," as the Yankees called them, first entered the Sierra late in 1848, after either trudging across the Colorado deserts or sailing via

[7] Doris Marion Wright, "The Making of Cosmopolitan California: An Analysis of Immigration, 1848–1870," California Historical Society Quarterly, XIX (Dec., 1940), 323–343; XX (March, 1941), 65–79.
[8] The travails of the Chileans in California are presented in Vicente Pérez Rosales, California Adventure, trans. by Edwin S. Morby and Arturo Torres-Rioseco (San Francisco, 1947); and Roberto Hernandez Cornejo, Los Chileños en San Francisco de California (Valparaiso, Chile, 1930).

Mazatlán. Some had sojourned in California earlier; in 1842, well before the advent of James Marshall, a Sonoran had discovered gold near San Fernando Mission. More visibly mestizo, less consciously Spanish than the Californians, they seemed "primitive" by local standards. Apache raiders kept them from their own mines and pastures, so that the Sonorans pounced on the California discovery as a panacea. The northern Mexican patróns themselves encouraged the migration of the peons by sponsoring expeditions of twenty or thirty underlings at a time, giving them full upkeep in return for half of their gold findings in California. The migration included so broad a spectrum of the population of Sonora and Sinaloa and was so large and continuous throughout 1850, that it compelled the governors of northern Mexico to admonish repeatedly about the dangers of life on gringo soil.

The Sonorans came on swiftly, heedless of any warnings, knowing that they had vital services to offer California—as prospectors and hired hands, as supply merchants and mule skinners, also as monte gamblers and prostitutes. The leading merchants of Altar and Horcasitas, Sonoran towns near the international boundary, stripped their shelves in the spring of 1849, loaded up every available pack animal, and scurried for the mines. There they sold everything they had brought, dug some gold, and shortly left their followers to return to Sonora for new stock or for quick investment in Mexican securities— much of this accomplished before most of the Yankee Argonauts had even arrived.[9]

Sonorans gravitated mainly toward the San Joaquin River tributaries, called the "southern mines" or "dry diggings," especially near a spot named in their honor, Sonora. Here they introduced Yankees to many of the rudimentary mining techniques that typified the early gold rush era. Sonorans somehow could probe the topsoil with knives and bring up nuggets, or work the *batea* (pan) to great advantage. Where water was scarce and quartz plentiful, as in the southern mines, they had the endurance to sit for hours and winnow dirt in their serapes, sometimes using their own gargantuan breath if the wind died down. They could

[9] José Francisco Velasco, *Noticias estadísticas del estado de Sonora, acompañadas de ligeras reflecsiones* . . . (Mexico, D.F., 1850), p. 281 ff. On the Sonoran miners and their technology see Sylvester Mowry, *Arizona and Sonora* (New York, 1864), p. 97 and *passim;* and Rodman W. Paul, *California Gold: The Beginning of Mining in the Far West* (Cambridge, 1947), pp. 26, 110–113, 212.

also improvise the *arastra* (mill), consisting of a mule harnessed to a long spoke treading in a circle and grinding ore under a heavy, flat boulder. Others eventually caught on to those techniques and machines and later surpassed them, but the Sonorans' sixth sense for finding gold and their willingness to endure physical hardship gave them great advantages. Talent made them conspicuously "lucky"—and, therefore, —subject to attack by jealous Yankees.

Although the Californios quietly withdrew from the Sierra and left the field to the Mexicans and the Yankees, the scene in the mines deserved their closest attention. For, the mines became the staging ground for widespread attacks on their ranchos and pueblos, the rehearsal place for broad-scale assaults on the Spanish-speaking.

The problem of precisely how to react to the remaining "Spaniards" made the Yankees squirm. They shifted from violence to legislation, from legislation to litigation, and back again to violence. Some wished to exploit, others to expel, and still others to control the Latin Americans. On occasion, some Yankees even proposed allowing them completely free access to the mines.

It would have given small comfort to Coronel, Vallejo, Reid, and other Californios to learn that good and decent men had inspired the purge trials of the winter and spring of 1849. Yet, in truth, a great deal of antiforeigner agitation originated from the most reputable new citizens—army officers, lawyers, merchants, clergy, and public officials. It is a fact that the first organized and officially sanctioned outburst against Spanish Americans came from three hundred "white-collar" Yankees. While stranded in Panama in January, 1849, on their way to San Francisco, they heard distressing rumors that "foreign plunderers" from all over the Pacific littoral had already siphoned off $4 million worth of gold in California; how much remained for "true citizens" thus was problematic. On a slight provocation, the Yankees called a public meeting to deal sternly with the interlopers. No less a dignitary than the justice of the Oregon Territory presided over the gathering, and in the background hovered General Persifor F. Smith, traveling to Monterey to take charge of the army. Smith drafted a circular declaring that, in California, he would "consider everyone who is not a citizen of the United States, who enters upon public land and digs for gold as a trespasser." This declaration won him three hundred vows of support.[10]

The miners, who twice confronted Coronel with the charge that "foreigners" had "no right" to dig gold, were simply enforcing Smith's hastily improvised "doctrine of trespass." In April, vigilantes at Sutter's Mill drove away masses of Chileans, Mexicans, and Peruvians; and during a similar purge along the Sacramento River on the Fourth of July lives were lost, property was destroyed, and foreigners' goods were sold at auction. More than a thousand victims, mainly Chileans, came pouring down into San Francisco shortly afterward, many of them embarking for home. "General Smith is blamed by everyone as the sole cause of the outrage." [11]

Smith beat a hasty retreat when he discovered that the consequences of the plunderers' activities had been grossly overrated: gold was still plentiful, and most of the dust already exported from California had found its way into the hands of American supply merchants. His successor, Brigadier General Bennet Riley, rode through the mines trying to undo some of the damage caused by the doctrine of trespass by telling Americans that technically all diggers were guests on government land, and that thereafter none should be denied access to its bounty.[12]

Resentment against the "greasers" mounted, however, a product of deep and abiding feelings of nationalism, racism, and despair over the debasement of free labor. The nationalism was partly a hangover from the war. Some men imagined seeing "whole battalions, armed to the teeth . . . moving through the heart of Mexico . . . gotten up by the great capitalists and friends of Santa Anna . . . rising in one solid mass whose cry is 'California's recovery or death!' " [13] Yankee veterans unhappy in the diggings and nostalgic for army comradery saw in the coming of the "greasers" the pretext for a "muss," whether for mayhem or for merriment. Northern Europeans—the Irish in particular—and Australians became implacable foes of the Spanish Americans, more so perhaps than many native-born citizens of the United States. The noto-

[10] The incident is described in Victor M. Berthold, The Pioneer Steamer California: 1848–1849 (Boston and New York, 1932), pp. 37–42 and passim; and by Smith to William Marcy, Jan. 7, 1849, in California and New Mexico, pp. 704, 707.
[11] Hugo Reid, July 18, 1849, quoted in Dakin, op. cit., pp. 174–175.
[12] Riley to R. Jones, Aug. 30, 1849, in California and New Mexico, pp. 788–789.
[13] New York Herald, April 3, 1849, quoted in Berthold, op. cit., p. 50.

rious San Francisco gang, the "Hounds," for example, which was staffed by former New York Volunteers and Australians, took particular delight in attacking the Chileans who came to San Francisco after fleeing enemies in the mountains.

The forty-niner's xenophobia also stemmed from fear of unfair economic competition. Back home, one could normally see who became rich, how rich, and by what means; a community could use institutional means to regulate the process and keep it fair. But on the periphery of civilization, controls broke down: men sometimes prospered by unfair means; the population upsurge, the ceaseless shuffling of men from camp to camp, and their scrambling for the top of the social ladder defied control by ordinary methods. Thus the forty-niner improvised new devices, even vigilante justice.

Fear of economic competition had some basis in reality. Sonoran peddlers marched into the mines and sold 10,000 pack mules in three years, thereby depressing the prices of mules (from $500 to $150 a head in a matter of weeks) and of freight rates (from $75 to $7 per hundredweight in two months). This reversal of fortunes evoked no complaint from the Yankee miners, who could buy onions, potatoes, and other supplies all the more cheaply and had come to associate Mexican mule bells with savory cooking odors and a few cheap comforts of life; but it brought, in 1850, a pained outcry from Stockton entrepreneurs, who sought mass expulsion of their business rivals. Moreover, when the Mexicans set to work as peons in the employ of their patróns, they did make themselves the target of the prospectors. Miners who began muttering against the Mexicans and plotting violence felt keenly conscious that the Spanish Americans were cheapening the value of labor.[14]

The treatment of immigrant Spanish Americans in the mines hinged also on the slavery question. They came into California precisely when the Yankees felt most irritated on this score and could see most clearly the parallels between Negroes and their masters, on the one hand, and peons and patróns, on the other. Yankee prospectors ejected from the mines with equal vigor any combination of bondsmen and masters. In

[14] Riley to Jones, Aug. 30, 1849, in *California and New Mexico*, pp. 788–789. See also Bayard Taylor, *Eldorado, or, Adventures in the Path of Empire* (New York, 1949 [1st ed., 1850]), pp. 67, 79.

July a prominent Texan, Thomas Jefferson Green, and his slaves were unceremoniously tossed out of Rose Bar on the Yuba River. The prospectors put into effect a local code prohibiting the mining operations of all master-servant teams, whatever their relationship. Three months later this provision cost the life of a Chilean and led to the ear cropping and whipping of Chileans and Mexicans who tried to oppose it.[15]

With California's entry into the Union as a free state, the plight of the Spanish Americans in the mines worsened momentarily. Their protagonists proclaimed that, if slaves were prohibited from the mines, then so should be the "refuse population from Chile, Peru and Mexico and other parts of the world [who are] . . . as bad as any of the free negroes of the North, or the worst slaves of the South." The apparent inconsistency in immigration policy annoyed both the friends and the enemies of slavery. In the first California legislature, nativists freely categorized the Pacific immigrants as a race whose morality and intelligence stood "but one degree above the beasts of the field." The State Assembly, in no uncertain terms (by a vote of twenty-two to two), asked Congress to bar from the mines all persons of foreign birth, *even* naturalized citizens.[16]

This extreme nativism soon brought about its own backlash. A fraction of the entrepreneurs in the mines began to worry less about the alleged dangers of unlimited immigration or of competition from "foreign capitalists" and more about the "disgregated, fractioned, broken up" techniques of mining; more about the possibilities of investing capital and hiring Mexican laborers, and less about expelling the interlopers. Usually outshouted at public meetings and outvoted in the legislature, this Yankee faction nonetheless had on its side the logic of economy and the ear of a few outspoken politicians who began a campaign to exploit, rather than exclude, aliens.[17]

[15] Allen B. Sherman, ed., "Sherman Was There: The Recollections of Major Edwin A. Sherman," California Historical Society *Quarterly,* XXIII (1944), 351–352; James J. Ayers, *Gold and Sunshine: Reminiscences of Early California* (Boston, 1922), pp. 49–63.

[16] J. Ross Browne, *Report of the Debates in the Convention of California, on the Formation of the State Constitution, in September and October, 1849* (Washington, 1850), p. 143 ff.; *Journals of the California Legislature, 1849–1850* (San Jose, 1850), pp. 803–811, 1013–1018.

[17] San Francisco merchants commissioned Felix P. Wierzbicki's *California As It Is and As It May Be* (San Francisco, 1849), which advocated measures to eliminate adventurism and stabilize the diggings. See also Claude Petty, "John S. Hittell and the Gospel of California," *Pacific Historical Review,* XXIV (1955), 5 ff.

Advocates of this new position were most numerous and effective in the southern mines. There, the Sonorans evicted from the northern placers late in 1849 found relative safety, hiring themselves out to Yankees who maintained loaded pistols, "cool eyes . . . [and] steady nerves" against possible opposition by other Yankees.[18] The Yankee patróns especially appreciated the Sonorans' skill and willingness to work for a daily wage of a dollar in food and a fraction of gold. "Greasers" worked speedily, when prompted, although work itself—and riches or savings—bored them, and gambling, drinking, dancing, and indolence cut down their work time. The argument ran as follows: The American, "with all his impatience of control, his impetuous temperament, his ambitions and yearning will . . . [never] be content to deny himself the pleasure of civilized life in the states for the sake of $4.00 to $3.00 per day, to develop the resources of the dry diggings"; the Mexican, on the other hand, is "milder in spirit, more contented to endure, more willing to suffer, more weak spirited, if you please," [19] but for those very reasons he is the man for the job. Although a mere "hewer of wood and drawer of water," [20] he would unlock California's wealth much as the Negro had done in the South. American freight shippers at the same time learned that the Mexican *arrieros* (mule skinners) were the most reliable of hired hands—skillful, proud of their work, and sure to get the pack train through the worst blizzard, over the toughest mountain trail. A genuine paternal fondness sometimes linked the arriero and his new Yankee patrón.

Yankee tradesmen of the southern mines came to see the Spanish Americans as particularly good customers. It occurred to them that, in contrast with the stingy Yankee who saved his money and sent it home, the Latin American invariably wanted to take home goods, not money; he spent all he had. Just as the Spaniard's eccentric work habits could be turned to the operator's profit, so could his spendthrift tendencies be turned to the advantage of the merchant. General Riley discovered that "Americans, by their superior intelligence and shrewdness in business, generally contrived to turn to their own benefit the earnings of Mexicans, Chileans and Peruvians." [21]

[18] Marysville Directory (n.p., 1858), pp. xv–xxvi; Taylor, *op. cit.*, pp. 66, 67, 75.
[19] *Times* (Stockton), Aug. 17, 1850.
[20] *Ibid.*, Nov. 23, 1850.
[21] To Jones, Aug. 30, 1849, in *California and New Mexico*, p. 788.

The tension between Yankee and Latin-American miners climaxed in the Foreign Miners' Tax Law of 1850, one of the most original if benighted laws ever passed in a California legislature.

Thomas Jefferson Green, its author, boasted that he personally could "maintain a better stomach at the killing of a Mexican" than at the crushing of a body louse.[22] A Texan, he had come to this opinion in a Mexican prison while brooding over the failure of a filibustering expedition. After a harrowing escape from the prison, Green published an account of his exploits, together with a tirade against all things Mexican (and Negro) and a proposal that the United States swallow up all of Mexico. He had come to California in the hope of using slaves to plant cotton, although the episode at the Yuba River smashed that idea completely. Because he had served in three Southern legislatures, however, and had a good reputation among Southerners, he easily won election as state senator from Sacramento.

Green had legendary powers of persuasion, even over men who disliked his social ideals. It was he who always gained adjournment of the California Senate to "more comfortable surroundings"—namely, his own bar—and thus earned his colleagues the sobriquet, "Legislature of the Thousand Drinks." In his tax bill—a kind of personal rejoinder to the men who had expelled him from Rose Bar for attempting to use Negro bondsmen—he proposed to issue mining permits to foreigners at a cost of $20 monthly (he later reduced it to $16). This tax, he thought, would bolster the bankrupt state treasury by $200,000 each month and would also encourage Yankee operators to buy licenses for their operatives, and to employ them "at a fair rate . . . until the labor is performed according to contract." The law would delight Americans no end and discourage mob action, or what Green grandly called "the interruption of the stronger power which is in the people."[23] This possibility so neatly wrapped up all the nagging problems of labor competition, foreign monopolies, taxation, bondage, immigration, and mob violence that the Assembly passed it nineteen to four and the Senate seven to four; the latter house, by a vote of eleven to two, also gave Green a special commendation for originating so "splendid" a plan.[24]

[22] *Journal of the Expedition against Mier* (New York, 1845), p. 269
[23] *Journals of the California Legislature, 1849–1850*, pp. 493–497.
[24] *Ibid.*, pp. 232 ff., 1106 ff.; *Cal. Stats.* (1850), p. 221.

Although later condemned as an intemperate and malicious act, "conceived in drink and brought forth in jollity," the Foreign Miners' Tax Law actually had quite sober intentions. Its main difficulty was that instead of flatly trying to either exploit, expel, or give free rein to the foreign-born, it tried to straddle the issue. It promised something for everybody: the prospector would be able to evict all "unprotected" aliens, the operator would be able to undercut the "agents of foreign bankers" who sponsored immigration, the government would receive money to pay its bills (among them, the expense vouchers of the legislature), the collectors would make a commission of $3 on each permit sold, and the immigrants themselves could claim the protection of the law if they paid their tax. On the face of it, one could hardly have asked for a more equitable solution.

Yet the Foreign Miners' Tax Law hardly worked that way at all. In Tuolumne County, where most of the potential taxpayers were entrenched, the impost caused outright defiance. Printed posters immediately denounced the tax and implored its intended victims to "put a bridle in the mouths of that horde who call themselves citizens of the United States, thereby profaning that country." [25] Two French radicals, schooled in the Revolution of 1848, engineered a rebellion and for its success needed the cooperation of the Mexicans. Although the Mexicans were gun-shy, they nevertheless went to tell the Yankees what was on the mind of all non-Yankees. An impressive array of 4,000 "aliens" —mostly Mexicans—congregated on the outskirts of Sonora on Sunday, May 19, to consider proper action against the law, which was to take effect the next day. To the collector's face the delegation flatly declared that the foreign-born might pay $3 or even $5 monthly, but not $20—a token sum for protection against rowdies, but not an entire fortune monthly. When the collector held his ground and demanded the full amount, most foreigners fled the town. [26] One remaining Mexican threatened the sheriff, or so it seemed to the bystander who killed him with a bowie knife. Local officials prohibited merchants from selling supplies to any foreign miners and spread an alarm to nearby camps to call up reinforcements for the forthcoming "war" at the county seat.

[25] *Daily Pacific News* (San Francisco), May 28, 1850.
[26] "Statement of [Collector] L. A. Besançon," *Journals of the California Legislature*, 1851, Senate, App. M, no. 2, p. 660.

One hundred and fifty war veterans promptly stopped work at Mormon Gulch, selected a captain, put on the remains of their uniforms, and, with regimental colors high, marched to Sonora for action. Sonora received them warmly with fulsome speeches, food, and free liquor. By nightfall the town seethed with inevitable rumors of Mexican incendiarism, assassination, and massacre. Officers posted pickets, stored weapons, and briefed the men for the next day's action. Sonora was under martial law.

Next morning, into the diggings marched four hundred Americans—a moving "engine of terror"—heading for Columbia Camp, the foreigners' headquarters. They collected tax money from a few affluent aliens and chased the rest away, with a warning to vacate the mines. One trooper recalls seeing "men, women and children—all packed up and moving, bag and baggage. Tents were being pulled down, houses and hovels gutted of their contents; mules, horses and jackasses were being hastily packed, while crowds were already in full retreat." [27] The posse finally arrested the two "hot-headed Frenchmen . . . of the red republican order," who started everything, fined them $5 for "treason," and dismissed them. Thus ended the "muss." The men liquored up for the road, hoisted the Stars and Stripes to the top of a pine tree, fired off a salute, and headed for home. Next day, about five hundred French and German forty-eighters stormed into Sonora shouting revolutionary slogans and vowing to liberate the Frenchmen. Upon hearing that the pair had been freed, the would-be liberators dispersed sheepishly.[28]

Sonora had just about recovered from the excitement of this "French Revolution" when a new attack broke over the heads of the Spanish-speaking. A series of robberies and violent deaths came to light near town in which the victims were Yankees and the murder weapons riatas; this made it easy to blame "foreigners of Spanish-American origin." Next, a Sonoran and his three Yaqui Indian retainers were caught burning two bodies and would have been lynched, but for the timely intervention of the justice of the peace and the sheriff, who remanded

[27] The quotation is from Walter Murray, a participant, writing in the Herald (Sonora), n.d., 1852, and reprinted in the Pioneer and Historical Review (San Jose), Aug. 11, 1877; see also Times (Stockton), May 19, 25, June 1, 1850; San Francisco Daily Alta California, May 24, 1850.
[28] Friedrich Gerstäcker, Scenes of Life in California, trans. by George Cosgrave (San Francisco, 1942), pp. 37–66.

the prisoners to the district court. On the morning of the court trial (July 15), the Mormon Gulch veterans again descended on Sonora in military order and spoiling for action. Informed that the prisoners might be hirelings of a "notorious Mexican chief" at Green Flat, they marched there, rounded up practically every male in sight, herded them back to Sonora, and literally corralled them for safekeeping overnight. In the morning, the justice of the peace investigated the "caze of murther against 110 Greasers . . . captured by 80 brave Americans," [29] but, having determined that the Mexicans were innocent newcomers, he let them go. After a momentary riot scene in the courtroom, the Sonoran, on bended knees, convinced the jury that he and his Indians had killed no one but had accidentally discovered the bodies and were trying to dispose of them according to Yaqui burial custom. The crowd dispersed grudgingly.

Unhappily, another gruesome death, uncovered the very next day, again made Sonora the prey of every rumor incriminating Latin Americans. Since all previous measures had failed to stop the atrocities, it was proposed to cleanse the hillsides thoroughly of every Spanish American with the least tinge of "evil." The present emergency demanded that "all Mexicans should suffer for a few." [30] The "better element" of Yankees in the southern mines, who normally recoiled from drastic measures, now feared that their territory was fast acquiring the reputation of a bandit refuge, which was bad for business, and felt impelled to join the broadside attack. Outshouting one dissenting voice, a large public meeting in Sonora voted to force all foreigners to deposit their arms with Americans and apply for permits of good conduct. All Latin Americans, except "respectable characters," were given fifteen days in which to depart. The Mormon Gulch veterans set to work enforcing these dicta with gusto.

The screening plan to expel the "obnoxious" Spanish Americans worked well. It reduced the danger of *bandido* attack and frightened off economic rivals. Between May and August, from five to fifteen thousand foreign-born diggers scattered from the southern mines. Mex-

[29] Judge Barry, quoted in Edna Buckbee, *The Saga of Old Tuolumne* (New York, 1935), p. 38.
[30] Enos Christman, *One Man's Gold: The Letters and Journals of a Forty-Niner* (New York, 1930), p. 176 ff.

icans went elsewhere looking for surcease of trouble but were dogged everywhere; eventually, they came streaming out of the Sierra, some showing signs of "pinching want." Even those who paid the extortionate $20 found that it bought very little protection, for if the collector neglected his monthly rounds their certificates lapsed, and if the Americans of one county refused to honor permits bought in another, the Spanish-speaking had little recourse but to leave. They knew that they alone of all foreign miners were being subjected to the tax: when they taunted the collectors to tax Irishmen, Frenchmen, and other Europeans they received no satisfactory reply. Masqueraders posing as collectors came into Mexican camps, solemnly tore up valid permits, and demanded money for new ones; when rebuffed, they auctioned off the victim's dirt and installed in his claim a "loyal citizen." One imposter carried off his charade so well at Don Pedro's Bar that he convinced a posse to help him chase away forty peons and their patrón and killed two Mexicans in the action, before his identity was uncovered.[31]

Even when seeking an escape from California, Mexicans found the Americans lying in wait for them. On the Colorado River, a United States Army lieutenant had express orders "to make all Sonorans passing out of California with gold, pay a duty . . . and for my trouble, to put the whole of it in my pocket." [32] A troop of California militiamen blandly confiscated from homebound Sonorans more than a hundred "stolen" mules and horses, ignoring the brand marks proving ownership and compelling the Mexicans to walk 300 miles, including 100 miles across desert.

In the preceding year misunderstanding, fear, and hatred had created an atmosphere so hostile to "Sonorans" as to sanction fraud and murder. Nonetheless, the argument for both protecting and exploiting the foreign miners once more gathered strength. The earliest and most effective counterattack against prejudice was made by the San Francisco Vigilance Committee of 1849, which summarily expelled the

[31] The tax troubles of the Spanish-speaking and of other "foreigners" are highlighted in the Stockton *Times,* July 27, Aug. 10, 1850; the Sacramento *Transcript,* Sept. 21, 1851; and in Richard Dillon, "Kanaka Colonies in California," *Pacific Historical Review,* XXIV (1955), *passim.*

[32] J. Cave Couts, *From San Diego to the Colorado in 1849 . . . Journals and Maps . . .* (Los Angeles, 1932), pp. 47–48.

"Hounds" from town and made amends to the Chileans who had been tormented by them. Thereafter many individuals took up the cause, speaking in behalf of civil law or laissez-faire competition or on grounds of simple revulsion against mob violence. Among those spokesmen were judges, editors, lawyers, a sheriff, a brigadier general, merchants, mine operators, and the French consul. Several sympathetic collectors ceased selling permits. Even the state attorney general disliked the tax so thoroughly that he refused to defend the collector prosecuted in the California Supreme Court and ignored the governor's threat to prosecute him for dereliction of duty.[33]

Xenophobia had injured its perpetrators as well as its victims. As Mexicans fled the southern mines in 1850, the profits of Yankee merchants plunged alarmingly. Eight-dollar crowbars in one afternoon dropped to fifty cents; a plot of land worth several thousand dollars went begging "for a few bits."[34] Out of sheer dollars-and-cents self-interest, if nothing else, businessmen collected money, hired a lawyer to sue the local collector, and circulated a mass petition asking the governor to lower the impost to $5; all but one merchant signed the document. In July and August, after the second wave of expulsions caused retail losses as high as $10,000 a day in three southern counties, merchants who had helped expel the "evil characters" during the bandit scare became aware that all Mexicans were fleeing, not merely the undesirables. A crowd gathered at Georgetown, down the road from Sonora, and went on record as denouncing antiforeigner vigilantes and as supporting civil law. As a result the Stockton Times reported that the screening plan enforced at Mormon Gulch and elsewhere was "speedily held in contempt."[35]

These forces had planned to persuade the governor to reduce the tax, the legislature to repeal it, or, best of all, the courts to nullify it. In the state Supreme Court they pleaded that it infringed the exclusive

[33] Stockton Times, Aug. 3, 10, Nov. 23, 1850; March 5, 12, 1851; Lang, op. cit., p. 89; Herald (Marysville), Sept. 6, 1850; J. Lombard to Patrice Dillon, Oct. 7, 1850, in A. P. Nasatir, ed., "A French Pessimist in California: The Correspondence of J. Lombard, Vice Consul of France, 1850–1852," California Historical Society Quarterly, XXI (1952), 143–146; Alta (San Francisco), March 5, 7, 22, 1851.
[34] Stockton Times, May 25, June 22, 1850.
[35] Ibid., Aug. 3, 10, 1850.

right of the federal government to govern federal lands and abridged
the protection granted to aliens by the state constitution and by two
treaties with Mexico. Neither of these arguments, however, swayed the
high tribunal, which advanced a philosophy of states' rights in all matters relating to the federal government. Two Southern attorneys convinced the court that a state (1) could rightfully tax federal lands, unless specifically prohibited from doing so, and (2) had police powers
to defend itself against undesirables. The court, in effect, agreed with
the author of the tax act, Green, who had grandly declared that congressional inaction on the California mines had thrown the state back
onto "universal laws . . . higher, greater, and stronger than the written constitution." Gratuitously, the court added that even had the law
violated a treaty—which had not been demonstrated—it might still be
valid, for state laws could take precedence over treaties.[36] Thus, the
Spanish Americans had unknowingly become the victims of the im-
ponderable and pervasive sectional controversies of the day.

Notwithstanding its new judicial seal of approval, the tax was a
practical failure, as even its original supporters admitted. The Mexican
was not the Negro slave; California was not Texas. The governor,
aware that the tax was reaping more resentment than revenue, cut the
rate to $20 for four months. Even after this corrective, however, the
state obtained only $30,000 instead of an expected $2,400,000. The collector in a county that had 15,000 potential taxpayers, sold only 525
permits and was so harrassed on his job that he resigned.[37] By 1851
Stockton's leading citizens had developed such loathing for the tax—"a
law for the killing of children to get their fat" [38]—that they decided to
rally the entire county and lobby in the state capital to obtain its repeal. This they accomplished early in 1851.

The tax had failed to make the state wealthy, to prevent mob action,
and to convert immigrants into hirelings as promised. It had eliminated
the Latin Americans already in California and curtailed new immigra-

---

[36] *The People ex rel. The Attorney General v. Naglee* (1851), 1 Cal. 232.
[37] Governor's "Annual Message to the Legislature," in *Senate Journal, 1851,* p.
33; Stockton *Times,* Jan. 18, 1851; "Statement of . . . Besançon," *op. cit.,* p.
616.
[38] Stockton *Times,* March 5, 1851.

tion, a result that did not altogether fill the original bill. Now, having pushed the tax aside, the boosters of the foreign miners hoped to summon them back and make amends. The Yankees had a sudden vision that with the law gone, tens of thousands of Latin Americans would come flooding out of Mexico and Chile and the California towns and wash up into the southern mines, thus opening a new era in gold mining.

That dream failed to materialize, however, since the Spanish Americans by now mistrusted the Yankees and suspected that gold was giving out. They withdrew to Los Angeles and other villages or returned home, informing their countrymen of the dangers of venturing forth into California. Of course, small parties of Spanish Americans continued to enter the diggings, rummaging about on their own hook and staying alert to the possibility of trouble. The one lone Mexican patrón who dared bring in peons in 1852 stood out so conspicuously that he became the center of an international incident. His case made the complete circuit to Mexico City, Washington, and back to California. The district attorney investigated it for the United States Secretary of War, who determined that, although the crowd of Americans who stopped the Mexican was "wholly unprincipled and deserving of punishment," Mexican nationals should seek reparations in the state courts, since the federal government took no responsibility for riots.[39] Thereafter, no patrón was courageous or indiscreet enough to enter the mines, and the Yankee triumph over "foreign capitalists" and "slaves" was complete.

In the long view of California history, the Mexican miners represent merely a link in a long chain of migrants who reach across the "Spanish borderland." They unwittingly followed the trail blazed by the Spanish soldier Juan Bautista Anza and used later by Mexican cholos and colonists. They foreshadowed the coming of the "wetbacks" and the braceros in the twentieth century. As ever, the Mexicans met with

[39] *Alta*, June and July, 1852, *passim;* I. S. K. Ogier to William L. Marcy, Nov. 15, 1853, in George Cosgrave, "A Diplomatic Incident on the Little Mariposa," California Historical Society *Quarterly*, XXI (Dec., 1942), 358–362; and Marcy to Manuel Larrainzar, May 25, April 28, 1853, in William R. Manning, ed., *Diplomatic Correspondence of the United States: Inter-American Affairs, 1831–1860* (Washington, D.C., 1937), IX, 129 ff.

mixed success in California, often defeat. They did find some gold, but had to fight for every ounce. That they escaped Yankee bondage was perhaps the most fortunate thing that happened to them.

The migration of the Mexican forty-niners affected the Californios in two ways: for one thing, it put the Yankees in an ugly frame of mind toward all the Spanish-speaking, including the native-born; for another, it sent the newcomers into the established old communities of California, where they fused imperceptibly with those born there. This tended to break down the old and somewhat artificial distinction between "native Californians" and "Mexicans." The fusion went on continuously thereafter.

The Mexican newcomers had, however, one major advantage over their California-born brethren; whereas they could utlimately evade the gringo enemy by returning home, the Californios, attacked on their own soil, could not.

IV

The Head
Pickled in Whiskey

BEFORE long, Chinese miners replaced the Mexicans at the bottom of the social heap. By 1851 it was the Orientals' turn to start paying the foreign miners' tax (revived at $3 to $5 monthly) and to scurry up and down the Sierra either to stay out of the way of angry Yankee prospectors or to hire themselves out to sympathetic Yankee mining operators. In effect, then, the Latin Americans, particularly the Sonorans, had paved the way for the Chinese question.

Far from abating, however, resentment against the Spanish Americans continued and even increased. For one thing, any expulsion of the Chinese automatically swept out other foreigners too, so that in 1852, when seven mining camps in a 50-mile radius blew up in fury against the "coolies," the Spanish-speaking also had to flee.[1] For another, hatred of the "greaser nation," Mexico, remained strong. Political campaigns, holiday oratory, filibustering rallies, and barroom arguments thrived on the constant diplomatic and border troubles with Mexico. These circumstances established throughout California a most unfavorable climate of opinion against all Latin Americans.

More frequently than any other matter, the "greaser's criminal conduct" kept cropping up in the mines as a pretext for expulsion. When it did, it spilled out of the mines and engulfed all Spanish Americans, in-

[1] San Francisco Daily Alta California, Jan. 8, Feb. 8, May 12, 14, 19, 26, 28, July 1, 8, 13, 1852; "Dame Shirley," pseud. [Louise Amelia Knapp Smith Clappe], The Shirley Letters from the California Mines, 1851–52, ed. by Carl I. Wheat (New York, 1949), 162 ff.; George Cosgrave, ed., "A Diplomatic Incident on the Little Mariposa," California Historical Society Quarterly, XXI (Dec., 1942), 358–362.

cluding Californios. In fact, when the rancheros read of the continuing agitation in the mines, they began to identify with the Latin-American immigrants to a greater extent than previously.

In the 1850's representatives of many minority groups suffered legal injustice in California, but none more painfully than the Mexicans and the Chileans. However badly the Yankee took to the Chinese, for example, he did not punish them for "innate immorality," as he did the Mexicans. Hubert Howe Bancroft's two-volume miscellany on popular tribunals clearly indicates the inordinately high number of Mexicans whipped, banished, or hanged from 1849 to 1860. As the San Francisco *Daily Alta California* sneered angrily in 1854, "it was almost a by-word in our midst, that none but Mexicans could be convicted of a capital offense." [2]

The mode of prosecuting the Latin Americans in and out of court in the gold rush years was generally uncompromising, indiscriminate, and abusive. They had to put up with the inequities inherent in both the regular judicial system and the lynch courts. Neither system could readily tolerate the law's delay, for miners had no time to dawdle over subtle arguments, mitigating circumstances, or conflicting testimony. The miner's punishments were harsh both in and out of court, since he tended to equate the crime of murder with other crimes such as horse theft and gold robbery. The vigilantes eschewed imprisonment, bail, or appeal with the stock arguments that ordinary courts were not in operation (rarely true), or that the regular law agents were corrupted and lax (quite often true). They thus inclined toward quick and final punishments such as whipping, branding, ear cropping, banishment, and hanging. Many of the regular courts demonstrated a form of justice comparably rugged to that of the lynch courts. [3]

Now, all of this applied equally to Mexicans and to any others who fell afoul the law. Yet Spanish Americans suffered special disadvantages: they had to put up with the language barrier, a difficulty Antionio Coronel had seen at Hangtown. The California Supreme Court took note of this problem in reversing the conviction of one

[2] Bancroft, *Popular Tribunals* (San Francisco, 1887), II, *passim; Alta,* March 18, 1854.
[3] For a concise essay on the vigilante impulse and illustrative examples, see John W. Caughey, ed., *Their Majesties the Mob* (Chicago, 1960), *passim.*

Jacinto Arao, charged with murder in a Plumas County court where not a soul but Arao spoke Spanish, and he knew no English. The high court ruled that "there is no statement of bill of exceptions, properly authenticated, and the attempted appeal upon the merits is characterized by ignorance of the formal rulings of this court and recklessness of human life, reprehensible in the extreme." [4]

"Greasers" had public opinion ranged against them from the outset: "To shoot these Greasers ain't the best way," one lyncher is quoted as saying. "Give 'em a fair jury trial, and rope 'em up with all the majesty of the law. That's the cure." [5] Even the regular courts in the Sierra put a heavier onus of guilt on the greaser's shoulders than on those of Yankees. For example, Tuolumne County judge R. C. Barry, a former Texan, noted during the "Sonoran Difficulties of 1850" that he "examined well into this case, as both [defendants] are greesers and there oths [sic] not to be taken as true." [6] Obviously, if a Mexican had testified against a gringo, Barry would have discarded his testimony completely. As Catholics, furthermore, Latin Americans condemned to die needed a priest to render final absolution—a service the mining courts rarely could supply. One lynch court that refused to summon a priest explained the need for haste: it indicated that the culprit, a Mexican horse thief, had bribed his way out of jail with stolen money in a town where several "Spaniards" had lately stolen about $3,000 and where an untold number of law officials had accepted bribes to let prisoners escape; the vigilantes were making an object lesson of him. [7] Each Latin American had to account not only for his own crime but also for the crimes of all other Latin Americans, and even for the derelictions of the sheriffs and the jailers.

The attack on the Spanish Americans in the mines assumed the characteristics of a moral crusade. Besides fearing the peons and masters who threatened the "purity of labor," the Yankees put themselves on guard against the "immoral" conduct of two other classes of Spanish Americans—prostitutes and bandits.

Among the provocations involving Spanish Americans, none was

[4] *Pioneer and Historical Review* (San Jose), July 29, 1879.
[5] Quoted in Caughey, *op. cit.*, p. 78.
[6] Quoted in Edna Buckbee, *The Saga of Old Tuolumne* (New York, 1935), pp. 32–33, 41.
[7] *Alta*, July 28, Aug. 2, 1853.

more incendiary than sexual rivalry. For years the Latin-American women were the most numerous in a community starved for feminine companionship. In addition to the Californian and Sonoran women who had come with their families, there were specially imported Latin-American women to work in the saloons, dancing the exotic fandango and selling drinks and themselves as well. Although the Spanish-American women seemed unprotected to the Yankees, and they were often all too jealously protected—by a brother, a husband, or a lover. The situation had certain parallels in the South of the United States, where Negro and white men struggled for the attentions of unprotected Negro women, except that the defense of feminine honor among Spanish Americans could be a deadly cult.

Sexual jealousy could, and did, swell into major violence, especially at the "Spanish houses" which soon dotted the entire northern landscape. A love triangle involving a Mexican mistress, a Mexican gambler, and a gringo kindled a sizable riot at Carson's Hill in June, 1851. The gambler was stabbed and his mistress was beaten, as war cries echoed from both the Mexican and Yankee camps. One gringo bystander was killed while engaged in a peace mission, and the Mexicans finally fled by the hundreds.[8] Instances of wife stealing caused special anxiety, even to the extent that the Mexican ambassador to the United States officially complained in Washington against the California mayor who seized "from a Mexican his legitimate wife to give her up to an American with whom she was intimate." [9]

Marriage between a gringo and a Latin-American woman, which did occasionally take place, also had its hazards. John S. Barclay and his wife, Martha Carlos of Columbia Camp, paid a heavy price for violating the prevailing social taboos. Barclay lost prestige in marrying her, for, as the newspaper delicately phrased it, his wife's house "was of ill fame, and Martha, the proprietress of easy virtue." On October 10, 1855, Barclay entered the place at the precise moment a drunken customer ("when free from liquor . . . a quiet, peaceable, and friendly citizen") heaved a chair at Martha in return for an innocent rebuke. Bar-

[8] *Ibid.*, June 18, 1851; July 30, 1853.
[9] José F. Ramirez to Robert P. Letcher, Nov. 19, 1851, in William R. Manning, ed., *Diplomatic Correspondence of the United States: Inter-American Affairs, 1831–1860* (Washington, 1937), IX, 432–433.

clay instantly shot and killed the man, to protect his wife. The town's leading politician thereupon inaugurated a lynch court, and a jury of twelve community leaders, ignoring the plea of justifiable homicide, voted to hang Barclay to "fulfill the Divine Law of 'An eye for an eye, a tooth for a tooth, a life for a life.'" The sheriff tried desperately to rescue the condemned man, but took a clubbing for his pains. The executioners tied the victim to a flume, which brought a "savage yell from the multitude," but neglected to tie back his arms, so that in falling he grabbed the rope. One bystander shouted "Let go, you ——— fool, let go!" Barclay paid with his life, as one reporter summed it up, because "in an evil hour he met the frail Martha, and, falling in love with her, married her." Professor John W. Caughey notes that by 1855 Columbia Camp had existed for seven years, "time enough for a good deal of progress in regularizing justice." [10]

Among many incidents with sexual connotations,[11] the hanging of the Mexican prostitute Juanita at Downieville in 1851 stands first, speaking volumes on the meaning of lynch law and of ethnic relations in the gold region. Downieville, with an uncommonly high ratio of saloons to customers, even for a mining camp, celebrated a particularly boisterous Fourth of July. That night a man named Cannon, reeling homeward in a drunken stupor, crashed down Juanita's cabin door and then went blithely home without causing any further damage. In the morning he returned, sober and apologetic, wishing to make amends (his friends said), but instead was met at the door by Juanita's paramour, the Mexican gambler José. Exactly what occurred next remains unclear, but evidently she heard Cannon utter an insult, grabbed a knife, and stabbed him to death. Americans seized Juanita and José and roused the town with cries of "Hang them!" A kangaroo court featuring a "prosecutor" and a twelve-man jury convened and stayed in session a good part of July the fifth. It recommended that José be merely exiled along with his "evil" friends, but sentenced Juanita to die. A few brave souls tried to prevent the lynching, since her crime was clearly unpremeditated and—she was a woman! Among them was

---

[10] Santa Barbara *Gazette*, Oct. 18, 1855; [Herbert O. Lang], *A History of Tuolumne County, California* (San Francisco, 1882), pp. 190–197; Caughey, *op. cit.*, p. 65.

[11] See "Dame Shirley," *op. cit.*, pp. 140–141, 158–160, 162 ff.

Stephen J. Field, a future justice of the United States Supreme Court, and a physician who did his best by declaring the woman pregnant.

These efforts accomplished nothing, however. The dead Cannon had been "a favorite, and there was considerable ill feeling toward Mexican gamblers and women generally." They took Juanita down to the bridge and improvised a gibbet out of the crossbeams and rope spans. She climbed a ladder unaided, notes an eyewitness, while below her stood "the hungriest, craziest, wildest mob . . . that I ever saw anywhere." [12] Maintaining infinitely more dignity than her executioners, Juanita adjusted the noose herself, even pulling a braid through the rope to tidy her hair. Two men wielding hatchets then cut the ropes and completed the hanging. Under a subsequent accusation of cowardliness, Downieville vigilantes sheepishly rationalized that the evil Juanita had corrupted innocent men before finally killing one of them, and that her death would cleanse the place of the bad characters who lately had troubled it.

Because Juanita was the only woman lynched in the mines, and one of the few in all frontier history, her case has remained symbolic to this day. Josiah Royce marks it as a nadir of California history, an instance of the depravity *not* of Mexicans, but of "respectable" Americans. Joseph Henry Jackson, after closely studying crime and punishment in the mines, observes that for the "Honest Miner" Juanita's hanging marked the end of innocence: it inaugurated a five-year era in which he either committed crimes or meted out punishments with particular fury and sadism.[13] This may well be true. For the Mexican in the mines, however, it represents a culmination, rather than a beginning, of violence. In light of the preceding two years of trouble, it seems altogether fitting that a *Mexican* woman should be so honored by gringos; if they had to punish Eve, then so much the better if she were a "greaser."

Yet, the evil Latin-American women seemed tame by comparison with the evil Latin-American men who roamed the Sierra in the 1850's

[12] David P. Barstow, quoted in Caughey, *op. cit.*, p. 49.
[13] Josiah Royce, *California from the Conquest in 1846 to the Second Vigilance Committee in San Francisco* (New York, 1948), pp. 290–295; Joseph Henry Jackson, *Anybody's Gold: The Story of California's Mining Towns* (New York, 1941), 102–106.

—the bandits. The *bandidos* fully matched the worst expectations that the gringos had of *all* Spanish Americans, irrespective of sex or nationality.

Endless theories have arisen that refute, defend, or explain the bandidos. Outright bigots, of course, simply charged them with the "innate depravity" of Mexico and let it go at that. Others saw in banditry the generalized, and perhaps justified, resentment of the Mexicans against their military defeat in 1847 or against the tax law and other injustices in the mines. In a sophisticated version of this rationale, Josiah Royce asserted that the Spanish Americans (including Californios) were an essentially amoral and childlike people who were not responsible for their conduct; the Yankees, a moral people, were to blame for provoking them. Carey McWilliams later speculated that the outbreak of crime in California came from a suppressed class struggle among Sonorans brutalized by cultural isolation and peonage. To these conjectures one might add as promising Margaret Mead's comment that crime among the Spanish Americans of the United States is often related to the destruction of village life. Florence Kluckhohn, in a similar vein, speculates that the sadism of some Spanish-American men represents the breakdown of the all-important relationship of brother to brother and father to son which pervades the entire culture.[14]

Whatever the merit of these conjectures, the bandido must be understood also as a product of social upheaval in Mexico. During the uncertain era that followed the revolutionary break with Spain, *caudillos* or banditlike chieftains roamed the countryside—a law unto themselves. Yankees who had fought them in the Mexican War recognized their special ferocity and learned, as Horace Bell put it, that south of the Rio Grande the line between "rebel and robber, pillager and patriot, was dimly defined." The resemblance of the California bandits to their Mexican counterparts was unmistakable.[15] By a curious coincidence, the heyday of the California bandido and the Mexican caudillo were to end simultaneously. The capture of Tiburcio Vasquez near Los Angeles

[14] Royce, *op. cit.*, p. 281; McWilliams, *North from Mexico: The Spanish-Speaking People of the United States* (Philadelphia, 1949), p. 128; Mead, in *Cultural Patterns and Technical Change* (New York, 1955), p. 170; Florence Kluckhohn, in *Variations in Value Orientations* (Evanston, Ill., 1961), p. 198.
[15] *Reminiscences of a Ranger* . . . (Santa Barbara, Calif., 1927), p. 100.

in 1876 put a halt to the deeds of the Spanish-speaking badmen in California in the very year when Mexican dictator Porfirio Díaz brought the caudillos to bay throughout Mexico.

The general alarm against Mexican badmen first sounded in 1850, about the time the foreign miners' tax was imposed. Suddenly the gringos began to notice that "amongst all the depredations, murders, robberies, etc. . . . not one had occurred amongst the foreigners or Mexicans—the Americans were the only victims." Occasionally, such sweeping indictments might later prove false. In at least one instance, however, the authorities learned that serious crimes were not committed by Mexicans but by some "half-breed Indians, some few Mexicans and Americans, and the larger portion of Sydney men" who had cleverly planted riatas as red herrings to confuse the issue.[16] Nevertheless, most bandits really were Mexicans.

By 1851 the California badmen began decimating the herds of longhorns being driven to market from ranchos in Napa, Sonoma, Monterey, and Contra Costa counties. Former Governor Peter H. Burnett recommended treating them as capital offenders, and the vigilantes agreed. Without much fanfare, for example, fifty vigilantes seized five Mexicans for rustling near Scott's Ferry along the San Joaquin River in late April, 1851, and hanged them twenty-four hours after they had confessed.[17] Hijackers increasingly deserted the mines, doubled back along the cattle trails, and ended up on the ranchos where they stole livestock and anything else they could find. Californios thus became involved in the trouble and, from that time forward, scarcely a week passed but that a ranchero was either charged with banditry or victimized by it.

Familiar Spanish surnames began appearing in news reports of bandits and their victims. On a winter's day in 1851, fifteen or twenty Americans sought shelter at a Pacheco rancho in the north and received every courtesy until suddenly, at gunpoint, they bound up the entire family and ran off with several thousand dollars. Señor Pacheco's bitterness multiplied some days later when another gringo, a tax collector, presented him with an assessment of $4,000, payable at once.

[16] Bancroft, *op. cit.*, I, 450, quoting a Stockton newspaper of June 5, 1851.
[17] *Alta*, Feb. 11, March 21, 1851; Jan. through May, 1851, *passim;* Marysville *Herald*, May 6, 1851.

Simultaneously, a gang of horse thieves was roaming the hills near Pacheco Pass and had already slain several men. The gang had in its ranks another Pacheco, aged twenty. This youth was caught pilfering a pair of boots from a store in the village of Martinez. Vigilantes took him prisoner, ignored his father's offer of $2,000 in ransom, roped him to a massive oak, and striped his back a hundred times with a whip. Such severe punishment for petty theft provoked some eighty Californios to threaten to burn down the town in retaliation. The Americans thereupon hid their valuables and withdrew arms from the armory, which lay across the water from Martinez, at Benicia. The crisis passed without further injury, but the horse thieves kept right on at their work.[18]

Unquestionably, the archetypal Mexican badman was the phantom-like "Joaquin," who terrorized Calaveras County and neighboring parts in the winter of 1852–53 and eventually became California's greatest legend. At first, Joaquin—whoever he was—seemed to specialize in attacking the Chinese, for some reason disliked by the Mexicans nearly as much as by the gringos. One early report has him kidnapping a Chinese to cook his meals. In mid-January, after weeks of sporadic forays, Joaquin stole several bags containing $50 or more and killed a Chinese who resisted. Five American horsemen gave chase, but were repulsed with losses. Enraged against all Mexicans, miners gathered at nearby Devil Springs and vowed "to exterminate the Mexican race from the country."[19] Thereupon, some Yankees seized one Mexican each at Yaqui's Camp and at Cherokee Ranch for extraneous reasons and strung them up immediately. Hundreds of miners thrust guns and knives into their belts, roamed angrily over the 5-mile region from San Andreas to Calaveras Forks, and methodically drove out the entire Mexican population—as prospectors had done in previous seasons— and confiscated all property. Forty vigilantes took off in pursuit of the Mexicans who reputedly numbered sixty, and although their quarry got away, they found four new bodies. In their frustration men kept

[18] J. Lombard, Feb. 10, 1851, in A. P. Nasatir, ed., "A French Pessimist in California: The Correspondence of J. Lombard, Vice-Consul of France, 1850–1852," California Historical Society Quarterly, XXXI (1952), 257–259; Alta, Feb. 24, March 2, 1851.
[19] Alta, Jan. 29, 1853.

meting out punishments for previously unpunished crimes. One group of vigilantes hanged an American at San Andreas for a serious crime; another seized a Mexican for allegedly murdering a pair of Indians at Camp Seco and then also punished two other Mexicans for robbing the Chinese.[20]

This sequence of events began the "Joaquin scare," an unprecedented hysteria of statewide dimensions. Blurred reports of Joaquin's presence came in from a zone of contagion stretching from the Consumnes River diggings in northern Amador County to Fort Miller far to the south. At Big Bar on the Consumnes, six Chinese were killed and robbed of $1,000, and the same amount was taken from other Chinese a short time later; a mail rider was assaulted; the body of a Chinese sprawled in the road, and a short distance away lay a mortally wounded American; now a solid camp of Chinese, now a stagecoach, now a lone teamster suffered. The bandidos evidently operated by a simple rule of thumb: steal everything valuable, leave no witnesses, never stop to fight. Time and again rangers gave chase but came home weary and disappointed. One group actually captured bandits' horses but let the culprits slip away and strew four more Chinese corpses on the road.

Four different ranger companies galloped out of Stockton, Jackson, and nearby towns, horrified by the killings and inspired by the $1,000 reward. Reports indicated vaguely that five Chinese were wounded and four more killed, either by "Irishmen or Mexicans," and that a few days later a band using similar tactics near Liberty Hall Ranch galloped in among two hundred Chinese, thoroughly panicked their camp, and seized the largest prize yet taken by bandits—$30,000. Rangers flitting in all directions never caught up with the enemy, although the Jackson contingent vented its spleen by hanging a Mexican for a completely unrelated crime. At Moquelumne Hill, miners seized another Mexican but brought him before Judge Creanor, who had him legally hanged for murder.[21]

At the end of March Joaquin disappeared over every horizon. By then many communities claimed him, sometimes a little proudly. Five

[20] Ibid., Jan. 26, 28, 29, 31, 1853; San Francisco Herald, Feb. 16, 1853.
[21] Alta, Feb. 14, 18, 20, 21, 28; March 2, 1853.

Frenchmen of Mariposa County, hijacked of $14,000 and then killed, reportedly were his victims, although San Diegans said positively that the bandit chief was then encamped near their town, while making a flying visit to Baja California. In San Francisco, rumors suggesting that "Joaquin Carrillo" was a prisoner in the city marshal's office quickly produced a mob near the jailhouse, but the captive turned out to be only an Italian seaman gone berserk. In the spring, the excitement over bandidos abated, although mention of the sobriquet "Joaquin" still brought chills to the neck of every miner, traveler, and teamster who had to go abroad alone in the remoter regions from Amador to San Diego. If a suspicious-looking stranger lingered in town, informants identified him positively as one of Joaquin's men, and if a brawl broke out or a wild bullet split a door, they always laid it to the Joaquin conspiracy.[22]

Supposedly, at the center of this conspiracy stood the mastermind himself, surnamed variously Muriati, Murieta, Ocomorenia, Valenzuela, Boteller, Botello, and Carrillo. "It is barely possible," the Los Angeles Star thought, "that THE Joaquin is included [in the list] . . . but if so his identity is destroyed and with it all the notoriety he has acquired." [23] Joaquin's identity was thus beclouded. Yet he was real enough to the Mariposans who lived in the heart of his stamping ground and who, in May, memorialized the state legislature to dispatch "twenty or twenty-five rangers, well armed and equipped, for the purpose of arresting Joaquin and his associate robbers."

Senator Pablo de la Guerra and Assemblyman Covarrubias cited the dangers of hunting a man so vaguely identified as Joaquin,[24] but the legislature, by a substantial majority, overrode their objections and created a special ranger company. The only concessions to the Californios were a three-month time limit for capturing Joaquin and elimination from the bill of a bounty on the badman's head. The governor thereupon put up a $1,000 reward on his own authority and gave the job of finding the quarry to a former army officer, Capt. Harry S. Love,

---

[22] *Ibid.*, March 20, 21, 1853; Los Angeles *Star*, May 28, 1853; June 11, 18, 1853; also Bell, *op. cit.*, p. 147 ff.
[23] June 4, 1853.
[24] *Senate Journal, 1853*, pp. 453–454, 555–556; Joseph Henry Jackson, *Bad Company* (New York, 1949), p. 17.

and twenty worthies, half of whom bore military titles and "all of whom had smelled powder either in Mexico or Texas." [25]

Predictably, the reward did not go unclaimed. Organized on the model of the Texas Rangers, Love's corpsmen chased the phantom bandit all over Mariposa County for nearly three months and then wandered southwestward into the Coast Range. In the last week of July, just before the bounty expired, Love's men flushed out a covey of suspicious-looking horsemen at Panoche Pass and in a lavish gunfight, since portrayed in a hundred or more scenarios, slew two of them. Convinced that the dead pair were Joaquín and his lieutenant, three-fingered Jack García, the rangers hacked off the head of one and the hand of the other and bottled them in alcohol provided by the surgeon at Fort Miller. To authorities eager for results, the grisly remains proved that Love deserved the accolades. (The authenticity of the head was "firmly" attested by a Sonoran, who "remembered" Joaquín from boyhood.) The legislature gave Captain Love $5,000 and, according to tradition, received a "gift" of $1,000 from the Chinese of San Francisco.[26]

When the news of Love's exploit reached Los Angeles, it was greeted with an incredulous and sardonic grin: "We strongly believe," wrote the *Star*, "that this head was put up in whiskey." Love was accused of seizing the most available head; Joaquín was positively *known* to be in the south on the *very* night of his alleged death. A local party of Sonorans and Californios had gone hunting wild mustangs in the north and had returned to Los Angeles after an unprovoked attack by Americans in which one of their party, Joaquín Valenzuela, who was not a badman, was killed.[27] The south never believed that Love had killed Joaquín and, in fact, later organized its own Joaquín-hunting ranger company.

This much is certain: Bandits ravaged Amador and Calaveras in 1853 and committed horrible crimes, but once Love brought in his trophies, organized terror subsided. But the rest is much less certain. For all his accolades, Love failed to establish that he had killed Joaquín or that the winter's atrocities were the work of a single brigand. Joaquín's very existence is questionable: he may have been

[25] Los Angeles *Star*, June 25, 1853.
[26] *Alta*, Aug. 14, 16, 1853.
[27] *Star*, Aug. 20, 1853; *Alta*, July 31, Aug. 12, 15, Sept. 1, 1853.

nothing more than a collective representation, created by a hundred anonymous truthtellers around a hundred campfires.

Yet, this is quibbling, for Joaquin Murieta became California's foremost folk legend; the truth may be doubtful but the myth is real.[28] His "life" was first published by an aspiring journalist, John Rollin Ridge, a habitué of the office of the San Francisco *Pioneer* who elaborated on a letter received there from "Dame Shirley" quoting a Mexican who vowed to bring "Death to all Yankees!" Ridge gives the brigand romantic prowess, aristocratic mien, and, most important, revenge as a motive. This Murieta is represented as a peace-loving miner, expelled from his diggings by lawless Yankees. For no good reason they tie him to a tree and whip him, rape his wife, and hang his brother for horse theft, which starts him on a career of retaliation against what Ridge sarcastically called the "*very* superior specimens of the much-vaunted Anglo-Saxon race!" (As a half-caste Cherokee Indian known as "Yellow Bird," Ridge was particularly sensitive to race prejudice.) The career of Joaquin vividly shows "that there is nothing so dangerous in its consequences as *injustice* to *individuals*—whether it derives from prejudice of color or any other source; that a wrong done to one man is a wrong done to society and the world."[29] This was too strong a homily for the 1850's, and the book sank out of sight until gringos could swallow it more readily.

The Ridge version of Joaquin gained little acceptance so long as bandit attacks continued in mining country, and they did so at least until 1856. Pancho Conde, alias Joaquin II, was arrested in Calaveras County in May, 1855, for killing and robbing the Chinese.[30] Later that year, a gang of eighteen to twenty-five horsemen, mostly Mexicans but headed by Americans, roamed Amador, Calaveras, and Mariposa counties. They killed nine people, including five gringos (one, a woman), two Chinese and two Indians, and broke into every safe in Drytown and drove out the community's inhabitants. Three Mexicans accused in this bandit orgy were hanged at Rancheria. As a follow-up, the Amador River communities decided to expel all "Spaniards" except those who passed a screening board composed of "six white Ameri-

[28] Jackson, *op. cit.*, p. 18.
[29] John Rollin Ridge [*pseud.* Yellow Bird], *The Life and Adventures of Joaquin Murieta* (Norman, Okla., 1955), p. 80.
[30] *Gazette* (Santa Barbara), May 24, 1855.

cans," and those who took responsibility for all members of their "race" who entered their homes. Vigilantes disarmed the Spanish-speaking and pocketed the receipts as expense money. Other communities along the river were invited to issue passports and expulsion orders; a company of a hundred men would carry out these orders, making sure to restrain the Indians and Chinese from taking revenge on the Mexicans and Chileans.[31]

Joaquín's head, the prize trophy of the struggle with the bandidos, became a museum piece in San Francisco. In 1856 its owner took it on a world tour, expecting to reap a $50,000 profit, and then brought it home. In a generation attuned to P. T. Barnum's freak shows or Buffalo Bill's Indian scalp collection, the pickled head remained a popular display in a San Francisco saloon,[32] only to vanish in the rubble of the 1906 earthquake.

Joaquín in his heyday seemed possessed of an uncanny ability to strike everywhere at once; to operate under many names and guises; and to agitate, organize, and unite all the Spanish-speaking in their antigringo crusade. Men believed in his ubiquitousness because the hostility between Anglo-Saxons and Latin Americans now took many forms and erupted on several fronts. Vast stretches of California became a no-man's-land, as foreboding as Apache country in New Mexico Territory. "When I see a Mexican approaching," reported an experienced California traveler in 1854, "I cock my rifle and cover him with it. At the same time calling to him to raise his hand away from his lasso which hangs at his saddle-bow. In this way I keep my rifle on him until he has passed and gone beyond lasso distance." [33] A few years earlier, meeting a Mexican on a lonely road had conjured up a picture of a comforting rancho or pueblo; by 1854, it invariably caused terror—not merely to miners but to Yankee settlers everywhere, even in the southern hamlets. In this grim frame of mind, the gringos came out of the mines and entered into combat with the Californios for control over the ranchos.

[31] Sacramento *Daily Union*, Aug. 8, 1856; San Francisco *Bulletin*, Aug. 18, 1856; Santa Barbara *Gazette*, Aug. 16, 1855; Marysville *Herald*, Aug. 16, 1855; *El Clamor Público* (Los Angeles), Aug. 28, 1855.
[32] Los Angeles *Star*, Feb. 14, 1856.
[33] William Ingraham Kip, *The Early Days of My Episcopate* (New York, 1892), p. 218.

V

The Northern Ranchos Decimated

A PUZZLE greeted the sojourner near San Leandro in the summer of 1853: Why should a fence patrol the desolate stretch of coastal road? Fences normally signal agricultural enterprise, yet this one surrounded no homes, no crops, no cattle—only a limitless expanse of ripe brown forage grass rolling inland toward a distant mountain range. Close inspection of the wooden barrier as it turned a corner and marched away from the highway, heading for the mountains, revealed that its purpose was negative—to prevent, rather than encourage, the use of the land. On the unenclosed property grazed a herd of gaunt-looking longhorns, sniffing hungrily at the unattainable feed and biting at soil as bare of grass as the dirt road itself.

Inquiry at nearby Union City or San Leandro clarified the mystery. The residents confirmed the suspicion that the fence was the work of settlers (more bluntly known as squatters), and that the cattle belonged to Californios. The land was claimed by the Peraltas and the Estudillos, who had occupied it since 1830, and by about 1,500 Americans who had hammered their stakes into it after 1851. The property had been in limbo since the beginnings of the Land Law of 1851. While the Californios pleaded their case before the Land Commission, the Americans watched and waited. Lawyers had meantime picked a flaw in an original claimant's will by means of which some settlers hoped to gain possession. Besides, the Americans knew that the legislature had recently granted settlers entry rights to land which "to the best of one's knowledge" was unused. The settlers thus put the law to

83

the test and spoke candidly of seeing the Peraltas "in hell" before re-moving their fences.

Here and everywhere near San Francisco Bay lives had been lost, property seized, and cattle killed, while the land itself lay idle. A lead-ing gubernatorial candidate complimented the San Leandro settlers and urged them to stay put until the Land Commission awarded a favorable decision. An aspiring local assembly candidate, who laugh-ingly boasted of once shooting a "Spanish cow" for "trespassing," prom-ised, if elected, to introduce for the settlers' relief a "fence act," an act preventing cattle from drinking at certain streams, and still another act compelling the old claimants—"semi-barbarians," he called them—to pay immediately for settlers' improvements. If they refused to pay, his law would eject them when their titles were confirmed and permit set-tlers to take possession.[1]

Nobody in California five years earlier seems to have anticipated this sort of social, political, and legal conflict. The Treaty of Guadalupe Hidalgo of 1848 had optimistically promised that the Californians would be "admitted . . . to the enjoyment of all the rights of the United States according to the principles of the Constitution; and . . . shall be maintained and protected in the free enjoyment of their liberty and property." [2] An early draft of the treaty had spelled out the provision on the California land titles, but for extraneous reasons the provision was later dropped. Yet both signatories implied that the dele-tion in no way compromised the Californians' rights. Secretary of State James Buchanan generously amplified this point, asserting that "if no stipulation whatever were contained in the Treaty to secure to the Mexican inhabitants and all others protection in the free enjoyment of their liberty, property and . . . religion . . . these would be amply guaranteed by the Constitution and laws of the United States. These invaluable blessings, under our form of government, do not result from Treaty stipulations, but from the very nature and character of our insti-

---

[1] San Francisco *Daily Alta California,* Jan. 14, July 14, 1853; Los Angeles *Star,* Aug. 6, 1853. A good general account of land tenure problems is W. W. Robinson's, *Land in California: The Story of Mission Lands, Ranchos, Squatters, Mining Claims, Railroad Grants, Land Scrip, Homesteads* (Berkeley and Los An-geles, 1948).

[2] George P. Hammond, ed., *The Treaty of Guadalupe Hidalgo, February Second, 1848* (Berkeley, 1949), p. 23 ff.

tutions." [3] The spirit, if not the letter, of the document promised full protection; its main fault thus was vagueness rather than prejudice against the Californians.

But, if the Treaty of Guadalupe Hidalgo itself did not create the land-tenure trouble of 1853, the Land Law of 1851 was more culpable. Of course, the originator of that act, Senator William Gwin, renounced all intention of harming the "happy and contented race" of Californians who faced a "prosperous and glorious" future; his bill would not cause them to feel "either distressed, oppressed or frightened." [4] Yet in it he proposed a fine-toothed combing of all the titles without exception, for he believed them to be largely inchoate and fraudulent—or so he said. The other California senator, John C. Frémont, believed that the defeat of Gwin's bill was of "vital importance to the security of our property" [5]—that is, of the property of the landed class—for he owned 44,000-acre gold-rich Rancho Mariposa. He discreetly kept his seat as an interested party, however, and let his father-in-law, Senator Thomas Hart Benton, take up the cudgels in behalf of the grantees.

Benton thundered that Gwin's bill was "the most abominable attempt at legislation that has ever appeared in a civilized nation"; [6] it would force the Californians into costly litigation and compel them to divide, sell, or simply give away parcels to pay their lawyers. They would arise in bloody insurrection and possibly assassinate Gwin himself. The Missouri senator presented an alternative bill, based on the premise that the present grants were generally sound. Let the law substantiate all the claims in one grand sweep, he proposed, and afterward let the challengers file suits in local courts to question the soundness of each individual holding. Gwin ignored Benton's first charge and said of the second that if any Californian killed him, Benton would have to bear the blame for having voiced such incendiary thoughts on the Senate floor.

Gwin's bill passed handily. As Senator Henry Clay declared in its be-

[3] To Minister of Foreign Relations of the Mexican Republic, March 18, 1848, in Hunter Miller, ed., *Treaties and Other International Acts of the United States of America* (Washington, 1937), V, 256.
[4] *Congressional Globe*, 31st Cong., 2d sess., 1850–1851, p. 159, and App., p. 48 ff.
[5] Cited in Paul W. Gates, "Adjudication of Spanish-Mexican Land Claims in California," *Huntington Library Quarterly*, XXI (May, 1958), 222.
[6] *Congressional Globe, op. cit.*, p. 368

half, while Californians deserved some consideration in the matter of land, the new "enterprising [Yankee] citizens" of the West deserved more.[7] As Gwin later admitted, what he had really sought in 1851 was an act to encourage his fellow Yankees to "homestead" directly on the land of the old claimants and thereby force the latter to pack up and relocate on public land. Had his modest proposal been enacted into law, the acres beyond the fence at San Leandro would have been occupied instead of withdrawn from entry—by Yankees. Yet the present act was a good start in the direction he eventually hoped to go.

In brief, the Land Law of 1851 established a three-man commission, the Board of Land Commissioners, to sit in San Francisco for two years (a period later extended) and weigh the proofs of all the titleholders who chose to come before it. Should the claimants or the government dispute the board's rulings, they could appeal to the district court and all the way to the United States Supreme Court. Both rejected and unclaimed land would revert to the public domain and could be seized by settlers. The board's function was to weed out the valid titles as defined by Spanish and Mexican law, the provisions of the Treaty of Guadalupe Hidalgo, the principles of equity, and the precedents of the United States Supreme Court.

The resulting disturbances differed in kind and order of magnitude from those Benton had predicted. He had not envisioned the squatterism, the waste of land, or the bodily attack on the Californians. Moreover, their expected uprising simply did not materialize. The real aggressors were not Benton, Gwin, or the Californians, but the Yankee Argonauts bursting with explosive energies. Tired of grubbing for gold, desiring to possess more nourishing soil, and feeling the weight of history on their side, they tried to adjust the land question swiftly and drastically. In fact, the Yankees' land hunger far outran the bounds of the Land Law.

Preliminary reports in 1849 showed great inequities in the land-tenure system. An estimated two hundred California families owned 14 million acres in parcels of from 1 to 11 leagues (nearly 4,500 acres to the league). This, cried the Yankee, was simply unfair. Many of the titles reportedly overlapped, or melted together in bewildering confu-

[7] *Ibid.*, p. 391.

sion; some had dubious legality. Governor Pico, it was rumored, had dreamed up some eighty new grants *after* the American occupation and had doled them out to his "worthless cronies"; certainly, all such grants must be retracted at once. The newly arrived Yankee argued that real estate in California, a province wrung from the enemy by blood, was formerly cheap; that "we [Americans] have actually made the land of its present value." [8] If rancheros deserved recompense for their acreage—and that was doubtful—then let them get only the prices current before July, 1846.

According to the traditions of humid-area agriculture in Anglo-America, ranchers—by comparison with farmers—generally stood accused of using land uneconomically. California provided an object lesson of this sort. While "idly living on a revenue" the rancheros were wasting "rich pasture land for unchecked herds." This situation could be remedied only by yeomen. Thus, with unfailing regularity, public spokesmen began intoning praises to the "hearty and industrious" farmers; the "hardy immigrants . . . the industrious settlers"; "the hardy and industrious settlers"; "the hardy and industrious hand which . . . turns the rich sod with the ploughshare"; "the sturdy New Englander, who with his family leaves the home of his childhood and goes into the wild woods of the far west or on to her unbroken prairies and builds himself up a new home among the haunts of the deer and the buffalo." [9]

However inappropriate for arid California, this poetic imagery served the purpose of evoking tradition, especially the freeholder tradition. It also advanced the Jacksonian idea that a few men of "immoderate wealth" and "special privilege" must not interfere with the equality of opportunity. In all fairness to the more well-intentioned squatters, it must be said that they probably did not mean to turn the Californians out into the cold. They proposed to let the rancheros keep as much land as an ordinary farmer—a quarter section—but to take away the "excess." While relinquishing their luxuries, the rancheros could learn

---

[8] *Alta,* March 4, 1853.
[9] See, for example, the phraseology used in the *Alta,* Jan. 18, June 25, Aug. 23, 1853; May 31, 1854; and in Governor John Bigler's message of 1856, cited in Robert Glass Cleland, *The Cattle on a Thousand Hills* (San Marino, Calif., 1951), pp. 123–124.

to share the "modest but respectable comforts" of the farmer; let them "look for their future advancement through the enterprise of their American fellow-citizen," one newspaper advised. Perhaps they could join agricultural societies and learn to "ply the sledge" themselves.[10]

To supplement the Land Law, which was only a beginning, the settlers wanted specific agrarian reforms; above all, they wanted protection for newcomers who hewed out farms on apparently unused private ranchos. To this end the settlers sought enactment of two laws: First, a law guaranteeing the right of occupancy, that is, permission to enter upon and improve "vacant" land with the guarantee of recovering the value of improvements from the titleholder should the court rule for the latter; second, a law of preemption, that is, a guarantee of the option to buy the land they had improved, should the courts reject the original claim, and to buy it at a minimum price (say, $1.25 an acre) before it went up for public auction. "Rights that had been . . . generally recognized elsewhere would," the American immigrants felt, "surely be granted in California by state and federal legislation."[11]

As it happened, Congress and the state legislature failed to satisfy the squatters; even the Land Law seemed inadequate. For a time the squatters actually demanded abolition of the Land Commission for its "dilatory behavior." Neither Gwin in Congress, John Bigler in the state house, nor the hosts of sympthetic local officials seemed to accomplish quite enough for them. A state preemption law did pass the legislature in April, 1852, permitting a settler to make $200 worth of improvements and then absent himself for a while without losing his presumed rights. (This explains the ghostly aspect of the landscape near San Leandro in the fall of 1853.) Gwin, moreover, in March, 1853, secured two encouraging congressional measures giving preemption to settlers on unsurveyed land and on land whose titles the United States Supreme Court might invalidate later.[12] Yet, despite these improvements, the absence of more immediate and more generous laws distressed the squatters and provoked excessive litigation and direct action, including violence.

[10] Santa Barbara *Gazette*, Oct. 11, 1855.
[11] Paul W. Gates, "California's Embattled Settlers," California Historical Society *Quarterly*, XLI (June, 1962), p. 104 ff.
[12] *Ibid.*, p. 100.

Only one scholar in the past century has risen to defend California's "embattled settlers" against their detractors. Professor Paul Gates argues that, although they sought the same moderate goals as most other frontiersmen, they got for their pains nothing but a blackened reputation. He blames a remote and confused Congress and an incompetent state legislature for California's difficulties, instead of Senator Gwin, the Land Law, or the settlers. The Californios, he adds, received more benefits from a sympathetic Land Commission and an able crew of attorneys than they deserved; the grantees lost far less land than they would admit and lost more of it by their own incompetence than at the hands of the settlers.[13] Professor Gates's revisionism has, however, evidently made no headway against the traditional interpretation, which is antisquatter. In a recent work, *California: A History*, Professor Andrew F. Rolle overrules Gates and quotes approvingly the verdict rendered by Henry George nearly a century ago in *Progress and Poverty*. The history of the California grants, George wrote, is a "history of greed, of perjury, of corruption, of spoliation and high-handed robbery." [14]

Clearly, the embattled settlers needed far less protection than did the embattled rancheros who were fewer in number, more ignorant of the judicial process, and altogether more vulnerable.

The ranchero never understood, much less accepted, the gringo's concept of land tenure. The Land Law, preemption and occupancy rights, and the "jungle-thickets" of land litigation made him not only violently angry but also mystified him. Even if he did comprehend the basic logic of owning land for speculative purposes or for family farming, the seeming heartlessness of the speculators and yeomen repelled him. Indeed, the more sanguine Californians had hoped to rent or to sell some land, raise cattle and crops on the remainder, and live according to custom—in a symbiotic relationship with the settlers. The relative peace and prosperity on the ranchos from 1848 to 1851 had reinforced such hopes; even the most pessimistic and farseeing Californians had not anticipated the wholesale land trouble after 1851.

The Californians felt sure they could prove their equity if given half

---

[13] *Ibid.*
[14] (New York, 1963), p. 306.

a chance. Even when they realized that the Yankee demanded solid, "gold-plated" documentary proof of ownership, which they had either never possessed or had misplaced or lost, the Californios nevertheless still banked on "common knowledge." Had not most of them earned their property through hard labor as soldiers and colonists? Salvador Vallejo, for one, dared any Yankees to say that he had not won his property fairly; and he proudly noted that none of them did. Were not herds and homes sound enough proofs of tenure? Was it justice that a man lose his patrimony because he lacked some papers?

As for the accusation that their land was vaguely defined, they agreed. Undeniably, most ranchos overlapped or were bounded by lines ambling indefinitely from perhaps a bullock's skull to a fork in a cow path, then to a brush hut and on to a sycamore, to end at a hatchet-blazed stump.[15] But then, in the early days no other boundaries had been necessary, and with a little patience most vagaries could be adjusted. What the Yankee had to understand was that California had been a wilderness, and that when colonists open a wilderness, judicial niceties hardly matter. What did matter was that men raise cattle and serve their king, God, and country, and this the Californios felt they had done.

As to the charge of fraud, the Californios avoided coming down to cases but retorted that, since land originally had been plentiful and easy to come by, no man had needed to forge papers or to lie to get his title, and few men had done so; the rancheros had executed all legal steps in "simplicity and good faith." [16] Although few Californios held a brief for Pio Pico, they refused flatly to agree that his eleventh-hour grants were illegal, since he had still been the rightful governor of California when he drew them up. But even if the Pico grants were questionable, how could the Yankees begin to doubt the legitimacy of solid old grants, such as that of the Peraltas, which went back twenty or more years and which any fool could plainly see were sound? Insofar as they admitted to swearing falsely in court, the Californios claimed that they used this Yankee trick only to defend otherwise legitimate

---

[15] These were the actual boundaries of Rancho San Antonio belonging to the Lugos; see Cleland, *op. cit.*, p. 29.

[16] Juan Bandini, "Documentos," MS, no. 123, 1853, Bancroft Library (Berkeley, Calif.).

claims, and only in desperation. If the "squatter courts" would accept none but the ironclad titles, what else could Californios do but "doctor" the record a little?

The Californians generally took an equally dim view of the personnel and the procedures of the land courts. The judges, the juries, and the "forensic judicature" of the courts were bad enough. Even worse, though, were the lawyers, who customarily picked at trivia, intimidated witnesses, flattered the jury, and even harangued the audience with patriotic speeches when they ran out of legitimate arguments. Land-law attorneys, in particular, seemed to give the lie to the professed beauties of Yankee justice.

Nevertheless, since most Californians scarcely understood English, much less the technical language of the courts, they had to depend greatly on their attorneys, whom they usually paid in land itself, and only rarely in cash. Sad to say, of the fifty or so attorneys who specialized in claim law in the 1850's, most were shysters who lacked not only honesty but also knowledge and experience. The names of William Carey Jones, Elisha Oscar Crosby, Henry W. Halleck, Henry Hittell, and Joseph Lancaster Brent nearly exhaust the list of worthy counsels. These few men pleaded for moderation. They wanted a legal compromise between the rights of the grantees and those of the settlers, not so much as spokesmen for an oppressed ethnic minority but as defenders of a Whiggish social philosophy. Since most of these honest lawyers owned land themselves, they crusaded with conviction for the defense of established property rights against upstart adventurers and scheming politicians. Their briefs, phamphlets, and articles articulated the only public defense the ruling class ever obtained in its time.[17]

Captain Halleck was the most successful of the land-claim lawyers and, to the Californians, the most important. The law firm of Halleck, Peachy, and Billings (and their silent "partner-resident" of Santa Barbara, Pablo de la Guerra) defended more titles than any other. In 1849, while still army secretary of state, Halleck had produced the first

---

[17] See Charles A. Barker, "Elisha Oscar Crosby: A California Lawyer in the Eighteen-Fifties," California Historical Society Quarterly, XXVII (June, 1948), 134–135. See also the anonymous pamphlet attributed to Jones, MS, F862.1.e9., Bancroft Library; and John S. Hittell, "Mexican Land Claims in California," Hutching's Illustrated California Magazine, II (July, 1857–June, 1858), pp. 442–448.

official report on California land matters, setting forth a negative interpretation. He believed that most California claims were inchoate and
the Pico grants totally invalid, if not openly fraudulent; this provided
grist for Gwin's mill. Paradoxically, however, Halleck never associated
himself with the Land Law; quite the contrary, he found it "harsh and
illiberal." [18]

Halleck originally solicited land cases eagerly, but his ardor for them
soon cooled. For one thing, his clients promised to find all manner of
corroborating documents but sent him very few. Such proofs as did
come to hand were often studded with obsolete legalisms which were
"almost impossible to translate well." [19] Besides, each case had its own
peculiarities and necessitated long and costly archival translations. The
Californians irked him by appearing in court with conniving lawyers
who presented claims "never before heard of," thereby damaging the
chances of legitimate claimants. Halleck's own clients proved to be "the
worst witnesses I ever saw, and when cross-examined by the government attorney . . . say something to completely destroy their testimony." [20] Twice he put Padre Jimeno before the Land Commission to
present evidence the padre alone could give, such as the year in which
a house had been built (a vital point), when a grantee had died, when
his children had died, or when his widow had remarried, but twice the
padre made "a miserable blundering mess . . . either from utter
stupidity or a desire to injure these claims." [21]

Most of all, Halleck berated the members of the Board of Land
Commissioners. At first, in March, 1852, he commended them for
"doing the best they can under the law," [22] but as they let the months
drift by without hinting at their intentions, he grew apprehensive. For
six long weeks they dawdled over testimony in a single case in which
all the main papers had been lost. A year later (April, 1853), two of
the three commissioners were removed "by Gwin and Weller to pro-
duce delay and give more influence to the squatters." [23] The replace-

---

[18] To Pablo de la Guerra, March 17, 1852, de la Guerra Collection, MS, Owen
Coy Room, University of Southern California (Los Angeles, Calif.). All of Halleck's letters cited in this chapter are to Pablo de la Guerra.
[19] Ibid., April 2, 1852.
[20] Ibid., March 1, 1852.
[21] Ibid., Feb. 24, 1854.
[22] Ibid., March 17, 1852.
[23] Ibid., April 23, 1852.

ments would have to study Spanish and learn the legal ropes, so that "the wheels are blocked again for five or six months at least." When the board reconvened, moreover, Halleck would have to reargue all the basic criteria: that a claim did not exceed 11 leagues, that it had been recorded properly, that it had been surveyed and occupied, that it had definite boundaries, and so forth.

He suspected John Bigler, the Democratic candidate for governor in 1853, of conniving with the new land commissioners, particularly when they slowed their work just before election time: "If the squatters succeed in electing Bigler, then farewell to land titles in California." When Bigler's election placed "the Squatter party . . . in the ascendancy" and the board then rejected eight claims and approved three, Halleck was convinced of a political conspiracy. He felt fortunate in having pleaded all three winners, but as he dredged through the board's decisions to pick up their meaning, he reported: "I tremble . . . especially for large grants." [24] Evidently, claimants whose land had never been surveyed or who never had attained "judicial possession" (that is, most of them) would have to demonstrate definite boundaries and proof of the construction of a house within one year after the initial grant. Perhaps, Halleck speculated, he should change his strategy and find even more reliable witnesses who would testify about boundaries and buildings. But, then again, Teodoro Arrelanes' Rancho El Rincón, which seemed to have "all the requisites," even judicial possession and nineteen years of occupancy, had been turned down simply because of vague boundaries, while Diego Olvera's Rancho Guadalupe, which every lawyer knew was lacking in most of the criteria, had been confirmed. Halleck, unable to fathom these decisions, wrote de la Guerra that he had "no further confidence in this Board." [25]

Although depressed, Halleck worked hard and refrained from taking his "pound of flesh" from the Californians as compensation for his setbacks. In the hard times of 1856, the widow Doña Carmen came crying to him "two or three times a day" that her late husband's creditors were wrecking her life. He did his utmost to keep the vultures from devouring her, yet he asked no fee of her. Concerning Doña Joaquina Alvarado he said that "if she is too poor to pay us anything we shall not

[24] Ibid., Aug. 25, Oct. 19, 1853.
[25] Ibid., Nov. 22, 1853.

molest her or sell her land; on this point she may rest content." [26]
Moreover, Halleck charged minimal prices: For confirming an 11-league grant he asked only $3,000, apart from $5,000 for expenses. His overall average was 2½ ¢ an acre, or at best 5 or 10 percent of the value of the land. For this reason, he dunned those of his winning clients who refused to pay their bills. Of Rancho Sespe Halleck wrote: "We worked like dogs in that case and gained it by the skin of our teeth. I know enough about that title to cause its rejection, and if they [its owners] treat us so meanly as to refuse our bill, I will defeat it" when it reaches the district court.[27] "I heartily regret that I ever touched a title in California," Halleck wrote bitterly after two years of labor.[28]

The total wealth devoured by lawyers and swept away by the raps of the gavel in judicial chambers is hard to judge. Benton's estimate of one-third of the rancheros' land runs too high; Professor Gates's figure of 5 or 10 percent seems too low; Theodore Hittell's projection of two-fifths to one-fourth probably comes closer to the truth.[29]

The Board of Land Commissioners itself generally was fair, but its entire operation, from January, 1852, until March, 1856, took far too long and produced eccentric decisions. Owing to its members' lack of fluency in Spanish, incompetency in Mexican law, and vulnerability to lawyers who dealt in technicalities alone, the board never discovered an equitable rule of thumb for measuring usufructuary interest.

The very act under which the board operated prevented an equitable outcome. The Land Law rested on a legal fiction, according to which the California titles were assumed to be so utterly confusing that only judges deliberating in Olympian detachment could distinguish valid from false claims. Actually, at a week's notice, dozens of trustworthy men of all nationalities—Thomas Larkin, Abel Stearns, William E. Hartnell, Pablo de la Guerra—could have drawn up lists and produced sketches of the best-known ranchos in their communities and told which were sound and which were not. Such pragmatic information, based on the "honesty and efficiency of average business clerks," [30]

[26] *Ibid.*, April 10, 1856; July 20, 1857.
[27] *Ibid.*, Nov. 10, 1853.
[28] *Ibid.*, May 23, 1853.
[29] Gates, *op. cit.*, p. 225 ff.
[30] Hubert Howe Bancroft, *History of California* (San Francisco, 1884–1890), VI, 581.

would have produced results quicker and no less sound than those of the Land Commission.

The Land Law prolonged an agony when speed was of the essence. As time dragged on, the gentry sustained outside the chamber of the Land Commission losses that were much more damaging than anything that went on inside. Ultimately, the Land Law did not cripple them half as much as the adventurism that accompanied the legal proceedings.

The Californians had to engage in relentless backyard guerrilla warfare with settlers bent on outright confiscation.[31] At first the settlers would encroach only on the outskirts of an estate, often taking up uninhabited land in good faith and paying rent for it, even though they refused to buy it. The first waves of settlers were quite tractable, but with each passing week in 1852 the number of settlers increased, and their field of battle grew wider and their mood more grim. Prospective farmers first headed for the green and fertile ranchos such as San Antonio, Napa, and Petaluma. Entrepreneurs could easily calculate from boats plying San Francisco Bay which points of land, inlets, and river outlets on these properties might make the best trading ports; they staked out their claims accordingly. The Peralta's Rancho San Antonio had the special advantage of fertile and naturally irrigated soil, thick stands of timber, and a strategic location directly east of San Francisco. Vallejo's Petaluma, besides its orchardlike appearance and proximity to the port city, was a proposed site of the state capital.

Bay-region settlers quit paying rent as soon as the Land Law took effect, on grounds that nobody owned the land. Initially, if a ranchero claimed 12 square leagues, they left him a sanctuary of 4 leagues and nibbled at the remaining 8, each squatter staking out 160 acres. In ad-

---

[31] *Alta,* Feb. 28, March 13, 14, 16, July 16, 1853; May 2, 1854; *Star,* Aug. 6, 1853; Transcript, *Peralta v. United States* (1910), Court of Appeals, Case No. 14766, Bancroft Library; Gertrude Atherton, *Golden Gate Country* (New York, 1945), p. 121; Edgar J. Hinkel and William E. McCann, *Oakland, 1852–1938: Some Phases of the Social, Political and Economic History* . . . (Oakland, 1939), II, 734 ff. Squatter trouble broke out also in Colusa, see *Alta,* May 26, 29, 1853; also in San Joaquin County, see *ibid.,* Aug. 12, 1853; and in San Francisco, see *ibid.,* July 22, 23, Aug. 2, 1853. See also Andrew F. Rolle, *An American in California: The Biography of William Heath Davis, 1822–1909* (San Marino, Calif., 1956), p. 111.

dition, they appropriated the rancheros' goods and crops for their own use or sold them in San Francisco. The Peralta squatters cut and milled orchard trees and took cattle to slaughter pens in an altogether businesslike fashion. Later they invaded the last 4 leagues, designated 160-acre parcels to the owner and his sons, and thus made yeomen out of ranchers. As though to emphasize their muscular reforms, they burned the Californians' crops, shot stray cattle, chased off vaqueros, tore down or occupied outlying buildings, blocked off gates, and fenced in access routes. Now and again, to show their "magnanimity," squatters leased range space to the claimants. But some rancheros could not fetch drinking water and firewood or hold a rodeo without a fight. Several Californios, like Señor Peña's son who went out to seed his father's field, and the thirty-year-old José Suñol, were killed. One sheriff died attempting to restore order.[32]

Meanwhile, mushrooming settlers' leagues institutionalized the breakup of the ranchos. The leagues sometimes hired professional squatters who used strong-arm methods on legitimate settlers as well as on claimants. After the Californios had fled in fear, land jobbers bought up and consolidated squatter claims. Intimidation often included third-party suits—suits supplementary to those submitted by claimants against the government. League attorneys produced numerous writs, injunctions, and counterclaims in the lower courts, sometimes valid but more often "smelling rankly of injustice and determined robbery." [33] In this way adventurers hoped to win a legal draw by some technicality, even if the courts confirmed the original titles.

When the squatters on Rancho San Antonio finally blocked off the very doorways to the Peralta homes, the old clan had to move from land it had occupied since the Spanish days. Salvador Vallejo also fled into exile, although he managed to salvage some cash. By selling some of his cattle, he paid his lawyers $80,000 to defend Napa. Although they secured him a favorable verdict before the Land Commission, the government's appeal to the district court gave the settlers courage to move into the remaining 4 leagues of the ranch. But, when they kept burning his crops, Salvador reached the limit of his patience: he sold

[32] Sacramento *Daily Union*, April 20, 1858, quoting Santa Rosa *Democrat*, April 9, 1858; San Jose *Pioneer and Historical Register*, 1879.
[33] *Alta*, Feb. 11, 1851.

his last 4 leagues and his home for a "paltry" $160,000 and moved to San Francisco.[34] His brother Mariano, although similarly besieged, stood fast pending court action.

By 1853, every rancho within a day's march of San Francisco Bay had its contingent of uninhibited nonpaying guests, and within the next three years ranchos in all seven northern counties—Sonoma, Napa, Solano, Contra Costa, Santa Clara, Santa Cruz, and Monterey —were to experience at least some of the typical settlers' agitation. For all the hullabaloo about "hearty settlers," however, yeomen did precious little farming in northern California in the early 1850's. Even the more honest settlers were unwilling to risk putting in fences, crops, and homes only to be ejected on short notice, or to be ordered to pay some as yet unstipulated price for land.

Probably even more pernicious than the squatters were the lawyers and adventurers who outsmarted the Californians while posing as their benefactors. Unlike the "Hallecks" of their days, they used any legal dodge to avail themselves of land and welcomed the Land Law as a smoke screen. Through friendly conversation and paperwork with the rancheros they sometimes accomplished more than a legion of armed squatters sniping from behind trees.

For all his suspicion of gringos, the typical Californian was intrigued by their worldly airs and freely opened his door to them. This naïveté took its toll, however. Swindlers hired on as secretaries, managers, or lawyers and ensnared the rancheros in "sure-fire" business deals. One smooth-talking lawyer, Horace Carpentier, and two of his associates, Edson Adams and James Moon, ingeniously divested the Peralta family of its 19,000-acre Rancho San Antonio, with an estimated worth of $3 million. Not content to stake out quarter sections, slaughter cattle, fell orchard trees, and otherwise harass the titleholder, Carpentier aimed for bigger stakes: control over the entire waterfront and the community it served. He craftily gained control over the settlers' league while at the same time acting as the Peraltas' "benefactor." He appeared in the family casas with a cross dangling from his neck, talked of religion, and unrolled legal papers that would "make the family rich." Happily for him, Vicente Peralta was going mad, but he was still rational

[34] "Notas historicas sobre California," 1874, MS, Bancroft Library, pp. 151–154.

enough to think he needed a manager for the purpose of leasing, selling, codeveloping, and defending the title in the courts. At one point Carpentier drew up for Peralta's signature a "lease" that later turned out to be a mortgage *against* the signer. When the don refused to pay, Carpentier bought the property he wanted at a sheriff's sale.

Carpentier's shrewd personal accession of some of the most valuable real estate on the eastern shore irked many members of the settlers' league. Nonetheless, he platted on Rancho San Antonio the town of Oakland, of which he became the first mayor, incidentally promising his constituents to stamp out bear-baiting and bullfighting which "belong to a people and a generation that are past." With his associates installed as aldermen, he made the town his private bailiwick. The Peraltas, meanwhile, started legal action to recover their land and were still doing so as late as 1910.[35] From Oakland's founding fathers they got little more than a street named after them.

Beside legal and financial counsel, a benefactor could play other roles—even that of husband: he need only seek out an estate held by a widow. More than likely the *señora* was entangled in a web of tax liens, litigation, debts, and ranching problems which threatened to destroy her home—a prospect that made her vulnerable. As a result, distaff property that remained intact after a few years of the Yankee régime was a rarity.

When José María Sanchez died suddenly in 1852, he left to his wife, Jurio, herds and property sprawling over two counties, gold dust amounting to $70,000, and a host of obligations and loosely managed enterprises. Having no sons to comfort her or to handle these bewildering details, she soon found herself surrounded by suitors and advisers who volunteered to do so. She married one of them, but he died within a year. The court appointed as executor of the estate an associate of her late husband, who, however, went to jail for defrauding the property of $30,000. The court next gave the job to two courthouse cronies, Louis Belcher and William Roach, who soon accused each other of further frauds amounting to $80,000 and began a vendetta which mushroomed until it enveloped politicians and moneymen up and down the

[35] *Alta*, Feb. 28 (quoting from *El Eco del Pacífico*, Feb. 23), March 1 (quoting from *El Eco*, Feb. 25), July 14, Aug. 5, 1853; *Bulletin* (San Francisco), July 1, 1876; *Chronicle* (San Francisco), March 26, 1879; Transcript, *Peralta v. United States* (1910), *op. cit.*

state. In 1856, when Belcher was traveling to San Francisco to summon the vigilantes to suppress his enemies, he was assassinated. Roach lived the life of a fugitive for nine years; as soon as he emerged from hiding, he was thrown into a well and drowned.

The Roach-Belcher feud claimed nine lives, including those of a sheriff, two deputies, a noted Mexican gunman, and the speaker of the state Senate, Isaac Wall, who had served as attorney for one of the contestants. Indeed, the only party spared a violent death was the widow Sanchez. She was "supplied" with two more husbands (her last, George Sanford, was popularly known as "George IV") who also died, one of them mysteriously. After thirteen years, the Sanchez holdings were completely segmented and alienated to this or that lawyer or mortgagor. After all her "allies" had died, the widow bought a small plot of land and settled down to live out her days quietly—and singly.[36]

The activity of Henry Miller, California's greatest land and cattle baron, illustrates yet a third method of gobbling up rancho land. The German-born butcher made his start by buying San Joaquin Valley cattle and bringing them to San Francisco. He soon branched out into the land business, however, in the hope of securing good sites for resting, watering, and fattening his herds along a trail that stretched from Santa Rita through Pacheco Pass and Gilroy all the way to San Francisco. Sometimes he rented grazing land; more often he used the technique of buying into a rancho that had several owners, retaining joint possession for a time, and then gradually easing out the co-owners or demanding a partition. The trick was to pay his associates no profits from the cattle trade and yet use all their land. Eventually, Miller and a partner of his named Charles Lux acquired all or substantial parts of fifteen northern Spanish-Mexican ranchos. These holdings constituted the core of the Miller and Lux empire, which eventually stretched in mosaic fashion from the Oregon to the Mexican border.[37]

A fourth and altogether painless method of acquiring rancho land in

[36] Paul P. Parker, "The Roach-Belcher Feud," California Historical Society Quarterly, XXIX (March, 1950), 19–28; Gazette (Santa Barbara), Oct. 4, 1855.
[37] The ranchos were Santa Rita, Buri Buri, Salsipuedes, Juristac, La Laguna, Bolsa de San Felipe, San Justo, Las Lomarias, Muertas, Aromitas y Agua Caliente, San Antonio, San Lorezo, Orestimba, Las Animas, and Tesquesquito. See Edward Treadwell, The Cattle King [Henry Miller]: A Dramatized Biography (New York, 1931), pp. 57–58.

California was through moneylending. The rancheros wanted nothing more desperately than cash to enable them to pay their legal fees and taxes and still live grandly, and they would almost certainly forfeit land rather than pay their debts. By foreclosing a mortgage, a moneylender might accomplish his end more painlessly than hosts of squatters and lawyers.

The export of gold from California, and certain other economic factors as yet badly understood, made cash scarce and capital dear. While titles lay in the "purgatory" of the Land Law, they had little worth as collateral and were good only for short-term, high-interest loans, with rates compounded monthly or even weekly. One claimant who needed cash for taxes and lawyers' fees was so hemmed in by squatters in 1853 that he could no longer raise and sell cattle and had to take a $10,000 mortgage payable at 10 percent monthly; *weekly* interest of 12 percent on loans and of 3 percent on mortgages was common in the 1850's.[38] Furthermore, any ranchero planning to borrow money normally had his compadres underwrite his note. When the note went unpaid, co-signers whose own finances were relatively sound were sucked into the vortex of debt. In Los Angeles County, Andrés and Pio Pico had involved so many of their friends that, when they themselves defaulted, they caused the severance of thousands of acres of rancho land.

In the old communities the gringo had at his disposal numerous ingenious ways of making a killing in land, some of them altogether lawful but no less damaging to the old order. A Scot named David Jacks, who was intrigued by reading Walter Colton's letters, decided to go to Monterey in 1849 while everybody else headed in the opposite direction. With a few thousand dollars' capital created by selling pistols in the mines, he began accumulating "worthless" county scrip (issued by the government in lieu of cash for salaries and debt obligations). When he redeemed $12,000 worth of scrip, he forced Monterey to hand over public land worth about $500,000. Californios who used the property as a commons for grazing and woodcutting were so outraged that they burned his enclosures, took potshots at him on lonely roads, and petitioned the state legislature for incorporation of the town to enable them to fight him more effectively. Jacks responded by simply repairing his fences, traveling with a bodyguard, and lobbying each year

[38] Cleland, *op. cit.*, p. 113.

among powerful friends in the legislature who blocked incorporation. Jacks also eyed private property. At sheriff's auctions he bought ranchos unwittingly defaulted for nonpayment of taxes, then sold them back to their disbelieving owners at a small but significant profit. He also lent rancheros money at the normally usurious rates and acquired one title after another when the mortgage payments lapsed. Within a decade Jacks owned 40,000 acres of Monterey land and became a philanthropist to the indigent, a political boss, and a pillar of his church. Yet Alvarado wrote that "as long as David Jacks has money and remains alive Monterey will never recover her lost prestige." [39]

Throughout northern California, scores of estates changed hands in the modes just described. The most tragic struggle for land, however, the one that distorted all the usual tendencies until it assumed the dimensions of a Spanish tragedy, involved the Berreyesa family. The scene of the battle was Rancho Milpitas, a green sward near San Jose where the bay divides the land. Yankee squatters began coming there in numbers in 1852. Like Vicente Peralta, Nicolás Berreyesa was going mad; the wartime deaths of his nephews and brother had undermined his stability. Now, as Horace Carpentier had done to Peralta, a cunning character named James Jakes took advantage of Nicolás Berreyesa's weakness. Jakes convinced the don and his three sons to respond to the Land Law by emulating the settlers and squatting on their own land. He even obligingly hired a surveyor to officially mark off one plot for each Berreyesa family. This accomplished, Jakes promptly claimed the vacated property, including Don Nicolás' adobe. Berreyesa sued to get it back but lost his case and had to pay $500 court costs. The pathetically deranged man thereupon sent protest letters to Governor Alvarado, believing that the governor still had some power in these matters.

The neighboring rancho belonging to the Alviso family also was at the mercy of a gringo "benefactor." This man, a butcher by trade, was engaged in pleading the title to the Alviso property before the Land Commission. He not only succeeded in confirming that title, but his

[39] Juan Bautista Alvardo, "Historia de California," MS, Bancroft Library, V, 49 ff.; Abrego, "Relación," in *Pioneer Sketches*, no. 9. Jacks' property was in constant litigation; see Monterey *Gazette*, Feb. 9, 1856; Dec. 18, 1863; Anne B. Fisher, *The Salinas: Upside-down River* (New York, 1945), p. 132.

measurements conveniently swallowed up a valuable piece of Berreyesa land, including buildings and crops. Don Nicolás filed a third-party suit but lost it. In this way, the butcher-lawyer systematically created a private fortune and was elected to the legislature.

This by no means ended the troubles of the Berreyesa family. Nemasio Berreyesa was having equal difficulty substantiating a title to the New Almadén quicksilver mine. One night masked raiders seized him, purportedly on a charge of murder, and hanged him from an oak near San Jose. Nemasio had not been the murdering kind, and the Berreyesas maintained that rival claimants hanged him simply to remove him from the scene. Two other Berreyesas were lynched, one in 1854 and the other in 1857. Furthermore, lawyers representing Don Nicolás before the United States Supreme Court disappeared in Washington along with irreplaceable documents, whereupon the don himself burned other papers in an insane rage. A year later, rival claimants ordered the family evicted from Milpitas. Two of Don Nicolás' sons who barricaded themselves against the town marshal were bodily ejected. They rented a home from the widow Alviso, but when she remarried, her Sonoran husband ejected the brothers.

That was not all, however. Three other Berreyesa brothers were bedridden with measles when a squatter deliberately grazed his cattle on their newly seeded fields, thus driving the men from their sickbeds to save their crops. The family's congenital weakness now caught up with them: all three became insane. One of them ran into the hills and nearly died of exposure, and another succumbed shortly thereafter in an asylum. In lucid moments the old man, brooding over the incredible tragedies that had befallen his kin since the Bear Flag Rebellion, begged the remainder of his dear ones to flee to Mexico while time permitted. They refused, however, in faint hope of a favorable decision in district court. In 1869, District Judge Ogden Hoffman ruled against them, although partly on the grounds that Nicolás had squatted on his own property. In 1873 the don died.

Three years later, the United States Supreme Court upheld Judge Hoffman's decision, and the seventy members of the once-powerful Berreyesa family, now completely landless and virtually penniless, threw themselves at the mercy of the San Jose town government and begged some small plot as a homesite. Concluding the saddest saga of all, Antonio Berreyesa estimated that of all the old families, his was the "one which most justly complained of the bad faith of the adventurers and squatters and of the treachery of American lawyers." [40]

In the north of California, then, the basis of landownership had changed drastically by 1856. Through armed struggle, legislation, litigation, financial manipulation, outright purchase, and innumerable other tactics, Yankees had obtained a good deal of interest in the land. The transfer of property destroyed the irenic vision provided by the Treaty of Guadalupe Hidalgo, which guaranteed the Californios the "free enjoyment of their liberty and property"—an obligation that did not worry many Yankees.

In the eyes of the Californios, on the other hand, the results of the land transfers amounted to something akin to social revolution. Whom did they blame? Doubtless each victim had his own answer, but it is noteworthy that many of them spoke of the land settlement as a massive betrayal. They charged the Mexican government with having sold them in 1848 as a "shepherd turns over his flock to a purchaser," and the gringo buyer with having led them to slaughter. Bitterly they alluded to the biblical tale of Joseph and his brothers; among Mexicans they were "Our Brothers Who Were Sold." [41]

[40] "Relación ... ," 1877, MS, Bancroft Library, p. 21; U.S. District Court, District of California, *United States v. Nicholas Berreyesa*, "Opinion of His Honor, Ogden Hoffman, District Judge, Rejecting the Claim" (San Francisco, 1869).
[41] Salvador Vallejo, "Notas historicas sobre California," 1874, MS, Bancroft Library.

VI

The Cow County
Ranchos in Limbo

Happily, while northern ranchos such as Milpitas and San Antonio were already so interlaced by fences and farms as to cease functioning normally, southern ranchos of comparable dimensions enjoyed relative peace. Life in the "cow counties" in 1853 went on as calmly as it had two decades earlier.

At Rancho Cañada de Santa Ana (in present-day Orange County), for example, the cacophony of barking dogs, clucking chickens, and shouting children bespoke the conventional way of life. Scores of employees buzzed about the place—wool combers, tanners, and vaqueros; a butter-and-cheese man, a baker, a harness maker, a shoemaker, a jeweler, a plasterer, a schoolmaster, a carpenter, and a majordomo; errand boys, shepherds, and cooks; also washerwomen, seamstresses gardeners, viniculturists, and assorted hangers-on from the neighboring Indian *ranchería*. It took ten steers a month to feed this veritable army. Besides, Santa Ana was the social center of the region and welcomed many guests.[1] When the proprietor peered down from the second story of his thirty-room adobe, he need never have feared that Yankees lurked in the orchard and threatened the security of his family. Southern California had few squatters and no squatter's fences.

The serenity of Rancho Santa Ana and of the entire area of the cow counties rested on social and geographic factors unique to the south of California. The lack of mineral wealth and of water in the southern

---

[1] Robert Glass Cleland, *The Cattle on a Thousand Hills: Southern California, 1850–1880* (San Marino, Calif., 1951), p. 53.

104

region deterred miners and farmers equally. Although adequate for ranching, southern California had insufficient rainfall for growing crops without irrigation, a basic deficiency that was to last another half-century. Entrepreneurs who came to California looking for urban market opportunities also generally turned elsewhere. Travelers passing through San Diego or Los Angeles normally wanted nothing more than a clean bed and a night's rest before heading northward for good. The few who did stay never mounted a serious attack on the old landed class.

Social peace enabled the southern rancheros to reap windfall profits from the early cattle trade, to pay taxes and lawyers' bills more readily than the northerners, and generally to live according to custom. The land question, unsupported by vast numbers of settlers who made it politically explosive in the north, took a different and more conciliatory form in the south.

This became evident at once in the rapport between the Land Commission and the landowners. In February, 1852, rancheros owning fifty-three southern titles met at Ignacio Coronel's home in Los Angeles and petitioned the commission to come south to hear their pleas and thus spare them a great loss of time and money in trips to San Francisco— spare them, in other words, what Benton had called the "march up . . . to Jerusalem to be taxed." They were prepared, if necessary, to send a three-man delegation to Washington to complain directly to President Millard Fillmore. Four-fifths of them were Californios, and they formed the first group in recent memory "in which the Americans were not the active agents and participants." They saw results, too, for the Land Commission did come south for one sitting, an event of such moment in Los Angeles that it produced a fiesta in the grand manner. Manuel Garfias acted as host in a celebration that, among other things, allowed the rancheros the opportunity of sizing up the Commission's three board members; the majority agreed that the gringos seemed honorable.[2]

The abajeños seem to have either received more of the favorable decisions awarded by the board than did the northerners or must have,

[2] Los Angeles *Star*, Feb. 26, 1852; W. W. Robinson, *Land in California* (Berkeley and Los Angeles, 1948), p. 85.

by and large, felt more complaisant about the unfavorable ones. For only occasionally did an unpopular decision cause a stir in the south, as when Judge Benjamin Hayes declared it inconceivable that the claim to Rancho Temescal, well defined and visibly occupied for years, could be voided in 1856 by a decree of the Southern District Court.[3] Most land cases came down from the judiciary in routine fashion. None of the third-party suits that so often exacerbated the northern land question arose in the southern local courts; Yankee inhabitants recognized the family ownership of land much as they recognized the family tenure of church pews—that is, tacitly and informally. In fact, the only really celebrated southern land suit was not an action under the Land Law, but a jury trial among members of the Dominguez family for control over Rancho San Pedro. No Yankee gained anything from that squabble, except perhaps the four lawyers involved.[4]

Undeniably, most southern communities did witness slight touches of squatter strife—precisely enough of it to remind the abajeños of serious happenings elsewhere in California. Rowdy settlers converted part of former San Gabriel Mission into a notorious saloon, which was frequented by assorted felons and by a justice of the peace who became famous for rendering decisions while playing cards. At nearby El Monte, a colony of Texans poached on land belonging to ranchers Workman, Rowland, and Temple. San Diego also had a squatter by 1853, reportedly "a good fellow and industrious and God-fearing." [5]

In Santa Barbara, the most unspoilt place in the cow counties, some former New York Volunteers under the leadership of Jack Powers laid siege to a large tract of mission land in 1853 and refused to budge. With church backing, Don Nicolás Den obtained a judgment against Powers which the California Supreme Court later sustained. "All classes were very much excited" in the normally placid village, "the Californians and Americans generally taking sides against each other." The sheriff's posse killed one Powers man and lost one of its own, Señor Leyva. After a second Yankee provocation, about fifty Californios proposed tearing down a billiard saloon "much frequented by Ameri-

[3] John C. Hough, "Abel Stearns, 1848–1871," unpublished MS, ed. by John Caughey, p. 96.
[4] Star, May 28, June 11, 1853.
[5] San Francisco Daily Alta California, Feb. 12, Aug. 23, 1853; Horace Bell, Reminiscences of a Ranger . . . (Santa Barbara, Calif., 1927), pp. 84, 367.

cans," but were restrained by the sheriff. Powers finally relented; he took a short-term lease from Den, harvested his last crop, and left for Los Angeles. There he fleeced the Californios in new ways, by playing cards with them and rustling their cattle on the sly.[6]

But for the Powers incident, none of this agrarianism disturbed the social peace of sourthern California to any great extent. At San Gabriel the Church eventually repossessed its mission buildings; at El Monte the squatters dutifully paid rent to Workman, Rowland, and Temple, a practice lately discarded by their northern contemporaries; and at San Diego the lone settler seemed more of a social oddity than a public nuisance. As for Santa Barbara, despite dire predictions of continuing trouble, that town sank back into the same languorous calm witnessed twenty years earlier by seaman Richard Henry Dana, Jr., and would enjoy it another two decades.

Nevertheless, if the settlers seldom used force or legal pyrotechnics to win land in the cow counties, neither were the owners able to convey their property in an altogether equitable manner. Before passage of the Land Law some owners had consummated notable deals, as, for example, when the Lugos and the Scpúlvedas sold 35,000 acres to the Mormons of San Bernardino. Afterward, though, in the south as well as in the north, the Land Law effectively inhibited land sales on the open market. As late as 1859 the Land Office had not issued a single southern patent. "Few if any, of the large rancho estates had been disposed of at legitimate sale; in fact, many of the choicest, at four bits an acre, had been entirely disregarded." [7]

Land did change hands, of course, but in ways detrimental to the ranchero. Instead of being sold in open-market arrangements, acreage was lost through mortgages, taxes, and personal expenses.

The south, for one thing, had its own share of gringo swindlers who did their best to ensnare land, gold, and personal property. For instance, Parker H. French, a "transcendent and misguided genius" who had been elected to the state legislature by befriending the rancheros

---

[6] Den's daughter recounts the episode in Katherine M. Bell, *Swinging the Censer* (Santa Barbara, Calif., 1931), pp. 134–164. See also Horace Bell, *op. cit.*, pp. 44–47; *Star*, May 7, 14, 28, 1853; and *Alta*, May 7, June 8, 1853.

[7] Alfred Robinson, *Life in California* . . . (San Francisco, 1891), p. 259; Harris Newmark, *Sixty Years in Southern California, 1853–1913* . . . (New York, 1916), p. 87.

of San Luis Obispo, nonetheless systematically bilked them. By using forged power of attorney, he sold and mortgaged nearly "every ranch in the county worth the trouble." The Lugos had comparable luck with their manager. He so beguiled the family with adventure tales, including interviews with African King "Mumbo Jumbo" and French Emperor Louis Napoleon, that they empowered him to deliver thousands of heads of cattle in the north, whereupon he absconded with the receipts and was never heard from again.[8]

Card playing also drained away wealth in flush times. Gringo gamblers preferred gold or cash but often played for land and personal property. Although the older Californios frowned on cards as a pastime worthy only of cholos, the younger generation had fewer scruples and frequently lost not only their own stakes but their fathers' as well. Whether the gamblers cheated or played straight, they usually beat the local novices hands down. One young Bandini lost as much as $10,000 while "locked up alone with those men." [9]

More than any other factor, the Californio's spendthrift tendency, encouraged by windfall profits in the early cattle trade, put him in financial hot water and caused him to part with more land than he wished. The end of the hide and tallow trade during the war and the start of the far more lucrative beef trade in the gold rush revolutionized the cattle business. The bony longhorn, once worth a dollar or two for its skin and fat, rose in value to $70 in 1849, when it became eating fare for the miners. Since the grower's costs remained about the same, he profited brilliantly. Even when the prices plunged to $16 a head in 1854, he still earned far more for his effort than did most gold diggers.

Prosperity fed into the old value system based on immediate spending, a process that had short-range advantages but long-range disadvantages. Rancheros sold herds swiftly and in great quantities, without a care for the "sore foot in a rainy day," as their parsimonious Yankee neighbors noted. Few took pains to fatten their herds before selling, restock their ranges, or develop auxiliary crops such as barley. Most rancheros simply spent cash prodigiously and mortgaged their future profits at usurious rates, in the baseless expectation of a continuing boom in cattle. Recognition of deep economic trouble

[8] Horace Bell, *op. cit.*, pp. 174–194, 267–272.
[9] C. R. Johnson to Abel Stearns, n.d., in Cleland, *op. cit.*, pp. 196–197.

came in 1855, when out-of-state growers introduced new herds and toppled the established prices, but by then it was often too late for the rancheros to make amends, even if they cared to do so.

In one way or another, the land-rich, money-poor Californians began to lose their land. Señor Yorba lost 1,000 varas when a county judge ordered a constable's sale for the relief of one of Yorba's creditors. A hard-pressed Manuel Dominguez in 1854 unwillingly deeded 24,000 acres at $12,000 to B. D. Wilson, W. T. B. Sanford, and J. G. Downey. Losing ground on the mortgage treadmill, Pio Pico in 1862 had paid moneylender Abel Stearns the principal on the $19,500 mortgage on Los Coyotes Rancho, but still owed him nearly as much interest. Meanwhile, as already mentioned, Don Pio Pico and his brother Andrés had entangled so many backers in their network of mortgage loans that, when the pair failed to meet their note payments, many rancheros of Los Angeles county with sound finances also were ruined. Señor Lugo became trapped that way: "Through the misfortune of giving my signature and my word as a bondsman for other people and giving my trust, etc., I sacrificed all my goods and even the house in which I lived." [10]

Even those Californios who, the Yankees felt, should have known better suffered. Don Manuel Garfias of San Pasqual, owner of immense lands and herds and a man of enough business acumen to be elected county treasurer of Los Angeles, nevertheless was too avid a *fiestero* and a "bad manager" [11]—faults that brought him to the verge of bankruptcy before long.

For the ranchero class as a whole, however, the situation looked far from hopeless. Of the twenty-five leading landholders of Los Angeles County, most still retained part or all of their property at the end of the 1850's. Even after a fratricidal legal trial, the Dominguez clan still shared 48,000 acres, and the segmented estate would remain in family control in the twentieth century. The Lugos also maintained their baronial realm. Patriarch Antonio María Lugo still owned 29,000 acres and $75,000 in personal property in the bad year of 1856, his seventy-fifth year. His sons, José María, José del Carmen, and Vicente still

[10] José del Carmen Lugo, "Vida de un ranchero ...," 1877, MS, Bancroft Library, pp. 129–130; *Star*, June 4, 1853.
[11] Harris Newmark, *op. cit.*, p. 36.

possessed a good part of their initial 37,000 acres. Bernardo Yorba had lost valuable land in and outside the city, but could ride 50 or 60 miles in one direction (in the present Orange County) without ever leaving his own property. Similarly, the Sepúlveda lands stretched away impressively toward the southwest of Los Angeles, 36,000 acres of the property facing the ocean at Palos Verdes. The Verdugo lands, close to 36,000 acres which flowed in and around the hills to the northeast of the town and which about a decade later were to go on the block for back taxes, in the meantime remained in family hands. Ricardo Véjar kept his part interest in the 22,000-acre Rancho San José, southeast of the town, before he had to sell a $29,000 parcel of it twenty years later. Manuel Garfias, albeit a bad manager, still held 13,000 or 14,000 acres in the late fifties. Even Pio Pico, worth 22,000 acres and $21,000 in personal property in 1851, was still not yet ruined.[12]

In general, then, notwithstanding debts, tax liens, extravagant expenses, subdivisions, and ownership changes, southern rancheros had less acute problems than their northern compadres. At the end of the first American decade they still held enough of their birthright to sustain the round of duties and pleasures that gave communal life its meaning.

If the Yankee refrained in southern California from the all-out agrarianism he had practiced in the north he did not thereby cease carping at the prevailing scheme of life. On the contrary, at every opportunity he expressed his contempt for the older economic system and, in the back of his mind, resolved to reform it.

Like the Berreyesa family in the north, the Bandini clan of Los Angeles and San Diego best exemplified the confrontation between new and old forces in southern California. The constant friction between Juan Bandini and his sons and daughters, on the one hand, and his three American sons-in-law—Abel Stearns, Charles H. Johnson, and J. Cave Couts—on the other, illustrates the "Americanization" of an old family. It came by small stages, on an intimate scale, through the operation of quiet and subtle influences.

Juan Bandini always imagined himself destined for a greater life

¹² *Ibid.*, p. 166 ff.

than isolation on the raw San Diego frontier. Like his far-northern contemporary, Mariano Vallejo, he sought salvation by embracing the new
régime. Frémont sensed this when he described him as a "slight and
thin person, sarcastic and cynical of speech . . . morbid because without outlet" and "glad of the relief from the monotony" occasioned by
the coming of the American forces.[13] The gold rush seemed to fulfill
Bandini's initial expectations that under American rule Californios
would prosper greatly.

With his land and cattle sprawled out from Tiajuana, Mexico, to the
San Bernardino Mountains, Juan Bandini was a ranchero on the grand
scale. Although no longer a politician, his holdings guaranteed him a
role as *cacique* (important personage) and social lion of the far south
of California. As befitted their station, he and his wife sponsored some
of the most illustrious fiestas of the cow countries. Moreover, Bandini
had grand notions about diversifying his operations, although he completely overestimated his capacity to adopt the new competitive business style. He invested $15,000 to build an inn and a general store near
his plaza town house in San Diego, so as to accommodate the gold
seekers passing that way from Mexico and the United States.

Those ambitious schemes exposed Bandini not only to the instability
of the cattle trade, which later was to threaten all his compatriots, but
also to the vicissitudes of commerce. In December, 1850, he borrowed
from a French gambler $10,000 at 4 percent monthly interest, expect-
ing to repay the loan in two months from cattle sales. When Bandini's
good intentions came to naught, the Frenchman granted him an extension at the same rate of interest, but required a mortgage on Bandini's
home and inn, which brought the entire obligation to $12,822.90, pay-
able in July, 1851. Early in 1851 Bandini was chagrined to discover
that "all of a sudden trade left us entirely";[14] evidently, the declining
Sonoran migration had pulled the rug from under him. Meanwhile, in
San Francisco he had contracted other bad deals, or, as his son-in-law
graphically put it, Don Juan mistakenly "fell in with some Jews who
rather got ahead of him."

[13] John Charles Frémont, *Memoirs of My Life* (Chicago and New York, 1887),
pp. 563–564.
[14] Johnson to Stearns, May 26, 1851, Stearns MSS, Huntington Library (San
Marino, Calif.).

The big item on his account ledger, the forthcoming mortgage payment to the French gambler, caused Bandini to take a hasty trip to
Rancho Guadalupe, near Tiajuana, to market beeves quickly. Upon his
arrival in April, however, he saw a rancho gone to seed, with "nothing
planted, and his cattle here, there and everywhere." Swiftly he hired a
new majordomo and new vaqueros and ordered them to cut out a large
portion of the 4,000 animals. This action ran directly against his son-in-
law's advice that he should save them as "a fine breeding stock," since
the cattle were too bony and nearly all cows.

However peeved at his son-in-law, Bandini nevertheless left him
temporary power of attorney. Johnson took the occasion of Bandini's
absence to describe the entire family crisis to Abel Stearns—Don Juan's
costly business schemes, the gambling proclivities of the don's young
sons, and the expenditures of Doña Refugia Bandini in preparing one
elegant fiesta after another even while feeling "awfully downcast"
about money matters. Johnson estimated that a loan of $2,000 and
proper management could save the Bandini estate and even make it
profit "handsomely." Noting that the power of attorney put "everything
in our own hands," he implored Stearns to "assist the old gent out of
this scrape; it had nearly killed him [Bandini] thinking of it." [15]
Stearns complied.

Johnson's business dealings with Bandini usually ended angrily.
Whenever Bandini suggested a new project, Johnson had to caution
realism. Because he considered the don obsessed with wild ideas and
a passion to win every argument, Johnson, in the interest of family
harmony, began to transact less and less business with him. In fact, although all three sons-in-law remained on cordial social terms with
Bandini, they soon began to carry on family affairs without consulting
him, whereupon he complained sadly of having lost respect.

The Yankees in the Bandini realm had similar collisions with their
brothers-in-law. When Juanito Bandini came to Stearns begging for
rancho work, Don Abel, good family man that he was, sent him to see
the manager of his Rancho Alamitos. Obligingly, manager Charles
Brinley hired Juanito. But, when the youth dragged along a ne'er-do-
well friend whose large family swarmed all over the ranch house, Brin-

<hr>

[15] Johnson to Stearns, June 7, 1853, in *ibid.*

ley fired him outright and ejected the strangers. Juanito later had an equally nasty and short-lived stint with Johnson, who told Stearns: "He can't take care of an iron axle cart he has now, much less a wagon; he has let the cart run without greasing . . . and it will cost at least fifteen dollars to repair it—ox carts are the things for his use." [16]

The Yankees in the Bandini realm found themselves at war also with an assortment of vaqueros, domestic servants, majordomos, and even with the neighboring rancheros. The "Spanish" world seemed filled with false pride, laziness, ingratitude. When most of the local labor supply drifted off to the mines, the remaining hands grew cocky, knowing that they could command higher wages in the labor market. Brinley felt that a dollar a day was an honest rate of pay and flatly rejected his vaqueros' demand for $2 for special work and $3 if they rode their own horses. Instead of granting a raise, Brinley hired "all the indians of three years old and upwards" who lived nearby and could ride a horse, and "bought" still others at the jail. He implored Stearns to "deputize someone to attend the auction that usually takes place at the prison on Monday's and buy me five or six Indians." [17]

J. Cave Couts, who managed another Stearns rancho, solved the labor problem at rodeo time by hiring vaqueros from the chief of the San Luis Indians. Couts made a down payment on twelve braves and promised each $12 to $15 a month. When the entire group was enticed onto another rancho at higher pay, Stearns demanded that the chief flog the youths and return the down payment. Yet Don Abel was a benevolent despot; when two other Indians escaped bondage and Couts sent his majordomo to haul them back in chains, Stearns counseled a more humane course, since escaping Indians never went far and could always be returned peaceably. [18]

Couts, finding the Californians every bit as inefficient at ranch work as the Indians, dealt with them accordingly. While once supervising a cattle drive up the coast, he fired two of them and cursed them out as "worthless, trifling, good for nothing." At the same time he demoted Majordomo Luis Arguëllo to the rank of vaquero, because Luis liked "to place himself on an equality with Baqueros" and consequently

[16] Johnson to Stearns, Jan. 11, 1853, in *ibid.*
[17] Brinley to Stearns, Aug. 30, 1852, in *ibid.*
[18] Cited in Hough, *op. cit.*, pp. 203–207.

could not discipline them. "I then told all hans [sic] that I was the boss and they should do as I said." Having appointed himself majordomo he found that "everything goes on smoothly. They all fear me." As for Arguëllo, "The Baqueros will Order him before Our Journey is over." [19]

Charles Brinley at Alamitos Rancho, the heart of Stearns's properties, also ranted against most of the Mexicans, Indians, and Californians who came within his sphere. He did not shrink from flatly accusing his neighbor, José Sepúlveda, one of the most highly esteemed men of the county, of selling 150 unbranded yearling cattle belonging to Stearns. Lest "robbery" by a highborn Californian encourage the "small fry" in the same course, Brinley wanted Don José to be "made an example of in this matter." One of the smaller fry, Joaquín Ruiz, was in fact building a house directly on the property line separating the Sepúlveda and Stearns estates, so as to "put his son there with a few cattle, and of course, rob all he can." [20]

Brinley grew "convinced that 'razon' and 'indio' is a distinction without a difference—they are all capricious and unreliable." Ranch hands ordinarily worked at specified chores and rested after they had finished. Not satisfied with this arrangement, Brinley tried assigning new tasks to idle hands, but they replied by deliberately slackening off. When the vaqueros learned the Yankee trick of bargaining for higher pay when labor was scarce, at rodeo time, he reared back at them for their impertinence. Stearns again cautioned moderation, but Brinley simply fired the majordomo. This signaled a walkout by the entire ranch crew, for the majordomo was a man to respect and fear; Brinley had come up against the all-powerful dependency relationship that typified the Spanish-American system of labor. Indebtedness complicated the strike, since the vaqueros owed Stearns money for cigars, boots, and other sundries advanced on their pay. Brinley filled the vacancies with stray Indians, who proved equally unworthy. Returning to his adobe after a day's work, bachelor Brinley had to prepare his own food, and at that rate ate only three solid meals in four days. "As I have in a measure turned shepherd, perhaps you will send me a pipe," he chided

[19] Couts to Stearns, July 13, 18, 1852, and to C. R. Johnson, July 17, 18, 1852, in Stearns MSS; Hough, *op. cit.*, p. 341.
[20] Brinley to Stearns, Oct. 2, 1852, Stearns MSS, Huntington Library.

Stearns; ". . . combining the romantic with the useful, serves to lighten labor." [21]

Zealous advocates of the new business ethos, Couts, Brinley, and Johnson represented the wave of the future in the cow counties. Yet they behaved strictly as boorish "intruders in a Mexican community," as John C. Hough has suggested.[22] Their Puritan ethic of labor and profit contributed to the emasculation of the local manhood. If Juanito Bandini, or Luis Arguëllo, or the majordomo of Alamitos Rancho ever became drunk and blindly turned on the nearest Yankee, it should not have come as a surprise, yet often did.

Abel Stearns profited from the decline of the old order. The set of his pockmarked face and the shape of his whitened mane told of the patriarch in him. Indeed, he was not only older and wealthier than his father-in-law but more successful than most men in California and therefore could presume to give Bandini advice. He saved the don's family home from the incubus of mortgage by paying the moneylender $13,000 (including a whopping $7,000 interest). Stearns lent Bandini a total of $24,000 in exchange for mortgages, particularly on Rancho Jurupa. He thus had earned the right to give advice, yet did not always temper advice with wisdom. When Bandini suffered additional losses in 1858, Stearns complaisantly advised the sale of another 1,000 head of cattle to realize cash. The don replied poignantly that by selling these, his last cattle, his career as ranchero would end and he did not know "what would become of myself." [23]

In fact, Don Juan had reached the end of his rope, and in August, 1859, gave up ownership of Jurupa to his son-in-law. He died three months later, a broken man. Peruvian-born, California-bred, he had enthusiastically turned Yankee late in life, only to suffer for it. He had lost his land, his money, his self-respect, his role as family head, and his station as a social arbiter of the community. Although insulated by 400 miles of desert and mountains from the sources of the Yankee violence that had injured his northern friends, and although buoyed up by gringo money and protected by gringo sons-in-law, he had nonetheless

[21] Brinley to Stearns, Sept. 5, 1852, in *ibid.*
[22] Hough, *op. cit.*, p. 264.
[23] Sept. 20, 1858, Stearns MSS, Huntington Library.

experienced as sure a personal disaster as any member of the Berreyesa family. Although, happily, his property remained with his daughters' husbands, Bandini's sense of defeat was thorough—all the more crushing because unexpected and administered by impersonal forces he could not master. In 1855, he quoted from the Scriptures to express the sense of alienation that typified his life:

> Our inheritance is turned to strangers—
> our houses to aliens.
> We have drunken our water for money—
> our wood is sold unto us.
> Our necks are under persecution—
> we labor and have no rest.[24]

Senator Pablo de la Guerra witnessed the same alienation from a central vantage point, the state capitol. His desk served, on the one hand, as a ranchero's wailing wall and, on the other, as a transmission point for information received from fellow legislators. From that spot, in the spring of 1856, the ranchero's position looked weaker than ever to him. Squatters were continuing their pressure tactics in the fields, cattle prices remained low, much to the disappointment of rancheros who needed cash desperately, and a seemingly vicious federal prosecutor promised a battle in the United States Supreme Court to reverse the hundreds of cases he had lost on a lower level. This procedure threatened to devour another third of the gentry's wealth and prolong the agony over titles for years. To top everything, cloakroom gossip indicated that settlers' lobbyists were again pressing for compensation.

Settlers demanded compensation! Senator de la Guerra never agreed that the weight of numbers gave Norteamericanos any just arguments against his own people, but he grudgingly admitted the right of certain settlers to partial recompense for their investment. He introduced a bill to that effect, but a legislative seemingly craving more than fair compensation defeated it. Settlers' advocates meantime produced a bill to convert into public land all acreage whose settlement of ownership was still pending in the courts.

Although an infrequent speaker, the impassioned de la Guerra arose

---

[24] Cleland, *op. cit.*, App.

to plead against this latest squatter bill and to defend those Californians who, he cried out,

. . . lay prostrate before the conqueror and ask for the protection of the few possessions which remain to them in the bad luck into which they had fallen . . . those who had been sold like sheep—those who were abandoned and sold by Mexico. They are unfamiliar with the prevalent language now spoken in their own country. They have no voice in this Senate, except such as I am now weakly speaking on their behalf. . . I have seen old men of sixty and seventy years of age weeping because they have been cast out of their ancestral home. They have been humiliated and insulted. They have been refused the privilege of cutting their own firewood. And all those who have committed these outrages have come here looking for protection. . . . the Senate sympathizes with them, though it does not hear the complaints of *la clase Espanole*. . . . after suffering all these injustices and enduring all kinds of injuries, now we find that the legislature is hungry to get from us our last penny, simply because the squatters are more numerous than we.[25]

The squatter bill nevertheless passed over de la Guerra's dissent, in plain violation of laws "human and divine"—an arbitrary, unjust, and merciless law inflicted by a powerful conqueror on his weak subject. It capped off all of the "madness and immorality" of the past seven years and showed that "each day our situation deteriorates without hope of remedy." Land matters had come to such a pass that Don Pablo prepared to bolt the chamber and hasten to Washington for the last-ditch stand of the rancheros.[26]

By this time the nadir of land troubles had come and passed, and better luck was in the offing. The United States attorney general soon declared in Washington that all pending suits concerning titles already upheld by the Land Commission and the district courts would be taken off the United States Supreme Court calendar. More than 150 claimants sighed in relief. Only eighteen cases remained for the high court to settle, and de la Guerra could cancel his trip to Washington. But, asked the Californians rhetorically, if the government had whittled its cases

[25] *El Clamor Público* (Los Angeles), April 26, 1856.
[26] Mariano G. Vallejo to Pablo de la Guerra, June 18, 1856, MS, trans., de la Guerra Collection, Owen Coy Room, University of Southern California (Los Angeles, Calif.).

down to eighteen, did this not prove the bankruptcy of a law that called into question all 813 titles?

A second bit of good news delighted the gentry in March, 1857, when the state Supreme Court invalidated the previous year's squatter law. Sheriffs began to hustle some of the settlers off the land, but most Yankees stayed put, greeted the sheriffs and surveyors with roughhouse tactics, and decided to yield ground only when the United States Supreme Court rendered its final decisions—a matter that might take years.

Ultimately, the high court was to reject only thirty-two claims involving about 700,000 acres. It overruled the Land Commission and the district courts and favored the original claimants in sixteen of the eighteen cases the government presented. These cases involved the sixteen most strategically located properties in Marin, Alameda, and Sonoma counties, such as Mariano Vallejo's 44,380-acre Rancho Petaluma and Domingo Peralta's San Ramón, honeycombed by thousands of farmsteads and the scene of bitter struggles.

Finally, five years, thousands of dollars, and countless heartaches later, some beleaguered claimants came within hailing distance of their patents. But even then they had one more bill to pay, for the Land Office ruled, no doubt as a lagniappe to accompany the presentation of patent, that the confirmees would have to survey their own and adjoining land at private expense. "When they receive patent," *El Clamor Público* of Los Angeles complained on August 15, 1857, "if they are not already ruined, they will be very close to it."

The latest Land Office dictum—coming on the heels of conflicting actions by the state legislature, the state Supreme Court, the United States attorney general, and the United States Supreme Court—instead of settling the issue, momentarily aggravated it. The settlers felt that each passing year increased their equity, and that they had earned something more than blunt eviction notices. When Mariano Vallejo proposed subdividing part of Rancho Petaluma for $35 to $50 an acre, some settlers praised his moderation and decided to buy, but when the Castros of Contra Costa declared that they would sell eighteen leagues at $100 per acre or lease it at $6, the settlers roundly condemned them for extortion. The price ran too high for most yeomen, and "the American farmer is not used to landlords," so that all those settlers "whose labor . . . [had] rendered the district a paradise" [27] were to stay until forcibly ejected.

Violence attended the final settlements. In 1858, when surveyors tried to draw the lines for lands confirmed to Peña, Fitch, and Berreyesa in Healdsburg, two hundred settlers first ambushed the surveyors, destroying their equipment, and then temporarily drove out the owners as well. A sheriff's posse armed with an ejectment order was no match for the 1,000 gun-carrying settlers who seized Domingo Peralta and held him hostage for a time. José Suñol was killed somewhere on confirmed land, shortly after his family had acquired title. [28]

The final stormy outburst reflected the yeomen's conviction that their government had betrayed them. Indeed, since 1851, Washington had neglected their interests almost as badly as those of the original owners; some yeomen had nothing to show for years of labor. The ultimate failure of the land settlement lay in its degradation of both the ordinary Yankee settler and the Californian. The actual results satisfied none but the speculators and adventurers who throve on delay and confusion. In large measure, Thomas Hart Benton's prediction on the floor of the United States Senate had come true: "Not the conquered alone, but the conquerors also . . . are to suffer."

[27] Sacramento *Daily Union*, April 13, 17, 1858.
[28] *Ibid.*, April 20, 1858; San Francisco *Bulletin*, Jan. 4, 1859.

VII

"Semi-Gringo"
Los Angeles

UNBELIEVABLE as it now seems, the sprawling megalopolis of Los Angeles was but a tiny village a century ago, more Mexican than Yankee in character.

By climbing Fort Hill (long since altered for a freeway) and by looking southeast one could encompass the entire hamlet and a hundred square miles of countryside at a single glance.[1] The natural setting particularly impressed the traveler who had just trekked across deserts. This, too, was unmistakably a desert scene such as one saw in Santa Fe or Sonora, Mexico, with only one tree showing its head for miles around; yet it was also something of an oasis. In the fall, precipitation carpeted the hills in greenery, turned gardens into a riot of color, and topped the eastern range of mountains with snow; all this was visible at the same moment as the ocean sparkling to the west.

Rural noises and odors came up from below—creaking caretas, barking dogs, galloping horses, a commotion in a country saloon; the stench of slaughtered cattle, dung, and tanned leather; and the milder odor of flowers and dust. The impression of a country village was reinforced visually by the careless blending of roads and gardens, orchards and vineyards and grazing land.

As the eye glanced across flattish, tiled rooftops, it alighted on the

---

[1] See the drawing by Charles Koppel (October 31, 1853), and an analysis of it in Ana Begue De Packman, "Land marks and Pioneers of Los Angeles in 1853," *Historical Society of Southern California Quarterly*, XXVI (1944), 56–95. See also Harris Newmark, *Sixty Years in Southern California, 1853–1913* . . . (New York, 1916), p. 30 ff. and *passim*, a book upon which this chapter relies heavily.

church, made prominent by an open expanse of land before it and by its bell tower and thin wooden cross. In 1853 scarcely any house in town stood out of earshot of the bell, which was a call to devotion, and an alarm system. (When pioneers later lived by the "chronometrical exactitude" of clocks and train whistles, some professed that they missed hearing the irregular tolling of the bell.) Above the small one-storied adobe structures, there jutted up about a dozen more imposing two-storied buildings, the homes of the richest *pobladores* (settlers). These features completed the downtown skyline.[2]

If this village had once had a master plan, its execution was faulty in most respects, except that the plaza ranging out before the church did serve as the community's focal point. Yet the plaza was altogether anti-climactic, for it had an amorphous shape and had been used as a town dump. Without rhyme or reason, buildings obstructed the streets or crowded one another where they could have been widely spaced. Roadways seemed to grope aimlessly through town looking for an exit to the nearby valleys, where other people lived who considered themselves Angeleños.

The discerning eye caught signs of change. Toward the west, white-washed clapboard demarked a Yankee settlement typical of the American West, while toward the east stood the adobe row houses reminiscent of Mexico. Placards emblazoned with "Sonora," "Chihuahua," or "Zacatecas" served as beacons to Mexican travelers. The Spanish-speaking element was gaining ground: one cluster of adobes was called Sonoratown. From Fort Hill one could hear but not see the activity on Nigger Alley (a corruption of *Calle de los Negros*), a narrow, one-block thoroughfare packed with gambling parlors, saloons, and brothels where all nationalities and classes mingled day and night. Los Angeles was Californian in the center, Mexican toward the east, Yankee in the west, and cosmopolitan everywhere. It would remain much the same until the first Southern Pacific Railroad engine roared to a halt below the plaza in the 1870's. "Semi-gringo," Horace Bell dubbed it, a town of mixed essences.

[2] These belonged to Ygnacio del Valle, Ygnacio Coronel, Cristóbal Aguilar, Pio Pico, José Antonio Carrillo, Vicente Sanchez, Tomás Sanchez, Vicente Lugo, Agustín Olvera, Francisco O'Campo, Francisco Gallardo, and the widow of José María Avila.

The Yankees felt confident of someday modernizing this spot, but meanwhile dissuaded Easterners from coming there if they hoped to rear their children properly. The village's human aspect seemed "very ugly," even to some settlers.[3] Domesticated creatures ambled about freely even in the best homes, which were cold and dark. And over everything man-made hung the "antiquated and dilapidated air" of Mexico. The cliché of the day was that the pueblo of *Nuestra Señora de los Angeles* contained no angels, unless they be fallen ones.[4]

Impressions gained by examining the town from the hills were reinforced by peering at faces and clothing, and by listening to voices on the streets below. Spanish Americans outnumbered Yankees: a total population of about 1,500 in Mexican days rose in 1852 to 2,500, of which only 75 persons had come from the United States. In 1853 Los Angeles attained a total of 3,500 to 4,000 souls, including about 300 Americanos; and in 1854 a total of 5,000 of whom 1,500 or 2,000 were resident Yankees, a few hundred transients, and the balance from Mexico and Europe. Sonorans fleeing the Sierra found work in Los Angeles as domestics, artisans, and vaqueros, or went into business as tradesmen, gamblers, and prostitutes. Luis Abarca, for example, a general merchant, prospered "until the advent of the [American] pioneers when he little by little became poorer and finally withdrew from business"; Refugio Botello dealt in cattle and meat, as did Francisco Solano, who became well-to-do at it; merchant Julian Chavez acquired hundreds of acres in the steep ravine northeast of the village and also earned a reputation as a "good, honest citizen"; Santiago Bolo ran a small grocery; Vicente Salcedo, the town's only roofer, had many clients during the rainy season but remained idle a good part of the year; and M. G. Santa Cruz groomed roosters and staged cockfights.[5]

Neophyte Indians, another "Spanish element," were also very much in evidence in Los Angeles in the 1850's; only in 1853 did whites out-

[3] Mrs. Hayes, March 31, 1853, in Benjamin Hayes, *Pioneer Notes . . . 1849–1875*, ed. by Marjorie Tisdale Wolcott (Los Angeles, 1929), p. 93; John W. Audubon, "Diary," Nov. 6, 1849, in Valeska Bari, ed., *The Course of Empire: . . . Accounts of California in the Days of the Gold Rush . . .* (New York, 1931), p. 127.

[4] Joseph Lancaster Brent, *The Lugo Case: A Personal Experience* (New Orleans, 1926), p. 3; Hayes, *op. cit.*, p. 92.

[5] H. Newmark, *op. cit.*, pp. 62, 93.

number them, and up to 3,700 Indians lived in the county. They frequented the saloons on Saturday, the jail on Sunday, and ranchos or ex-missions during the week. Or they went skulking back to their own rancherias which, for a time, dotted the scenery everywhere. The presence of the Indians, the high birthrate of Californians, and the influx of Sonorans allowed the Latin-American element to hold its own in the total population. Until the 1870's it remained an absolute majority.

Americans thus occupied a minority status in southern California's leading community. While this never stopped them from dominating the government or the business scene, it did cause them to seek a modus vivendi with the Spanish-speaking, a social relationship long characteristic of the cow counties.

Yankee tolerance for the Spanish-speaking came partly from the cash nexus, for Yankee cattle buyers, moneylenders, and merchants had to assure their bread and butter. Common sense dictated that Californios and Mexicans be met on their own ground, whenever possible. Some gringos ventured into business or professional alliances with Spanish-speaking partners. John Temple retained Ygnacio García as his confidential business agent in a general store catering to the serape trade. W. W. Twist made Blas Aguilar partner in a similar enterprise. District Attorney I. S. K. Ogier joined Peruvian attorney Señor Rojo in a law partnership. Latin Americans contributed to these enterprises a knowledge of Spanish, a host of personal connections, and some money, while Yankees added a knowledge of English, new laws, and business techniques—in short, it was a symbiotic combination.

For years business enterprises retained the old-fashioned style of trade. Merchants selling to the "natives" continued the traditional "soft sell," extended credit generously, and willingly rode out to the ranchos to peddle goods, just as in the time of the hide and tallow trade. The rancheros remained infrequent though big spenders, who always honored their debts. The Yankee tradesman had little choice but to slow down his pace to theirs. For five years the town went without a horse and buggy, and the slow, wooden-wheeled, ox-drawn careta remained the common mode of drayage. Not until the storekeeper heard its creaky axel or yapping canine escort and saw its whirl of dust did he interrupt his billiards or cards and primp his goods for sale.

To function properly, Yankees in all walks of life had to learn "Spanish" ways. Willingly or not, many spoke a serviceable Spanish, wore odd pieces of local garb, used Mexican saddles (although not the Spanish bit, which seemed too cruel), measured real estate by leagues and varas, fastened fences with riatas, and lived in adobe homes. They drank Mexican wine, ate Mexican food, smoked Mexican tobacco, and, of course, learned to woo the local women. On the other hand, such mores as they found utterly intolerable they would circumvent, if possible. For example, the Yankee town fathers tried to dissuade the Mexican women from washing clothes in the *zanja*, the town's chief source of water, or at least to do their washing on the edge of the ditch; but lectures on hygiene generally produced only blank stares. Fortunately, a Yankee who began carting clean river water from house to house came to his countrymen's relief. By and large, however, Americans learned the necessity of doing as "the Romans" did, at least until they could change conditions in their favor.

The harmony of the "races" rested on more than the cash nexus; it received a great deal from the Mexicanized Yankees of the cow counties, who pointed the way to amelioration. These Americans were few in number, but economically entrenched and socially respected. In fact, two dozen of them owned one-third of southern California's developed land in estates as large as 60,000 acres.[6] Benito Wilson, Ricardo Den, Don Abel Stearns, Guillermo Wolfskill, Juan Griffin, Estevan Foster and others answering to Spanish Christian names constituted a class of village elders. Although some newcomers begrudged them their wealth and some Latin Americans questioned their loyalty to the "true" California, these elders had many Californio friends and the respect of their fellow Yankees out of appreciation for their wartime patriotism. As a result, the ranchers automatically exercised a quiet, steadying influence on the southland, especially in a crisis.

Mixed marriage also created ethnic alliances, although the importance of this point has been questioned. Realists have noted that the mixed unions occurred rarely, and almost always when Yankee women were scarce and native-born women abundant—and acceptably Caucasian and rich into the bargain. A Yankee woman almost never married a native-born man. Tension in such families as Bandini's,

* *Ibid.*, p. 166 ff.

moreover, raises doubts whether mixed marriage guaranteed ethnic harmony. Be that as it may, whether the groom married for romance or for status, he accepted many elements of the old culture, just as had the sea traders in the old days. He attended his wife's church, willingly entered her family circle, and let her raise the children in the old style. The bride's people, especially her father, usually liked their Yankee relative (although they might despise the rest of his "race"), so long as he behaved as a good family man. The weddings of Messrs. Delano, Smythe, Mott, Foster, Woodward, and Carson to Señoritas Véjar, Yorba, Sepúlveda, Bandini, Pico, and Dominguez were celebrated with exceptional verve in the first years of the new era. Happily, the offspring of such unions gained acceptance into society as readily as their parents.[7] In general, the presence of this minority made the Yankee conquest smoother than it might otherwise have been.

The urge to rise above racial and national barriers came naturally to the élite of Los Angeles. The members of mixed families and business partnerships, Yankee ranchers with Spanish nicknames, and "respectable" businessmen—indeed, all businessmen except gamblers—held themselves aloof from the common herd. They formed a remarkably cosmopolitan class: an alliance of Californians, Mexicans, and South Americans; of Yankees, Britons, Frenchmen, and Germans; of mestizos and whites; of merchants, gentry, and lawyers; of Protestants, Catholics, and a sprinkling of Jews. Harris Newmark, a German Jewish pioneer of 1853 who felt altogether welcome in the homes of the Catholic Californios, could distinguish only two classes, "the respectable and the evil elements." The respectable ones "came together because they esteemed each other and liked one another's company," and could cultivate "warm, stimulating friendships" without giving a thought to race or to "foolish caste distinctions." Against the "evil element" of all races, they were "ready to fight to the last ditch for the protection of our families and the preservation of our homes."[8]

Bitter experiences further unified the "respectables." For the Washington's Birthday Ball of 1852, Abel Stearns invited all the "best" Cali-

---

[7] One Yankee, William C. Dryden, married two Californios: Dolores Nieto, in 1851, and, after her death, Anita Dominguez; see *ibid.*, pp. 50–52.

[8] *Op. cit.*, pp. 184–185; Boyle Workman expressed similar affinities in *The City That Grew* [Los Angeles] . . . (Los Angeles, 1935), p. 45.

fornios to his home, but deliberately snubbed the Yankee gamblers of the town. Claiming closer affinity to the Father of His Country than the Californios, the gamblers tried to crash the party, first with a battering ram and then with a small cannon. At this point, Andrés Pico leaned out of a window and with his pistol picked off two insurgents, throwing the town for several days afterward into fear of a bloodbath.[9] Similar clashes with the lower order of Mexicans also solidified the respectable element.

The "walk-in-without-knocking" friendships of several hundred Anglo-Americans and Spanish Americans, which created a channel for the flow of good feelings in Los Angeles, was partly a result of the religious composition of the town. A good many Yankee Catholics settled in Los Angeles and attended church functions as regularly as their Spanish-speaking coreligionists. The Catholic church remained the only organized religious body until 1854, when a Yankee preacher launched the first Protestant congregation in a converted saloon. But even thereafter, the Catholic flock remained ethnically mixed. Non-Catholics, moreover, were markedly tolerant toward Catholics, which also helped the town endure the transition years.

To advance the harmony of the races, gringos campaigned to make the Californios into patriotic Yankee citizens. To this end, the Fourth of July ritual became particularly important. The most memorable celebration of the Fourth occurred in 1853; unlike the ill-fated Washington's Birthday Ball of that winter, it would be attended by all Angeleños. The preparations committee wisely selected San Pedro as the celebration site, near where the United States Navy had effected its "liberation" in 1846, and near the Dominguez and Sepúlveda estates which could supply lavish quantities of food and drink. The festivities ran two days, much in the old California manner. From a hundred miles around, Yankees, Californios, Mexicans, Frenchmen, Britons, Germans, and Indians came to make obeisance to Freedom. Yankees telling campfire tales about the marines buried at nearby Dead Man's Isle were outdone by Californios boasting how they had outsmarted Commodore Stockton at that spot and pinned his force to the beach for days. The festivities were punctuated by alternate rounds of "The Star

[9] Cleland, *The Cattle on a Thousand Hills* (San Marino, Calif., 1951), p. 94.

Spangled Banner," the "Marseillaise," and the Mexican "Ponchada," and the celebrants ate, drank, and danced according to all the customs and toasted in all the languages represented. Los Angeles would see other celebrations of the Glorious Fourth, such as the parade in 1855 in which Californios marched or rode ten abreast, but none would match the festivities of 1853 in cosmopolitanism. By about 1855, moreover, Independence Day had become less consciously an international celebration and more narrowly Yankee in spirit.[10]

"Everybody in Los Angeles seemed rich" in the early 1850's, asserts Horace Bell; "everybody *was* rich and money was more plentiful at that time than in any other place of like size, I venture to say in the whole world." "Up to the year 1853," adds José del Carmen Lugo as if to refine the argument, "I was in good circumstances. Although I did not have money, I had plenty of land and other things of value." [11]

Whether measurable in money or its equivalent, the extraordinary wealth that came from selling beef in the gold mines provided the necessary solvent for the mixing of the gringo and Californio elements; wealth dissolved many differences. All Angeleños enjoyed the unique distinction of having an organized town life situated far enough away from the north to avoid the customary arrogance of the forty-niners, and yet close enough to siphon off the real wealth that was dredged from the Sierra. No other old-line community profited to the same degree from the gold rush.

Amid newfound opulence, the Spanish-speaking of southern California entered what should be called a "cut-flower" phase of their evolution. Though war had cut their cultural roots, life showed few outward signs of discoloration or rot. Abajeños could temporarily ignore the desperate straits of relatives elsewhere and carry on their daily affairs as usual, secure from any feeling that their native soil had been permanently disturbed. In fact, some abajeños felt better off now than amid the incessant wars and rebellions of the Mexican era.

The bellwethers of the Californio community, the *ricos*, reflected this

[10] Horace Bell, *Reminiscences of a Ranger* . . . (Santa Barbara, Calif., 1927), pp. 126–127. Newmark, *op. cit.*, pp. 157, 163; Los Angeles *Star*, June 5, 1858.

[11] Bell, *op. cit.*, p. 10; Lugo, "Vida de un ranchero ... ," 1877, MS, Bancroft Library (Berkeley, Calif.).

attitude in their mode of living between 1849 and 1855. As against the lean years of the waning Mexican era, their purchasing and recreational spending between 1852 and 1855 ran very high, perhaps reaching its highest level ever. If they had ever lacked the wherewithal to feel fulfilled as grandees, they now had it. Former poor men stuffed their pantries and wine cellars, bought goods from Yankee peddlers to their heart's content, gave generous handouts to friends, strangers, and servants, and generally spent—or "wasted," as puritans clucked—their wealth freely. Don Antonio Lugo, son of a common soldier, owned a bridle outfit inlaid with $1,500 worth of silver and used it in his daily chores, even at a time when he was strapped for cash. Pablo de la Guerra in 1851 splurged $80 on a single chair for his father, even while expensive litigation got under way.[12] Rancheros snapped up costly European laces and silks for their wives to convert into *rebozos* and gowns that would be trailed about on clay floors in daily use. The variety and richness of personal effects were limited more by what Yankees imported than by what Californios would buy, for they bought almost anything. Those knowledgeable in Mexican history likened Los Angeles to Zacatecas 300 years earlier, when poor Mexicans had struck it rich in the "gold rush" of 1548.

The best-attended public celebrations, the longest weddings, and the most carefully staged sporting events belong to the halcyon years before 1855. Horse racing, for example: old California never saw a more spectacular contest than the one involving jockeys José Sepúlveda and Pio Pico, in October of 1852. Widespread advance notice brought to the scene not only a large crowd but also gambling money that had come all the way from San Francisco, and eventually reached a total of $25,000 in cash and an almost equal amount in stallions, mares, heifers, calves, sheep and land. Sepúlveda's wife staked each of her house servants to $50 in betting money and personally held in her kerchief a fortune in gold slugs. When the starter shrieked "*¡Santiago!*" the contestants dashed onto a 9-mile course and Sepúlveda, riding an imported Australian mare, Black Swan, flew home 75 yards ahead of Pico,

[12] José Antonio Menendez to Pablo de la Guerra, March 4, 1851, MS, de la Guerra Collection, Owen Coy Room, University of Southern California (Los Angeles, Calif.).

mounted on the California-bred Sarco. Don Pio lost $1,600 in cash and 300 head of cattle.[13]

The number of fiestas was legion. Usually they took place in a town house or a rancho casa large enough to embrace in its courtyard a multitude of guests, even those whom a Yankee quaintly identified as the "plain people . . . always so responsive to music and its accompanying pleasures." When religiously inspired, a fiesta had to be held close enough to the church to permit a procession at the end of the services. For these functions, the flower of society came to town by ox-cart or on horseback from any distance. The regal Petra Pilar Sepúlveda required half a day for the drive from San Pedro and customarily migrated with an entourage of servants, trunks stuffed with gowns and jewels, and mattresses piled high for their stay at the wretched Bella Union Hotel. Her wedding in 1853 had lasted five days and nights, and its lavishness had made a deep impression on gringos. At the typical fiesta, dancing, singing, and eating proceeded all night and well into the following morning, perhaps even into the next evening, or at least until Juan Bandini, Antonio María Lugo, or Nicholas Den had finished competing at the *jota*, bolero, fandango, or waltz.

At the climax of the fiesta came the flirtation called the *cascarón*. The object was to catch a victim unawares and crack open on his head an eggshell filled with some harmless substance; he or she would then try to get even. Ordinarily, confetti or cologne water filled the egg, but in the good years gold dust, even gold leaf, fluttered down on some heads. This delightful extravagance invariably made gringos gasp. Later, cologne and confetti came back into use. Thus, in a sense, the cascarón was a barometer of the community's opulence. As time passed, however, the dances were being danced with less and less finesse, until the true fiesta disappeared altogether.[14]

---

[13] H. Newmark, *op. cit.*, pp. 160–161; Cleland, *op. cit.*, pp. 88–99; Bell, *op. cit.*, p. 197 ff. For news of another like event, see Los Angeles *Star*, May 20, 1853.
[14] H. Newmark, *op. cit.*, pp. 71, 135.

VIII

"Serapes and Split Breeches" in Politics

A CALIFORNIO ordinarily knew little about the sister province of New Mexico. Yet, had he gone about eight hundred miles to the east of Los Angeles along the Old Spanish Trail, he would have been astonished to find 50,000 to 75,000 Spanish-speaking compatriots enduring many familiar trials—and coming out comparatively well. From Santa Fe south to the Mesilla Valley on the Mexican border, he would have witnessed instructive examples of the same gringo conquest over things Spanish and Mexican, although unaccompanied by the frenetic atmosphere of the gold rush.

Life in New Mexico was poorer, slower, and quieter than in California, but for those very reasons also more favorable to the native stock. Most impressive from a Californio's viewpoint was the way the New Mexicans managed to acquire and hold political power with the approval of their new gringo overlords. The patróns casually but firmly occupied the middle and upper echelons of government from the 1850's on and remained there even into the twentieth century.

Distinctive conditions created in New Mexico the symbiotic relationship known as the "boss-patrón system." First of all, the "lost colony" of New Mexico long remained a territory, an administrative arrangement that kept the government small, stable, and under the remote control of federal authorities instead of that of the local gringos, who had fewer qualms about repressing the "natives." Second, the New Mexicans for a long period retained an undisputed numerical dominance over gringos; in the 1850's the New Mexicans numbered between 50,000 and 75,000 in a total population of 100,000—a proportion that was to continue for nearly a century. The patrón class, moreover, kept control over most of its land and peons, the wellspring of genuine social power. The docility of most New Mexicans toward their leaders contributed as essential an ingredient to politics as did the alliance of the patróns with the Yankees. So long as the Spanish-speaking gentry delivered the vote, Yankee merchants, editors, lawyers, and ex-army officers who actually pulled the strings in Santa Fe and Washington gave patronage to the New Mexicans gladly and protected the institution of peonage.

Leaving aside the question as to whether they put their authority to the best possible uses, the patróns nevertheless showed a notable ability for self-leadership. For half a century after 1857, the Otero family, for example, had an undisputed foothold on the top rung of Santa Fe politics. Miguel Antonio Otero served as territorial representative in Congress through the Civil War; his son, Miguel II, remained territorial governor from 1897 to 1906.[1]

The Californios started with the same potential as the New Mexicans but never came close to realizing it. California's rapid leap into statehood, the monumental increase in its Yankee population, the alienation of the cow counties from the north, the cataclysmic struggle over land —all operated to the political detriment of the Californios. Nevertheless, certain marked similarities to New Mexico developed in southern California, where the Spanish-speaking played an active role in local politics in the troublous 1850's and thereafter.

In the semigringo south of California, the Spanish-speaking had a numerical majority until the 1870's. Even in the absence of a patrón class, the Yankees looked on this superiority as both a challenge and an opportunity of assuring their own political dominance. They enthusiastically sidled up to the natives, courting them politically with gifts of

---

[1] See, for example, Loomis Morton Ganaway, *New Mexico and the Sectional Controversy, 1846–1861* (Albuquerque, N.M., 1944), pp. 60–62, 67, 70–74, 113, 123. But, cf. Sister Mary Loyola, *The American Occupation of New Mexico, 1821–1852* (Albuquerque, N.M., 1939), p. 148. Miguel Antonio Otero documents his astonishing career in three works, *My Life on the Frontier, 1864–1882* . . . (New York, 1935); *My Life on the Frontier, 1882–1897* . . . (Albuquerque, N.M., 1939); and *My Nine Years as Governor of the Territory of New Mexico, 1897–1906* (Albuquerque, N.M., 1940).

money, legal aid, and the spoils of office. Ward heelers canvassed Los Angeles as they would have any "foreign" ward in St. Louis, New York, or Boston, allowing only for the differences created by special frontier conditions.

In Los Angeles the new, integrated politics began haltingly between 1847 and 1852, but thereafter moved with a surer pace. By May, 1849, the last doctrinarie "pro-Mexicans" had resigned from the military government in favor of "pro-Yankees." First Alcalde Stephen C. Foster reigned alongside Second Alcalde José del Carmen Lugo, only to be succeeded by the equally harmonious team of Abel Stearns and Juan Sepúlveda. The permanent system of local government originated in 1850, creating a stampede of office seekers, while the preparations for the presidential election of 1852 created political partisanship and thus the organized wooing of the "Mexican vote."

The electoral contests of 1852 and 1853 in Los Angeles had the same fiesta spirit as the Glorious Fourth celebrations of those years, reflecting again the prosperity, cosmopolitanism, and material well-being of the early 1850's. Although the municipality cast an infinitesimal 363 votes in 1853, and although the county did scarcely better with 1,003—in a state that cast a total of 71,189 votes [2]—no community in California saw a livelier or more thoroughly organized campaign.

Both Whigs and Democrats engaged in high-jinx tactics to sway the voters. The issues were so muddled and the party labels so meaningless that the voters had to be harangued down to the very last moment. Since citizenship was a vaguely defined status, arguments arose constantly at the polling window (Ygnacio del Valle's town house) that So-and-So was born in Mexico, or was an Indian or a transient, and thus ineligible to vote. Irregularities occurred often. By 1853 it was an open secret that the standard rate of bribery was a dollar a vote. Rumor told of an entire Indian tribe illegally exercising the franchise, of a steamship passenger list being stuffed into the ballot box, and of dark-skinned voters being "whitewashed" for a second round of balloting. One Los Angeles Democrat persuaded some of the Spanish-speaking voters that Whig presidential nominee, General Winfield Scott, hated

[2] Benjamin D. Hayes, *Pioneer Notes . . . 1849–1875*, ed. by Marjorie Tisdale Wolcott (Los Angeles, 1929), p. 87.

Catholic Mexico, whereas Democrat Franklin Pierce, a good Catholic, simply wished to aid his Mexican coreligionists.

One of the most famous incidents in Los Angeles political history occurred on election eve in 1852. An enterprising Whig stumper bodily herded together a crowd of Sonorans, lower-class Californios, and Indians, locked them into a corral in Boyle Heights, and filled them with liquor to ensure their presence for the morning's balloting. When the Democrats got wind of this, boss Tomás Sanchez sped to the scene, tossed off an impromptu speech, and immediately put the Democratic brand on those hapless voters.

Despite the momentary strength of the Whig party on the national scene, most of southern California went Yankee and democratic at one and the same moment. Perhaps the Democrats had the edge over their opponents because they felt less inhibited in dealing with "foreign" voters. In any event, a few hard-working party regulars such as Judge Benjamin Hayes and Joseph Lancaster Brent accomplished Democratic ascendancy in Los Angeles by 1853. Hayes had the supreme advantage of being a Catholic, and both he and Brent also profited from taking an active interest in the rancheros' legal well-being. As loyal compañeros of the dons, they built a political following effortlessly, on the basis of casual friendship.

In a system reminiscent of New Mexico's, the Democratic caciques of southern California operated through the ricos to reach underlings long accustomed to following their "betters" in public matters. For example, once Brent had clinched the vote of his client, Señor Verdugo, he could also bank on the votes of the don's thirteen sons and bevy of servants and relatives. The Whigs had the same opportunities, but they could do little to break up the early friendships established by the Democrats. This core of ricos and gringos, especially gringos who came from the Old South, created a Democratic majority which long withstood the shifting tides of California politics.[3]

Doubtless, many Latin Americans remained indifferent to politics, except as instructed by their caciques or as attracted by the holiday atmosphere of election eve, and most of them failed to see any of the

[3] Harris Newmark, *Sixty Years in Southern California, 1853–1913* . . . (New York, 1916), pp. 42, 43, 50–51; Horace Bell, *Reminiscences of a Ranger* . . . (Santa Barbara, Calif., 1927), pp. 94–97.

larger issues. Some simply enjoyed being on the receiving end of a bargain with the Yankees; the spoils of office appealed to others as its own end. A few, however, did see the exercise of the franchise as a duty, like the Mexican who appeared at the polling place in a Sierra mining town and, when asked by an incredulous Yankee whether he really intended to vote, replied in Spanish, with an authoritative twist of his serape: "Why not? Am I not now an American?" [4]

Liberals saw the prevailing situation as an opportunity to "bring better luck to Californios." They actively embraced the new politics, although it represented a radical departure for them, since in olden California no such autonomous organizations as political parties had ever existed. Those who took politics seriously stood for election on all levels of government.

The Spanish-speaking took a prominent part in the formative municipal and county elections in Los Angeles. Antonio Coronel, the Mexican-born schoolteacher transformed by Sierra gold into a wealthy Californio, became the city's first superintendent of schools in 1852 and its mayor in 1853. He simultaneously acquired the hat of chairman of the Democratic County Committee, and brought to the state convention that year a solidly Catholic delegation; this launched him on a thirty-year political career. His father, Ignacio, was elected county assessor in 1853, while Dons Manuel Requeña and Pio Pico became city councilmen (together with five gringos).

Californios filled lesser posts, too. In 1852, five of them were elected justices of the peace in the city, and in all the outlying townships, except Mormon San Bernardino, they easily dominated the Yankees. The townships of San Jose, Santa Ana, and San Salvador chose Californios exclusively to serve as justices of the peace and election judges. Although in the 1852 contest organizing the County Board of Supervisors Yankees defeated four Californio candidates, in 1854 J. Sepúlveda and C. Aguilar gained entry into the board, two of whose three remaining seats were held by Yankee ranchers (S. C. Foster and D. W. Alexander). In addition, of the twenty-three juezes del campo, sixteen were Californios.[5]

---

[4] Bayard Taylor, *Eldorado, or, Adventures in the Path of Empire* (New York, 1849), p. 190.
[5] *Los Angeles Star*, June 25, Aug. 6, Oct. 30, Nov. 6, 1852; June 4, 1853; San Francisco *Daily Alta California*, May 25, 1853.

Santa Barbara's gentry had an even more pronounced political dominance, although they had originally worked through the Whig Party organization and had only gradually switched to the Democrats. Four caciques, the two de la Guerra brothers and José María Covarrubias and Joaquín Carrillo, virtually controlled politics. They never shared but a few crumbs with the local Yankees, a stance that truly reflected the rancheros' economic and numerical strength in Santa Barbara. In the presidential election of 1852, Whig nominee Winfield Scott won 112 votes in San Luis Obispo and Santa Barbara, while Democrat Franklin Pierce won only 11. Pablo de la Guerra and M. Pacheco were first elected to state office as Whigs. In 1853 the Whig nominee for governor won 137 votes and the Democratic nominee, 9—in direct contrast with the statewide trend. The Whig vote remained strong in 1854, but, owing to the vicissitudes of national politics after the death of President Harrison, the party lost its strength shortly afterward. The Barbareños now swung completely around to the Democratic ticket and tried to determine which of the party's many factions was most promising.

Illustrative of the totality of the Californios' control in Santa Barbara is the roster of government personnel in the year 1855. The mayor was Pablo de la Guerra, and a quorum on the Common Council normally consisted of A. M. de la Guerra, J. C. Carrillo, and Señor Palma y Mesa; since none of those posts consumed much time, Carrillo served also as surveyor and port inspector and de la Guerra as county assessor. In May, Fernando Tico, Pablo de la Guerra, and Ramón Mateo were elected to the county Board of Supervisors, thereby taking that body out of Yankee hands; Californios now held the reins of city and county government. Covarrubias remained state assemblyman and presided over the Democratic County Committee, whose other members were the brothers Pablo and Antonio María de la Guerra, Juan and Joaquín Carrillo, and George D. Fisher and Russell Heath. Unlike Los Angeles, Santa Barbara showed little excitement over politics (nor over anything else, for that matter). When Don Pablo resigned as mayor because of illness, the voters ignored the scheduled special election so completely that it had to be postponed. They finally chose José Carrillo as their new mayor, from a list that also included Joaquín Carrillo and a Yankee newcomer. The Democratic county convention that year selected eleven Latin Americans and two Yankees to serve as delegates to the state convention. For the fall election the party nominated a slate of fifteen Latin Americans and five gringos. No less than six different Carrillos dabbled in politics. The influence of the Californios extended into the judiciary, since the district judge was Joaquín Carrillo and the grand jury had eighteen men with Spanish surnames (including three members of the Judge's clan) and only six Yankees.[6]

The sternest challenge to the Californios of the cow counties came in 1855, from the Know-Nothings—translated mischievously into Spanish as "*Ignorantes*." Although the American Party in California later proved to be more concerned with the Chinese, practically every plank of its 1855 platform posed a potential threat to the Spanish-speaking. The Know-Nothings pledged to fight against free immigration, "Romanism" in government, and "foreign influence" in the schools and in the state militia.[7] If victorious, they could possibly block the influx of Mexican migrants, purge the government of Californios (Catholic to a man), stymie the public education of native-born children, or somehow interfere with religious expression. They might also forcibly disband Andrés Pico's recently formed California Lancers, a troop of Los Angeles horsemen which paraded next to W. W. Twist's Yankee militia at all public functions. As a result, Californios who never before had voted took the trouble to do so now, in recognition of the seriousness of the issues. Suddenly the circus aspect of politics gave way to a somber mood.

The outcome of the 1855 election gratified the abajeños. Not one local candidate dared wear the American Party label publicly, and gringos who privately espoused Know-Nothingism restricted themselves to small quips only, such as their allusion to the Democrats as a "confused mass of serapes and split breeches"; the nativists went no further, at least not openly.[8] In Los Angeles seven of the twenty-three delegates to the state Democratic convention were of Latin-American origin. Some of the Californios running on the "Democratic ticket—the liberal ticket" won office handily. Antonio Coronel became county

[6] Annie L. Morrison and John Haydon, *History of San Luis Obispo County and Environs* . . . (Los Angeles, 1907), p. 60. For an account of a hotly contested election in 1852, see *Star*, Nov. 13, 1852; Santa Barbara *Gazette*, May 23, 31, June 7, 14, 21, 28, July 19, 26, Aug. 16, 23, 30, Sept. 6, Oct. 18, 1855.

[7] *El Clamor Público* (Los Angeles), Sept. 4, 1855.

[8] *Ibid.*, Aug. 28, 1855.

assessor and Cristóbal Aguilar and Agustín Olvera county supervisors, alongside Yankee candidates who were "very popular among Californios." [9]

As for the statewide offices, while California voters as a whole elected Know-Nothing J. Neely Johnson to the governorship and gave him a platoon of Ignorante followers—the lieutenant governor, the superior court judge, the comptroller, the treasurer, the attorney general, the land surveyor, the state printer, and state senators and assemblymen, Los Angeles and San Bernardino counties bucked the trend. Democratic candidate Bigler received 1,243 votes to Johnson's 570; the town of Los Angeles itself gave 397 to Bigler and 234 to Johnson. The only solid pocket of Americanism in the southland was El Monte, stronghold of Texans and confirmed anti-Mexicans, which gave Johnson 125 votes to Bigler's 54.[10]

The most thorough rout of the Know-Nothings occurred in Santa Barbara. The Democrats as a whole breezed to victory by a three-to-one margin over independent and Know-Nothing rivals, and Democrats with Spanish surnames won by a margin of five to one. For example, the García brothers were elected constables in the second township with respective votes of 174 and 168, defeating the Hagan brothers who received only 47 and 26. José Covarrubias retained his assembly seat with 305 votes to 55 for Lee, his nearest rival. A temperance proposal to "purify" the Barbareños' drinking customs was soundly beaten, receiving only 39 favorable votes to 248 opposed.[11] In the former Whig stronghold of San Luis Obispo, the story was much the same: 118 for Bigler and 45 for Johnson.

The participation of Californios in politics and government had geographic limits. If, owing to wealth, family connections, landownership, or the backing of a bloc of Spanish-speaking voters, a Californio played a central part in the power structure of his pueblo, that part ended the moment he left home. Should he venture into the state capital, he found himself practically in enemy territory and could expect the worst. In San Jose he did far worse than his brethren in Santa Fe; no

[9] *Ibid.*, Sept. 11, 1855.
[10] *Ibid.*, Sept. 11, 18, 25, Oct. 16, 1855.
[11] Santa Barbara *Gazette*, Sept. 6, 1855.

Californio could persevere long enough in the capital to become the political peer of the Oteros of New Mexico.

The Californios came hobbling into the Yankee era without any statewide leaders. Because of weaknesses inherent in the old ruling circles, not even the native-born governors ever enjoyed anything approaching universal respect. What is worse, several of the most able, popular, and deeply committed políticos simply disappeared from public view. When José Castro returned from self-exile in 1848, he found the Yankees so angry at him that he prudently slipped into ranchero's garb and lived quietly at San Juan Bautista and Monterey. In 1856, at the age of forty-six, the old desire for public service got the better of him and he went to Baja California to fill the position of *sub-jefe político* and commandant of Baja California. A poor man and a virtual illiterate, Don José had once enjoyed considerable popularity among the northern lower classes. Larkin rated him a leader of "quick, inventive, intriguing and natural talents," so that his loss to Californios was considerable. Bancroft estimated that "nine tenths of all that has been said against him [Don José] by American writers has no foundation in truth." [12] José Castro died in Mexico in 1860, either in a brawl or at the hands of an assassin.

José Antonio Carrillo's retirement also crippled the native Californians, for he had been an able alcalde, an instigator of rebellion, a manipulator of factions, and a generally scrappy fighter for what he took to be the cause of liberty. Bancroft appraised him as a man "of good information, particularly in Law, of much influence, of a busy, restless and reckless disposition and more feared for his satirical manner than otherwise." [13] He died in Santa Barbara in 1862 at the age of sixty-six, having had no further involvement in government after his stint in the constitutional convention of 1849.

Juan Alvarado, whom Larkin once judged to be "a man of the best general knowledge, information and talent" (except under the influence of liquor), hardly took part in the Mexican War and became, at

---

[12] Thomas Oliver Larkin, "Notes on the Personal Character of the Principal Men," in *The Larkin Papers, 1845–1846,* IV, ed. by George P. Hammond (Berkeley and Los Angeles, 1953), 327; Hubert Howe Bancroft, *History of California* (San Francisco, 1884–1890), II, 751–752.

[13] Bancroft, *op. cit.,* II, 745–746.

the age of thirty-four, merely a ranchero. While still a youth in his teens he had filled the responsible jobs of secretary to the California junta and customhouse clerk and had participated in the successful coup against Governor Victoria; not long afterward he overthrew Governor Nicolás Gutiérriez and became governor himself.[14] The new politics, however, so repelled Alvarado that he went into retirement; he even advised younger men to stay out of politics. The only honor he had ever gotten out of it, he grumbled, was that his landlord, when asking for the rent, addressed him as "Your Excellency, the Governor." His chief association with gringos thereafter was to fight them as squatters. In twenty years of litigation he had managed to preserve but a small part of one rancho, and he spent his last years at the Castro adobe in San Pablo, which he had inherited from his wife.[15]

Yet, if some of the important native-born leaders stepped down or were shunted aside, the younger, spryer, or more acculturated men decided to stand for statewide offices. Pablo and Antonio María de la Guerra and José María Covarrubias of Santa Barbara, Andrés Pico and Ygnacio del Valle of Los Angeles, Mariano Vallejo of Sonoma, and M. Pacheco of San Luis Obispo found a niche in one or more of the first three legislative sessions. The Californios reached peak strength in the first session, during which Mariano Vallejo, Pablo de la Guerra, and their "Yankee compadre," Alexander Hope, served in a senate of only eighteen seats and could at least make their voices heard before they were voted down. At the same time, that crowd-pleaser, Covarrubias, sat in the thirty-five-man state Assembly.

Even in the second session, in 1851, the Californios and their friends were still active in state politics. Andrés Pico, Mariano Vallejo, and Pablo de la Guerra, together with D. W. Alexander and Abel Stearns, traveled in the company of the "Whig committee of correspondence," which met in the capital in March of 1851; Stearns presided over the group. In a deliberate pitch for the "Mexican vote," the Whig nominee for lieutenant governor nearly bowed out in favor of Mariano Vallejo.[16]

[14] *Ibid.*, pp. 693–694; Larkin, *op. cit.*, IV, 328.
[15] "History of California," 1876, MS, Bancroft Library (Berkeley, Calif.), V, 150
[16] John Wilson to Mariano Vallejo, April 7, 1851, in Mariano Guadalupe Vallejo, "Documentos para la historia de California," 1874, MS, no. 423, Bancroft Library, XIII.

Vallejo, in the abstract still the gringo's pet Californio, had some stature. During the 1850 legislative session, John C. Frémont had once made a point of coming to Mariano's rooms. First he belatedly apologized for his own wartime conduct, explaining that, once reduced to a "captain in name, but not in fact," he could not liberate Vallejo from the Bear Flaggers' clutches. Then he came to the point: Would Don Mariano vote for him for United States senator? Since Vallejo thought Frémont a remarkable figure—bold, persevering, contrite, and apparently sincere—he did pledge his vote, only to regret it later. Mariano's brother Salvador, incidentally, never wavered in his conviction that Frémont was simply a "thief, coward and begger" who showed his usual "cheek" by courting Mariano with "flattery and falsehoods." [17]

The election of 1851 was something of a turning point. It eliminated from the state Senate all the nativos, including the ambitious Mariano Vallejo. Although the Californios regained a narrow beachhead the following year, their numbers in the legislature remained small from that time forward and their authority infinitesimal. The only consolation for the 1851 rout was the election to the state Senate of the friendly Yankee ranchers from the south, S. C. Foster, Alex Hope, and J. J. Warner, and of Andrés Pico to the Assembly. Ignacio del Valle, Pablo de la Guerra, M. Pacheco, Andrés Pico, and José María Covarrubias took their legislative seats in 1852, but in the meantime the size of the legislature had grown to twenty-five senators and sixty-three assemblymen, thus further diminishing the relative weight of both Yankee southerners and Californios.

During the year that followed, 1853, only three Californios—Pablo de la Guerra, J. M. Covarrubias, and M. Pacheco—and the Yankee, Foster, held seats. The kingmakers of California politics in the capital now scarcely gave the cow county representatives a thought. In the legislature one heard constant talk that southern California would be stamped out "like an unresisting insect," that it was "only a drop of water in an ocean," and that the north was "teetotally and universally against anything Spanish."

Even on the symbolic level the Californios now received far fewer

[17] Salvador Vallejo, "Notas históricas sobre California," 1874, MS, Bancroft Library, pp. 106–107; Mariano G. Vallejo, "Recuerdos históricos y personales tocante a la Alta California ... 1769–1849," 1875, MS, Bancroft Library, V, 222.

genuflections than at the constitutional convention. Mariano Vallejo, still admired and feared for his independence and wealth, nevertheless had little chance of earning reelection in the squatter stronghold of Sonoma and was forced to retire from politics; occasionally, he came to lobby in the capital. After offering to donate to California 156 acres on Carquinez Strait as a site for a permanent capital and $350,000 in cash to build an entire complex of government buildings, he haunted the scene to sell his idea. Overwhelmed by its magnitude, a legislative committee declared the offer "more like a legacy of a prince to his people than a free donation of a private planter to a great state." [18] But needling opponents questioned Vallejo's ownership of the land, then embroiled in litigation, and mentioned alternative geographic locations for the capital, thereby killing the proposal. Vallejo thus sustained another in a long series of rebuffs from the very Yankees he had always tried to please.

Antonio María and Pablo de la Guerra of Santa Barbara exemplified that small band of Californios who hung on tenaciously at the capital, despite vehement opposition. Family wealth, a working knowledge of English, a theoretical understanding of Yankee institutions, and a background in the liberal politics of the 1840's prompted them to try their hand at the new politics. Pablo served as state senator in the first legislature (and returned later for another term), while Antonio María had a term in the senate that met in January of 1852.

As he set out for the "new world" of the north, Antonio vowed to his brother to "write something of my *compañeros* that will entertain you." [19] He did so in a series of lively letters which illuminate the Californio's sense of alienation outside his home precincts. One anecdote worth writing home about originated with his Los Angeles kinsman, Ygnacio del Valle. On arriving at the plaza of the government house, Senator del Valle suddenly saw "how far these demons, the Yankees, have gone" in dominating the Californians. Among the boys milling around, eating sweets, and selling newspapers, one small Yankee, perhaps nine years old, sacrificed half of his tin of molasses for a news-

[18] Myrtle M. McKittrick, *Vallejo: Son of California* (Portland, Ore., 1944), pp. 298–300.
[19] Jan. 19, 1852, MS, trans., de la Guerra Collection, Owen Coy Room, University of Southern California (Los Angeles, Calif.).

paper. He promptly unfolded the massive sheets and disappeared behind them to digest the latest news. This display of Yankee precocity
contrasted horribly with the backwardness of native-born youngsters.
"No wonder they eat us alive!" Don Ygnacio exclaimed.[20]

How the abajeños might keep from being devoured during the 1852
legislative session was no small matter. One factor mitigated in their
behalf, however: the confusion of state politics, which allowed for a
certain give-and-take on privileged, local matters. The fratricidal struggle within the Democratic Party, the breakup of the Whigs, the feud
over the nomination of a United States senator, and the forthcoming
presidential election gave an independent senator a chance to ma-
neuver for advantage—but he had to know the ropes. Antonio María
de la Guerra naturally looked to influential friends for help, particularly Henry Halleck's law partner, Senator Archibald Peachy; he also
tried to build on the earlier experiences of his brother in the California
Senate. Some of his countrymen preferred Don Antonio to drop his
Democratic allegiance altogether and instead to steer an independent
course, watching "all parties equally carefully." Antonio personally felt,
however, that the best chances lay in working within the Democratic
fold.[21]

Antonio took note of the popularity of Senator Andrés Pico and
Assemblyman José Covarrubias. When the legislature wished to compliment the twenty or so "distinguished soldiers" in its midst, it gave
due consideration to both former Mexican officers. "General" Covarrubias was being groomed by the Locofoco Democrats for the post of
major general in the militia, which pleased Antonio, yet brought out the
cynic in him. He promised Covarrubias the pair of "gold epaulettes in
my trunk, though my first vote will be against him, because here even
the dogs are called General. . . . The actual generals of the state have
been treated as robbers in the chambers, and perhaps they deserve
it." [22]

The more substantive measures that engaged Antonio María de la
Guerra's attention were the bills concerning tax equalization, state
divison, control of rodeos, and the appointment of a judge in the Sec-

[20] Ibid., Feb. 5, 1852.
[21] Ibid., Jan. 29, Feb. 20, 21, 22, 23, 1852.
[22] Ibid., Feb. 5, 1852.

ond District Court of Santa Barbara. He introduced a bill to extend the cattle-branding season, which passed. Since the jurisdiction of the Second District Court embraced all touchy aspects of the law, especially land litigation, and thus made the judgeship a key post, the Democratic administration decided to throw it to a Santa Barbaran. Late one night, Senators Broderick and Cook (the latter Mariano Vallejo's business partner) banged on Antonio's door to get his help in quashing the imminent appointment of a Yankee, a man of a rival clique. Antonio did help block the Yankee from the judgeship (and from other posts as well, for he considered him generally "no good"). "The members of the legislature favored us very much on this subject," he reported, until suddenly two party strong men, Bigler and McDougal, proposed abolishing some of the judicial districts altogether, including the second. Don Antonio raised a storm with his contact men, Senators Van Buren and Clark, who took the matter to higher-ups. Strangely enough, Governor McDougal shortly became "very different and amiable" on this question; the judgeship was saved and eventually went to Joaquín Carrillo.[23]

Despite an occasional feather in his cap such as this, Antonio María de la Guerra remained acutely aware of his own limitations in a new world inhabited by vaguely hostile men. About gringos he remained a thoroughgoing skeptic. "Your recommended friends have received me like Yankees," he told Pablo acidly; despite our delivering the Santa Barbara vote, "they did not seem willing to do anything." [24] Even Archibald Peachy, whose law firm was handling the de la Guerra family's affairs, was too much the gringo. When Antonio decided to back David Broderick for United States senator, Peachy besieged Pablo to change his brother's mind, because Broderick was the squatters' candidate. Antonio adamantly replied that, if he voted Peachy's way, "we will make enemies and will be pushed into a corner." [25]

Gringo politics looked altogether comical and frustrating to the Californio. No sooner had the 1852 session convened on January 12 than it ground to a halt. For six days the upper house debated the credentials of three newly arrived men claiming one seat, whose occupant was to

[23] Ibid., March 2, 1852.
[24] Ibid.
[25] Ibid., Jan. 29, 1852.

be a party to the bitterly contested election of a United States senator. The solons laboriously scrutinized the English and Spanish versions of the state constitution without determining which senator-elect might sit legally. The approach of George Washington's Birthday and the state Democratic convention in the capital caused additional laxity in the chamber: a quorum was lost, and "boisterous laughter" and a "burlesque" mood invaded the house. Meanwhile, a particularly heated committee fight concerning the San Francisco water lots threatened to freeze the legislature's deadlock permanently. Having put the real estate in private hands the preceding year, the legislature now was entertaining a proposal to get it back, a move Antonio regarded as a "perfidious" assault on private property. Insiders whispered that the water-lot dispute and other controversies foreshadowed a new state constitutional convention that would permanently split California in two—a possibility that at the time seemed imminent and real.

On February 13 of the same year, the Democratic organization convened for business that proved to be equally stormy, amusing, and ineffectual. No sooner was a chairman elected than a "feast of inkstands" broke out in the corridor—a fight provoked by Senator David Broderick, the stormy petrel of California politics, who received a piece of furniture in the eye which narrowly missed blinding him. When a "delegation" of women rustled into the hall, the men grew exceptionally boisterous; "You can imagine the noise and rattle there must be." [26] The finale was the unexpected election of José Covarrubias as delegate to the national Democratic Convention in Baltimore. The Santa Barbara assemblyman was named by acclamation, yet the episode miffed Antonio de la Guerra because it helped the wrong faction, the "locofocoismo," and was engineered by the convention chairman without consulting him. Amid "screams and noise" and hat throwing, the tongue-tied Covarrubias went to the stand for a speech but could manage only a few words.

The recent high jinx provided relief from the boredom and disappointment of the legislature and ended on a note of appreciation for a Californio, albeit the wrong one. But nothing brightened Antonio

[26] *Ibid.*, Feb. 24, 1852.

María de la Guerra's bleak view of the Yankee legislative process, as the session reconvened for more of the same. (The disputed senate seat, incidentally, was declared vacant.) The trip north cost Don Antonio in excess of $10,000 owing to inflated living costs and money scarcity; the six days of "vacation" alone cost $150 and forced him to sell $110 notes for $45 simply to cover bills. Meantime, "nothing, nothing, nothing, has been, nothing is doing, and nothing will be done" (February 23); ". . . we will retire as we came, without having done anything" (March 5).

Antonio reported one final sidelight to his brother. The legislature had reconvened in a new hall, to escape the bedbugs infesting the first spot, but "came out worse, as we have here something more besides." (He did not specify.) Andrés Pico feared "what the *señoras* will say when they learn that we are full of these vermin." The recently wed Ygnacio del Valle also felt "quite nervous" on the subject and informed Antonio he "vows he will never come to the Legislature again." This vow he kept, incidentally, for at the session's end he left the hungry vermin (and Yankee children) and returned for good to his bride and rancho.[27] His senate seat went to a Yankee, which lowered the representation of Californios in state government from five to four. Ygnacio would, however, remain active in local government until his death three decades later.

Antonio María de la Guerra also left the capital permanently. Santa Barbara was, however, a safe constituency for a de la Guerra, and Antonio's brother Pablo went to claim the senate seat. For the rest of the decade Pablo de la Guerra and Andrés Pico remained the only experienced rancheros on the top political rung.

Don Pablo also felt isolated in the capital, even by something so elementary as the language problem. As a freshman senator in 1851 he ventured to write his first English letter, in which he noted his preference for Spanish, "the language of God, which I understand tolerably as I intend to become a Saint one of these days and to speak with Him." English, on the other hand, "the idiom of birds, I do not know . . . with such a perfection as I have neither beak nor wings, things

[27] *Ibid.*, Feb. 20, 1852.

. . . I believe inherent to every Yankee . . . notwithstanding that I am one of them, yet its deficiency in me I think is because I am an unwilling one." [28]

His feelings of isolation continued and his effectiveness had declined in his second term, yet Pablo kept his ears open and made his desk a clearinghouse for all sorts of information, complaints, and petitions for patronage. Judge Carrillo complained of working late nights to whittle down a vast backlog of court cases and requested legislation to lighten the load (1854); José M. Covarrubias passed along the tip that friends would like a law licensing billiards; J. M. Bonilla sought Pablo's endorsement as a replacement for Judge Muñoz (1861); gubernatorial hopeful Eugene Casserly wanted Pablo's vote in the state Democratic convention; Charles Fernald thanked Pablo for supporting a certain mineral-lands bill and later asked his help at the convention in getting the nod for United States district judge; Salvador Vallejo presented a petition bearing a hundred names asking the pardon of a German imprisoned in San Quentin (Don Pablo was on the state Prison Board); a Mrs. Aylesworth asked his aid in getting the confirmation of a river island in San Joaquin County; Gwin Democrats in San Luis Obispo bombarded Pablo with petitions and notices of public meetings requesting that he help stall the vote for a replacement for Gwin.[29]

A discouraged Pablo de la Guerra nearly threw in the sponge several times and had to be coaxed back into his senatorial chair. "For our friendship and our religion," Mariano Vallejo urged him in January, 1854, to stay in his senate seat until after the election of a United States senator. "It may be the last time that we will be represented in the legislature of California and it is necessary for you not to abandon the position. : . . I am your uncle who appreciates you and wishes you all good." In 1856 Pablo again talked of resigning, to plead land cases before the United States Supreme Court. Uncle Mariano, a trifle wiser

---

[28] To Archibald Peachy, Dec. 14, 1851, in *ibid*.

[29] In *ibid*., Joaquin Carrillo to Pablo de la Guerra, May, 5, 1854; J. M. Covarrubias to M. de la Fayette, Feb. 3, 1854; José Antonio de la Guerra to Pablo de la Guerra, Feb. 8, 1861; Eugene Casserly to Pablo de la Guerra, June 6, 1861; Fernald to Pablo de la Guerra, April 29, June 5, 1861; Salvador Vallejo to Pablo de la Guerra, May 2, 1861; Aylesworth to Pablo de la Guerra, April 9, 1861; Ely Hubbard to Pablo de la Guerra, Feb. 28, 1854; and P. B. Reading to Pablo de la Guerra, Feb. 24, 1854.

through his own disappointments, again implored him to stay, intimating that Pablo was the wrong man for the job of legal advocate, not for lack of eloquence but of influence in Washington. "It is necessary to be very intricate and demoniacal for that business, for which I will say it is necessary to be very delicate and honest." And if Pablo were to leave, "who will represent us here in the Senate? Shall we leave a seat free to the K. N. [Know-Nothings]? I ask you to meditate well about it." [30] Perhaps Don Pablo did, for he remained in his seat.

Between 1850 and 1856, and even later, the Spanish-speaking of California, like those of New Mexico, sought and obtained practically every imaginable public office, important or otherwise. In southern California and elsewhere they served as tax assessors, election referees, surveyors, court clerks, and translators; as party delegates and national committeemen; as town constables, councilmen, and mayors; as assemblymen and senators; as trial jurors and coroner's jurors; and as justices of the peace, judges of the plains, and district judges. On the side they delivered speeches, gave endorsements, bought and sold votes, and pressured hirelings, relatives, and friends in the prescribed manner. That so many Californios willingly exerted leadership in a hostile and unfamiliar environment is particularly striking in light of the notable scarcity of leadership among the Spanish-speaking Californians in more recent decades.

Precisely what the leaders sought and what they accomplished for their followers is another matter. Meantime, the Californios' total estrangement from politics was in the offing, even in southern California.

[30] In *ibid.*, July 26, 1854; June 18, 1856.

IX

Race War
in Los Angeles,
1850-1856

I<small>F</small> the Yankees and the Californios of the cow counties found certain areas of respect for each other, one matter in particular —the problem of crime and punishment—divided them with razorlike sharpness. The trouble began about 1850 and built up to a crescendo by 1856, when Los Angeles County suffered nearly as badly from disrespect for law and order as did Amador and Alameda counties, and perhaps worse, since it had more to lose. By then the community had been so often cut along ethnic lines as to make the social alliance of the "better element" the most tenuous of relationships.

Nobody knows precisely what contribution Californios, as opposed to Mexicans, Indians, or Yankees, made to the general pool of criminals in California. Accounts that tend to glorify Californios preclude any possibility that the native-born dirtied their hands much with major crimes. Some of the more sensational published accounts of the gold rush, on the other hand, embroidered imaginary bandit escapades which unjustly blackened family names such as Carrillo, Armijo, and the like. Most native Californians preferred to think of crime as imported by cholos rather than brewed domestically by Californians, or derived from the lower class and the Indians instead of the upper class, or indigenous to plebeian Los Angeles and not to patrician Santa Barbara. (As early as 1782, the Franciscans complained of an infestation of thieves in the pueblo of Los Angeles.) In point of fact, highway

Field hands identified as Californios on the porch of the former San Fernando Mission, probably in the 1880's.

LABORERS. *Above:* Adobe brick makers at Casa Verdugo. *Below, left:* A vaquero at San Jan, near Los Angeles. *Below, right:* A Neophyte Indian serving as a zanjero (keeper of the irrigation ditch).

Top, left: Pio Pico at ninety years of age. *Top, right:* Andrés Pico. *Above, left:* Juan
B. Alvarado. *Above, right:* Mariano G. Vallejo.

Top, left: José Antonio Carrillo. *Top, right:* José Sepúlveda, *ca.* 1890. *Above, left:* Pablo de la Guerra. *Above, right:* Ygnacio del Valle.

Top, left: Bishop Tadeo Amat of Los Angeles. *Top, right:* Joseph Lancaster Brent, *ca.* 1860. *Above, left:* Reginaldo del Valle. *Above, right:* Stephen C. (Estevan) Foster.

FAMILY SCENES. *Top:* Fiftieth wedding anniversary of Jeronimo and Catalina Lopez, pioneer settlers of the San Fernando Valley. *Above:* Hilario Ybarra and family at home, Upper Main Street, Los Angeles, 1890.

Above: Juan Bandini and daughter Margarita. *Below:* Antonio F. Coronel and wife, Doña Mariana, in old regalia, *ca.* 1886.

Above: Tiburcio Vasquez, celebrated California-born bandit. *Below:* A hanging on October 4, 1871, at Temple and New High Streets, Los Angeles.

RANCHOS IN TRANSITION. *Above:* Vicente Lugo with his family and servants, 1892. Sound roof suggests affluence in the second generation. *Below:* Pio Pico's former adobe on the Whittier Road, *ca.* 1900. In contrast with the Lugo residence, the Pico home shows signs of decay.

Above: General view of the Sanchez Rancho, Baldwin Hills, 1924. *Below:* The encroachment of Los Angeles can be seen in the distance. Close-up of two-story Sanchez adobe, built in 1856.

Rancho Camulos, near Newhall, 1885, property of the Del Valle family. Setting of Helen Hunt Jackson's *Ramona* (1884). *Above:* General view. *Below:* Sheep wash.

RECREATION. *Right:* Guitar playing at Rancho Camulos. *Below:* "Caballeros" in the Los Angeles Fiesta of 1903. *Bottom:* Dancers led by Eugenio R. Plummer.

SAN FERNANDO MISSION. *Top:* Convento in 1882, before restoration. *Middle:* Same, after restoration *Left:* Neophyte Indians, 1890, reputed to be mother, 130 years old (left), and daughter, 100 years old (right).

Los Angeles street scenes. *Top:* Koppel's drawing of the town from Fort Hill, 1853. The Plaza is middle left, beyond the church steeple. *Above:* The Plaza, looking east, *ca.* 1890. *Below:* "Nigger Alley" *(Calle de los negros),* showing part of the Pico House hotel, *ca.* 1870.

SONORATOWN, LOS ANGELES. *Above:* General view, 1885. *Below:* Adobe building contrasts with newer brick structure, New High and Ord Streets, in the 1880's. Note signs advertising Wrigley gum and a Mexican theatrical performance.

Above: Mexican ice cream vendor, Los Angeles. *Below:* Dancers in Olvera Street, Los Angeles, 1920. Possibly a celebration of "Cinco de Mayo."

robbery occurred rarely in old California, even if only because brigands had few outlets for cattle or other booty, so that the old California was unquestionably safer for life and property than the new.[1]

It is, nevertheless, true that in the early Yankee years some Californios took to the highway and earned bad reputations entirely on their own hook. Disaffected youths found many reasons and opportunities to turn to crime and had many Mexican and Yankee badmen to imitate, should they lack initiative. Veterans of the rebellions and wars of the 1840's went into hiding in the 1850's and remained there as "patrons of San Dimas," the patron saint of thieves. Bernardo García, who disappeared after killing two Bear Flag soldiers in 1847, remained an outlaw; he allegedly hired on as Joaquin's lieutenant and died with him in 1853. Ex-soldier Salomón Pico became chieftain of a gang of Californios, Mexicans, Yankees, and Indians who gave the ranchos of Santa Barbara and Monterey a good working-over. On April 18, 1851, vigilantes captured Don Salomón and two of his associates, including an American named Otis, and turned them over to the authorities. Just before Antonio de la Guerra deposited bail, Pico escaped and made his way south, perhaps to Baja California, and purportedly became head of a new gang of robbers; Otis had no friends to go to bat for him and sat behind bars. For years to come the shadows of Bernardo García and Salomón Pico hovered over all the unsolved crimes committed in southern California.[2]

In American Los Angeles the criminal element had already run wild by February, 1850, when a despairing alcalde, Ygnacio del Valle, called for the help of United States dragoons, but never got it. The trend continued, and in the thirteen months from August, 1850, to October, 1851, the county experienced the astronomical number of forty-four homicides, which must have set some sort of record, considering that the entire population was below 2,300.[3]

The most singular crime in the Los Angeles region, the murder of an Irishman and his Indian servant in the Cajon Pass in 1850, was laid to

---

[1] J. Tyrwitt Brooks, *pseud.* [Henry Vizitelli], author of *Four Months among the Gold-Finders in California* (New York, 1849), a fraudulent travel account, originated the myth that Andreas Armijo and Tomás María Carrillo were the first robbers.

[2] San Francisco *Daily Alta California,* April 29, 1851.

[3] Los Angeles *Star,* Oct. 11, 1851.

the members of one of the leading old families, the Lugos.[4] On the day of the crime, Don José del Carmen Lugo, his three sons, and about fifty vaqueros had traversed the Cajon Pass, chasing Indian horse thieves; this made them suspect. A Sonoran vaquero belonging to the Lugo party confessed that he, another Mexican, and the three Lugo boys—Francisco, Chico, and Benito—had done the dirty work; that the Irishman had purposely misled the chase into a canyon where Indians lay in ambush and killed a member of the search party. Thus, the motive of the Lugos was revenge. The three scions of the wealthy southern family fiercely denied the charge and had twenty witnesses to back them. They went free without indictment, although many Yankees remained convinced of their guilt. In what may have been a personal vendetta, County Attorney Scott nevertheless prosecuted them in April, 1851. Once, while lodging at the Lugo home, Scott had had a falling-out with his wife, lost his temper, and struck her. The Lugo boys had restrained him physically, which he had taken as a deliberate humiliation. In any event, Scott indicted the boys, and Don José retained Joseph Lancaster Brent to defend them. The gringo lawyer was convinced of their innocence and sized up the case as a possible travesty of justice. For this service, Brent allegedly got a handsome $20,000 retainer.

Even more alarming than a prejudiced prosecutor and an inflamed public opinion was the arrival in town of twenty-five meddlesome ruffians led by John "Red" Irving, a once-illustrious Texas Ranger and a cavalry captain during the Mexican War. Irving claimed to be heading for Sonora to fight Apaches at Mexico's invitation (although skeptics thought him going "in search of ladies fair and pastures green"). The night before the Lugos were to post bail, Irving's lieutenant accosted Brent to demand $10,000 for spiriting the boys from jail and taking them safely to Sonora, if they were not to be lynched. Brent persuaded Don José to reject the blackmail and offered a counterplan to protect

---

[4] Joseph Lancaster Brent, *The Lugo Case: A Personal Experience* (New Orleans, 1926). See also Horace Bell, *Reminiscences of a Ranger* . . . (Santa Barbara, Calif., 1927), p. 12 ff.; Benjamin D. Hayes, *Pioneer Notes* . . . *1849–1875,* ed. by Marjorie Tisdale Wolcott (Los Angeles, 1929), pp. 75–81; *Alta,* June 4, 17, 1851; Benjamn D. Hayes, Scrapbooks, MS, Bancroft Library (Los Angeles, Calif.), I, 106–112; and José del Carmen Lugo, "Vida de un Ranchero ... ," 1877, MS, Bancroft Library, pp. 71–75.

the boys at their release. Although fearful of igniting a general "race war," Brent that night enlisted seventy-five armed Californians and Sonorans and quietly stationed them behind a wall near the courthouse to await the boys' release. By a stroke of luck, some state militia on an Indian-hunting expedition rode out of the morning fog. Its commander at first refused to interfere in local affairs, but Brent persuaded him simply to deliver the bailees into the hands of friends. The trick worked. Irving complimented Brent on his resourcefulness, but broadly hinted that he would "give the Lugos hell" anyway.

Irving's men soon resumed their Mexican expedition, and the town breathed easier. While passing Chino on May 24, however, they stole horses, killed cattle, and reportedly threatened to ravish some women. Several Angeleños hastened to Chino to investigate, while others rode quickly to summon General Joshua H. Bean's dragoons stationed north of the city. Irving still craved the Lugos' blood or money and, hearing of Bean's approach, decided on a ruse. He sent a Sonoran into the San Bernardino Mountains to spread the lie among the Coahuilla Indians that two hundred white men were on the warpath to exterminate the foothill tribes. Irving hoped that the Coahuillas would divert or smash Bean's force while his own men doubled back to sack the Lugo ranchos. Fortunately, a friend of the Lugos overheard the conspirators in a saloon and forewarned the family, who fled their ranchos with all their valuables. The Irving gang tore into trunks and personal effects, only to find nothing of interest. While they were engrossed in their search, they noticed the Coahuillas surrounding them in silence. As the bandits rode off to plunder yet another Lugo home, the Indians followed them steadily, but stayed beyond pistol range. Unknown to Irving's men, Justice of the Peace José María Lugo, the Coahuillas' old protector, had secretly dispatched them there for police action. By cunning or by luck the Indians lured the bandits into a blind mountain canyon and, armed with boulders and bows and arrows, slew them to a man.

When the Angeleños got wind of this event, they nervously dispatched posses to the scene. First to arrive was S. C. Foster's contingent of Californios and Yankees who had ridden from Chino, where they learned that Irving's gang had done little more than steal beef on the hoof. Emerging into the steep canyon, they cringed at seeing eleven dead gringos, with heads bashed in and clothing stripped, and the carrion crows already feasting. Furiously, the Americans turned on Foster and cursed his wife's family, the Lugos, for having stirred up savage Indians against white men. However evil, they said, Irving's men deserved the white man's justice, not that of barbarians. The posse had almost come to blows when fifty dragoons arrived and saved the day. The respected General Bean calmed the disputants and "prevented a general war which must have proved . . . disastrous." [5]

Clearly, here was an example of the overlapping of old and new judicial philosophies. A six-man coroner's jury with a Californio majority concluded that Justice Lugo and his Indian police had exceeded their office, although they had given the gang its just desert for threatening to "give the Lugos hell." The jury refrained from censuring Lugo, but that name, already tarnished by the suspicion of guilt against the three sons, was blackened further.

The Yankees resolved to prevent a recurrence of old-style summary justice by "Spaniards" and "savages." As the Yankee Indian agent later reported, "doubtless, the Indians thought they were acting in obedience to the authorities," as in years gone by. "The necessity for correcting their ideas on this subject, is evident. . . . they ought never to be allowed to meddle with the punishment of whites for public offenses." [6]

The incident had a sequel. Chico, Francisco, and Benito Lugo skipped bail, which left the murders of the Irishman and the Indian, like most other crimes, unsolved. No sooner had a new justice of the peace announced a plan to rearrest the trio than an unknown assassin fired several shots into his office. One bullet tore clean through the hat of County Attorney Hayes, the justice's office mate, who theorized on the sequence of events. He believed that the would-be killer had meant to revenge the death of a Californian named Domingo Jaime, recently killed by an American, Ned Hines, who was never prosecuted for his black deed and had eventually skipped bail. Hayes philosophized that "when the murderers of Californians can escape, like Ned Hines a few days ago, I do not wonder that revenge is sought, and no distinction is

[5] John Walton Caughey, ed., *The Indians of Southern California in 1852* (San Marino, Calif., 1952), pp. 10–11.
[6] *Loc. cit.*

made between innocent and guilty, [just] so that he be an American."
The citizenry concluded that the Lugos had engineered the shooting.
The fresh trail of the unknown horsemen did, in fact, lead Sheriff
Barton to the Lugo rancho, although not to the assailant, who eluded
capture. Hayes later concluded that Salomón Pico and Benito Lugo
were the culprits.[7]

More than a year later, lawyer Brent brought the Lugo boys out of
hiding to clear their names. A court officially exonerated them, although in Los Angeles the suspicion never died that the mountain killings and the attempted assassination of a judicial officer were their
handiwork. Angeleños long remembered the Lugo incident, because of
its panoramic sweep and its elaborate involvement of Indians, Yankees,
and Californios. It was also the first prosecution for murder—and unsuccessful at that.

By the middle fifties, the structure of law enforcement in Los Angeles County looked impressively ornate on paper. It consisted of a district and a city prosecutor; sixteen justices of the peace who held forth
in the outlying townships, supported by thirty-two constables; a sheriff,
a subsheriff, and a deputy sheriff for the county; a city marshal, his
deputies, and the city police, not to mention the mayor and six councilmen who were empowered to make laws and encourage their enforcement; a jailer and a coroner to investigate deaths with the aid of juries;
twenty-three judges of the plains, who had the powers of a rural police
and could even hang a man for stealing stock; the County Board of
Supervisors, responsible for the general well-being of the county; a district judge with power to hang without a jury; a court of sessions
staffed by three justices and a county judge, with a jury for each case;
and a grand jury which could be formed at will and had wide discre-
tionary powers in criminal cases. Here ruled more men, one Spanish
American wryly observed, than a company of dragoons, or about the
same number as had accompanied Hernán Cortés in his conquest of
Montezuma's empire.

Yet this veritable army of public officials failed to secure even a
modicum of public respect. Office seekers lunged after available titles,

[7] *Op. cit.*, p. 78.

but shirked their duties if a job entailed any danger. Only the mournfully efficient coroners' juries operated competently; they gave their findings to the law courts, the "graveyards" of all criminal matters. Participation in the law-enforcement process was so dangerous that for months at a time the office of sheriff had no takers, even at a yearly salary of $10,000.[8]

The resulting proliferation of crime netted for Los Angeles one of the worst reputations of any gold rush town; northern detractors thought of it as a place combining jaded opulence with rampant drinking, murder, and brutality—the kind of disorder associated with mixed breeds and the stagnant cow county culture. For the north to make invidious comparisons was surely an instance of the pot calling the kettle black, but Los Angeles could do little else but admit its failings. In truth, for five years and more it failed to cope with troublemakers—the transient army of Argonauts, neophyte Indians on a Saturday-night binge, runaway criminals from the north, wild Indian marauders lurking in the hills, teamsters and cattle buyers flaunting their money, gamblers, and restless native-born youths.

With few exceptions, confessed the Los Angeles *Star*, murderers went unidentified, and, if identified, went unprosecuted; if they were prosecuted, they got off somehow, even if only by escaping on bail. "With all our natural beauties and advantages there is no country where human life is of so little account. Men hack one another to pieces with pistols and other cutlery, as if God's image were of no more worth than the life of one of the two or three thousand ownerless dogs that prowl about our streets and make night hideous." [9] Things came to such a pass that breakfast small talk commonly began with "Well, how many killed last night?" According to tradition, the town averaged one homicide a night, but even at the rate of one a week, Los Angeles was annihilating a sizable proportion of its scanty population.

Like the San Franciscans, Angeleños preoccupied with the failure of public morality resorted to popular tribunals. Vigilante justice had a distinctiveness in Los Angeles, however, in that every important lynch-law episode and most minor ones involved the Spanish-speaking. This

---

[8] Bell, *op. cit.*, p. 13.
[9] Feb. 26, 1852, a remark prompted by the pistol duel at the Washington's Birthday Ball.

tended to split the Spanish-speaking themselves: the "better element" polarized around Andrés Pico, Tomás Sanchez, and other ricos who helped the vigilantes, while the "lower element" generally remained leaderless but indignant, so long as the Yankees tried to bring them to task without also punishing gringo wrongdoers. Even the most formless and short-tempered mob, moreover, recognized in its own perverse way the problem of ethnic balance. Once, for example, a mob snatched from the San Gabriel jail a Yankee slated to hang for theft and sentenced him instead to seventy-eight lashes on the bare back; simultaneously, for a Sonoran who had cut up a countryman in a brawl they prescribed fifty lashes. The Mexican "begged the privilege of being whipped first, saying that he was a man of honor . . . [and] had only used his knife when insulted." An Indian appointed by the mob flayed him with a willow switch with "an air of intense satisfaction." The Yankee also had his pride and refused to be flogged by a lowly Indian. An unsuspecting American volunteered for the job, but when he had finished the spectators rewarded him with a blanket-bouncing that knocked him cold. The Los Angeles *Star* felt repelled by the episode, particularly because the constable stood by and watched, unmoved.[10]

Still another special feature of the cow county lynchings lay in the character of the lynchers. At El Monte lived one key group, an enclave of Texans who had served in the Texas Rangers during the Mexican War, and who, in any event, considered themselves experts at "dealing with" Mexicans. Going by the name of rangers and not vigilantes, they generally tendered their services to the vigilante committees or to the sheriffs, but sometimes took separate action. Another group, the vigilante committeemen, generally included "respectables"—old-time ranchers, merchants, lawyers, and government officials. Since they owned land titles or had a smattering of legal knowledge, the town looked to them for leadership. At the height of a crisis they contributed an element of caution and always sought the support of the better classes of Californios—no mean contribution, considering the deep hatreds of the El Monte group and the potential danger of the mob. Yet, as to why they could not exert the same authority within, instead of outside, the law remains unclear. Harris Newmark attempts a feeble

[10] Bell, *op. cit.*, p. 40; *Star*, Feb. 12, 1853.

answer when he says that "the safety of the better classes in these troublous times often demanded quick and determined action, and stern necessity knew no law. . . . milder courses than those of the vigilance committees of our young community could hardly have been followed with wisdom and safety." [11]

Vigilante justice began with a bang in the summer of 1852.[12] In mid-July of that year the legal authorities delivered to Los Angeles three Latin Americans wanted for murdering two Yankee cattle buyers. One of the trio was Doroteo Zavaleta, a soldier's son, born and reared locally. A clod rather than a depraved character, Zavaleta had stolen oxen, cattle, and horses from Bernardo Yorba's rancho and wood from Manuel Garfias' property, for which he was arrested. Zavaleta broke jail with two Sonorans, one of them Jesús Rivas, a cold-blooded character. Seeking aid from Zavaleta's brother, the trio fled to San Juan Capistrano "to go away from this part of the country." There, however, they chanced upon a pair of American cattle buyers, whom Rivas decided to rob and kill. Zavaleta later testified that he absolutely rejected the idea of murder, particularly when his brother agreed to give them horses for their trip to Mexico. After robbing the Americans of $500 Zavaleta wanted to flee, but Rivas saw the danger of this plan and committed the final deed. Later he claimed that Zavaleta had incited the murder and had killed one of the pair.

With decorum unsurpassed in San Francisco, Los Angeles convened its own vigilante committee. Abel Stearns, initiator of the proceedings, served as chairman; Señor Rojo and Mr. Sanford took the minutes; and Mr. Dryden translated them. Alex Bell, Francisco Mellus, and Manuel Garfias selected a jury of seven Yankees and five Latin Americans (José Antonio Yorba, Andrés Pico, Dolores Sepúlveda, Felipe Lugo, and Julian Chavez). A committee of public safety (Manuel Requeña, Matthew Keller, J. R. Scott, Lewis Granger, Rojo, and John G. Downey) took the prisoners' confessions in English and Spanish. The jury returned a verdict of first-degree murder for Zavaleta and Rivas, and the next morning the town witnessed its first "grand" lynching.

---

[11] *Sixty Years in California, 1853–1913* . . . (New York, 1916).
[12] What follows is taken from the *Star*, July 24, 31, 1852. Actually, the first person hanged in the county was an Indian, for the murder of an Indian; see *ibid.*, April 3, 1852.

Thus ended the first popular tribunal, which for its ethnic makeup and judiciousness won the approval even of the Californios. Ideally, Manuel Garfias, as an interested party, should not have helped select a jury, and a clever defense lawyer might have empaneled lower-class Latin Americans to offset the obvious class prejudice against the prisoners. It is very likely, though, that a regular jury would have rendered the same verdicts—all the more reason to wonder why the town refused to allow the law courts to function normally.

A second vigilance committee was formed after the murder of the estimable Joshua H. Bean, four months later, on November 7, 1852, near former San Gabriel Mission. This time the entire town, rather than the vigilantes alone, pressed the issue, for Bean was a courageous and popular figure, unlike his notorious brother, Judge Roy Bean, "the Law West of the Pecos." Actually, two bodies convened: a central committee consisting of two gringos and M. C. Rojo, and a committee at large composed of Rojo and six gringos. These were as respectable a group of vigilantes as could be found anywhere.[13] Salomón Pico's name arose in connection with the crime, and rangers arrested and jailed several Sonorans and a young Californian thought to be allied with him—"Eleuterio," the cobbler Cipriano Sandoval of San Gabriel, Juan Rico, Reyes Feliz, and the Indian, Felipe Reid, adopted son of Hugo Reid. Young Reid maintained his innocence, but Sandoval claimed that he had stumbled into him in the darkness, that Reid at first had blurted out his guilt but then denied it and finally had tried to bribe him to seal his lips. Reyes Feliz also pleaded innocence, but so frantically that he confessed a previous crime. For ten days the committee grilled the dazed suspects, separately and together, analyzing and reanalyzing the testimony and seeking corroboration for new points. Although unsure of themselves, the vigilantes nonetheless felt that they had the culprits at hand and rested their case before the town.

The tribunal that meted out justice was utterly chaotic. After hearing the evidence about Reyes Feliz, a "ferocious looking gambler" mounted a chair and moved that Feliz be hanged; the crowd assented. The same verdict was meted out to Sandoval, about whom little was actually

[13] D. W. Alexander, M. Goodman, H. Hancock, J. L. Brent, J. G. Downey, and Col. Stuart; see *ibid.*, Nov. 13, 27, 1852.

known. Reid was turned over to regular officials for disposal, although many suspected him because of his known rivalry with Bean for the attentions of an Indian woman. On Sunday the town climbed toward a gray sky to gather before the gibbet on Fort Hill. The two prisoners were led up by a priest (and accompanied by yet a third Latin American caught attempting murder that very morning when the public's dander was up). Before a silent crowd, Sandoval reasserted that he had no connection with this or any other murder and prayed for the Lord's forgiveness for himself and his tormentors. He kissed the crucifix and then was hanged. Says Horace Bell: "A peal of thunder announced the end of the tragedy," and heavy rain began to fall, whereupon the crowd retired quietly to the local saloons.[14] The words of cobbler Sandoval and the thunder later were to nettle the town's conscience; years afterward, the true killer made a deathbed confession,[15] which belatedly made some Angeleños wary of vigilante proceedings.

The third vigilante action, in 1853, concerned Mexican bandits. At the first rumor that the bandido chieftain Joaquin might be attending a fandango at the Moreno adobe, the pugnacious Texans from El Monte got into fighting regalia and went to investigate. "Immediately taken into custody by an overwhelming array of black-eyed Senoritas," [16] the "Texas rangers" neglected their mission. Additional bandit activity two months later led to the formation of Captain Hope's Rangers. Only five of Hope's twenty-three gringo horsemen were among the town's respectables. Although mainly Texans again, they politely tendered their services to Mexican Mayor Antonio Coronel and gladly accepted a gift of a hundred broken horses from Pio Pico and Ygnacio del Valle.[17] Upon hearing that Joaquin was definitely within city limits, writes the ranger historian Bell, the company sallied forth at midnight to "search every suspicious house and place within the city limits." Men scoured Nigger Alley, Sonoratown, the vineyards, and all nearby suburban huts, but without result, except that one party retrieved a stolen jackass.

Bandido depredations, even murders, continued. By late August the

[14] Op. cit., pp. 8–10, 27, 29.
[15] Caughey, ed., op. cit., p. xvii.
[16] Bell, op. cit., pp. 30–32.
[17] Los Angeles Star, Aug. 6, 1853; A. W. Hope, et al., to Coronel, MS, Coronel Collection (n.d.), Los Angeles County Museum.

volunteer mounted police numbered a hundred men, including Agustín Olvera, Juan Sepúlveda, F. L. Guirado, and new gringo worthies.[18] When a visiting cattle buyer was murdered by his Sonoran interpreter, Vergara, they pursued the felon for 90 miles, driving him into the clutches of the soldiers stationed at Yuma, who killed him. He was not yet quite dead when another Sonoran, named Senate, killed Marshal Whaling and escaped. With new resolve, the rangers chased from one canyon to another in every direction, seeking the trail of the will-o'-the-wisp, Joaquin.

One night twenty-one unidentified bandidos broke into the home of a Frenchman named Lelong and murdered him. They raided the "Spanish houses" in Sonoratown, abducted some girls to a nearby headquarters, and escaped. By October, "rumors of a Mexican invasion and an expulsion of the gringos" evolved into a state of siege and a business standstill. Finally, rangers trapped eight bandits in a cornfield —one of them a woman—but they had no connection with Lelong's murderer. The district attorney told the town that "it was not our hang" and packed the captives off to their own stamping ground of San Luis Obispo for appropriate treatment.[19]

The recent violent occurrences began to sink down into the endless annals of unsolved crimes, when guilt devolved on two missing Sonorans, Luis Burgos (lately allied with Vergara) and Senate, whose last known act was to stab a man and flee for his life. Judge Hayes feared that putting a reward on their heads would create a "bad state of society" among the Latin Americans, but Sheriff Barton nonetheless offered $500 for the culprits, dead or alive, for the crimes of murder theft, and rape. The reward was claimed by a Californio who brought in the bodies of Burgos and Senate neatly arranged in a careta.[20] He offered no explanation, but the key to the whole mystery was discovered soon afterward, when a Sonoran sold a watch that formerly had belonged to Lelong. This was Atanacio Moreno who, under close questioning, confessed to having led the recent bandido troop, including Senate and Burgos, whom he had killed after a falling-out. On April 5 Judge Hayes sentenced Moreno to fifteen years. "He took the sentence

[18] Downey, S. C. Foster, Banning, Hayes, and Brent.
[19] Bell, *op. cit.*, pp. 147–165.
[20] Hayes, *op. cit.*, p. 101; *Alta*, Feb. 5, 1854.

with perfect composure," noted the judge.[21] This interrupted (but did not end) the checkered career of a "tall, straight, fine appearing white man, belonging to the best blood of Sonora . . . [who had once] stood well in society, and was highly respected." [22]

Not until February, 1854, after a six-year judicial interregnum, did Los Angeles witness its first bona fide execution. The victim was a Mexican, Ygnacio Herrara, who had "killed one of his own race, about a woman!" Thousands attended the historic event, including many Latin Americans who admitted Herrara's guilt but cursed Hayes's death sentence and wondered if he would henceforth punish gringo killers with equal severity. Hayes himself took the event in stride and merely wrote of the Mexican's repentance and of the prayerful attitude of the entire Catholic population. "At their request, candles were burnt there [at the scaffold] last night and today he was buried with martial music and religious rites." [23]

Plainly, by 1854 the Spanish-speaking of Los Angeles felt oppressed by a double standard of justice such as some of them had previously experienced in the gold mines. One sees here in embryo resentments about "Anglo justice" similar to those that have incited Mexican-Americans in more recent times.

The time had come when many Latin Americans had quietly resolved to equalize the situation at any cost, as they demonstrated during the double execution that occurred in January, 1855. Among the criminals who crossed Hayes's path was a mestizo named Félix Alvitre, who in November, 1854, confessed murdering a Yankee at El Monte. After a jury trial Hayes sentenced him to die on January 12, 1855, thus allowing a reasonable time for appeal to higher courts. In sentencing Alvitre, the judge spoke sharp words, not for Alvitre's ears alone, but "for the benefit of his young countrymen, who are betraying too many signs of hostility to Americanos." [24] With an eye to ethnic symmetry, Hayes sentenced the cowboy Dave Brown for killing a fellow American in a drunken stupor. The judge also ordered him hanged two

[21] Op. cit., p. 126.
[22] Bell, op. cit., pp. 155–162.
[23] Op. cit., p. 104; San Francisco Alta, Feb. 22, 1854.
[24] Hayes, op. cit., p. 107. See also Bell, op. cit., pp. 155–162, and H. Newmark, op. cit., pp. 68–69.

months later, but an impatient crowd seized Brown for immediate execution. At that point, Mayor Stephen Foster rescued Brown but also promised the mob that, if a higher court reversed the decision, he would immediately resign as mayor and resume the interrupted lynching bee.

When January 12, 1855, rolled around, Brown's lawyer brought from the California Supreme Court a stay of execution, but there was no word of leniency for Alvitre. So far, none of the vagaries of justice had erupted into pitched battle among the races. The execution of Herrera and Sandoval, the killing of Domingo Jaime, the escape of Ned Hines, and the crimes of Moreno's bandits had torn, but not shredded, the fabric of society. But when the hangman executed the wretched Alvitre in the jailyard (and bungled the job by allowing the body to writhe to the ground), the picture changed. Spanish Americans would not cavil over his guilt, but neither would they any longer tolerate a gringo killer slipping free while a Mexican one was hanged, in this instance horribly so. Taking a trick from the gringo's hat, they went en masse to make Foster redeem his pledge. True to his word, the mayor resigned, called a public meeting, and announced himself ready to help lynch Brown. After hearing a round of speeches, a mob of Latin Americans and Yankees stormed the jail. Sheriff Barton called upon General Andrés Pico to help restore order, but Foster's crowd was too determined and simply took Brown out.

Juan Gonzales, a lowly Mexican who would soon go to prison for horse theft, was supposed to trip the cord and hang Brown, but when the prisoner objected to being dispatched by "a lot of greasers," Foster gave the job to a "genuine American." Through a piece of advance journalism, the weekly *Southern Californian* gave the crowd a handy program of the day's doings. To meet the departing steamer, it went to press in the morning with a full "description" of the forthcoming lynching, even Brown's confession. With its task done, the crowd unanimously reelected "Don Estevan" Foster as mayor.

One week later a returning vessel brought Alvitre's stay of execution, the fatal delay having resulted from the slowness of the mails and a red-tape mix-up in the capital. Folk history ridicules Foster and intimates that the episode made him break down "under a brooding remourse"; nevertheless, the Spanish-speaking still thought him altogether "upright, honorable, [and] effective," and supported his reelection. According to the Spanish-language weekly *El Clamor Público*, "our fellow citizens are in agreement with the summary justice" Foster administered. Without such men as he in the saddle, clever lawyers and corrupt juries let the most evil criminals go completely free. A deliberately sluggish court is "the most ridiculous farce and the most infamous disgrace which a nation can endure." If the courts falter, then "*¡Bien hecho* (well done)!" [25] to those who do its work.

The worst yet lay ahead for Los Angeles. So far as ethnic relations are concerned, unquestionably the ugliest week after the time of Captain Gillespie was that of July 19 to 26, 1856. Business lay dead, the town was split along racial lines, and every man went armed, expecting the outbreak of a "Mexican revolution." Again Spanish Americans took legal matters into their own hands to solve the six-year problem of the nonprosecution of Yankee evildoers, or so they said.

The trouble began on a Saturday night, when Deputy Constable William W. Jenkins tried to repossess a guitar belonging to Señor Ruiz, who was in arrears on a small debt. In the instrument the woman of the house had left a personal letter which she begged the constable to return to her. Just then Ruiz entered and seized Jenkins from the rear to protect her. The panicky constable reached for his pistol, swung around, and fired. Ruiz collapsed, lingered for a day while painfully bidding each of his many companions good-bye, and died the next evening. What particularly "exasperated the spirit of all Mexicans" was that Ruiz was no criminal like Alvitre, but a hardworking family man and a man of parts. He had recently had the honor of delivering the Mexican Independence Day oration. They interpreted the death of the thirty-three-year-old Ruiz as needless, wanton, inexcusable.

On Monday the court convened momentarily to arraign Jenkins but then adjourned for "the largest [funeral] procession of its kind ever seen in Los Angeles." Americans who read dangerous resentment on the faces of the mourners immediately strapped on their guns. At the inevitable graveside meeting, Ruiz' more irate friends tried to arouse

[25] *El Clamor Público* (Los Angeles), May 31, 1856.

the crowd to seize Jenkins, who was behind bars but was due for bail. Temperate Californios and Yankees dissuaded them from violence and instead established a committee to protect the jail and see that justice was done. But when the peace committee departed, anger overcame the remaining mourners.[26]

At sundown "the lowest and most abandoned Sonorians and Mexicans" (the words of the *Star*) gathered on the hill, and again the next night, still admittedly confused about how to right the wrongs of their existence.[27] Various points of view were represented among the hundred persons in attendance, but firebrands, sneering that Mexicans had "too long blindly followed" the lead of Yankees in legal matters, gained the upper hand. "Archconspirator" M. Carriaga, a Frenchman who made a "wholesale and violent denunciation of Americans," assumed the role of leader. He did not intend to lynch Jenkins, as the Yankees feared, but only to seize and hold him for trial so as to prevent a Ned Hines disappearing act.

To do so, the rebels would need arms. By distracting the attention of the village priest, they searched his yard and made off with a few old guns stored there since the war. Once they had congregated in full strength on their hill the remonstrances of Juan Padilla, Pedro Romero, José Rubio, and Tomás Sanchez could not dissuade them from action. At midnight, aided by a bright moon, they came down for a parlay with Sheriff Getman, reiterating that they merely wanted to hold Jenkins for trial. Getman would not hear of it and, with five deputies and ample supporters, dug in for attack. Although the sheriff sustained a head wound, he counterattacked and chased the rebels out of town, dispersing them in two directions.

By Wednesday morning a dozen Latin Americans sat in jail, among them a good many who had nothing whatever to do with the attack. Meantime, suburban Yankees as usual had interpreted the violence as the threat of a broad-gauged Mexican rebellion, bundled up their children, and flocked to town for protection. Thirty-six El Monte men arrived for action and were received with loud cheers. A public meeting at ten in the morning established the town's defenses.

[26] *Ibid.*, July 26, Aug. 2, 9, 16, 23, 1856; *Star*, July 26, Aug. 2, 23, 1856.
[27] *Ibid.*, Aug. 2, 1856.

Just then the San Franciscans were in the throes of their most sophisticated vigilante activity, and their Los Angeles country cousins followed suit. The Angeleños produced a new committee of their own, with Judge Norton presiding and H. N. Alexander serving as recording secretary. Among the first business was a rousing welcome for Andrés Pico, who came to the rostrum to offer full cooperation in the restoration of order. The resolutions committee included nine gringos and four Latin Americans (A. F. Coronel, A. Pico, T. Sanchez, and Señor Padilla). Clearly echoing the San Franciscans, the Angeleños resolved that, whereas the town harbored "a great number of knaves, thieves and assassins," the committee would take testimony concerning suspicious characters, seize them or put them at liberty at will, and form military companies, yet refrain from shedding blood or taking life unless the proper authorities refused to act. All townsmen would go unarmed unless on duty with one of the military companies—such companies to be directed by the sheriff and a mixed council of nineteen men.[28] A majority vote of the committee would be required to expel a man from the community, and 500 English and 500 Spanish circulars would be printed to explain the emergency.

Four military companies were formed. In addition to the El Monte rangers, the town organized the city guards, the citizens' company, and a fourth band, comprising twenty Californios led by Andrés Pico. Seventy miles of hard riding to the south brought Pico's men face to face with Carriaga, whom they retrieved as a prize. Los Angeles slept uneasily that night as two Mexicans fired wild shots at Yankees for no apparent reason and then put spurs to flanks and escaped. The committee thereupon reconvened and ordered the rangers to sweep the countryside again for hidden rebels. The "Monte boys" located Vicente Guerrero's son and practically dragged him to a spot where he might locate hidden confederates, especially his father, another conspirator. Hayes issued warrants for the arrest of several outlaws, including his own good friend, Guerrero, a family grocer and property owner as universally respected as his dead friend Ruiz. As Hayes himself admitted, "there never was any harm in . . . Vincentillio." Terrified and lonely, the refugee Guerrero paused in Juan Bandini's home in San Diego, told

---

[28] Including gringos Dryden, Mellus, B. D. Wilson, Forester, J. G. Downey, and Stearns and Latin Americans A. F. Coronel, T. Sanchez, Olvera, and Aguilar.

the tearful story of his compadre's death and his own role in the rebellion, and then fled home to Mexico.[29]

Just before Hayes grilled Carriaga, news arrived of the execution of the miscreants Hetherington and Brace by the San Francisco vigilance committee, whose "contagious influence" therefore reached its height in Los Angeles. Judge Hayes took the opportunity to plead for due process of law. He cited two outstanding allegations against the Frenchman: fomenting revolution and attempting assault. On the first point he could find no evidence, and thus could see no purpose for the vigilantes. He reminded Americans that they had supplied three "memorable examples" of vigilante executions which Mexicans had tried to imitate, most recently in the Alvitre-Brown case. He informed the aggrieved Mexicans, moreover, that they should have availed themselves of the grand jury, since "violence . . . ends only in ruination." He accused both sides of condemning "a single individual for the offense of a multitude." Meanwhile he commended the sheriff for good sense and forbearance. As for the second charge against Carriaga, Hayes had him indicted for assault with intent to kill (the sheriff), set him free on $2,000 bail, and turned him over to the grand jury. In so doing Hayes urged Los Angeles to honor the grand jury and not the vigilantes, and therefore was one of the few Angeleños who ever seriously opposed vigilante law.

William Jenkins was in his early twenties, tall, lean, fair, with a command of Spanish. His popularity was at least great enough to encourage him to stand for marshal in the preceding election. When brought into court, he seemed confident of getting off lightly. Hayes indicted him for unpremeditated homicide, set him free on bail, and remanded him to the grand jury. To this release the Latin Americans took exception, especially since that very week the previous city marshal had been tried in absentia for killing a man and skipping bail.

Jenkins' case went to trial in the district court, Judge Hayes presiding, on an indictment for second-degree murder, for which the maximum penalty was twelve years. The sheriff brought in forty-eight prospective jurors, every last one of them unknown Yankees, probably most of them new. The trial hinged on the testimony of the only two witnesses, Ruiz' landlady, María Candelaria Pollorena, and Cesaria

Navarro, a woman who had seen the fracas begin before fleeing to safety with her children. Jenkins' attorney, the redoubtable Judge Scott, in a two-hour cross-examination impugned Señorita Pollorena's veracity. Testimony by men like B. D. Wilson tended to show that "her general character is very bad," so that Scott could allege that she had conspired with Ruiz to attack Jenkins and protect the stolen guitar.

Hayes acknowledged the unreliability of the leading witness but observed that Señora Navarro was of good character and had introduced corroborating testimony. He gave long and careful instructions to the jury, weighing the basic legal issues—the difference between premeditated and unpremeditated homicide, the responsibility of public officials like Jenkins to enforce civil rather than criminal law, the evaluation of the testimony of character witnesses, and the meaning of self-defense; he even reminded the jurors of the need for equal justice to rich and poor. The jury, by contrast, in five minutes returned a verdict of not guilty. Jenkins went free and returned to work as deputy constable. Fortunately, the grand jury then tactfully quashed the indictments against Carriaga and released the imprisoned Mexicans, by that token restoring the town's equilibrium.[30]

F. P. Ramirez, editor of *El Clamor Público,* by no means fully sympathized with Carriaga's tactics, but he justified them under the circumstances and railed against the Yankee vigilantes and their secret night work. Most of the gringo committeemen had intentions of "hypocritically damagaing" the Spanish-speaking, he charged, and would have done so but for the restraint of a few decent men among them. Mexicans, not Yankees, were carrying on the high traditions of the San Francisco vigilantes; "the death of Ruiz was for Los Angeles what the killing of James King of William was for San Francisco." Thankfully, Mexicans who once "begged favors on bended knees, now . . . seek *justice* and *liberty* by their own efforts." Too bad, though, that they lacked numbers and gained nothing by their effort; "we remain at the same place as before." Los Angeles still desperately needed genuine security and unity among its diverse nationalities.

Meantime, Ramirez heard the Yankees using an inflammatory term, "war of the races," to describe the excitements of the day.[31]

[30] *El Clamor Público* (Los Angeles), Aug. 23, 1856.
[31] *Ibid.,* May 9, 1857.

X

Cow County
Bandidos, 1856-1859

Into a town already steaming with resentment about lack of civil order and civil rights, in 1857 came one more explosive ingredient: bandits—not phantom bandits, but real and brazen ones. During the three years since the demise of Vergara, Senate, Burgos, and Moreno in 1853, the Angeleños had not been able to retire at night without worrying about organized robberies, knifings, shootings, or riots troubling their sleep, but never about bandidos. So convinced did Ben Hayes feel about the southland's freedom from highwaymen early in 1856 that he confidently assured a stranger to expect perfect safety "on the road." In October, though, the situation worsened, and for the next several years all such assurances were to have a hollow ring.

The trouble began when the twenty-one-year-old Mexican Juan Flores broke out of San Quentin, where he was serving a term for horse stealing in Los Angeles. Unreconstructed by his stay in jail, he resolved to return to the scene of his original exploits and commit even greater ones. These new crimes inaugurated southern California's most extensive vigilante action and brought "race" relations to a new low.

A young man of strong personal magnetism, Flores and his lieutenant, Pancho Daniel, assembled the largest bandit aggregation ever seen in California; more than fifty Spanish Americans from the territory between San Luis Obispo and San Juan Capistrano joined the ring. Some came along for specific personal motives, such as Andrés Fontes who craved revenge against Sheriff Barton of Los Angeles, who supposedly had jailed Fontes for defending an Indian woman against the sheriff's own lust; Fontes would remain with the gang only until he concluded his personal vendetta. Others, including many decent and orderly men, enlisted for more generalized causes. The War of the Reform had just broken out in Mexico, which gave a glimmer of legitimacy to guerrilla action and convinced some men to join Flores for vaguely political motives.[1]

Needing supplies and protection, Flores decided to operate out of San Juan Capistrano, where innocence still clung like a lace *rebozo*. Gringo rancher Juan Forster flatly turned down Flores' entreaties for aid. When the German settler Charles Fluggart did so too, the bandits killed and robbed him and, as a neighbor said, sat down to eat the dead man's dinner while the blood drained from his body. Firing pistols, shrieking antigringo curses, and galloping about wildly, they broke into three shops, whose proprietors Miguel Krasewski, Manuel García, and Henry Charles fled for their lives. Before escaping, Krasewski witnessed enigmatic handshakes and overheard grim references to 500 confederate Mexicans lurking in the hills for the start of a massive invasion of the southland.

When words of the dark doings at Capistrano reached Los Angeles, the attack assumed the proportions of a full-fledged political rebellion. Accompanied by six assistants, Sheriff Barton set out to investigate. While he paused at José Sepúlveda's rancho, the don warned him against chancing the bleak hills to the south with so few men, but the sheriff pushed on anyway. The price he paid was heavy: with the vengeful Fontes in the lead, the bandidos jumped out of ambush and kept up a 12-mile galloping pistol duel in which Barton and two deputies, as well as three of the robbers, were killed.

When the survivors straggled home, the Angeleños assumed that the outlaws were on their way "to murder the white people." They set up a committee of safety, a committee of vigilance, and a foot patrol; requested backing from soldiers at Fort Tejon and provisions from the San Diego cavalry post; organized parties of mounted rangers; and

---

[1] The Flores episode is described in Horace Bell, *On the Old West Coast: Being Further Reminiscences of a Ranger* (New York, 1930), pp. 401–410; Harris Newmark, *Sixty Years in Southern California, 1853–1913* . . . (New York, 1916), pp. 205 ff.; Los Angeles *Star*, Feb. 21, March 27, May 9, Dec. 12, 19, 1857; Feb. 20, 1858; *El Clamor Público* (Los Angeles), Jan. 31, Feb. 7, 21, March 7, 14, 1857; Antonio F. Coronel, "Cosas de California ... ," 1877, MS, Bancroft Library (Berkeley, Calif.), p. 208.

tucked away the women and children in Armory Hall, bolting the windows. A wagon detail retrieved the corpses in coffins for burial on Sunday.[2]

At the funeral most of the Spanish-speaking remained discreetly in the background, although the behavior of their countrymen pricked their conscience. By indiscriminately robbing and killing Americans, Californians, a Frenchman, and a Jew, declared *El Clamor Público*, the Flores gang showed that it was "without principles, without religion and without piety." Now is the time to recognize that "our society is linked with indissoluble bonds to that of the Americans." Let us "lay aside all animosity" toward them, forget their past injustices, and demonstrate that we are "loyal citizens and good patriots." We must refrain from hiding the badmen and instead help the authorities punish them as a lesson to others.[3] In a burst of good faith, a band of Californios, supplied with sixty horses by Tomás Sanchez and Andrés Pico and led by General Pico himself, rode away from the funeral to flush the Mexicans and Californians from their lair. The "El Monte boys" followed Pico's rangers on Tuesday morning, as did a party of French and German settlers, another of gringos from Los Angeles, and still another from San Bernardino. Charged with coordinating the assault, the General enlisted the aid of Indian scouts, who quickly located the enemy camp below San Juan.

No less than 119 rangers and Indians converged on the outlaws. When this force sprang into action, part of their quarry escaped but the remainder stumbled over low-lying hills directly into the clutches of other waiting rangers. On a flanking movement to cut off escapees, the El Monte rangers captured Flores and his lieutenant, Pancho Daniel, but the pair wormed free that night. To avoid further escapes, the El Monte men encamped at Los Nietos, simply hanged their next nine captives—José Santos, Diego Navarro, Pedro Lopez, Juan Valenzuela, Jesús Espinosa, Encarnación Berreyesa, and three others whose names they failed to note. Pico, too, feared "to risk the safety of his prisoners" and hanged Juan Silvas ("El Catabo") and an infamous Sonoran, Guerro Ardillero, whom he had seized the day before. To search for the rest of their prey, Pico, Tomás Sanchez, and Juan Sepúl-

[2] H. Newmark, *op. cit.*, p. 205.
[3] Jan. 31, 1857.

veda split up and for the next eleven days ransacked the entire countryside northward along Los Angeles River. To their dismay they
encountered Californios who, "either from sympathy or fear, aided the
murdering robbers and so made their pursuit doubly difficult." [4] Meanwhile, the gang split up and dodged northward instead of toward the
border. A house-by-house, canyon-by-canyon search at Simi, Cahuenga
Pass, and in the San Gabriel Valley finally led to the gang's capture—
that is, all but Daniel.

As the exhausted vigilantes handed the prisoners to the committee of
safety, incendiary news came from San Gabriel. Witnesses reported
that the El Monte rangers, behaving like "voracious lions rushing in
upon unfortunate victims with a frenzied appetite," had unjustly
hanged three *hijos del país*—Juan Valenzuela, Pedro Lopez, and Diego
Navarro, good family men only incidentally allied with the bandidos.
Navarro's father reported that the "drunken and blood-thirsty mob"
threw tar on his roof, threatened to burn his house, and finally rammed
the door to haul away his son. They hanged the innocent boy next to
three dangling corpses, and, when his torn noose dropped him to the
ground alive, they shot him. His wife arrived at that very moment, and
Navarro died in her arms.

At certain times, *El Clamor* wrote, when public authorities fail, the
people "in all their majesty" are justified in enforcing the law, but
never against innocent victims. "In all countries which go by the name
'civilized' there is one distinction between virtue and vice, namely that
one man must not pay for the fault of others." One week later reliable
information absolved the lynched men from a major role in this or any
other crime.[5]

The weather grew unseasonably and unbearably hot. All regular
business ceased, fifty-two suspects crammed the jail, and four armed
companies lounged in the streets chatting about their recent labors,
especially the dispatching of eleven "Spaniards." Meanwhile, eyes
gravitated toward the vigilantes, presided over by Judge Scott, the in-
veterate prosecutor of bandidos, as they worked on the shaded veranda
of the Montgomery Hotel and stayed in public view to avoid all taint
of secrecy. Citizens drifted into town from the suburbs for the public

[4] H. Newmark, *op. cit.*, p. 209.
[5] *El Clamor Público*, Jan. 31, Feb. 7, 1857.

meeting that would act on the committee's findings. Behind bars Flores was the model prisoner, calm in the face of certain death and courteous toward curiosity seekers. He parried their questions nicely: When asked what a thief's life was like, he replied good-naturedly, "Become one and see!" [6] Judge Scott finally presented the vigilantes' decision, which was to hand over most of the accused to the regular courts for routine handling, "their crimes being only attempts at murder, burglaries, and horse stealing," but to hang Flores at once. An overwhelming "Aye" vote backed these decisions. Some townsmen wanted to dispatch three more Mexicans, two for horse theft and one for attempted murder, but the French community in particular urged caution so that the assemblage turned the idea down by a vote of 257 to 395.

The newly appointed sheriff feigned taking custody of Flores, although when the jailer blocked his way, he left good-naturedly. On February 14 the committee marched on the jail, easily overcame the guard, and proceeded with Flores to Fort Hill and a new gallows. Four military companies led by Twist, Faraget, Pico, and Stanley escorted him through a quiet throng of 3,000 observers. Flanked by two priests, Flores strode up the hill with firm steps, still looking "as composed as any one in the crowd. . . . He was a young man . . . of pleasing countenance. There was nothing in his appearance to indicate the formidable criminal he had proved himself to be." [7] Through an interpreter, Flores told the crowd that he had committed many crimes, bore no ill will toward anyone, and was ready to die; to a few countrymen he whispered instructions about his body. The noose, made from the riata of one of Barton's martyred deputies, hung too short to kill Flores at once and caused a protracted death. This technical "oversight" expressed a "pettiness of heart," El Clamor thought, even though the hanging itself was justified as an example to evildoers.

Entirely without pomp or circumstance, vigilantes that same day hanged the Mexican "Blanco" for attempting to stab Sheriff Twist. Next day they found bandido José Jesús Espinosa lurking in a nearby canyon, brought him to town, and strung him up at once; on a third

[6] Ibid., Feb. 21, 1857.
[7] Los Angeles Star, Feb. 21, 1857. According to El Clamor Público (Los Angeles), Feb. 21, 1857, the Americans were led by J. S. Griffin, the Germans by J. Waskel, the French by C. Plasant, and the El Monte contingent by Mr. Thompson.

day they did the same to Lenardo Lopez, a laborer from San Luis Obispo. Lopez protested his innocence to the very end. The attending priest tried to contradict him, but since everyone had known Lopez as a law-abiding citizen before his fling with Flores, many felt that he was being made a sacrificial lamb; at worst, he had stolen a horse. One badman, "El Chino" Varela, went scot-free because he was *very respectably connected*—a brother-in-law of Ygnacio del Valle and a cousin of Judge Sepúlveda.[8] Considering the committee's leniency toward Varela and others, the white-heat lynchings by the El Monte Texans looked worse than ever.

From up north came burning resentment about the hanging of the hapless Encarnación Berreyesa. His first brush with vigilantes had occurred on the ancestral Rancho San Vicente, near Santa Clara, in July, 1854, when gringos accused him of killing an American. A Santa Clara vigilance committee broke into his adobe, dragged him out, and, in the presence of his wife and children, jolted his noose torturously to wring out clues of the killing. Discovering his ignorance, they let him go, but then went and kidnapped his brother Nemesio. On July 22 Nemesio's body was found suspended off the ground. Contrary to public opinion, the San Jose coroner's inquest adjudged both Berreyesas innocent of the crime. This judgment did not stop the vigilantes, however, who forced the five Berreyesa boys and their families to seek safety elsewhere, one in Mexico and the others in the southern counties.

In Santa Barbara, Encarnación was afflicted with his family's congenital mental illness. Brother Nemesio's death, his own ordeal, and his family's assorted miseries deranged him from time to time, yet he was essentially pathetic rather than dangerous. His executioners, evidently residents of San Buenaventura or Santa Barbara who were fired up by the current excitement, never charged Encarnación with helping Flores, but solely with killing the Santa Clara man. As a kinsman noted, they could neither cite the murdered man's name, the place of the crime, nor the names of witnesses. A Yankee witness subsequently corroborated that lynchers had killed Encarnación under cover of darkness, without offering proof of guilt or time for defense, much less mercy. His executioners tried publishing an anonymous letter incrimi-

[8] Coronel, *op. cit.*, pp. 204, 209.

nating him in the death of a Frenchman, but *El Clamor Público* refused to print it and challenged the Venturans to speak up manfully and publicly. Encarnación's neighbors collected $100 for his widow and children. The Berreyesas could reel off the names of eight kinsmen (fathers, sons, nephews, cousins) whom the Yankee had "hurled repentently to appear before the tribunal of their Creator": José R., Nemesio, Juan, and Encarnación Berreyesa; Francisco and Ramón de Haro; José Suñol; and José Galindo.[9]

The last of the badmen, Pancho Daniel, managed to evade capture until March, 1858, when he stumbled into the hands of the law.[10] His presence created a sensation. Judge Hayes exercised unusual caution by convening a pretrial hearing to see if Daniel could receive a fair trial in a town rife with threats and rumors of lynching. His Honor asked witnesses whether they thought the accused could go free without losing his life. Skeptical after hearing inconclusive replies, Hayes nevertheless inaugurated the trial. His doubts about the possibilities of justice were borne out by an anonymous committee, "probably acting on behalf of a larger body of citizens," which broke into the jail before dawn on November 30, shrouded Daniel's eyes with a black kerchief, and strung him from a roof beam. In the Mexican quarter feeling ran high against the vigilantes although, according to the Los Angeles *Star*, nothing indicated that "the respectable portion of the Californians was dissatisfied with the result."[11]

Concerning the split between Californios and Americanos in Los Angeles during the Flores-Daniel rebellion, Antonio Coronel spoke reassuringly. If the affair initially opened a breach in the village, he explained, the exemplary behavior of Don Tomás Sanchez and General Andrés Pico in scourging the badmen healed it and produced a "complete reconciliation."[12] Coronel here touches a partial truth: Sanchez and Pico, who gladly rode with Texans to track down "their own kind," thereby won the gringos' everlasting gratitude. Among the few Californios ever to reach positions of armed power in gringo government,

[9] *El Clamor Público* (Los Angeles), March 28 (citing the San Francisco *Herald*), and May 9, 1857.
[10] Los Angeles *Star*, March 27, 1858.
[11] Benjamin D. Hayes, "Criminal Trials at Los Angeles: Blotter Notes of Honorable Ben Hayes," Documents, Bancroft Library, pp. 88–92; *Star*, Dec. 4, 1858.
[12] Coronel, *op. cit.*, pp. 204, 209.

Sanchez soon became sheriff, while Pico assured himself a brigadiership in the California militia and election as state assemblyman. Despite Don Antonio's optimism, however—the optimism of a Mexican with a stake in society—a great many Spanish-speaking expressed indifference, and even sympathy, toward Flores but telling coolness toward Pico and Sanchez. "It is very sad," a correspondent of *El Clamor* observed some months earlier, "to see the asperity and antipathy that reigns among Mexicans in California—they have no union—they have no fraternity—everywhere is hatred and this is principally observed among the majority of *hijos del país* who behave with more animosity towards the Mexicans who were not born in California than towards the Indians. . . . This will pass," he concluded philosophically, "because in California everything passes." [13] It had, however, not passed at the time of the Flores incident. In the larger sense, Mexicans were nearly as alienated from Californians as Californians were from Yankees.

In 1857 a similar vigilante-bandit confrontation rocked Santa Barbara. There, however, the Spanish-speaking resisted the Yankee "justice-seekers" more successfully. Whereas the forces of order had prevailed on Fort Hill with the cooperation of the ricos, Santa Barbara's vigilantes and public officials had to reckon without substantial aid from ricos and with considerable opposition from the lower class.

Santa Barbara's calm, as beguiling as its pastel sky, was occasionally shattered by social turbulence as strong as the ocean that raged offshore. Although Jack Powers fled the village in 1853 and allowed it to sink back into lassitude, not all criminals disappeared with him. The number of felonies ran high, considering the small size of the population, and grew alarmingly in 1857. The greenhorn editor of the Santa Barbara *Gazette* thought he saw a pattern of crime waves. "We must look upon the idlers of a community for those who constitute the criminals," he said, as he proposed a stiff vagrancy law. [14]

Gradually, the peaceful countryside near the mouth of the Nacimiento River became known as a "dark and bloody ground," which travelers had best avoid. Two Basque cattle buyers were murdered there in November, 1857, purportedly by Jack Powers and his new

[13] "El Curioso," in *El Clamor Público*, Aug. 22, 1857
[14] June 14, 1855.

company of badmen, including Pío Linares, Nieves Robles, Huero Rafael (alias Rafial Money, alias Rafael Herrada), and a Californian named Froilen.[15] Froilen and Robles seemed to have wormed their way into the Basques' confidence, selling them stolen cattle and then hiring out as vaqueros, ostensibly to drive the cattle northward. At a prearranged time, Powers appeared with Linares and Rafael and shot and robbed the Basques of $3,500. The plan went off so smoothly that twenty days passed before the bodies came to light.

The authorities got hold of Robles and indicted him, but they simply could not convince a jury of Latin Americans of his guilt. As the Yankee Santa Barbaran, Walter Murray, explained:

Robles was a Californian. The Americans did not move. It was nobody but a Frenchman who had been killed. The French talked lynch; the Californians threatened that in case they did it, every Frenchman in the country should be killed. The best lawyer of the country . . . was appointed District Attorney. The proof was light. The jury, a packed California one. One of the jurors was, at the time, a fugitive from the charge of murder. Another was an accomplice in the very crime for which Robles was tried. One frustrating aspect of life in Santa Barbara was that the American citizens of this county are but a corporal's guard. The Californians and their Mexican defendants are the great bulk of the community. We are helpless. At an election, or at the empaneling of a jury, it is very easy for an unwashed greaser to swear that he came to this country before the treaty with Mexico. That oath makes him a good citizen, and he takes his seat in the jury box.[16]

Outside the courtroom, the Californios lightheartedly conceded Robles' guilt (and in later years he himself confessed), but some added that the Frenchmen who had knowingly bought stolen goods deserved their fate. As the Spanish saying went, "The thief who kills a thief deserves 100 years' relief." While Robles passed through the throng a free man, the Yankees could do little but keep up "a devil of a thinking. . . . it was getting hot, and . . . it would soon be time to stir."

Seven months later the Yankees faced a similar situation and did stir. Two more Frenchmen, Bartolo Baratie and M. J. Borel, who had recently migrated from Oakland with their wives, died violently. Nine

[15] A full account by the head vigilante, Walter Murray, was serialized in the San Francisco *Bulletin* in 1858, and quoted verbatim in [Myron Angel], *History of San Luis Obispo County* (Oakland, 1883), pp. 293–304.
[16] *Ibid.*, pp. 293–295.

Spanish Americans working as a gang and including some previous suspects—Pío Linares, Froilen, Servin, Desiderjo Grijalva, Huero Rafael, Miguel Blanco, Chico Martinez, Santos Peralta, Luciano Tapia (a Mesteño Indian), and Jesús Calenzuela—were implicated. They had ingratiated themselves into the Baratie household, stayed the night as guests, and in the morning robbed the proprietors of $2,700. Finally the gang killed Boratie and Borel and shared the money, but bungled the job by leaving clues everywhere. They spared Mme Baratie's life though she had seen everything, and designated the Indian Tapia to escort her to San Juan Bautista and put her on the Oakland stage.

The authorities first seized Chico Martinez and locked him up in jail, where he was a sitting duck for an anonymous party of callers. "Satisfied of the determination of the greaser population to set justice at defiance," they hanged him and later proved him guilty. The sheriff and fifteen men set out after Linares, allegedly the "arch conspirator . . . whose father before him was a robber and a murderer, and whose whole family is tainted with crime." But Linares had too sound an alibi and had to be let go. Although the sheriff and his men failed momentarily to catch any other culprits, they had the good fortune to run into Joaquín Valenzuela (alias Joaquín Ocomorenia, one of the five famous Joaquins), completely innocent of the crime at hand but with a price on his head for others. They carted their special prize back to San Luis and prepared him for death. Valenzuela asked for mercy for his friends and, displaying the proper aplomb for a "Joaquin," warned all Spanish Americans to keep their secrets more carefully; then he was hanged.

The vigilantes meanwhile discovered that the gang had slain yet another man, a Yankee hunter who either had seen too much or simply stood accused of "having light skin." Mme Baratie's Indian escort, having delivered her to safety, was riding home when he fell afoul of another posse, which hauled him back to San Luis Obispo. Looking for mercy he blurted out as much as he knew, which was a great deal, but nevertheless he "was hung in broad daylight . . . as a warning to all miscreants." As the lady's escape seemed odd, tongues began to wag that she was an accomplice, until she surprised the town by alighting from the steamer a few days later and displaying sufficient grief to clear her name.

Emboldened by success, the Santa Barbara Yankees decided on June

6 to liquidate the murderers of Graciano and Obiesa, if they could find them, and also all other available miscreants. The most serious effect of vigilantism thus displayed itself: the snowballing of vengeance. For the broad-gauged purge they wanted from the Californios the sort of help that had smashed Flores in Los Angeles. A delegation went to state Senator Romualdo Pacheco and Judge José María Muñoz, asking them to raise a posse. Muñoz had helped the vigilantes by grilling the prisoners and taking their testimony, but he and Pacheco backed away from deeper involvement. "Gentlemen," they replied, "ourselves, our arms and our animals are at your disposal. [But] . . . the Californians will not be influenced by us . . . to go in search of these men. Some of them [bandidos] are our countrymen" and relatives. Only a handful of nativos enlisted. Head vigilante Walter Murray charged that the Californians secretly opposed the purge and "breathed curses not loud but deep" against it: "They would tomorrow clear the whole gang in a court of law." [17]

Next, the vigilantes went after José Antonio García, the only available accomplice in the murder of Obiesa and Graciano. Taken into custody, García wrote his mother in Mexico and dictated a confession detailing the crime and the extent of Jack Powers' leadership, but asserted that he regretted having participated in the killing. "To all appearances truly penitent, and exhorting his friends to take warning by his fate, and to avoid evil companions," García was executed. Enlarged to 150 strong, the vigilantes set out that very night to hunt down several gang members hiding in a nearby wood. The brigade spread out and systematically tramped through the brush until they gunned down Linares and Blanco and captured Grijalva and others. The next day the town interred the dead bandidos and a martyred vigilante, and on the following day hanged yet another pair of badmen, both of whom confessed guilt, exhorting their countrymen to "keep away from bad company," and acknowledged the fairness of their captors.

These events finally inspired some Californios to participate in the final mop-up campaign. Romualdo Pacheco managed to raise a posse of eighteen Californians and New Mexicans. By heading for Los Angeles on the trail of the escaping Huero Rafael, they gave the other vigilantes a chance to track down Powers, Nieves Robles, and Eduviguez. With the "natives" thus aroused, Murray foresaw less respite for bad-men. Many "half-honest Spaniards" heretofore had consented to crimes "because they saw no hope for a redressal of them, and had not the energy to stand aloof from them." Now things would be different: After the committee completed its task and disbanded, there would be "less money spent . . . in the billiard-rooms and drinking houses, and on gambling tables," where so many crimes had been hatched.

Both remnants of the Powers gang fled steadily southward, staying well out in front of the ranger columns. They picked up additional cohorts from among the local Spanish-speaking youths and headed through San Bernardino and out toward Mexico, where they finally disappeared. One northern newspaper urged the vigilantes to seize the gang below the border, for Mexico certainly would not do so.[18]

This ended the fighting and inaugurated the postmortem. From all sides came both criticism of and support for the Santa Barbara Yankees, with the press drawing parallels to the work of the recent San Francisco vigilance committee. *El Clamor Público*'s attack on the vigi-lantes received amens from two San Francisco newspapers (the *Bulle-tin* and the *Herald*). Editor Ramirez charged Americans with using in-sufficient evidence, particularly against Robles who gave an altogether reasonable account of himself. Their execution of Joaquín Valenzuela, moreover, went far beyond their original mandate and was contempti-ble; they had brutally mishandled Pío Linares' family by throwing a faggot on the roof to smoke out Rafael who, as the inhabitants kept saying, was not there; and they had grilled Linares unfairly for a man who had not even been at the scene of the crime. Courts should have administered justice, Ramirez maintained, instead of a crowd sodden with whiskey.

This last reproach cut the vigilantes to the quick. As group spokes-man, Murray answered Ramirez point by point and took his final lunge at the editor himself. Every vigilante, he declared, was "a better citizen than the *El Clamor* editor ever can be until he plucks out that Mexican heart of his and substitutes an American one in its place." Murray, al-

[18] *Ibid.*, p. 299.

though capable of goodwill toward the Spanish-speaking (as he had shown in 1850 in reporting the Sonoran tax difficulties), had turned completely bitter.[19]

Two years later similar bad blood existed in Santa Barbara, as both Californios and gringos again took the law into their own hands. In fact, the Californios never felt more vengeful than on August 24, 1859, when they learned that the lifeless forms of Francisco Badillo, aged sixty, and of his son, aged twenty-six, were hanging from an oak in Carpinteria, 13 miles down the coast.[20] Some forty or fifty of them mounted up and raced to the scene and, upon hearing the old man's two teen-aged boys describe the gruesome hanging, went after the culprits, members of the Nedever family. As a matter of record, the Californios had never wasted much love on Badillo, an unreconstructed Mexican convict who had sold cattle to both armies in 1847, had once faked a theft upon himself, and recently had been suspected of cattle theft. Of Badillo and his son, Juan Alvarado said, "blood will tell!" [21] Nonetheless, the Barbareños would not lightly tolerate a lynching by Yankees.

They caught up with suspect George Nedever, tore him from his horse, stabbed him, pumped bullets into him, and had all but killed him when the sheriff arrived and took him to safety. The officer arrested John Nedever, close kin of the suspect, put him under a mixed guard of Californians and Yankees, and had the grand jury arraign him as a murder suspect. Judge Joaquín Carrillo set bail at $20,000. Young George, however, who miraculously hung onto life, successfully established his innocence. This led to the arrest of his assailants, Guillermo Carrillo (one of the judge's relatives), Francisco Leyba, Eugenio Lugo, José María Gutiérrez, and Manuel Zurita. The grand jury, composed of Californios, Mexicans, Yankees, and a few Frenchmen for good measure, weighed the evidence carefully for five days and then freed all the prisoners without indictment. The legal score satisfied both sides, until a new vigilance committee of Irishmen and Americans decreed George Nedever's attackers "dangerous to the well-being of

[19] Ibid., p. 301; El Clamor Público (Los Angeles), Aug. 22, 1857.
[20] El Clamor Público (Los Angeles), Sept. 17, 24, Oct. 22, 1859.
[21] "Historia de California," 1876, MS, Bancroft Library, V, 252–253.

society" and gave them a stipulated time to get out of town. Lugo, Dominguez, Gutiérrez, and Felipe Badillo fled as ordered. Fortunately, these were the final scalps delivered to Judge Lynch in Santa Barbara.

XI

El Clamor Público:
Sentiments of Treason

DESPERATION echoed in the editorial column of *El Clamor Público* in the crisis of August, 1856. *"Oh! fatalidad!"* it exclaimed. "Mexicans alone have been the victims of the people's insane fury! Mexicans alone have been sacrificed on the gibbet and launched into eternity . . . ! This," it added with ironic emphasis, "is the *liberty* and *equality* of our adopted land!" Scan the history of the state since the gold discovery, and one must conclude that *"California is lost to all Spanish-Americans."* [1]

The author of these sentiments was not Juan Bandini or Pablo de la Guerra or any other oldster, but a twenty-year-old Californio, Francisco P. Ramirez, who for the four years from 1855 to 1859 was the new self-styled champion of the Spanish Americans in California.[2] A good deal of his fervor, bombast, and eloquence stemmed from his youth and his awareness of the difficulties of the younger generation. A baby when his elders were fighting rebellions, a boy during the gold rush, a youth who had neither land or cattle, nor stature in the better classes, Ramirez nevertheless somehow managed to articulate the views of most Californios in the 1850's.

---

[1] Aug. 2, 1856. Citations in this chapter are from *El Clamor Público* (Los Angeles) unless otherwise noted.

[2] The few known details about Ramirez are mentioned in Harris Newmark, *Sixty Years in Southern Califorinia, 1853–1913* . . . (New York, 1916), p. 156; and Muir Dawson, "Southern California Newspapers, 1851–1876: A Short History and Census," Historical Society of Southern California *Quarterly*, XXXII (March, June, 1950), 23. The only extant file of *El Clamor Público* is at the Huntington Library (San Marino, Calif.).

Francisco's journalistic career began as a printer's devil or compositor for *La Estrella*, the Spanish page of the Los Angeles *Star*. This job irritated him, however, because he had to handle copy tinged with a seemingly repellent gringo chauvinism. Yearning to counteract the *Star*'s editorials, he quit his job and in June, 1855, began turning out a one-sheet Spanish-language weekly, devoted to the advancement of Spanish-speaking Californians. *El Clamor Público*—"The Public Outcry"—the town's third newspaper and the first in Spanish, went to press each Thursday and sold at $5 a year.

Ramirez' newspaper venture proved something of a milestone in the evolution of the Latin-American community, if not in the history of Los Angeles journalism, for the Spanish-speaking desperately needed a publication to carry a torch for them. If they wished, they could read the Spanish page of the Los Angeles *Star* or of the *Southern Californian* (Los Angeles), or, from San Francisco, *El Eco del Pacífico* and *La Crónica*. These last two, however, appealed to northerners; moreover, *El Eco* consisted of but one page in a French weekly, and *La Crónica* ceased publication in 1856. The editor of *El Clamor* meant to appeal not only to Latin Americans but also to Frenchmen, who in Los Angeles alone numbered about four hundred. He was fluent in French and English, as well as in Spanish. Since his sheet was a curiosity to news-hungry Yankees who could read a hobbling Spanish or who wanted to advertise for the "serape trade," Ramirez acquired that much more support in the cow counties. In his first year of publication, in fact, he complained of having more Yankee than Californio readers.[3]

However much he crusaded against certain gringos, Francisco nevertheless shared many of their fundamental ideals. Like Alvarado, Castro, Vallejo, and other Californians before him, the liberal ideas that molded his thinking were common coinage in every Western nation in his time, including the United States. By dedicating his paper to "political independence," "moral and material progress," and a "regime of law and order," he chose the very catchwords that any Yankee editor might fly beneath the masthead. He paid homage to the "magnanimous spirit and grandiose ideals" of the Yankee Constitution and the Decla-

[3] June 19, July 10, 1855.

ration of Independence, and to the nation's dedication to popular government, economic progress, civil rights, and the "arts of peace."[4] Ramirez, in short, in his own curious way expressed the liberal-democratic ethos of Jefferson and Jackson.

Like every editor he boosted the fortunes of his own state and region. California's future looked bright to him even in the depths of the 1855 depression, although he wished that the settlers would turn their energies to agriculture and Congress would turn its to sanctioning the transcontinental railway, so as to assure that rosy future. With the natural beauties of Switzerland and the soil fertility of the Nile Valley, California could not help but prosper.[5] For the betterment of the southern region he championed division of the state, compulsory reduction of monetary interest, and reorganization of Los Angeles taxes —three reforms that had the support of a majority of Angeleños.

Moved by a deep commitment to liberalism, Ramirez reported on and evaluated, however briefly, all the reform movements and social enthusiasms current in the United States during the middle period. Over the years he editorialized on bloomers and prostitution; Know-Nothingism and anti-Catholicism; prison reform and death penalties; medical quackery and Mormonism; Manifest Destiny and filibusterism; and on laws concerning temperance, vagrancy, and Sabbatarianism. Most unusual for Los Angeles, he concerned himself with Negro rights, opposing not only the extension of slavery into new soil but slavery itself. He even denounced a legislative attempt to proscribe the rights of the free Negro in California. By printing travel accounts hostile to the Southern states, he took a position on the sectional conflict which, in Los Angeles, was downright radical.[6]

Ramirez had to contend not only with all the disadvantages of publishing a frontier newspaper, not to mention his own inexperience and overenthusiasm, but also with the hostility of the gringos and the illiteracy of his main potential audience. As journalism his paper left much to be desired. Editorials blended freely with news reports, until the reader could scarcely distinguish fact from analysis. On slack news days, bad fiction, doggerel, and dull aphorisms ate up much space.

[4] June 19, 1855.
[5] Loc. cit.
[6] See, for example, July 24, 1855; March 1, 1856.

Misspellings, fractured grammar, broken type, and typographical errors plagued many editions. Advertisements crowded out news; choppy bits of second- and third-hand reports frustrated the reader's quest for bare facts; and key stories often lacked a follow-up.

Most of these faults typified the condition of every struggling newspaper in the West. What set *El Clamor Público* apart from the others, however, was its championing of the cause of the Spanish-speaking and its editorial overtones of Latin-American radicalism. One suspects that, before becoming a newspaper man, young Francisco had gone to school in Mexico and traveled in Mexican revolutionary circles.

El Clamor nicely captured the distressed mood of the Latin Americans of southern California; it gave them remarkably good news coverage and a public forum for their ideals. If Manuel Reytes felt outraged by the Yankee's selfish use of the word "American," he could write a dissertation urging that the "sacrosanct" term should embrace all peoples of the Western Hemisphere—Latin Americans as well as Anglo-Americans. If the anonymous writer signing himself "Consistencia" wished to dilate on the gringo legal profession and publicly swear off ever voting for a lawyer again, or if "Uno Mexicano" wished simply to unburden himself generally about the assorted miseries of his people in California, the columns of *El Clamor* were open and waiting.[7] When Enrique Avila wanted Andrés Pico to stop meddling in politics, when Nesario Dominguez wanted to defend himself from the charge of cowardice, when Señor Oso wanted to warn cattle thieves that he would kill them if they ever returned to annoy him, when Mellus & Company wished to announce the arrival of a new shipment of goods—*El Clamor* was the perfect vehicle for a public notice.[8]

Ramirez sought to educate both Yankees and Spanish Americans about the progress of Latin-American liberalism. He carried a good deal of news about Mexico, where, in 1855, revolution again hit full stride with the emergence of President Ignacio Comonfort, cut from a more heroic mold than the deposed Santa Anna. Ramirez plainly thought that the events surrounding Comonfort's administration would give the Mexicans living in the California "Diaspora" renewed inspiration to cope with their own lives. To this end, *El Clamor* gave the

[7] April 25, 1857; June 19, 1855.
[8] June 13, 1857.

fullest possible coverage to celebrations of Mexican Independence Day in California; typically, in 1855 he printed word for word a lengthy patriotic oration delivered in Los Angeles on September 27 by the same Señor Ruiz whom Constable Jenkins later killed.

A practicing Catholic, Ramirez was nevertheless also a rationalist and a secularist and little disposed to mysticism. The new Mexican constitution of 1856, with its moderate solution to the religious question, particularly pleased Francisco and he printed it verbatim. He believed in religious toleration in the United States, and in a peaceful accommodation between Church and state in Latin America, instead of a war to the death between them.[9] He found the Mexican priests of Los Angeles too fanatical for his personal taste, yet he defended the Church against its would-be enemies. He criticized doctrinaire anticlericalists and gave straight, full, and favorable coverage to all local charity drives, parochial-school functions, and religious celebrations. Thus, his paper closely mirrored the mild Catholicism of the younger Californios, but even the more pious older ones would have found in its pages little to complain of. Indeed, neither would most Protestants and Jews.

Crusading editor Ramirez licensed himself to serve his people in many ways. As their chronicler he revived little-known historical facts, such as how Sonorans had discovered gold in Mexican California long before the advent of Señor James Marshall. As their public defender he chronicled all their expulsions from the mines, lynchings, and courtroom difficulties. As moral critic, he presumed to tell his fellow youths how to comport themselves. And as instructor in civics, he did what he could to initiate novice citizens into the workings and traditions of their new government. He published thumbnail sketches of the American presidents (Jefferson was a favorite), the full Declaration of Independence, texts of state laws pertinent to the Spanish-speaking, and reports of current affairs in the nation at large.

Above all, Ramirez played to the hilt the role of political mentor to the Spanish-speaking. In those days, all California newspapers depended heavily on political subsidies (or state funds, for the publication of laws), and his weekly clearly had Republican money from the

[9] May 10, Aug. 16, Sept. 6, 1856.

outset; without the Republican Party it probably would not have come into existence. Besides, he obviously believed sincerely that Californios must participate more actively and intelligently in politics. He needled them both for their apathy and for the way they voted, when they bothered to do so. They should vote regularly and "independently," he held; the habit of voting the straight Democratic ticket brought results as bad as the "six plagues of Egypt." [10] (Yet no man voted a straighter Republican ticket than he.) While all politicians seemed more or less dishonorable to him, those of Los Angeles seemed to stand a head higher than the rest, and therefore deserved support.

Naturally, the brash young editor would win no popularity contests among the Yankees of Los Angeles. To "chivalry" Democrats, to the defenders of slavery, to the glandular haters of the "greasers," and to ordinary Yankees unaccustomed to hearing back talk from Mexicans, Ramirez seemed something of a Jacobin. His filiopietism, free-soilism, and civil libertarianism frequently annoyed the *Star*, which accused him of exaggerating the bad treatment Latin Americans got from Yankees, of encouraging racial warfare, and of giving Californians dangerous ideas. Ramirez, on the other hand, kept an ear cocked for the faintest dissonance from the *Star* and, on the slightest provocation, crossed editorial swords. On one occasion, for example, he lambasted the *Star*'s report that "last Saturday night the *tendencies of our Mexican population toward armed riot, scuffling and robbery, seemed to develop completely*." To make wholesale insults against all Mexicans because some had transgressed typified, in Ramirez' view, the "evaporations of the depraved imagination" of the *Star;* thankfully, the better classes of *norte Americanos* were more fair-minded.[11]

El Clamor's trumpet blasts for improved civil rights grated on the ears of at least one gringo who considered himself an ally of the Californios, namely, Joseph Lancaster Brent. In 1857 Los Angeles Assemblyman Brent accused *El Clamor* of "disseminating sentiments of treason and antipathy among the native population." *El Clamor* lit into him (and into the *Star* for using "sycophantic invectives" to back Brent); Ramirez asked rhetorically how *El Clamor* could be accused of treason for simply raising an outcry for a despairing people and seek-

[10] Aug. 6, 1859.
[11] Dec. 26, 1857.

ing restitution for outrage. Was it treason to describe the tremors of "a thousand hearts . . . a thousand eyes filled with tears . . . a thousand hands" of the Californios who see their fathers and brothers tortured in the presence of innocent children? If this be treason, he cried, saints preserve us! [12]

The rationalist-minded Ramirez naturally put great stock in education, especially public education, a benefit in which his people were woefully deficient. Thus he praised the Californios who sent their children to school and roundly scored the many who kept them at home. Only at school do "American children begin to know their independence and liberty" he emphasized. Even girls should be educated, he believed, so that as women they would not be infantile or ignorant, and would not be looked upon merely as the playthings of their capricious husbands. A mother, he thought, should be educated to exert proper moral influence on her children, especially her sons, to whom she imparts the first semblance of knowledge before sending them off to serve *la patria*.[13]

While expounding on education, Ramirez revealed himself as an advocate of assimilation and a believer in practical rather than classical knowledge. Writing in English, he told his compatriots that "we are Native California Americans born on the soil and we can exclaim with the Poet, this is 'OUR OWN, OUR NATIVE LAND.' " But like it or not, we are now under the American flag, he added, "and there is every probability that we shall remain so for all time to come. . . . [Therefore] let us divest ourselves of all bygone traditions, and become Americanized all over—in language, in manners, in customs and habits." This shift was necessary "upon grounds of principle and expediency." For want of knowledge about the prevailing customs, "we have seen our countrymen . . . fleeced out of their flocks and herds, ranches and money by cunning 'sharpers' who have taken advantage of their simplicity and their verdancy." Common law, statute law, and the "fixed institutions" of the nation go back to English tradition and are published exclusively in the English language; freedom of the press and the right to a jury trial are "founded upon the sage maxims of British Statesmen"—all this the Californians must learn. German and French

[12] May 2, 1857, quoting Brent's letter of April 15, 1857.
[13] Feb. 9, 1856.

immigrants soon acquire a knowledge of English: "Why not Mexicans, and those of Castilian descent?"

As a first remedial step, all adults might subscribe to *El Clamor* and study the new Spanish-English page. But more important, Ramirez urged, "let us husband our resources; be careful of our means, and spend what we have to spare in *educating our children,* and bring them up in a thorough training of the English tongue. . . . We must learn [*sic*] them useful trades and professions, stimulate them to excel in the sciences and other utilitarian occupations." [14]

Ramirez gradually revealed his preference for a revolutionary brand of liberalism. Stretching a point a bit, in 1859 he identified the Republican Party with the libertarian forces of France, Italy, Germany, and Ireland. To Frémont, the Republican standard-bearer, he gave the epitaph of the Irish insurrectionist, Robert Emmet—"genius of universal emancipation"—and then ticked off an impressive list of revolutionaries and militant reformers who probably would have voted the Republican ticket: Daniel O'Connel, Lafayette, Washington, Montgomery, Lord Byron, Bolivar, Hidalgo, and, to round out the list, Bartolomé Las Casas. "Courage friends! stand by the virtues of the noble Las Casas, and all will be well. Those who are not for us are against us." [15]

Although his radicalism must have made the conservative Californios cringe a little, Ramirez could count on at least a small liberal following. Ramón Carrillo, writing for the County Republican Committee, implored the readers of *El Clamor* to heed the example of the Italian Republican army, and from one of its slogans he paraphrased: "Californios! from the heights of heaven our ancestors look down with pride." Let us "guard in our hearts the sacred words of Liberty and Independence"; and, "Let us give to our sons the example of morality, virtue and patriotism which our fathers gave to us." [16]

In surveying the human condition, most nineteenth-century liberals would have agreed with Francisco Ramirez when he philosophized that "in this century, nations tend toward peace . . . and humanity." [17]

[14] June 18, 1859, in English.
[15] June 18, 25, 1859.
[16] Aug. 13, 1859.
[17] Dec. 5, 1857.

California's immediate moral predicament, however, demonstrated a palpable scarcity of peace and humanity; daily life presented so many instances of bloodshed and inhumanity as to confound the belief in the idea of moral progress. Although not visibly shaken in his belief about the world at large, Ramirez must have had his doubts about California. In particular, he was deeply concerned with the problem of law and order as it pertained to the Spanish-speaking.

In branding practically the entire Yankee system of law as hypocritical, unfair, and even brutal to the Spanish-speaking, Ramirez was expressing not a minority opinion as in his politics, but the general sentiment of the Latin Americans of California. If the Yankees averred that "Spaniards" were profoundly and irredeemably dissolute, the Spanish-speaking such as Ramirez and scores of correspondents who wrote to him countered that the Yankees failed to live up to common standards of decency, much less to their professed constitutional ideals. Latin Americans especially resented the accusation that, as a class of people, they inclined more readily toward crime than Yankees. They thought of themselves as an essentially law-abiding people—the few Joaquins notwithstanding. To the charge that Mexico was the most disorderly nation in the world, they retorted that no community on earth valued life less than Yankee California.[18] Moreover, they also believed that the Yankees, especially the Yankee newspaper editors, who judged them by the conduct of a few *borachos* (drunkards), were grossly unfair.[19] The *Star* reported that of 110 men convicted in Los Angeles courts in 1856, 57 were Mexicans and 11 were Californios;[20] whether this reflected stronger enforcement against the Spanish-speaking or a greater inclination to wrongdoing, the Yankees probably felt that it proved their point. This kind of evidence, however, never convinced *La Crónica* or *El Clamor* that Latin Americans committed crimes more often than Yankees. As proof they alluded to reports in every one of their editions of Yankee "killings, plunders and outrages of all kinds" against Spanish-speaking people.

Yet, in another connection and in a more reflective mood, Ramirez for one did not gainsay his own people's crimes but tried to account for them. It struck him one night as he watched three sixteen-year-old

[18] Oct. 29, 1859.
[19] April 5, 1856.
[20] Los Angeles *Star*, Aug. 9, 1856.

Californios lounging in a saloon, playing cards and drinking, that most of the criminals were young. Of the *maleditos* whom the Yankees had executed more or less justifiably before February, 1857, Flores, Espinosa, Catabo, Zavaleta, Rivas, Alvitre, and Herrera were youths or men scarcely over thirty years. And what impelled them to misdeeds? Gambling! Flores, for example, had lost all his stolen money at cards, and his followers too had "committed crime only for this fascinating passion of gambling."

California, Ramirez believed, was happier when it was poorer and younger. The Arguëllos and Estudillos had once provided "firm and prudent leadership" based on the knowledge that "wealth mothers pride, extravagance, laziness . . . and loss of decent habits." But the inspirational teachings of the older generation had grown feeble, and the surviving elders neglected to instruct the young and thereby lost faith among them. "We say frankly: our own youths are more inclined than others to imitate blindly the bad customs of others. They do not have that ability to resist the temptation which for the most part had preserved our fathers during many spiritual dangers."

Let the young men seek honest labor, Ramirez preached, let them "go work on the ranchos—sow maize, wheat, etc.—find some useful occupation, instead of idling time in these detestable taverns and gambling houses.—Work, work and thirst for independence. . . . riches are not the greatest happiness [that] one may aspire to." [21] This prescription, worthy of *Poor Richard's Almanac,* curiously resembled the sneering advice that many Yankees were giving Spanish Americans. But in answer to the Yankee's premise that "Spaniards" were innately weak, Ramirez postulated a strength of character antedating their defeat.

The Californios stood accused of obstructing justice by sheltering known criminals. This weakness Ramirez provisionally admitted and deplored, but he explained that many of the Spanish-speaking committed this evil out of sheer ignorance of the criminal code—a code the gringo lawmakers stubbornly refused to publish in Spanish! At this juncture, he did his bit to rectify matters by reproducing the statute concerning the sheltering of criminals. [22] He never ceased harping on the need for a systematic publication of all laws, in booklets and in

[21] Feb. 21, 1857.
[22] July 19, Aug. 16, 1856; March 7, 1857.

newspapers, in the mother tongue of the more than 30,000 Spanish-speaking—a need written into the state constitution but constantly evaded by legislators and governors.

As Ramirez saw it, then, the essential blame for the present crisis of crime and punishment lay elsewhere than with Californios or Mexicans, or even the mass of Yankees. It lay with those Yankees who violated their nation's high ideals, especially lawyers, sheriffs, jurymen, and judges. Too many of the latter, Ramirez felt, listened to only one side of a case and gave the decision to lawyers "so conscienceless as to take the bread from a man's mouth . . . destroy [his] happiness . . . and reduce him to beggary" without feeling the slightest remorse.[23] Elected officials should also bear the blame, he asserted, particularly the ones who sat on their hands. "*Quien calla otorga*" ("Silence gives consent").[24] Laws existed to punish every known outrage, he conceded, but not authorities to enforce them; law is a "progressive element" in the United States, he granted on one occasion, but its enforcers are a regressive force. As a result, the authorities often failed to prosecute, the courts ignored the decisions of the Supreme Court, and the guilty escaped punishment on technicalities.[25]

Ramirez liked to dilate on the jury system, the death penalty, prison reform, and the governor's pardoning power. As a legal buff he lacked a certain consistency, however. Whereas he urged the abolition of capital punishment, he also saw good in the terrifying aspect of a hanging. When a San Francisco newspaper proposed that executions take place within prison walls rather than in public, Ramirez demurred, with the assertion that secret executions smacked of the Inquisition and that public hangings, chastened by an attending clergyman, warned evil men of their fate. Such terrible scenes prevent crime by chilling the imagination; through the eyes the heart is touched.[26] Meanwhile prison life must be overhauled so as to reform criminals instead of simply hardening them. Curiously, he opposed the governor's power to pardon and commute sentences—even though the incumbent governor was using them to free *Californios*—because such executive action

[23] Dec. 22, 1855.
[24] Quoting *La Crónica* (San Francisco), Sept. 18, 1855.
[25] Nov. 4, Dec. 15, 1855.
[26] Dec. 5, 1857; March 27, 1858.

negated "a power superior to law." No earthly force should let hard-core criminals return to society; the right hand (the governor) should not undo the work of the left (the courts).[27]

In his frustration over the handling of Spanish-speaking prisoners, Ramirez eventually questioned the operation of the jury system itself. To insist, as the courts then did, that twelve men must always render unanimous decisions is "worse than madness," since a single dissent, honestly motivated or otherwise, lets the guilty party off. As he understood it, the British were about to correct this flaw in the judicial process by adopting the majority vote in jury trials, and Americans ought to do likewise. The current practice of disqualifying jurors before a trial also hobbled justice, Ramirez argued unconvincingly, because the juror unfamiliar with the full accusations can hardly know whether or not he has yet formed an opinion.[28]

But nothing taxed Ramirez' logic more severely than the question of popular justice, which he followed closely but apparently never understood. In offering some reflections on the Flores episode, Ramirez bit into the Jacksonian maxim, "The voice of the people is the voice of God." With this proposition he could "generally agree," unless it entailed what he called "blood-justice." Then, of course, popular justice goes bad; a "wild rabble out for blood and vengeance" never speaks the will of the people. He had a list of good and bad instances: The people's voice had rung true when Justice Lugo and his Indian police had stamped out the Irving gang in 1850, when the vigilantes had executed Zavaleta and Rivas, when Mayor Foster had had Dave Brown lynched, and finally when Andrés Pico had executed "only known bandits" at San Juan. The people's voice had faltered, however, in condoning the escape of the murderer Ned Hines and in supporting the wanton murder of Berreyesa at Los Nietos. *Vox populi* had had one of its worst moments when numbers of Angeleños had voted to sacrifice Flores' wretched accomplices for stealing a horse or so; and one of its best moments when the French, who are "exemplary" friends of justice, had used their influence to have the motion voted down.[29] Ramirez complained not of vigilantes as such, but of their mood and motive.

[27] May 24, 1856; Dec. 5, 1857; Jan. 29, Feb. 5, 1859.
[28] Jan. 29, 1859.
[29] Feb. 21, 1857.

As for the San Francisco vigilance committee of 1856, Ramirez condoned its work without hesitation. This opinion put him on a par with most Californians, regardless of ethnic or social background. The committee of 1856 was necessary and good, the "only . . . beautifully fortunate exception" to the rule that vigilante justice is an unmitigated evil. Ramirez had known James King of William, the editor of the San Francisco *Evening Bulletin,* whose murder touched off the San Francisco committee trial. Ramirez revered him as a journalist and as a man imbued with a "courtesy to foreigners." In hanging the assassin James P. Casey (and another miscreant, Cora, on the same day), the vigilantes had acted in a manner "just, inexorable and true," precisely as had the *Angeleños* who had dispatched cowboy Brown immediately on hearing the news from the Bay city.[30]

Like most contemporaries and most historians, then, Ramirez became hopelessly ensnared in the dilemmas of vigilante law. Other Californios such as Mariano Vallejo, who condemned the treatment of the Spanish-speaking at the hands of lynch courts, also found reasons to approve the 1856 episode in San Francisco.

As a newspaper, *El Clamor Público* always showed superficial signs of success. It attracted nearly as much advertising as the *Star,* the bulk of it from Yankee merchants. In 1856 it had moved into Aliso Street, nearer the heart of town, to attract walk-in customers wanting something printed in English, French, or Spanish. Later it used smaller type and squeezed more news onto its pages, and before the 1859 election it appeared twice a week. But how many regular cash-paying subscribers Ramirez could bank on, or whether his accounts ever were in the black, he never revealed. After the 1859 election he went to San Francisco, hinting that he would there tap new financial sources enabling him to print additional pages. Meanwhile, as an interim good-bye, Ramirez published backslapping notices culled from other newspapers, including one that cited him as a "youth of brilliant promise." [31]

Although these evidences might seem to augur well for *El Clamor,* the end was nearer than its editor let on. In the 1859 election, in which Ramirez had run for assemblyman, the voters showed what they thought of his editorial policy by allowing him scarcely one-quarter of

[30] May 31, 1856.
[31] June 18, 1859.

the total votes cast. Evidently his money-hunting expedition to San Francisco had failed, for, on the last day of 1859, he printed a brief swan-song editorial and closed down his press for good. Most directly, the cause of Ramirez' journalistic demise lay in his trumpeting the cause of free-soil Republicanism in a proslavery and Democratic town. Suddenly shedding a few crocodile tears for its fallen rival, the Los Angeles *Star* granted that Ramirez had conducted *El Clamor* with "marked ability" despite his youth, to which "may be attributed the heated and injudicious attacks on the American government and people which from time to time have appeared in the paper." [32]

Unless he left his press to the Los Angeles *News,* which took over his office, Ramirez may have taken it with him when he went to Mexico. There he served as the official state printer of Sonora from 1860 to 1862. By 1864 he was back in Los Angeles, serving as postmaster, and in 1865 he was official state translator—two patronage awards presented by a Republican administration for prewar services. When the next Spanish-language weekly *(La Crónica)* was launched in Los Angeles in 1872, Francisco edited it for a time, but thereafter one hears nothing of him in Los Angeles.[33]

[32] *Star,* Jan. 7, 1860.
[33] Henry D. Barrows, "Los Angeles Postmasters, 1850–1900," Historical Society of Southern California *Annual Publications* (1900–1902), V, 49; Dawson, *op. cit.,* pp. 30–31.

XII

California Lost,
1855-1859

F RANCISCO RAMIREZ may have sounded too brash for most of his elders. Yet, since his newspaper had the sad duty of chronicling the five worst years of the confrontation with the Yankees, 1855 to 1859, even the most restrained Californios must have cheered a little each time they unfolded a copy of *El Clamor Público* and read its editor's comments.

In southern California, those years produced the Ruiz-Jenkins affair, the Brown-Alvitre flare-up, the Flores episode, and the Powers-gang violence. On the statewide level, the same period saw the final thrust of the squatters, the onslaught of the Know-Nothing Party, the upsurge of racism, and the arrival of filibusterism. For intensity of feeling, compression in time, and geographic scope no violence had yet matched that of these years in California. Logic suggests that the gringos, having separated the Mexican peon from his master and the ranchero from a good bit of his property, should have begun easing the pressure on the Spanish-speaking; instead, their anxiety seemed to increase as it spilled down from the Sierra, spread outward from squatter country, and covered California to its southernmost border.

Precisely why Hispanophobia reached a peak just then is difficult to decide, except that in the late 1850's the nation as a whole seemed to experience a crescendo of tribal emotions, which evidently found their way into the Far West. Furthermore, by 1854 the poor man's dream of sudden riches in the gold mines had faded into drudgery and disappointment. In addition, the California economy began dragging its feet, until by 1855 it walked at snail's pace, so that hard times made

195

men restless. Experts attributed the depression to the draining away of specie in payment for imports and to the extravagance of business speculations after 1849. Although essentially a monetary problem, the crisis soon encompassed all economic sectors, so that by 1856, from San Francisco to San Diego, men complained of "dull and hard times. Rent low, land cheap, and very little business." [1]

The depression acted directly on the Californios in lowering land values and cattle prices, and in undermining a social system based on extravagant spending. Fiestas were held more rarely and seemed duller than ever. Santa Barbara's Holy Week festival of 1854 reached a climax when a militia company ceremoniously "executed" the Judas effigy, and although the town did not know this was to be its final Holy Week celebration, its mood was notably restrained. Still, the urge to ignore economic reality ran strong among the gentry. Juan Avila and Pio Pico staged elaborate horse races in 1858 to test their steeds, Coyote and Azuela, although both men were hard pressed by creditors and lawyers and everyone knew that the betting was "ruinously high" for those days. This ended the horse-racing fad, at least until the Yankees revived it decades later. Los Angeles staged the last bullfight that same year, and in 1860 the town joined the statewide bandwagon and formally outlawed the sport. (The Yankees, however, substituted a new diversion, a baseball club.) In 1859 fiesteros booked the shoddy Bella Union Hotel for the annual Christmas celebration, but the attendance was slim and spiritless. [2]

The dance in particular suffered decline. The true fandango, Newmark notes ruefully, lasted "only for the first few years after I came [in 1853]. . . . Little by little it went out of fashion, perhaps in part because of the skill required for its performance. Balls and hops, however, for a long time were carelessly called by that name." Saloons, brothels, and gambling parlors still held affairs called "fandangos," but the *aficionado* recognized them as base corruptions. The Common

[1] Henry W. Halleck to Pablo de la Guerra, April, 1856, MS, de la Guerra Collection, Owen Coy Room, University of Southern California (Los Angeles, Calif.); *El Clamor Público* (Los Angeles), March 23, 1855; Robert Glass Cleland, *The Cattle on a Thousand Hills* (San Marino, Calif., 1951), p. 102 ff.

[2] Horace Bell, *Reminiscences of a Ranger* . . . (Santa Barbara, Calif., 1927), pp. 295–297; Los Angeles *Star*, Dec. 18, 1858; Harris Newmark, *Sixty Years in Southern California, 1853–1913* . . . (New York, 1916), pp. 161, 256.

Council in 1861 put a $10 tax on each such event to see if it could tame them down.[3] Increasingly, the Yankees found the old customs "quaint" and would stop to stare in amazement at what formerly they had taken for granted. Thus, the falling economic fortunes of the Californios speeded up the inevitable change in the style of recreations.

As the Californios began to put up a brave front to simulate limitless wealth, the more sensitive gringos who saw the truth kept silent. When Doña Vincenta Sepúlveda spoke to Ben Hayes of spending $200 for her daughter's new dress, the judge went home and confided in his diary that it was "none of my business, of course. But I could not avoid a pang of regret at this probable extravagance, which makes so much against the real usefulness of society that might characterize the Californian ladies, even with the present wrecks of their estates." In contrast, the more blunt and impersonal Santa Barbara *Gazette* did not scruple to moralize publicly in the same vein by reminding the Californians that the "golden age" was giving way to the "age of iron," and that sons must turn away from their fathers' pursuits, or perish.[4]

The Californios' economic and social decline was accompanied by their legislative and political decline. Naturally, the introduction of the Anglo-American legal system in 1850 and the accompanying repeal of all Spanish and Mexican statutes and institutions (except the juezes del campo) caused the native-born some discomfort and insecurity. But, whereas the initial transformation represented the inevitable change of systems, later enactments sometimes seemed intent on mischief-making alone.

Under the lash of an ill-defined puritanism and nativism, the 1855 legislature passed six laws—sumptuary, labor, and immigration— which bluntly or obliquely injured the Spanish-speaking. The first was a Sunday law prohibiting the operation of any "bull, bear, cock or prize fights, horse race, circus, theatre, bowling alley, gambling house, room or saloon, or any place of barbarous or noisy amusements on the Sabbath," on pain of a $10 to $500 fine;[5] the second was a separate gambling-control act.[6] Two additional statutes had marginal implica-

---

[3] H. Newmark, *op. cit.*, pp. 136–137.
[4] Hayes, *Pioneer Notes . . . 1849–1875*, ed. by Marjorie Tisdale Wolcott (Los Angeles, 1929), pp. 75, 173; Santa Barbara *Gazette*, June 14, 1855.
[5] *Cal. Stats.* (1855). p. 50; this statute was repealed in 1858.
[6] *Ibid.*, pp. 124–125.

tions for Latin Americans: a $50 head tax to discourage the immigra-
tion of people ineligible for citizenship (primarily the Chinese, but the
statute was vaguely worded), and a new foreign miners' tax of $5 a
month.[7] The 1855 legislature produced also an antivagrancy act, freely
called the "Greaser law" (the epithet "greaser" appeared in the act itself until struck out by amendment the next year).[8] The legislature
presented to the voters, moreover, a temperance referendum, which
the Spanish-speaking properly regarded as a direct slap at their customary celebration of holidays.[9] The session closed, finally, with its
members refusing to provide for the Spanish translation of laws, as
stipulated in the constitution. Although the legislative branch was re-
sponding to larger impulses than simple Hispanophobia—the growing
anti-Chinese sentiment, for example, and a nationwide Sabbatarian
movement—the Californios nevertheless felt more conscious of the
enmity of the 1855 legislature than of that of any other, even the Know-
Nothing legislature of the following year.

The Yankees also revealed their current mood in cow county politics,
heretofore a relatively benign field of culture contact. By 1855, "race
war" took much of the fun out of electioneering. Ignorante and vigilante curses and Spanish epithets destroyed the pleasantries that earlier
had accompanied the voting ritual; big smiling speeches and robust
fiestas on election eve gave way to straight, hard politics with the
gloves off.

The presidential election of 1856 held particular interest for Californios, although in a far different way than the election of 1852, in which
a frolicsome indifference to issues had prevailed. Their "old friend"
John C. Frémont suddenly reappeared as candidate for president, running on a brand-new ticket, that of the Republican Party. The fact that
his name automatically conjured up ugly memories throughout most of
old California, and that he had to mend fences there before making
any headway, enlivened the campaign. Even Mariano Vallejo, his

[7] *Ibid.,* p. 216.
[8] *Ibid.,* pp. 217–218.
[9] *Ibid.,* p. 220. In the summer of 1855, one of the innumerable diatribes leveled
at "foreigners" suggested disfranchisement of the Mexicans. See Marysville *Herald,*
Aug. 11, 25, Sept. 4, 1855.

staunch supporter in the senatorial race of 1851, had meantime cooled toward him: "I have seen the error [in supporting him] in the result of his election," a penitent Mariano reported.[10] Yet the Republican Party managers thought that, with a little luck, the "magnanimous conqueror" might have a fighting chance among the Californians, owing to the potential weaknesses of the other parties. The American Party could not win a single vote among the Spanish-speaking, the Whigs had grown increasingly feeble since 1852, and the Democratic Party, although friendly to Californians and capable of handing out patronage, nevertheless also embraced innumerable racists, squatters, and filibusterers who alienated the Spanish-speaking.

Francisco Ramirez, for one, overnight converted to Republicanism and Frémont. He argued that Democratic President Franklin Pierce had sanctioned gringo filibustering in Nicaragua and had threatened a high-handed take-over in Spanish Cuba, and also that Pierce's would-be successor, James Buchanan, had expressed vicious sentiments toward non–Anglo-Saxons, in particular opposing the annexation of Texas because Negroes and dark-skinned Mexicans might mingle too freely there. All Democrats, Ramirez observed, condemned Latin Americans and Negroes because of the incidental conditions of their birth; by contrast, Frémont opposed slavery's extension. Here was a man widely traveled, conversant with diverse nationalities, cosmopolitan in outlook, and intimately connected with California's history. His published works, his senatorial vote against the Land Law of 1851, his advocacy of the transcontinental railroad, his leadership of the cross-country military surveys—all these indicated his dedication to California's betterment. Taking a few liberties with history, Ramirez added that during the Mexican War Frémont had defied the filibusteros.[11]

Frémont's wartime conduct unavoidably opened him to criticism. The Democrats hurled against him the charge that in 1847 he had opened a "public harem" in Los Angeles for liaisons with local "sisters, mothers and daughters." This tale El Clamor Público squelched as a product of the Los Angeles Star's "fertile and perverted" imagination,

[10] "Recuerdos históricos ... 1769–1849," 1875, MS, Bancroft Library, V, 221–222.
[11] El Clamor Público (Los Angeles), June 28, Aug. 16, 30, Sept. 6, 27, 1856.

and as an intentional insult the Californios should remember on election day.[12] Second, the Democrats charged that as a wartime commander Frémont had connived with a San Fernando Valley rancher, Señor de Celis, to confiscate and sell cattle, split the profits, and make the government foot the bill under the heading of requisitions. What substance lay beneath this accusation is unclear, although the rancher's son searchingly explained and denied all.

The third and most telling accusation against Frémont came from Don José de los Santos Berreyesa, who asserted that the conqueror had personally directed the "cruel and unsoldierly" killing of the de Haro twins and their aged uncle Berreyesa. The atrocity story had leaped from mouth to ear in every old casa and had gained added color because of the beating that the Berreyesas later took from squatters and lynchers. Another Berreyesa came to Frémont's rescue, however, and recalled that Kit Carson, not Frémont, had been the officer in charge on the fateful day. Republican Victor Castro testified as the de Haros' field commander that the twins had been acting under military discipline and were thus subject to enemy sanctions, yet that someone other than Frémont must have ordered them killed, because Frémont was always "humane and gentlemanly." Thirty-four leading Angeleños published a letter attesting Frémont's good conduct, twenty-eight Californios of San Jose did likewise, and José L. Sepúlveda penned a lengthy epistle praising both Frémont and God for a merciful conquest.[13]

The presidential contest and the contests for lesser offices arose against a background of increasing hostility to Californio political influence. On the eve of balloting, Yankee superpatriots called a special convention in Los Angeles to consider the possibility of splitting the county in two, as a means of increasing the influence of gringos near the town. Happily for the Spanish-speaking, this plot bogged down in parliamentary technicalities. The xenophobic mood of the day showed itself with open slander against mayoralty candidate Antonio Coronel. A Democratic associate was astounded to hear fellow Democrats speak nastily of "el negro Coronel." Open racism among Democrats was a

[12] *Ibid.*, Sept. 13, 1856.
[13] *Ibid.*, Sept. 6, 27, Oct. 4, 11, Nov. 1, 1856; Los Angeles *Star*, Sept. 27, Oct. 4, 18, 1856.

new wrinkle in village politics, since it had formerly been restricted to the Ignorantes, who at least had had the good sense to keep their caustic remarks private. Former Mayor Coronel lost to John G. Nichols, a relative newcomer.[14]

Politicians had short-circuited Coronel once before, although more discreetly. In 1853 he had come up for possible appointment to the post of subagent for Indian affairs in southern California, a federal position, only to be vetoed by his "friend" Judge Hayes. Hayes indicated privately to Senator Atcheson in Washington that, since his "rather popular, clever and sprightly" acquaintance, Coronel, was a Mexican by birth, his "appointment would be no extraordinary compliment to the 'native Californian.'" Moreover, "a 'Californian' will not accept an offer to which any similar responsibility [to that of Indian agent] is attached," he explained further. "You could not get one, for example, to run for sheriff or constable—not because he could not be elected; but for the reason that he naturally shuns civil posts of difficulty or danger." Besides, the rancheros tended toward "misrule, oppression, and injustice" in regard to the Indians; a man like Coronel would encourage the exploitation of Indian gang labor. His unfamiliarity with English constituted another disadvantage, for the Indian agent was supposed to educate the natives. "It is no disparagement of his other qualities to say frankly," Hayes added, "that he has not that degree of *moral courage* requisite for an Indian agent in California," an officer needing "iron firmness" to "execute the laws without respect to local caprices or interest or prejudices." Hayes's final objection concerned the subordinates in the agency; as no laws could be enforced "by any but an American against Americans," Coronel's American aides "will either resign, or they will control him; which I suppose is not the spirit of the law. . . . I should tremble for the poor Indian subjected to them."[15] The post finally went to a Yankee. Hayes's confidential discourse on southern California's ethnic relations calls into question much of his own election-day oratory about brotherhood.

Prejudice against Californios, muted in the early days of the régime

[14] Quoted in *El Clamor Público* (Los Angeles), Oct. 4, 1856. See also Los Angeles *Star*, Oct. 25, Nov. 15, 22, 1856.
[15] Jan. 14, 1853, in John W. Caughey, ed., *The Indians of Southern California in 1852* (San Marino, Calif., 1952), pp. 82–84.

but blatant by 1856, sounded readily in the courts as well as in political circles. Manuel Dominguez—signer of the California Constitution of 1849, landowner, county supervisor from Los Angeles, and one of the most respected Californios—in April of 1857 came up against the color bar in a San Francisco courtroom. Before Dominguez could testify for a defendant, a gringo lawyer arose to point out that Dominguez' Indian blood legally barred him from the witness stand. The judge agreed and dismissed Dominguez from the stand. In denouncing the ruling against one of California's founding fathers, Pablo de la Guerra made one of his rare senate speeches and his colleague, Senator Shaw of Los Angeles, arose to back him. *El Clamor* reminded the Yankees that even in gringo veins there ran some drops of Indian and Negro blood and that the "epoch of the bluebloods," if it ever existed, had now passed. *El Eco* called the expulsion "anti-republican and anti-liberal" and again scored Americans for mouthing high ideals about everything and everyone except the Spanish Americans.[16]

On another occasion (in 1858), a constable seized former Governor Pico and literally dragged him off to appear in a San Francisco court to testify in a relatively minor legal matter.[17] Few incidents better underscore the deterioration of social and legal conditions in the late 1850's than the public snubbing of the mestizos Dominguez, Coronel, and Pico.

The Republicans tried hard to capitalize on the Californios' awareness of prejudice, but to little avail. In 1856 Buchanan easily beat Frémont in southern California, and the Democratic Party, having weathered challenges from Whigs, Know-Nothings, and Republicans, remained solidly entrenched at all levels. In 1857 the Republicans stormed the polls in Los Angeles again, with equally bad results. In the gubernatorial election their man Edward Stanley received but 82 votes in the entire county, as against 1,294 for Democrat John Weller. Republican apologist Ramirez weakly attributed Stanley's annihilation to his prosquatter speeches, which insulted the titleholders. Somewhat more to the point, Ramirez complimented the "secret and smooth" Democratic machine for operating too efficiently for Republican novices. The Democrats nominated more men with Spanish surnames in

[16] *El Clamor Público* (Los Angeles), April 25, 1857, citing *El Eco del Pacífico*.
[17] *Ibid.*, July 30, 1859.

1857 than in 1855, and these made a fair showing, especially in county elections. The voters unanimously installed Julian Chavez, Tomás Sanchez, and Francisco O'Campo on the five-man Board of Supervisors and made Juan Sepúlveda tax assessor. On the level of honorifics, fifteen of thirty-three election judges were Californios, six Californios became justices of the peace, and another five, constables. In losing the contest for a state assembly seat, Andrés Pico gave Henry Hancock a close race, with 1,401 votes to 1,355.[18] A year later, in 1858, Francisco Ramirez tried to unseat incumbent Assemblyman Hancock, but General Pico garnered 1,234 votes, Hancock, 1,013, and the editor only 499. Chortling at Ramirez' rout, the Los Angeles *Star* complimented the town for giving a body blow to the "pernicious principles" of "Black Republicanism," a remark Ramirez interpreted as a racist smear.[19]

By 1859 the California Democratic organization, like its parent body in the East, had cracked at the seams owing to its inability to contain the slavery question. Internal bickering inescapably affected the Californios. To cite some examples: José Rubio of Los Angeles exchanged fisticuffs with a rival factionist, John G. Downey, the Democratic candidate for lieutenant governor, and tried to spoil Downey's chances by naming himself for the same office. Also, when the state legislature voted at the behest of proslavery Senator William Gwin to condemn free-soil Senator David Broderick for his stand on the Kansas question, cow county legislators wavered. Although sympathetic to Gwin, state Senators Thom, Gregory, and Pacheco abstained. Finally, the "Gwin machine" of Los Angeles—run by Joseph L. Brent, Andrés Pico, and Tomás Sanchez—lost some headway at the nominating convention of 1859. The Californio delegates from San Jose and La Ballona townships balked at seating certain delegates and refused to support Sanchez, the "Chivalry" candidate for sheriff.

With the Democrats weakening, a coalition of former Whigs, Republicans, and independents tried to take advantage of the situation by announcing a "People's Ticket." They ran Californios and gringo ranchers for a number of key offices: Ramirez for assemblyman; Abel

[18] *Ibid.*, Aug. 22, Sept. 5, 1857. Coronel had been appointed to the Common Council in May; see MS, L116/ 531, Coronel Collection, Los Angeles County Museum.
[19] Los Angeles *Star*, Aug. 21, Sept. 4, 11, 1858.

Stearns, "Guillermo" Workman, "Juan" Temple, Manuel Requeña, and Santiago Martinez for county supervisors; "Juan" Forster for assessor; and "Guillermo" Wolfskill for administrator. The *Star* accused Señor Martinez and his associates of election irregularities and *El Clamor* defended them, but editor Ramirez won only 692 of 2,245 ballots cast for assemblyman, and the remainder of the ticket did about as badly. Sanchez, quite popular since his participation in the Mexican War and the antibandido campaign, won the sheriff's race handily.[20] The Democratic Party thus retained local strength, even as it prepared to "go underground" in the Civil War.

The debate on slavery put the Californians at a special disadvantage, as is revealed in one particular legislative matter which culminated in 1859. The southern Californians had long sought division of the state; they wanted establishment of an independent territory comprising the region from San Luis Obispo or Santa Barbara south. By that method, cow county leaders of both "races" hoped to relieve themselves of burdensome state taxes, which brought them little in return, and of other northern discriminations such as detrimental freight rates and the egress of capital. For the Californios separation surely would have meant an increase in political influence and self-control. All things being equal, many northerners contemptuous of the south would willingly have bidden the cow counties farewell. In May, 1858, and again in February, 1859, Assemblyman Pico pressed the issue until he succeeded in getting the legislature to adopt a statewide referendum asking the voters to approve or disapprove the *principle* of forming a new southern territory, the "Territory of Colorado," which would include San Luis Obispo, Santa Barbara, Los Angeles, San Diego, and San Bernardino counties. Although the electorate voted "Aye," state separation in 1859 nevertheless became hopelessly entangled with the politics of sectionalism and slavery. The San Francisco *Herald,* in opposing the measure, expressed some typical preoccupations:

Californios are a degraded race; a part of them are so black that one needs much work to distinguish them from Indians; there is little difference between them and the Negro race; in the event a Territorial government would be established in the south very soon they would establish friendship with

---

[20] *El Clamor Público* (Los Angeles), June 25, July 9, 16, 30, Aug. 6, 13, Sept. 3, 17, 1859.

the Negro slaves, would be united with one another, until all would be amalgamated and all would be slaves! [21]

Despite a popular mandate, therefore, the legislature balked at state separation and killed the idea. This disappointed practically all abajeños except the editor of *El Clamor*, who, out of his opposition to slavery, felt pleased.

All these issues raised the real problem of where the Californios stood in reference to slavery. The Yankee assumed that, since rancheros exploited Indian bondsmen in a plantation-like environment, they supported bondage as a matter of principle. It was a reasonable assumption. Californians fell heir to a rigid class system and to a religion that did not condemn slavery as a moral wrong but only frowned on its worst abuses. As a result, even the Californios needed reminding that their own José Antonio Carrillo had signed the Mexican constitution which first ended slavery in the Republic. But although the Californios cherished class distinctions, they overlooked racial distinctions as Yankees knew them. (An American Negro once found a ready niche in Los Angeles: Peter Biggs, Negro barber and groom who arrived with the army in 1846, married a California woman and became fully accepted into society—so much so that, when one night he danced with the belle of the fiesta, a white woman, he nearly gave a Southern gringo apoplexy.) [22] Socially committed to a hierarchic system, historically associated with abolitionism, emotionally inclined toward racial tolerance, and politically linked with advocates of slavery, the Californios had, to say the least, an equivocal position.

As of 1860, politics had failed to bring the Spanish-speaking any substantial advantage in their struggle for survival. Even the activists among them grew cynical at their frustrations, and the passivists became resigned. As Judge Ben Hayes noted,

. . for half the burthens they have borne and half the losses they have sustained from defective government or a mal-administration, since the year 1850, the clamor of the same number of "American-born" citizens would have been infinitely louder and more methodical; and, for that reason, would have had greater effect upon the politicians that have wielded our destinies. But the Californians vent their griefs too reservedly. It is only to their friends

[21] N.d., quoted in *ibid.*, Feb. 26, 1859.
[22] Bell, *op. cit.*, pp. 22–27.

they unbosom themselves, and always very quietly. As yet they have not come universally to appreciate their position as a component of *the people.* And to me this has always been a subject of regret, and, often, of inconvenience, not to say labor.[23]

Of course, Hayes would have "inconvenienced" himself to give them only honorific posts involving their concordance and prestige instead of initiative and power. Yet he hit the mark squarely in suggesting that, but for a handful among them, the Californios rarely complained loudly enough. Too many accepted the political status quo or fought it only halfheartedly; not rebellion, but indifference or loyalty to the system typified the political style of the majority.

To add to their troubles, the Spanish-speaking witnessed in the late 1850's a mounting ideological campaign against Mexico, culminating in a rash of gringo filibustering, which dovetailed with political nativism.

Gringos generally assumed in the 1850's that Mexico was a "very sick" nation, as sick as Turkey in Europe,[24] and in need of "Yankee medicine." Catchphrases such as "Young America," "Universal Empire," and "Manifest Destiny" still resounded loudly in the California press and at public meetings, signifying a continuing passion for another pound of Latin-American flesh. The election of President Pierce started a lively annexation fever. A debate arose as to how much of Mexico to seize—Sonora, Baja California, or the entire country—and by what means—war, negotiation, or filibuster. Even the San Francisco *Daily Alta California,* the state's most levelheaded newspaper, advocated irredentism: "That Mexico must be Americanized is clear to every thinking man. . . . There is little moral wrong in depriving Santa Anna of the sovereignty of his province which has so little love for him as lower California." While not disputing the theoretical merits of Americanizing Mexico, the *Alta* preferred a diplomatic solution. The chief disadvantage it saw in grabbing Sonora was that its 80,000 voters would menace the Yankee body politic like an alien army. They would prove far inferior to the 5,000 enfranchised *Alta Californios* "who, it is well known, far excelled all other Mexicans in manliness, natural intelligence, courage, size and strength." American institutions would ill suit

[23] *Op. cit.,* pp. 113–114.
[24] San Francisco *Bulletin,* June 16, 1858.

foreign nations, and ingestion of Sonora would evoke new land-title and Indian troubles and aggravate the slavery question.[25]

Not content merely to debate the pros and cons of the "Mexican problem," certain activists went to work solving it. The most celebrated adventurer, William Walker, the "grey-eyed man of destiny," sailed from San Francisco in December, 1853 to the accompaniment of an elaborate fanfare, taking with him 240 "liberators" and two boatloads of supplies. On the docks he left behind an even larger contingent of sympathizers itching to join him at the first sign of success. (Some of his Texas-border raiders had seen service as vigilantes in southern California.) He selected Baja California as the beachhead for his "Twin Republics of Baja California and Sonora." Once in power there he planned to hop over and snatch Sonora and then apply for recognition from President Pierce, who reportedly wanted to acquire both Mexican provinces "without the expense or danger of war." Although a popular favorite, Walker had a reputation in certain quarters as a "sly, devilish sly" fellow. A fear of him prompted the *Alta* to warn that "the true interest and welfare of the province [of Baja California] requires absorption by the United States by honorable and just negotiation." [26]

Walker counted on the aid of the *Baja Californios,* reportedly as disenchanted with the Mexican government as the Alta Californios had been about 1846. As a result he underestimated the strength of the Mexican régime, especially of the two young army officers, Melendrez and Nicochea, who refused to be liberated and crushed Walker's entire cabal with surprising ease. Juan Bandini, while no lover of the Baja California régime, nevertheless eagerly joined its defense. Since Walker was planning to plunder Rancho Guadalupe, the Bandini property near Tiajuana, Don Juan, his sons, and about thirty aides rode down below the border town, intercepted Walker, and chased him back into Alta California. A few Walkerites stayed behind and settled down quietly (some married Mexican women), but the ragtag of the expedition came back up through southern California. There they got the cold eye from paisanos, but no worse punishment; San Francisco welcomed them home as heroes. Although two of Walker's lieutenants

[25] San Francisco *Daily Alta California,* June 10, 13, 15, July 10, 23, 1853; Jan. 11, March 10, 1854.
[26] *Ibid.,* Jan. 3, 14, 30, Feb. 3, 1854; Bell, *op. cit.,* pp. 103–104, 211–212.

were fined $1,500 for violating Mexican sovereignty, Walker himself went scot-free after a perfunctory trial.[27]

To the pro-and-con discussion about filibusterism, the Spanish-speaking added their own small but vehement protest. Juan Bandini, whose complaints about Yankees by then could have filled a sizable ledger, wrote a personal memoir about the Walker episode, hoping to lay bare the guilt of the California authorities, who winked at such international lawlessness. Manuel Reytes, a Mexican settler of Los Angeles with a gift for irony, tried a slightly different approach. After reading Walker's pronunciamiento calling for a rebellion of the Latin Americans, he invented a mock proclamation of his own: "Whereas," he began, "California, ever since the redemptive conquest of Hernan Cortes, has been an integral part of Mexico," and whereas it has vast riches, is peopled by numerous non–Anglo-Saxons, is accessible by sea to the South Pacific (and so on for a total of eighteen items), then be it resolved that the Europeans and Latin Americans of California should rise up, throw off the Yankee yoke and form their own independent "Tropic State." But if irony was misplaced on insensitive gringos, other correspondents in the Spanish press spoke more bluntly.[28] When a San Francisco newspaper wrote glibly of the cruelty, anarchy, and backwardness of the "Spanish race," *El Eco del Pacífico* reviewed California's own disorders—corruption in government, failure to punish criminals, and torment of Latin Americans—and rhetorically asked, "Which of the two races has more in it that is vile and degenerate?"[29]

Between 1856 and 1859 one could hardly scan a California newspaper without seeing a slur on Mexico's honor, a plan or a rumor of filibuster, or advocacy of colonization somewhere to the south. Each time a bandido fled below the border, an Apache tribe raided Arizona, a miner struck it rich in the borderland, or a Washington diplomat argued with his Mexican counterpart, some Yankee Californian proposed an attack on Mexico.

In January, 1857, the Angeleños caught another glimpse of filibusteros. Two northern parties totaling sixty men came strutting through town and marched out to San Pedro and San Diego. Although

[27] San Francisco *Daily Alta California,* Feb. 6, 18, March 16, 1854.
[28] *El Clamor Público* (Los Angeles), July 24, 1858.
[29] *Ibid.,* Sept. 24, 1859, quoting *El Eco del Pacífico* (San Francisco), n.d.

professing to be miners, carpenters, and other peace-loving folk, they were transporting arms and "a vast quantity of powder." To *El Clamor Público* they looked suspicious. If they seemed a shade less ugly than the Walkerites, these "buccaneers" nevertheless planned to march through Gadsdonia and Sonora and "give the *coup de main*" at Guaymas. Other Los Angeles newspapers tried to correct *El Clamor's* jaundiced view. Noting that the leader, Henry A. Crabb, a respectable Yankee lawyer and state senator (married to a propertied Sonoran woman), was a world removed from the high-handed and vindictive Walker, they argued that Sonora should open its doors to him.[30] Yet *El Clamor* remained unconvinced.

After a showdown near Altar, Sonora, Crabb suffered tragedy. With little provocation, a brutal Mexican governor seized and executed him together with fifty-eight followers. This savagery called forth a violent storm of words against all the Spanish-speaking. Yankees convinced of Crabb's good intentions charged that the new governor had betrayed him (in retrospect this seems very nearly true) in a fit of "cowardly treason." Crabb's death was "nothing but brutal murder," remarked the Sacramento *Daily Bee.* "The day of retribution will come," added the San Joaquin *Republican,* and Americans would remember Altar as another Alamo, another San Jacinto, another Goliad. Indeed, retribution came swiftly to the Mexican miners in the California town of Eldorado, when the Yankee miners gave them the *quid pro quo* for Crabb's death—a quick notice to leave the country or make ready for forcible expulsion.[31] *El Eco del Pacífico*, in giving its own version of the Sonora annihilation, cursed Crabb's people as "revolutionaries, *filibusteros* and thieves." [32]

Meanwhile, *El Clamor* printed miscellaneous news items pertinent to the continuing filibusterism. First it cited Walker's new "civilizing" mission in Nicaragua. Later came a rumor of a projected invasion of Sonora by Sam Houston. A year after the Crabb affair, former Senator Gwin declared he had a yen to free Crabb's Mexican brother-in-law, a prisoner of the Sonoran governor.[33] A Sonoran student enrolled at

[30] *El Clamor Público* (Los Angeles), Jan. 31, Feb. 7, 1857; April 27, 1859.
[31] Quoted in *ibid.*, June 13, 1857.
[32] Quoted in *ibid.*, May 30, 1857. See also Los Angeles *Star,* Oct. 9, 1858.
[33] *El Clamor Público* (Los Angeles), Aug. 7, 1858.

New York's Fordham College wrote to a San Francisco newspaper, advising his native province to sell itself to the United States, whereupon *El Eco* denounced him for mouthing the foul sentiments of the "Young America" movement and wondered whether his parents now recognized the folly of sending their son to be corrupted in an American school.[34]

El Clamor particularly resented the seeming complicity of the (Democratic) presidents of the United States in the infringement of the rights of a friendly power. The Los Angeles weekly branded President Pierce a "moral accomplice" of Walker; in 1859, when James Buchanan spoke of Latin America and Spain in a manner "bellicose, offensive, menacing," *El Clamor* again grew incensed.[35] In the interest of repressing the Apaches whom Mexico could not control, Buchanan proposed a Yankee military protectorate over Sonora and Chihuahua. This address, coming right after Crabb's death, encouraged jingoist sword rattling in California and provided the Republicans with a way of illustrating to the Spanish-speaking the perfidy of the Democrats. *El Clamor* traced the Apache danger to Yankee military ineptitude and warned that Buchanan's "sarcastic protectorate" would make a mockery of the Monroe Doctrine.[36] Just before the 1859 election, Ramirez took malicious delight in printing and reprinting the more inflammatory parts of Buchanan's speech.

Perhaps the best answer to their Job-like sorrows and afflictions was for the Californians to leave home altogether and start life anew on more friendly Mexican soil: perhaps "Exodus from Egypt" was the solution. In the bad times after 1855, some Californians at least toyed with this idea.

Several colonizing expeditions had gone forth to Mexico officially or semiofficially (Crabb's, for example), but the idea of sending out Californios was novel. Don José Islas, a citizen of Mazatlán who had made an unsuccessful tour of the California mines in 1855, first broached it as he made ready to return home to Mexico. He wished to lure back with him 500 to 1,000 families to establish a frontier haven in the Depart-

[34] Quoted in *ibid.*, Aug. 14, 1858.
[35] *Ibid.*, July 12, 1856; Jan. 15, 1859.
[36] *Ibid.*, Jan. 29, 1859.

ment of Sonora. A man of revolutionary dedication rather than an adventurer, Islas had a good reputation; at last, "a genius has participated in our sad outcry," affirmed a Mexican acquaintance.[37] In San Francisco he established an organizing junta with Juan Bautista Alvarado as president, and received endorsement from Manuel, José, and Guillermo Castro; from Mariano Vallejo; and from Andrés, Antonio María, and Francisco Pico. He argued that in Sonora Californios would enjoy the protection of "liberal laws" and the practice of their own language, religion, and customs. All they needed was a willingness to go there, stem the "barbarous Apache," and start a fresh life. Sonora's fertile soil could support a "useful, energetic population, schooled by contact with the Saxon race." [38]

By August, 1855, Islas had won the blessing of the Mexican government, which had earlier issued a standing invitation to European immigrants but now felt doubly fortunate in attracting settlers of "our own race." He received from the Sonoran village of Ures a donation of 200 fanegas of wheat and 100 head of cattle and obtained elsewhere a promise of acreage suitable for the cultivation of livestock, cotton, sugar, indigo, and mulberry trees; he could also guarantee the settlers subsoil rights.

After enlisting only a sprinkling of followers in San Jose, Islas led his peripatetic colony into Los Angeles on May 5, 1856. Already behind schedule, he met further resistance and delay, but remained convinced that 25,000 Spanish Americans would emigrate within four or five years, and therefore gave himself the rest of the month to pry loose some Angeleños. Editor Ramirez anticipated that 200 or 300 of them would soon join the expedition. Although normally a California booster and an advocate of assimilation, he asserted that "California has fallen into the hands of ambitious sons of North America" who wished to expel the old settlers, vilify their religion, and deface their customs. Since the Californians now lived in a foreign nation that offered only bad prospects and poor treatment, let them go instead to the "country

<hr>

[37] *Ibid.*, May 17, 1856. See also Colonization Society MSS (especially those written by Secretary Francisco Casanueva, Feb. 12, 14, 15, March 4, 5, and May 4), 1855, in Cowan Collection, 104/24, UCLA, Special Collections (Los Angeles, Calif.).

[38] *El Clamor Público* (Los Angeles), Oct. 23, 1855.

of their birth; where they can live with their wives, sons and daughters; where finally, they can enjoy the rights of free citizens." Islas'·project was "neither sordid speculation nor . . . purely philanthropic" nonsense but an opportunity for self-betterment and patriotic service.[39] To the doubters he addressed one question in the edition of·May 17, 1856: "Are the *Californios* now as happy as when they belonged to the Republic of Mexico . . . ?"

To this question, Ramirez received argumentative replies. A Sonoran warned prospective émigrés that Mexico never kept its promises and would disappoint them. They would fall into the clutches of the Sonoran jefes who needed cannon fodder for their sordid battles. Besides, he added, "bear in mind that in California things are not as bad as they have been painted. . . . Los Angeles has always been the asylum of the inhabitants of Sonora and has been the place where they have found good wages, hospitality and positive joys." [40] A Californio seconded the Sonoran's warning: although not questioning Islas' patriotism, he urged Ramirez to awaken from his dream. The "sad republic" of Mexico cannot honor its promise to support a Sonoran colony, he cautioned, since Sonora was overrun not only by Apaches but by a "*turba* of undisciplined soldiers and mercenaries [who] have ruined the people with levies and contributions." Were we happier before? Certainly! But "who caused our misery and who put us into the hands of foreigners? . . . Was it we, who . . . hurled ourselves into the battles of Los Gutierres, El Chino and San Pascual?—or [was it] our [Mexican] brothers who sold us, as they say of Joseph's brother? You answer us that, Señor Editor!"

Despite the nay-sayers, the colonists met on July 16 and, after toasting the health of Mexican President Comonfort and Comandante Islas, established a departure date of September 8. They resolved to celebrate Mexican Independence Day two months later on the desert near the Rio Grande.[41] For a time they became disorganized in the shuffle of the Crabb affair, but by February, 1857, they had launched their colony at El Saric and Tubatuma, 100 miles south of Tucson, Arizona, in the direction of Hermosillo. Their first tangible asset was a silver

[39] *Ibid.*, May 10, 1856.
[40] *Ibid.*, May 17, 1856.
[41] *Ibid.*, July 19, Aug. 30, 1856.

mine, which they had claimed for $5.[42] By September, 1858, the "starving time" had evidently passed for "300 people, more or less," of both sexes and all ages, with the total increasing "every day." While admitting that at first the inadequate protection against Apaches, the disinterested governor, and the bloody civil war had caused the colonists grief, a spokesman now boasted that "we live very happily and breathe [the] pure and agreeable air of this beautiful climate." The colonists, engaged in farming, cattle raising, day labor, hunting, and fishing and in the silver mine which "offered the most positive hopes of bettering our situation," were already enjoying "subsistence from our labor." [43] The new governor showed greater partiality to them than his predecessor, the civil war had ended, and the suppression of the Apache had begun, so that in its present "tranquility . . . Sonora is the salvation of the Spanish-Americans who grieve in California."

Another junta emerged in Los Angeles in October, 1858, with plans for a new colony on a separate location. Its members were "mostly Mexicans," [44] such as its president, Manuel Reytes, and its secretary, schoolmaster Pioquinto Davila. This project had as much trouble getting launched as the first, until in the summer of 1859 the Mexican consul at San Francisco favored it with a promise of free transportation as far as Guaymas. He contracted a vessel to leave San Francisco with 100 colonists—preferably entire families—in time to touch San Pedro about the first of August.[45] What success this venture had remains unclear, but it definitely failed to excite the Californios. Perhaps they looked askance at the Sonoran jefes or hoped that the local land problem was clearing up; or perhaps they felt a generalized loyalty to their native province, despite its many disappointments. Whatever the reason, the Californios plainly showed by their coolness to the colonizing idea that they never seriously accepted exile as a cure for their ills, but preferred, for better or for worse, to stay at home.

[42] Ibid., April 18, 1857.
[43] Ibid., Oct. 2, 1858.
[44] Ibid., Oct. 16, 1858; Los Angeles Star, Oct. 9, 1858.
[45] J. Alcaraz y Torrez to Miguel Pesqueiera, July 22, 1859, in El Clamor Público (Los Angeles), Aug. 6, 1859.

XIII

Catholicism
in a "Medium State"

I AM . . . in a medium state—neither good nor bad. Not bad, because no one opposes me, [or] well, because these people in the Church are not in a state I would wish." This lamentation of Padre Domingo Serrano's in a letter to José de la Guerra in 1856 [1] betokens the conditions not only of his own village chapel in San Buenaventura but of most of the old churches. Indeed, it suggests the predicament of Hispanic Catholicism throughout California in the early Yankee years.

After secularization of the missions and after the death of California's first bishop in 1846, Catholicism had suffered "near extinction." [2] The religious community had emerged from the Mexican War and the early gold rush practically leaderless and without funds and with but a "corporal's guard" of padres (twenty-one, to be precise), who operated in a state of virtual paralysis. Only the arrival of Bishop Joseph S. Alemany in 1850 ended the "iron years" of Church history and raised conditions to a "medium state."

As for the California-born laity, nothing in their response to the new predicament suggests deep religious trauma. The more critical religious changes had occurred two decades earlier, with the decline of the Franciscan theocracy and the rise of liberalism. The Californios naturally never felt any particular remorse at the ebbing of missionary power; nor had they cultivated any fealty to the new regular clergy as

[1] Oct. 13, 1856, MS, de la Guerra Collection, Owen Coy Room, University of Southern California (Los Angeles, Calif.).
[2] John Bernard McGloin, S.J., "The California Catholic Church in Transition, 1846–1850," California Historical Society *Quarterly*, XLII (March, 1963), 39.

represented by California's first bishop, García Diego, whose tenure of office had lasted but a few years. Meantime they had, in fact, rid themselves of the more traditional Hispanic Catholic devotions.

These developments prepared the Californios for the next step, the advent of Protestanism. The coming of the "blond-haired heretics" they seem to have taken pretty much in stride, although the sight of a man of the cloth strolling with a wife and child on his arm did seem a bit odd at first. They evidently neither "returned to religion" as a source of comfort from their new social woes, nor broke away from the Church because of the temptations of the new life. They still adhered to the minimum rites, although without a conviction deep enough to satisfy the clergy. Wives and children attended Mass more often than their menfolk, and with more apparent feeling, although even feminine worship brought occasional priestly reproof, as when Padre Serrano complained that "very few" women normally assisted his services and "not one" man, except during Sunday Mass; if either the church or its padre is "well or bad, it makes little difference" to any of the laity.

Of course, religious practice varied from one household to the next, but one may take as typical the attitude of Mariano Vallejo, who flatly refused to pay a tithe to the bishop, scoffed at the doctrine of papal infallibility, and yet supported the Sonoma church generously and almost single-handedly. Long exposure to Yankee Protestants and to rationalist and secularist ideas had weaned him from orthodoxy, yet he remained a Catholic. José de la Guerra, by contrast, a God-fearing Spaniard of Santa Barbara, could still converse with priests about such matters as priestly alienation—which is why Padre Serrano corresponded with him. But then, Don José was of a dying breed.

To be sure, nativists caused the Church some anxious moments. Archbishop Alemany in 1856, the heyday of the Know-Nothings, felt that "we suffer very much from those who interpret the law . . . in an anti-Catholic manner." [3] Private citizens bent on embarrassing the Church also caused anxiety. When Padre Sorentine of Mission Carmel and a crew of Christian Indians exhumed Junípero Serra's remains for a proper burial, the town of Monterey tuned out en masse to watch, including ruffians who pilfered sacred objects from the open grave.[4]

[3] Sept. 2, 1856, MS, de la Guerra Collection (USC).
[4] Cayetano Sorentine to Bishop Amat, March 12, 1856, in *ibid.*

The horrified Indians dropped their tools and nearly stoned the dese-crators while the priest went for the sheriff. The political discrimination of which Alemany complains was, however, short-lived. As for the bar-baric souvenir hunting at Serra's grave, it was an isolated incident that, from hindsight, merely denotes the latency of Serra as a symbolic fig-ure; the gringo's romantic adoration of Spanish Catholicism lay strictly in the future. Happily, the Protestants did not crusade against the Church as they had in other times, in other parts of the gringo nation. In fact, the only clause of the Treaty of Guadalupe Hidalgo they hon-ored in the observance and not in the breach was the one guaranteeing religious equality.

Unknown to most of the local Catholics, much less to the Protestants, a deliberate program of reform was molding the Church in California in subtle but important ways. It stemmed from Baltimore, seat of Catholic power in the United States, where the hierarchy was currently pressing "forward the complete uniformity of Church life in the United States." [5] Specifically, the Church sought to convert "its huge [Euro-pean] immigrant flocks to American ways" and to assimilate the Mexi-can Catholics of the new Southwest. To these ends, the Plenary Coun-cil of Bishops of May, 1852, formulated a program which eventually found its way into the far Western diocese. In effect, the Eastern lead-ership enjoined the Church in California, first of all, to gain control over the Pious Fund, a vast monetary credit salted away by the Mexi-can government, which might put the Far Western diocese on a solid financial footing; second, to introduce the tithe; and, third, to ensure effective control over former mission property.

The missions stood as a living monument to the decline of Hispanic Catholicism. As ever, the padres still held forth at Santa Barbara, San Fernando, San Gabriel, San Diego, and San Jaun Capistrano, but the institutions themselves were a shadow of their former being. The gente de razón shunned mission chapels and left them strictly to the several thousand Christian Indians, who continued to hover in the shadows. Gringo tourists visited the grounds to watch special Indian pageants, although ordinarily they, too, stayed clear. Mission walls had listed and

⁵ John Tracy Ellis, *American Catholicism* (Chicago, 1956), pp. 40, 80.

fallen, gardens had gone to seed, gravestones lay where they had toppled, bare stumps showed where orchard trees had been felled for firewood. Grazing lands either stood idle or were occupied by ranchers or
squatters. The Church, busy elsewhere with more promising prospects,
had little reason to earmark any new funds for the missions.

Although the Pious Fund and control of mission lands hardly involved the Californios, other key phases of the "Americanization" program touched them directly and personally. They soon witnessed
changes in church personnel, increased financial demands, diocesan
reorganization, and the introduction of typically Baltimorean Church
institutions such as parochial schools, orphanages, hospitals, and newspaper publicity. That the Church had a new grand design seems to
have escaped the notice of the average communicant, but few Catholics could avoid feeling the resultant effects.

Bishop Alemany, who originally had come to shepherd the Californios, injected vigorous leadership into the religious community, such as
they had not seen since the days of Father Duran. Alemany soon left
Monterey, however, for a bigger and tougher assignment as archbishop
of San Francisco. His replacement was Bishop Tadeo Amat. Since
Monterey had fallen into decline, the diocesan headquarters was
moved to Santa Barbara, the richest and least spoilt old-line community. There, Amat became the chief religious preceptor of 10,000 or so
Californios living south of San Francisco Bay. The move pointed in the
right direction, although Amat later came to prefer Los Angeles for his
official residence and moved there in June, 1858. Although poorer, Los
Angeles was growing more rapidly and needed guidance.[6]

With the installation of the new, American-based clergy, the leading
Mexican priests withdrew from California or assumed new posts. The
Zacatecas Franciscan College removed Father Gonzales Rubio, former
vicar-general of the diocese. The mere announcement of his removal in
1855 came as a thunderclap to the more pious Santa Barbarans, especially the Indians and the older faithful who had known him in better
days; even non-Catholics liked him. Friends unfamiliar with the problem of national jurisdiction petitioned Alemany and Amat to let Father
Gonzales stay, but without success. In a scene reminiscent of Helen

---

[6] San Francisco *Bulletin*, June 28, 1858.

Hunt Jackson's *Ramona* and symbolic of the mutability of Spanish-American Catholicism in California, sobbing parishioners kissed the Vicar's frock and tried to prevent him from clambering into a rowboat to meet the departing steamer.[7]

The Los Angeles Plaza church, the Asistencia of Our Lady of Angels, presided over the liveliest old religious community in the state and retained a central place in village life for another decade or more. By contrast with typical Catholic celebrations in the United States, Los Angeles festivities occurred more frequently, emphasized different religious occasions, lasted longer, and had relatively more participants. Holy Week in March, Corpus Christi in May or June, Communion and San Juan Bautista Day in June, Assumption of the Virgin in August, the celebration of Nuestra Señora's day in September, Immaculate Conception in December, and, of course, Christmas—these celebrations continued as public fiestas well into the 1850's.[8] The Assumption fiesta of August, 1857, lasting three days, included a bullfight, in which *el toro* gored a horse and killed a man.[9] On June 3, 1858, Corpus Christi began with two morning Masses, which were followed by an afternoon procession. When the laity and the clergy emerged from the church, the hundred white-robed girls of the Catholic orphanage walked to the cadence of a musical band and the escort of Twist's Southern Rifles and the mounted California Lancers with swords drawn. They toured the plaza, passing under flowering arches and pausing for benedictions before bejeweled altars near the homes of Doña Benicia Sotelo, Ignacio del Valle, and Agustín Olvera. Finally, the girls filed back into the church and out again to the orphanage.[10]

Christmas, the winter's "principal event," brought Church activities to a peak in Los Angeles. Indian jailbirds paved the way for the fiesta by carting from the plaza a year's accumulation of trash. After Mass, the town usually witnessed a tableau of the journey of the Three Wise

---

[7] *El Clamor Público* (Los Angeles), Jan. 20, 1855; Feb. 9, 1856; A. M. de la Guerra to Pablo de la Guerra, Jan. 21, 1856, MS. de la Guerra Collection (USC).

[8] *El Clamor Público* (Los Angeles), March 29, June 28, 1856; April 11, 25, 1857; May 15, 1858; June 25, 1859. For a brief history of the plaza church see Marco Newmark, "The Story of Religion in Los Angeles, 1781–1900," *Historical Society of Southern California Quarterly*, XXVIII (March, 1946), 36–38.

[9] Los Angeles *Star*, Aug. 22, 1857.

[10] *Ibid.*, May 28, June 5, 1858; *Bulletin*, June 14, 1858.

Men, or of *Los Pastores,* the presentation of the shepherds before the crib of the Infant, enacted by children and adults strolling from house to house around the plaza. This evocative Old World procession charmed strangers; to Newmark it recalled pleasant childhood memories of Bavaria.[11]

The transition years of the 1850's brought, however, a share of trouble to the religious community, especially internally. The old-fashioned cremonial practices sometimes annoyed the more sophisticated youths. For example, the same Christmas festivites that so beguiled gringos left some Californios cold or evoked a feeling of revulsion. The enactment of the very *Los Pastores* that had impressed the Jew Newmark seemed to Francisco Ramirez, in 1855, an "anachronism." The imitation of the Wise Men he found downright "disgusting," and the processioners' chants "unintelligible and insulting"—perhaps even to the Almighty himself; mumbo jumbo was good entertainment for Indians, he thought, but not for civilized men. He knew that his editorial would irk many Californio participants, yet he intimated that he had company in his resentment.[12]

More critical among the internal difficulties of the community was the eruption of disputes over monetary procedures. The Californios had never had to support the clergy out of their own pockets until Alemany imposed the tithe, and even then they balked noticeably. Soon, priests complaining bitterly about the withholding of the tithes forced Alemany to announce that disobedient Californios "will have no priest to serve them," unless they mend their ways. At the heart of the matter lay a canon law prescribing the payment of the *diezmo* strictly in cash, which the rancheros professed themselves unable to raise; they preferred to pay in kind. The sympathetic Alemany applied to Rome for a special dispensation for cattle breeders, but meanwhile, out of consideration for the local padres, enforced the cash tithe.[13]

Catholics were soon airing their linen publicly as a matter of course. Padre Anocleto Lestrade, a representative of the Church in Los Angeles, sermonized against recalcitrants, singling out Don Francisco

[11] *El Clamor Público* (Los Angeles), Dec. 29, 1855; Harris Newmark, *Sixty Years in Southern California, 1853–1913* . . . (New York, 1916), pp. 101–102.
[12] *El Clamor Público* (Los Angeles), Dec. 29, 1855; Jan. 5, 1856.
[13] Joseph Alemany to José de la Guerra y Noreiga, Sept. 20, Oct. 15, 1853, in *ibid.*

Mellus as a sinner whose nonpayment of the tithe had prevented him, the priest, from leaving town on holy affairs. Mellus happened to be near bankruptcy; moreover, since Mellus was absent and his wife sat alone in the pew, Lestrade's outburst offended some members of the congregation. *El Clamor Público* took the priest to task for assuming that "everybody who goes to hear him preach is an idiot." The padre later apologized to Señora Mellus.

Father Lestrade also came under attack for other monetary policies. His ceremonial rates—$300 for a funeral of forty mourners and $50 or more for a fair-sized wedding—angered several of his flock. Most of our people, wrote *El Clamor* in an unusually jaundiced tone, "are so stupid and fanatic that in order to avoid scandal they pay these extortions without a murmur," although a defiant few resort to secular ceremonies such as civil marriage. Moreover, the sacristan thoughtlessly jangled the poor box in the middle of the services, which repelled the devout and embarrassed the poor; let the box sit near the door, *El Clamor* suggested, and let each pay according to the dictates of his conscience. Bishop Amat shortly thereafter received a petition from disgruntled Angeleño parishioners asking more reasonable charges for church services.[14]

On March 29, 1856, Estevan Muñoz published a blistering manifesto concerning a churchly financial matter. One day, he explained, "under the call of Death" he stopped at former Mission San Gabriel for the final rites of his church. The priest, however, announced that Muñoz would receive neither confession nor absolution in that or any other California church unless he repaid a long-standing debt of $1,766 he owed the Church as an administrator of mission property; nothing less than an affidavit of payment witnessed by three persons would reinstate him into the good graces of the Church. Muñoz publicized the matter to show the world, as he noted acidly, the true cost of absolution.[15]

In addition to these lapses, the Californios' charity donations were becoming niggardly. In 1854 two Santa Barbara priests devised a plan to house a "college for apostolic missionaries" in the adobe vacated by José Antonio Aguirre, who had moved to San Diego. They wanted

[14] *Ibid.*, Dec. 29, 1855; Jan. 19, 1856.
[15] *Ibid.*, March 29, 1856.

Aguirre to sell them the property at a nominal price as a religious donation, and entrusted to José de la Guerra the task of converting Aguirre to the plan. Aguirre lauded the project as "saintly and pious work," but nevertheless politely declined to sell the house, as he intended to leave it to his children. He gave de la Guerra a scriptural reply, the rhetoric best known to the old Spaniard: "At the end of my days that are numbered," he intoned,

I intend giving my children the few things that God has given me. It is true, as our Lord says, "give and it shall be given unto you," but it is also certain that He says: "Speaking of charity to your neighbors, give alms to those who need it but give out of what you do not need."

The house represented a need, he added. Thus, "my dear Don José . . . it is impossible for me to comply with the request." When the Spaniard pleaded again, Aguirre replied more bluntly: "Putting aside the language and mystic quotations I will tell you in words plain and profane with [the] frankness for which you well know me"—he would not sell. Finally, however, he did agree to lease the property. He thus gave the school a start, but in January, 1856, it closed its doors for lack of funds.[16]

The "race war" of the mid-1850's generated its share of religious tension in Los Angeles, as is revealed in the "cemetery desecration" of 1856, a conflict that occurred in the interval between the Brown-Alvitre and Flores-Barton episodes. In June, a newly arrived party of Mexicans went before their priest to obtain permission to bury the body of a woman who had died on the way to California. When the cleric realized that she had died in sin, he absolutely forbade a church burial. This refusal angered the Mexicans, about forty of whom stole into the churchyard that night and, contrary to the priest's strict warning, dug a grave and put the body to rest. In the morning, the enraged padre went to court charging them with desecrating holy ground. American Catholics, enraged at the "indiscretion" of their Mexican coreligionists in this episode and in the recent lynching of Dave Brown, charged that the "entire Mexican race" was a "mutinous rabble." Latin Americans normally unfriendly to the priest this time came to his defense and crit-

---

[16] José Antonio Aguirre to José de la Guerra y Noreiga, March 1, 23, 1854, MS, de la Guerra Collection (USC).

icized the unruly Mexicans, although they also denounced the outburst of the Yankee Catholics.

The issue went before a jury. The priest demanded civil protection against desecration, but the Mexicans retorted that, since the church cemetery was orignally part of the adjoining public burial ground, the action was legal. The jurymen, mostly Yankee youths, ruled for the defendants, and the judge ordered the priest to pay the court costs. This last twist especially outraged the Californians, already smoldering with resentment at the operation of the local courts. Several among them deplored the episode as an attack on religion, as an insult to the priest, and as proof—if further proof be needed—of the weakness, malfeasance, and prejudice of the men administering California law.[17]

Aside from internal strife, Los Angeles Catholics had to put up with the barbs of the anti-Catholics. The private thoughts of some Yankees fairly bristled with hatred toward papism. On a Sunday afternoon in April, 1855, the Reverend James Woods sat down to describe to the folks back home the "bedlam" attending the "Sabbath breaking" on Main Street. Near his doorstep a neglected child was bawling for its mother, dogs were fighting, and one man was trying to run down another with his horse; "what a spectacle for a country laying claims to christianity. . . ." The afternoon's main attraction, the horse races, are "the fruits of popery—the only form of religion known among the Spaniards of this region." The "horses are very fine and richly caparisoned. But the men are a dark complexioned set with darker minds and morals. I preached this morning upon the destruction of Sodom and Gomorroh [sic] and had I wanted material for supposed scenes in those cities I could have found them in the very scenes" before his eyes.[18]

However bigoted, Mr. Woods at least had the decency not to preach his hatred aloud, thus leaving his anti-Catholicism muted and private. One Protestant, however, breached the peace with the Catholics— William Money, a self-styled physician, astrologer, historian, and

[17] Ibid., June 28. July 5, 1856.
[18] Lindley Bynam. ed., "Los Angeles in 1854–1855: The Diary of Reverend James Woods," Historical Society of Southern California Quarterly, XXIII (1941), 82–84.

theologian. Money arrived in Los Angeles in 1840, via Sonora, where he had been expelled for showing disrespect for the Church. "Bishop" Money preached and wrote incessantly (not only against Catholics but also against Jews and Mormons). In one manifesto he asked the papists to purge their church of fifty-two "abuses," in exchange for which he magnanimously promised to bring his own flock back into the fold. Bishop Amat obviously saw no humor in Money's offer and stooped to reply to him: "I send you a word of warning. . . . Discontinue your struggles with a giant that can strangle you without exertion." [19]

Most Angeleños never took Money seriously, however, as either physician, minister, or practitioner of any of his other "professions." His "Reformed New Testament Church," the town's first offbeat religious sect, tried to attract Californios by installing Ramon Tirado as "President of the Council" and Francisco Contreras as "Secretary." Money's church converted ten or twelve of the native-born, which made a fair-sized Protestant congregation for those days but did not constitute a mass conversion from Catholicism. Whereas criticizing the clergy or practicing a slipshod Catholicism came easily to some Californios, turning Protestant did not. Happily, the town as a whole took Money for a harmless crank, an idiot savant, and never let him disturb its essentially calm religious temper.

Notwithstanding dissensions, the southern diocese gained coherence as it gained guidance. Another Americanizing reform, the introduction of newspaper publicity, fell to the local weeklies. Although too poor to support its own newspaper, the bishopric could rely on *El Clamor Público* and the *Star* to publicize its work. The Spanish-language weekly, for all its antagonism toward certain clergymen, dutifully noted the comings and goings of the bishop, described church fiestas (although one and the same description of Holy Week appeared word for word in two successive years), and publicized fund raisings.[20] It defended the Church from detractors everywhere in the nation (although it let "Bishop" Money have his say in print) and also kept the

[19] William B. Rice, *William Money: A Southern California Savant* (Los Angeles, 1943), pp. 41–42.

[20] *El Clamor Público* (Los Angeles), Sept. 6, 13, Oct. 18, Dec. 26, 1857.

community informed of religious happenings throughout the state, such as the dedication of new churches, colleges, seminaries, and schools.[21]

The American Catholic hierarchy held no institution in higher esteem than an orphanage, and now slated one for the village of Los Angeles. The formative work fell to the Sisters of Charity, an American service order founded in Maryland by Blessed Elizabeth Seton (a convert from Episcopalianism). As nurses in the Baltimore cholera epidemic of 1832, the Sisters had earned the reputation of a humane, non-sectarian society and thus became an important adjunct of the Baltimore hierarchy in its new work of assimilation.[22] Bishop Amat called a special meeting in the Los Angeles parish house in December, 1855, to create a home for a contingent of Sisters who were already en route to the Far West. The gringos Stearns, Downey, Hayes, Drown, Alexander, and Foster, and Californios Vignes, Coronel, Requeña, del Valle, and Olvera, pledged money and support in raising a countywide subscription.[23]

Six Sisters of Charity—three Americans and three Spaniards fluent in French—arrived shortly after the New Year. The committee ushered them around the town in search of a likely location, until they selected a house with vineyard and orchard belonging to B. D. Wilson, for which they agreed to pay $8,000 (half in cash and the balance within a year). Their site put the Sisters within hailing distance of the local church, in a neighborhood of orphans and school-age children, and afforded them an income from wine grapes and a supply of fresh fruit and vegetables. The "Institución Caritativa de Los Angeles" opened in a matter of days as a girls' orphanage and school, with plans for a hospital and for branches in San Diego and Santa Barbara. El Clamor rejoiced that native-born children would triumph over destitution and ignorance, but noted that the Sisters sorely needed $6,000 for an additional house. This sum, El Clamor suggested, could easily come from a dozen wealthy rancheros, although perhaps the entire community should share the burden, even the poorest members. Indeed, the

[21] Ibid., June 25, 1859.
[22] Ellis. op. cit., pp. 56–57.
[23] El Clamor Público (Los Angeles), Dec. 22, 1855.

orphanage project stirred up such civic pride as to induce Protestants and even Jews to donate money to the fund.[24]

The orphanage pupils took their midyear public examinations in February, and observers reported them doing well in English and Spanish exercises. Encouraged, *El Clamor* urged the Common Council to subsidize the Sisters. While the village government would not go that far, it did provide free land for the proposed charity hospital (in operation by 1859).[25] After 1856, no public function—religious or civic —was complete without a parade of the Sisters and their wards. At the Mayday Festival of 1857, 140 girls preened in white dresses presented themselves to the public. Several delivered Spanish, English, or French recitations; Susan Avila was crowned Queen of the May and spoke "beautifully" in English. Bishop Amat's short Spanish oration lauded the institution and urged public support. Religious instruction, he thought, provided a special blessing for future womanhood; Californians would be second to none in talent and ingenuity when guided on the path of true knowledge. The Lord protect the Sisters of Charity! [26]

As another main phase of religious acculturation, Bishop Amat inaugurated a boys' parochial school for Los Angeles. This project coincided with a long-felt need of Spanish-American leaders, both secular and religious. The diehard liberal, of course, preferred sending his child to public school and leaving religious education in the home, while the more tradition-bound wanted his child to have simultaneous instruction in basic subjects and the catechism. Yet Spanish Americans of all degrees of religious commitment sought better schooling than was then available—schooling in both Spanish and English, instead of merely in one or the other. Bilingual education of any sort was the common goal of all Spanish-American spokesmen; refinements in course content were of secondary importance.

Proponents of education for the Spanish-speaking had to contend with a twofold resistance, however. First, they faced the inertia of old-fashioned parents who felt lackadaisical about schooling their off-

---

[24] *Ibid.*, Jan. 12, 1856; Boyle Workman, *The City That Grew* [Los Angeles] . . . (Los Angeles, 1935), pp. 43, 57–59.

[25] *El Clamor Público* (Los Angeles), March 1, 1856, April 25, 1857, Oct. 1, 1859.

[26] *Ibid.*, May 2, 1857; Los Angeles *Star*, May 2, 1857.

spring. This group illustrates what Margaret Mead has termed the "mañana pattern": even while approving such progressive ideals as schooling, Latin Americans nevertheless act slowly and postpone enrollment for "tomorrow." [27] Second, educationists had to overcome an equally strong Yankee opposition. In 1855 the state Bureau of Public Instruction stipulated that all schools must teach strictly in English. This linguistic purism went hand in hand with the nativist sentiments expressed in that year's legislature, including the suspension of the publication of state laws in Spanish.

Catholics and Protestants fought over the language issue. Archbishop Alemany, in a rare political venture, tried to line up support for a "liberal and impartial" candidate for superintendent of public instruction in 1856. Santa Barbara, where three-fifths of the 1,200 inhabitants spoke only Spanish in 1855, succeeded in retaining Spanish instruction. The Yankee editor of that town's *Gazette* tried to get the teacher sacked for his ignorance of English but failed; thereafter, the public school was conducted exclusively in Spanish. (After a year's publication, the editor of the *Gazette* dropped his Spanish page with the disingenuous explanation that the "upper classes" were adopting English and that his faulty Spanish was a "disagreeable burden.") [28]

Los Angeles found the language problem more acute. By 1855 the town had 500 school-age children (most of them Californios and Mexicans), a budget of $3,000 for education, a paid teacher, and a three-man school commission (including Californio Manuel Requeña), but it offered only sporadic instruction, and all of it in English. When the school repudiated Spanish instruction, a public-spirited Mexican, Antonio Jimeno del Recio, offered to teach Spanish-speaking children at the town's expense, in the curate's home, until the Church could summon some Jesuit fathers to take over. Stearns pushed del Recio's proposal through the town council, enabling the Spanish class to go into operation, but it lasted only briefly, until its limited funds ran out.[29]

Next, an interested party named J. R. de Neilson in the winter of 1856 undertook to create a bilingual Catholic school for boys. The

[27] *Cultural Patterns and Technical Change* (New York, 1955), p. 174.
[28] Dec. 20, 1855.
[29] Hubert Howe Bancroft, Reference Notes, spring binder, "Education . . . 1847–1885." MS, Bancroft Library (Berkeley, Calif.); *El Clamor Público* (Los Angeles), Jan. 24, 1857.

scholars attended classes in Luis Vignes' printshop, weekday mornings from nine to twelve and afternoons from two to four, studying English, arithmetic, geography, reading, writing, drawing, as well as religious themes. De Neilson kept lowering the tuition to boost enrollment, but even at $1 a month many parents found the cost steep. His school never had more than thirty-five pupils, including some whom he supported gratis, and began faltering within a year. Antonio Coronel and other Spanish Americans petitioned for a new public subsidy to help indigent children learn their own language, Spanish. They argued that de Neilson needed only a small salary from the Common Council to inculcate religious ideals, piety, and justice among the "*pueblo español.*" This argument was, however, singularly unpersuasive, since it came up against the principle of separation of Church and state. The petition therefore failed, the school closed, and most of the Spanish-speaking children stayed at home.[30]

When Bishop Amat moved to Los Angeles in June, 1858, he immediately contracted for a parochial school and an "ecclesiastical seminary." He also installed a far more popular priest, the Very Reverend Bernardo Raho, who promised to open the grammar school if he could but locate 100 subscribers willing to pay 50 cents a month for instruction in "our tongue and religion." It took him six months, but in January of 1859 Raho initiated the "Escuela Parroquial de Nuestra Señora de Los Angeles," although at a tuition of $2 a month ($4 for French instruction). By April the school had boarders as well as day students, and a Mexican headmaster, Pioquinto Davila. That some gringos accepted bilingualism is suggested by the fact that "many of the first families of the city, Catholic, Jewish, and Protestant, sent their children to school there." For example, among the students slated to receive prizes in July, 1859, were some named Newmark, Greenbaum, Abraham, and Goldwater; others, Johnson, Abel, and Brown. The majority, of course, had Spanish and French family names. The curriculum included handwriting, spelling, history, Spanish and Spanish translation, reading, arithmetic, deportment, and Christian doctrine, a subject from which non-Catholics were excused.[31]

Spanish-American parents who preferred secular education and

[30] *El Clamor Público* (Los Angeles), Feb. 9, March 8, Nov. 1, 1856; Jan. 31, 1857.
[31] *Ibid.*, Jan. 15, April 30, July 30, 1859.

could overlook the language handicap sent their children to the public school, which by year's end had sixty-four boys and girls from six to twelve years old, studying under Miss Hoyt's tutelage. Yankee parents complained occasionally that she had difficulty coping with the Spanish (and French) children to the detriment of Yankee children, although admittedly she was doing her best and the Spaniards were picking up English swiftly.[32]

Thus, southern California's Catholic school system began as a reaction to nativism. A century later a similar Anglo-Saxon cultural purism continued to annoy the Spanish-speaking, who discovered that the schools in the Mexican-American neighborhoods still eschewed teaching Spanish, except as an "elective."

One might guess from the Yankee's broad-guage attacks on the Spanish Americans in the 1850's that he would sooner or later launch an organized religious crusade against Catholicism. Yet he did not. The strongest drive for religious conformity in California came from *within* the Church, which appeared in the role of prime mover for acculturation. Perhaps the nativists felt satisfied with the Catholics' drive for self-reform; in any event, they offered only token opposition to the Church. Throughout the transition years, the Californio thus found it easier to retain his identity as a Catholic than as a miner, rancher, voter, or naturalized citizen.

[32] *Ibid.*, Feb. 20, 1858; Dec. 24, 1859.

XIV

Upheavals-Political
and Natural,
1860-1864

By 1859, the most tempestuous decade in the Californios' experience had come to a close. The impact of the new constitution and of new legislation, the unprecedented immigration, the rise and fall of the cattle boom, the heyday of the squatters and the operation of the Land Law, and the contest between bandits and vigilantes lay in the past. There followed in the sixties a notably less violent time but one that was, in a different way, nearly as fateful.

Of the outstanding episodes of the 1860's which impinged on the lives of the Californios, two were political—the American Civil War and the revolutionary contest between Benito Juárez and Ferdinand Maximilian in Mexico; another two were in the realm of natural catastrophes—a flood and a drought. The net result was a hastening of both acculturation and economic deterioration in the older communities, especially in the south of California.

When the Civil War erupted in the United States, the War of the Reform in Mexico, which had begun with the liberal constitution of 1857, had taken on a new form—an effort of the Mexican liberals to overthrow their French masters. This turn of events had a tonic effect on the Californios. It drove many of them out of their political apathy and into a state of activism. By and large, they responded favorably to

229

the new Mexican liberalism and to the Union cause, although some exhibited conservative tendencies and Confederate sympathies.

The Republican administration in Washington had good reason to fear for the safety of the Southwest. The long indefensible border with Mexico, the anti-Unionism of the Mexican government, the activity of Southerners in places such as Los Angeles, the unknown loyalty of the conquered New Mexicans and Californios, the concentration of Mormon strength in Utah—all these aspects threatened the hegemony of the region. Late in 1861 a small Confederate force entered Arizona and seized the government. Spanish-speaking New Mexicans meantime either flirted with politicians favoring slavery or espoused proslavery ideas.[1] In southern California the circle of Buchanan Democrats, which virtually controlled Los Angeles, included Sheriff Tomás Sanchez and state Senator Andrés Pico. Because Andrés was a popular military figure and a high officer in the state militia and had a brother with supposed influence among the Californios, the Union Army in June, 1861, demanded that both he and Pio Pico "define their relations to the union and the Federal Government." Pio Pico retorted that he proudly supported Lincoln, and Don Andrés replied that he respected "the Constitution and the Union entire, to maintain which I would cheerfully offer as a soldier, my sword, and as a citizen, my fortune."[2] General Pico's recantation convinced the administration of his goodwill, and they resolved to make use of him.

As a show of muscle in the shaky Southwest, the administration resolved to form a battalion of "Native Cavalry" in California and to offer its command to General Pico. Ill health forced Pico to reject a commission, although the plans for such a contingent went ahead and other Californios responded warmly. Salvador Vallejo of Napa accepted a major's commission and took command of the Native Cavalry, while lesser officers went about the state on a recruiting drive to establish four companies. Captain José R. Pico of Company A addressed an assemblage of the Spanish-speaking at San Jose and blended two themes, the defense of liberty at home and abroad. "Sons of Califor-

---

[1] Loomis Morton Ganaway, *New Mexico and the Sectional Controversy, 1846–1861* (Albuquerque, N.M., 1944), *passim*.

[2] Los Angeles *Star*, June 15, 1861; Leo P. Kibby, "California Soldiers in the Civil War," California Historical Society *Quarterly*, XL (1961), 344, 349.

nia!" he began in a rhetoric recalling the speeches of twenty years earlier,

Our country calls, and we must obey. This rebellion of the southern states must be crushed. They must come back into the Union, and pay obedience to the Stars and Stripes. United, we will become the freest and mightiest republic on earth. Crowned monarchs must be driven away from the sacred continent of free America.

Then he lapsed into rhyme:

> Strike for your altars and your fires!
> Strike for the green graves of your sires!
> Strike for our Union's emblem grand,
> Star Spangled Banner, God, and your native land! [3]

The gringo press warmed to the sight of the Californios mounting their horses, sometimes flourishing their famous lances, and rallying to the Stars and Stripes instead of to the Mexican or the Confederate flag. Captain Pico recruited a full company at San Jose, San Juan Bautista, and San Francisco. José Antonio Sanchez (offsetting the work of his Confederate kinsman of Los Angeles, Tomás Sanchez), did likewise at Monterey and Watsonville. Antonio María de la Guerra mustered in ninety Spanish-speaking soldiers at Santa Barbara (although he personally did not enlist). In Los Angeles a blue uniform was nearly as unpopular in 1862 as it had been in 1846, but some Californios were among the 163 Union recruits who hailed from that town.[4] To fill out the complement of Californio officers, a Señor Soto later was made a captain and Romualdo Pacheco of San Luis Obispo became brigadier general of the force.

The Native Cavalry was substantial in size but somewhat misnamed. Between 1862 and 1865 it attained a strength of 483 enlisted men, eight captains, and sixteen lieutenants, of a total of about 3,000 Union volunteers from California. The "native" troops listed their occupations as ranchers, farmers, carpenters, laborers, and shoemakers; there were also present in the ranks a musician, a butcher, a cook, a teamster, and

---

[3] Aurora Hunt, "California Volunteers on Border Patrol, Texas and Mexico, 1862–1866," *Historical Society of Southern California Quarterly*, XXX (Dec., 1948), 266; H. S. Foote, *Pen Pictures from the Garden of the World, or, Santa Clara County, California* (Chicago, 1888), p. 137.

[4] Hunt, *op. cit.*, pp. 266–267; Monterey *Gazette*, Feb. 5, 1864.

a sailor. Most enlistees ranged between eighteen and thirty-four years of age, although the oldest was forty-three. Many were illiterate; several Castros and Carrillos could but sign their names with an "X." The nationality of the native companies, however, was deceiving, for the muster rolls show that most of the enlisted men were Mexicans and South Americans rather than Californians. (One volunteer even hailed from Sardinia.) The sixteen lieutenants came from Anglo-American families, albeit local families closely allied with the Californios. When Vallejo resigned his post late in the war, he was replaced by Major John C. Cremony, a gringo.[5]

The 1st Battalion of the Native Cavalry marched out of California together with their Yankee comrades to patrol the Colorado River region and to the Mexican border as far east as Texas, to head off a supposed linkup between the Confederates and the French Imperialists of Mexico. They were charged with guarding telegraph lines, isolated settlements, and road travelers, and with capturing army deserters heading across the border. The entire tour of duty was something less than eventful; although the men clashed sporadically with Apache Indians, they never saw the main enemy.[6] They garrisoned Fort Yuma for a time, in boredom and in sweltering heat. Porfirio Jimenez probably expressed a consensus when he wrote home to Santa Barbara, "for Heaven's sake never come out this way if you can help it. You will surely melt. The thermometer is 112 in the shade every day [in August], with no wind. Scorpions thick as molasses and flies still more. When we want to drink cool water we have to boil it and drink it immediately or else it gets hotter." Jimenez had a slightly more lively time of it when he and Captain Pico and thirty men actually penetrated Sonora to hunt down deserting Union soldiers. When Pico's men ran into a French-officered Mexican patrol which had caught the deserters, Pico demanded the culprits' surrender. The Frenchman said that Pico first would have to acknowledge the legitimacy of the Im-

[5] Clodomiro Soberanes, "Documentos para la historia de California," 1874, MS, Bancroft Library (Berkeley, Calif.), pp. 195–196, 207–209; *Star*, Sept. 3, 1864; Thomas Savage, "Documentos para la historia de California," 1877, MS, Bancroft Library, I, 120–126; *Gazette* (Monterey), Feb. 5, 1864; "Report of Adjutant-General of the State of California," in *Journals of the Senate and Assembly, 1865–1866* (San Jose and Sacramento), App., pp. 584–599.
[6] Hunt, *op. cit.*, p. 267 ff.

perial Government. Pico stiffly refused to comply and instead swore his sympathy for Juárez. The French officer finally let the deserters go, but gave them eight hours to get back across the border without getting caught by Pico.[7]

Major Salvador Vallejo remained in the field apparently until 1863 and was discharged in February, 1865. He considered his tour of duty "devoid of interest"; when asked for details, he replied in his usual crusty fashion, "I shall pass them in silence." Truthfully, what mattered the most was his entry into the service and not his service record, for his acceptance of a commission represented the most extreme political reconstruction in Vallejo's entire generation. A dyed-in-the-wool cynic about Yankees and all things Yankee, Salvador had been a lifelong critic of his brother, who was a friend to all Yankees. He had never participated in gringo public affairs and had lately devoted a good bit of his time to the hateful fight against squatters. But an overriding sense of duty had driven Salvador out of retirement and into a Yankee uniform. Not that he particularly wished to see the Negro slaves freed, he explained, or the South reduced to humiliation—these matters were of secondary importance—but he keenly wanted to help restore the Union to its full size and majesty because it was the world's strongest bulwark against the European despotism of the sort then rampant in Mexico.[8]

Californios on desert garrison duty helped to disperse the Confederate effort in Arizona and New Mexico, a valuable though small and unglamorous accomplishment in the total war effort. Their countrymen who had stayed at home sometimes also became strongly involved in Civil War issues, especially in Los Angeles and Santa Barbara.

In Los Angeles, the Democrats had kept Lincoln's vote down to 356 in the election of 1860, while allowing his opponents 1,700 votes. A Confederate flag flew overhead on July Fourth, 1865, the first such holiday after the firing on Fort Sumter. One of the Californios' best friends, Joseph Lancaster Brent, enlisted in the Confederate Army and went to Louisiana for frontline duty. Servulio Varela, the Mexican

[7] Porfirio Jimenez to Pablo de la Guerra, Aug. 3, 1865, MS, de la Guerra Collection, Owen Coy Room, University of Southern California (Los Angeles, Calif.); Hunt, op. cit., p. 274.
[8] "Notas históricas sobre California," 1874, MS, Bancroft Library, pp. 154–155.

rebel hero of 1847, followed Brent's example and also left for the South. (He was to return with a wooden leg.) Tomás Sanchez— veteran of San Pasqual, prominent ranchero, bandit fighter, and Democratic boss—also enlisted in the Confederate Army, as a second lieutenant, although he never left town for active duty. Before the war, the state had issued rifles and sabers to the Los Angeles Mounted Rifles and to the *Lanceros de los Angeles,* a twelve-man constabulary of Californios captained by Juan Sepúlveda. When both militia organizations developed Union sympathies, "Chivalry" Sheriff Sanchez let the weaponry slip into the hands of a new Gray militia, and thence to Arizona and out of the grasp of the Union Army. Andrés Pico and Romualdo Pacheco tried to retrieve it, but too late.[9] So went the Civil War in the heart of the cow counties.

In light of this and much more, in 1864 the San Francisco *Alta California* charged that at least a third of the Spanish Americans of Los Angeles were "copperheads." This assertion contained a kernel of truth, although it would have had greater relevance a few years earlier. The charge left two-thirds of the Spanish-speaking unaccounted for; half of these were probably altogether apolitical, or completely dependent upon the word of their patróns, while the rest were in a changeable frame of mind and becoming increasingly Unionist.

Santa Barbara, too, witnessed a gradual consolidation of Unionism both in and out of Californio ranks. The clearest indication of the sentiments of the Californios in that town came during a lively election campaign in 1863. The political contest centered on the effort of Pablo de la Guerra to unseat incumbent District Judge Benjamin Hayes, a leader of the "Chivalry" faction. As state senator in the previous decade, Don Pablo himself had straddled the slavery question and hovered between the Gwin and Broderick factions. Some Barbareños still reproached him as a "Chivalry" man and perhaps he nearly deserved that label, although after 1856 he seems to have swung closer to the orbit of Senator David Broderick, leader of the Free Soilers. Pablo

[9] Percival J. Cooney, "Southern California in Civil War Days," Historical Society of Southern California *Annual Publications,* XIII (1924), 54–68; Edward A. Dickson, "How the Republican Party Was Organized in California," Historical Society of Southern California *Quarterly,* XXX (Sept., 1948), 197–212; Leo P. Kibby, *op. cit.,* pp. 343–350.

remained a Democrat and an anti-Republican, but after 1861 he definitely supported the Union, as did his brother Antonio María, who recruited one of the native companies.

Happily, the Unionists began encouraging Don Pablo's candidacy. Dr. Hayward, a Los Angeles physician who had won many Californios as friends after his work in the smallpox epidemic, spoke on behalf of the Union League and of Andrés Pico and Romualdo Pacheco, when he urged Don Pablo to announce his candidacy promptly, since Judge Hayes and another possible candidate were trying to make headway with the Unionists. Meanwhile, Hayward wrote, "I am studiously fomenting discord between the Californians and the French, on the invasion of Mexico, and trying to show the Californians that the U.S. Government is friendly to Mexico, while the French and Confederates are acting in concert with each other." [10]

Pablo de la Guerra's campaign faced serious difficulties. The electoral district he had to cover stretched hundreds of miles from San Luis Obispo to San Diego and from San Fernando to Yuma. Incumbent Hayes had ridden his circuit for years and had enough friends in Los Angeles, San Diego, and even Yuma to consider the south his bailiwick. The Carrillo and Pico families of Santa Barbara would align their strength against their sometime enemies, the de la Guerras; in fact, onetime Judge Joaquín Carrillo now decided to try to regain that office. Although a poor politician and thus a less serious contender than Hayes, Joaquín threatened to steal nativo votes.

Nevertheless, Pablo and Antonio de la Guerra made a strong political twosome and felt equal to the job. When backed by brother Francisco, papa José ("El Capitán," patriarch of Santa Barbara), and numerous relatives, they had money, experience, power (Antonio was Santa Barbara's mayor) and prestige among the poor. As a former state senator, Antonio had learned the gray art of politics sufficiently well to serve as his brother's campaign manager. Francisco became legman at Carpinteria and Simi. The de la Guerras took charge also of the campaign of Miguel Covarrubias, a family friend who was running for the Assembly in Santa Barbara. Following the customary gringo

[10] A. B. Hayward to Pablo de la Guerra, June 24, 1863, MS, de la Guerra Collection (USC).

practice, Don Pablo went into seclusion and left the fight to his seconds.

The de la Guerra machine functioned as smoothly as any ever seen in southern California. The ward heelers went through all the motions of hardened professionals, even spying out the opposition. Antonio's agents learned precisely when Joaquín's men posted letters and to what destination; he used every occasion—even a wedding—for politicking and kept his ears open for all manner of gossip. "Williams, the lawyer, told me the other night that . . . [Alfred] Robinson had told him that you, in his presence, had said that you drank for the Triumph of the South. This I do not believe, but it is well to know." [11] Antonio's chief tactic was to keep a running tabulation of possible voting strengths and weaknesses, and send aides or go himself to shore up doubtful precincts. When two of his lieutenants came down from the north to report that Las Cruces and Los Alamos were safe but Santa Ynéz was doubtful, Antonio shifted forces. Señor Torrovito of Montecito, originally pledged to Don Pablo, had just come out for Hayes; whereupon Don Antonio reported to his brother that "tomorrow [October 12] I will be in Montecito." [12]

Antonio de la Guerra received a petition from Sanchez and numerous other Californios begging Pablo to withdraw in Hayes's favor, but promptly discarded it. Outside Los Angeles, Antonio kept the native vote in his pocket by evoking feelings of respect, kinship, and honor. For example, "Don Geronimo" wavered in his fealty to Pablo de la Guerra yet refused to campaign for the enemy, having earlier "given his sacred word." Ygnacio Sepúlveda, although one of the signers of the pro-Hayes petition, would vote for Pablo because, Antonio reported, "you were a brother of his brother-in-law," but Covarrubias was nothing to Ygnacio and would not get Sepúlveda's vote. "Old Demasio," on the other hand, teetered the wrong way after initially supporting Pablo because, he said, "he can not abandon Joaquín [Carrillo] as he was recommended to him by the deceased Domingo." [13]

Antonio de la Guerra expected Hayes to sweep Los Angeles and San

[11] *Ibid.*, Sept. 25, 1863.
[12] *Ibid.*, Oct. 11, 1863.
[13] *Ibid.*, Sept. 25, 1863.

Diego, and his own brother, Pablo, to take Santa Barbara and San Luis Obispo, but he foresaw a hard scrap elsewhere. At Santa Ynéz, for example, the supporters of Hayes rented an inn, a saloon, and a stable near the polls, keeping open house there for three days before the balloting and paying as much as $50 a vote. "This was more than we expected," Antonio noted. Carpinteria also "had the gold in grand style . . . and the ones who figured in it were your opponents." For example, Francisco Ayalya was offered $100 to work and vote against Don Pablo. Even in Santa Barbara the "gold was distributed in handfuls." Don Ricardo Den, who generally kept clear of politics, spent $500 to defeat his foe, Pablo de la Guerra, and a Mr. McGuire persuaded Luis Carrillo to vote against Covarrubias by presenting Luis with "a few pounds of rice and flour." Antonio's people applied the same kind of pressure: Juan Olivas, an indifferent voter who owed Pablo's supporter Brinkerhoff $10, had the debt canceled on the promise to deliver his own vote and the votes of his five sons. The opposition had more money to spend—in all, about $3,000—but Antonio's people did their best with limited resources.[14]

Until September 25 the progress of this hottest election campaign in memory pleased Antonio de la Guerra, who estimated a 400-vote plurality for his brother Pablo and a victory for the Union. The Union Leagues of Los Angeles, San Bernardino, San Luis Obispo, and San Diego backed Pablo, but the one in Santa Barbara harbored political enemies who questioned his Unionism and increasingly tended toward Joaquín Carrillo. Even Ramón Pacheco referred to Antonio as a "secessionist," a charge that rankled. In any event, the proper strategy was to make Pablo seem more Unionist than Democrat. "Williams wrote a speech for you to make," Antonio observed, but Antonio vetoed it "as he is somewhat excited for the Democracy. He admits I had good reason and tore it up." [15]

Early in October, however, the Santa Barbara Union League ceased hovering between Carrillo and de la Guerra and came down to roost in Joaquín Carrillo's camp, alleging that Pablo was a "Doughface" and a "Chiv." The Unionists "will give their vote to Joaquín, so as not to give

[14] *Ibid.*, Oct. 23, 1863.
[15] *Ibid.*, Oct. 11, 1863.

it to you." League member Hughes waved the bloody shirt by printing incendiary charges against Don Pablo. On October 13 Antonio wrote that "things are getting very hot here." [16] Only the Californios continued to support his brother, and some of them were awaiting Pablo's reply to Hughes before committing themselves finally.

At a Santa Barbara Democratic rally, "El Capitán" mounted a table and delivered so rousing a speech for his son Pablo and for Covarrubias that even the Yankees cheered him. "The indignation rose to such a pitch that the crowd wanted to go and get Hughes out of his house. I opposed it and tried to calm the alarm, which was great." Covarrubias, an intemperate and ineffectual speaker, also arose to orate despite Francisco's strong-arm efforts. He cursed McGuire roundly, which somehow pleased the crowd, and "the whole world changed for our side." [17] McGuire next day came back with a tongue-lashing for the de la Guerra–Covarrubias ticket, but meanwhile he had to repudiate Hughes's campaign smear and deny ever attacking Pablo's character. This tactic won him converts. On election eve, Joaquín Carrillo realized that he would lose and withdrew in Hayes's favor. For some reason, the excitable Covarrubias also sought to quit the race, but nobody accepted his resignation. When the balloting began, Ricardo Den tried storming the election table for a last-minute tirade against Pablo de la Guerra, but "Mayor" Don Antonio publicly ordered the marshal to arrest Ricardo if he did so, thus forcing the proud Don Ricardo to skulk away enraged.[18]

The balloting occurred on October 23, but the tabulation proceeded so slowly that on November 1 the outcome still hung in the balance and excitement still ran high:

Every time the stage arrives from below [wrote Antonio María] the plaza [in Santa Barbara] is crowded with *Californios,* all desperate to know something. Friday night when the mail arrived, a passenger said Hayes won by 14 votes and it was pitiful to see the faces of our *paisanos.* They were all dumbfounded until I read your letter to them. Then the screaming was immense; they wanted to use the cannon but I would not consent. You cannot

[16] *Ibid.,* Oct. 6, 1863.
[17] *Ibid.,* Oct. 16, 1863.
[18] *Ibid.,* Oct. 23, 1863.

imagine the anxiety for your election—as much among the women as among the men.

In San Buenaventura they celebrated your triumph and after taking all the food they wanted they filled a barrel of beer that they could not finish.[19]

At San Luis Obispo the county supervisors haggled endlessly over the contents of the ballot box and could not make a final count. Antonio sent attorney Archibald Peachy to browbeat them with legalisms, but without luck. A de la Guerra supporter reported that Supervisor José Mariano Bonilla was "a rascal and very angry," and that it would be Pablo's first duty, if elected, to force Bonilla to count the Obispo ballots. By a late estimate (November 2) Pablo had lost there, with 131 votes to Hayes's 183, also at San Bernardino where Hayes's majority was 106 votes, and in Los Angeles where it was 76.[20]

These complications notwithstanding, Pablo de la Guerra finally did win the judgeship. He took San Pedro and San Fernando—by trickery, Hayes charged. At San Diego, where the incumbent was supposed to win, Pablo received 25 votes more, thanks mainly to Uncle José Joaquín Ortega, who reported that "although your adversaries worked very hard, an old uncle with three friends accompanying him were more active than all put together."[21] At San Buenaventura Pablo got 93, Hayes, 29, and Joaquín Carrillo, 2 votes. Covarrubias, however, ruined his chances for election with his bad campaign manners, losing even Santa Barbara by 14 votes. Pablo lost Carpinteria where opposition money flowed generously and his campaign workers were outnumbered. The decisive margin of victory lay at home, in the Californio vote: "In Santa Barbara your vote was from the Californians and a few Americans," and amounted to 419 to Joaquín's 16 and Hayes's 45. Of 644 ballots cast in the entire district, only 19 contained no vote for district judge.[22]

Northern Californios also came alive in the wake of war and revolution. Some who had been consigned to political oblivion for years rose up again. With renewed prestige and hope, Salvador Vallejo dabbled

[19] *Ibid.*, Nov. 1, 1863.
[20] Walter Murray to Pablo de la Guerra, Nov. 2, 1863, in *ibid.*
[21] To Pablo de la Guerra, Oct. 30, 1863, in *ibid.*
[22] Eugene Lies to Pablo de la Guerra, Dec. 19, 1863, in *ibid.*

in politics, going in 1863 to Sacramento with Manuel Torres and others to make his weight felt in the election of a United States senator. "At one time they [the Californios] speak well of one candidate and another time of another. . . . it is time lost for them to be here," a Yankee legislator observed.[23] Perhaps so, although they could not resist the temptation. Mariano Vallejo, exiled a decade earlier by Yankee voters, had been a Republican since 1856; now that the Republican Party dominated the scene, he was elected mayor of Sonoma in 1860. Squatters still nagged him in and out of court, but with reduced success at election time.

Land problems continued to plague Californios, such as the Vallejos. Although Mariano had once discouraged his nephew Pablo de la Guerra from going to Washington, D.C., to defend California land titles, because Pablo would be a "lamb among wolves" at the capital, the political climate had improved sufficiently for Mariano to consider making such a pilgrimage himself. Combining business and pleasure, he went first to look up his son Platón, a Union Army surgeon serving near Washington. He toured the military camps, renewing acquaintances with former lieutenants who had meantime climbed high in the ranks. Back in the days after the Mexican War, when a fiesta was a rare treat in an otherwise dull tour of duty in California, lieutenants William Tecumseh Sherman, Henry W. Halleck, Joe Hooker, Phil Sheridan, and Ulysses Grant had visited Sonoma as guests of Don Mariano. Vallejo thus enjoyed distinguished treatment in the East.

Since the administration felt obliged to appease the Southwestern Spanish Americans and keep them from going Confederate, it even granted Mariano an audience with Lincoln. Vallejo broached the land problem with the President and questioned the possibility of securing federal help for a California–Mexico railway. They spoke of many things. "The Yankees are a wonderful people—wonderful!" Vallejo exclaimed, as he warmed to the occasion. "Wherever they go, they make improvements. If they were to emigrate in large numbers to hell itself they would irrigate it, plant trees and flower gardens, build reservoirs and fountains and make everything beautiful and pleasant, so that by the time we get there, we can sit at a marble-top table and eat ice

---

[23] R. I. Hill to Pablo de la Guerra, Jan. 2, 1863, in *ibid.*

cream." Lincoln, it is said, was duly amused and added this item to his inexhaustible repertoire of anecdotes.[24]

To oblige the Californio, the Republican Congress passed a relief act stipulating that any settler on Vallejo's domain wishing a quick and secure land title should pay him $1.25 an acre. With this palliative the issue ended; Vallejo had not obtained the patents to his land, which is what he had sought to accomplish in Washington. His childern urged him to press his litigation all the way into the United States Supreme Court, but he replied, "I brought this on myself" by encouraging Yankee immigration. "It was best for the country, and . . . I can stand it. *Quien llama el toro aguante la coronado*—Whoso calls the bull must look out for the horns." [25]

As the war progressed, the Democratic Party weakened and the Republicans blossomed. The Californios drifted with these changes. In general they enjoyed a notable rise in political prominence, particularly in southern California, although some leaders dropped by the wayside and others had to change their party affiliation. Tomás Sanchez' career ended during the war; Andrés Pico, Manuel Requeña, José Mascarel, and Abel Stearns, on the other hand, founded the Lincoln-Johnson Club in Los Angeles. In March, 1864, a secret junta of Unionists met at Agustín Olvera's casa to draw up a slate of candidates for the county elections. Victorious by a considerable majority, Olvera became county judge; Ygnacio del Valle, recorder; and Manuel Garfias, treasurer. Judge Hayes, who meantime had parted company with the "Chivalry" faction, became district attorney on the same ticket. "Native Californians were then in the ascendancy," he noted. For the swearing-in ceremonies Don Ygnacio prepared "a sort of altar surmounted by a large crucifix and with a cushion to kneel upon." The Californios took office "according to the old style," but when Catholic Hayes spurned the ritual, del Valle felt "somewhat shocked at our cold, unsentimental form on such a *gran ocasíon*." Although Olvera and Garfias knew little English, Olvera proceeded to study and learn it. Hayes translated key laws into Spanish with the editorial help of Antonio Coronel (town

---

[24] Emily Browne Powell, "A Modern Knight: Reminiscences of General M. G. Vallejo," *Harper's New Monthly Magazine*, LXXXVI (Dec., 1892 to May, 1893), 788.

[25] Myrtle McKittrick, *Vallejo, Son of California* (Portland, Ore., 1944), p. 333.

councilman during most of the 1860's), and the "green" hands "soon made as good officers as the County has ever had." [26]

Californios thus replaced gringos in political office in Santa Barbara and Los Angeles, reversing the trend of the late 1850's. Clearly they had not yet completely lost their penchant for self-leadership and could capitalize on the new political possibilities; despite previous defeats, the patricians' sense of duty was still alive.

Had revolution not erupted in Mexico in the 1860's, the Californios might have felt far more indifferent to current affairs, but the uprising of Benito Juárez had the effect of sharpening all political issues, clarifying all social struggles. No Californio with hopes for the Union could feel indifferent to events in Mexico, but to sympathizers of the Gray as well as of the Blue, the anti-French rebellion in Mexico seemed a mere extension of the domestic struggle. Indeed, the two struggles overlapped diplomatically, for the French invaders took advantage of United States weakness to come into power in the first place, and stayed as long as they did because of the inability of the United States to make good the threat of its Monroe Doctrine. Meanwhile, some Californians had to chose between two combat arenas; while Salvador Vallejo and his nephew Platón served the Union Army, Platón's brother Udislao went to Mexico and enlisted under Juárez.

To capitalize on potential sympathies in California, Juárez dispatched the Comandante of Sinaloa, General Placidio Vega, to San Francisco to raise volunteers and collect matériel for the liberation and generally to stir up interest in Mexico's cause. Vega had in his favor the Yankees' traditional antipathy toward European involvement in the Western Hemisphere, as well as their innate sense of republicanism. But, since Lincoln feared driving the French régime into a Confederate alliance, Juárez found Yankee officialdom quite cool to requests for government support for the Mexican rebels. He also had to face the opposition of Mexican conservatives, who plumped for Emperor Maximillian in the Bay city. Vega sparred verbally with the editor of the imperialist weekly *El Eco del Pacífico* and finally sued him for libel. He could, however, bank on support from *La Voz de Méjico*, a San Francisco weekly catering to Juárez supporters. Its editor breathed liberal

---

[26] Benjamin D. Hayes, *Pioneer Notes*, . . . *1849–1875*, ed. by Marjorie Tisdale Wolcott (Los Angeles, 1929), p. 211.

fire and, at one point, tried to split the California clergy over political matters.[27]

As for raising funds among the Californios, Vega found that few had money to spare, although many offered warm sympathy. Mariano Vallejo donated some cash, but the drought of 1863 prevented him from making a really generous donation. His best gift was the use of his name, which unlocked other doors to Vega. This advantage, combined with the backing of Salvio and Romualdo Pacheco and of Agustín and Victor Castro, enabled Vega to raise about $500 each month in 1864; even better, he collected $24,000 from San Francisco businessmen. In 1864 the Civil War evolved to the point where the administration could finally toy with open support for the Mexican rebels. A San Francisco mass meeting drew 6,000 spectators. Republican leaders like Romualdo Pacheco and Senator James A. MacDougal supported Vega's mission until he raised his total receipts to $209,000—again mostly from Yankee businessmen in San Francisco and San Diego. According to folklore, however, tragedy befell this treasure when one of the Mexican emissaries entrusted with its delivery to Juárez buried it secretly and then died, leaving two of his companions who searched for it to accuse each other of stealing it. The money never was found; it evidently still lies buried in the ground, perhaps at San Bruno.[28]

Vega also busied himself collecting arms and enlisting troops for the liberation, but in this endeavor he ran into nearly as much trouble as in raising funds. Mexican patriotic and benevolent societies mushroomed wherever Mexicans lived in the 1860's, even in the ghostly town of Sonora, and by May, 1865, these societies formed one and a half regiments of volunteers, including some Californios. Union Army veterans who volunteered to fight in Mexico were guaranteed a $2,000 cash bounty and a Mexican land grant up to 1 square mile. By then the United States government had succumbed to last-minute French pressure and halted the troop exodus; only a few of the enlistees reached Mexico, by an overland route. A local supplier lost patience awaiting an overdue payment from Vega and sued him for $2,000. Even when

[27] Richard Henry Morefield, "The Mexican Adaptation in American California, 1846–1875" (M.A. thesis, University of California, Berkeley, 1955), p. 90.
[28] Horace Bell, *On the Old West Coast: Being Further Reminiscences of a Ranger* (New York, 1930), pp. 67–69.

Washington finally approved a gun export, balky San Francisco customs officers impounded the shipment.[29] Vega thus largely failed in his California mission.

Regardless of whether a Vega could profit from it or not, the Juárez revolution had left its impact on California. The patriotic societies of the 1860's remained active afterward. The bolder political tastes of the Mexican community encouraged the growth of new and larger Spanish-language newspapers, both conservative and liberal, which reached a more attentive readership than Francisco Ramirez had ever found. After the 1860's, the Spanish-speaking of California unfailingly celebrated September Sixteenth, commemorating Mexican independence from Spain, and *Cinco de Mayo*, marking the overthrow of the French; both secular holidays captured the general public fancy. The Los Angeles Juarez Society marked the death of Benito Juárez, July 18, 1872, by a solemn meeting, and a twenty-gun salute two days in a row; September Sixteenth that year saw a parade of 400 in Los Angeles. California-born Refugio Botello acted as grand marshal in the festivities made possible by a collection of more than $300 from people of all nationalities. San Francisco, San Jose, and even Santa Barbara witnessed similar celebrations.[30]

Civil war in two nations touched the Californios purely on the level of ideology, since they sustained no recorded losses worse than Servulio Varela's amputated leg. But, by an irony of fate, they suffered a physical disaster as great as if they had stood in the path of Sherman's march to the sea. It came in the form of an earth-scorching, life-killing drought which lasted for two years, 1862 through 1863, and which is as important a milestone in the history of pastoral California as secularization of the missions and land litigation.

The cattle economy had sagged badly long before the real trouble began. "Everybody in this town is broke," wrote Pedro C. Carrillo of Santa Barbara in June, 1861. "Cattle can be bought at any price, real estate is not worth anything."[31] Six months later, meteorological dis-

[29] Morefield, *op. cit.*, pp. 92–93, 102, 108.
[30] *La Crónica* (Los Angeles), Aug. 31, Sept. 21, 1872
[31] To Abel Sterns, June 6, 1861, Stearns MSS, Huntington Library (San Marino, Calif.).

turbances began with a furious rainstorm and destructive floods. The sky opened on November 11 and poured rain virtually without letup for fifteen days. The flow began again December 24, drenching the Christmas and New Year celebrations; lasting for the next month, it deposited an estimated 50 inches of rain before it ceased. On January 27, 1862, clear skies allowed a reconnaissance of Santa Barbara, a "town made of paper," and revealed losses of $10,000 to $12,000 in drowned stock, broken fences, uprooted orchard trees, and water-logged homes. At San Buenaventura a 3-foot stream had coursed down the main street, tearing from high ground boulders that wiped away all houses in their path with the exception of three or four casas, in which everybody huddled. "Every day and night," a resident reported, "we would hear strange noises: homes and corrals falling." A landslide killed one man.[32]

The story repeated itself along every river or stream south of the Tehachapi Mountains and along many rivers in the north. Los Angeles merchants sloshed about in water up to their waists trying to save their goods. Water swept away the city's precious waterworks. Mail deliveries ceased for a month; some wag put a "To Let" sign on the post office. The San Gabriel River, gushing wildly from the foothills, jumped its banks, swallowing irrigation ditches, fruit trees, homes; it tore off a corner of Pio Pico's place. Water buried vineyards and, after it had receded, left an equally damaging residue of sand. In Agua Mansa, an isolated village of New Mexicans, the Santa Ana River wiped out every structure but the church on high ground, where the inhabitants found safe refuge. The sun peeked out briefly on two separate days, prompting the *Star* to headline a "Phenomenon." Only two blessings in disguise came from this catastrophe: the water delivered to lower ground loads of driftwood, which could be converted into firewood; and it produced good grass in the spring of 1862. Cattle fattened on it sold at $8 to $12 a head, the highest price in years.[33]

Northern California also endured a flood of biblical proportions. En-

[32] Francisco de la Guerra to Pablo de la Guerra, Jan. 27, 1862, MS, de la Guerra Collection (USC).
[33] *Star*, Dec. 6, 1861; Harris Newmark, *Sixty Years in Southern California, 1853–1913* . . . (New York, 1916), p. 309; James M. Guinn, "Exceptional Years: A History of California Floods and Droughts," Historical Society of Southern California *Annual Publications,* I (1890), 36.

tire valleys lay under water; massive streams changed their courses. After a visit to the Central Valley, a competent geologist estimated that "America has never before seen such desolation by flood." [34] Perhaps he exaggerated, although the Californios had never seen anything like it. Neither have any Californians since then, except when the Colorado River jumped its banks and nearly blotted out the Imperial Valley in 1906.

Severe drought followed the flood. After the summer fodder of 1862 had given out, cattle and sheep found little nourishment for the next three years. Longhorns looked bony, grew weak, and died in large numbers. A steer would stumble into a dry arroyo vainly sniffing water, be too feeble to climb out, and become a feast for buzzards; only his hide was salvageable. Instead of Cleland's "Cattle on a Thousand Hills," travelers saw bleaching bones everywhere. In Los Angeles normal trade halted—merchants had nothing to sell. The city made no tax assessment during 1863 and 1864 and could not even auction land for delinquent taxes, so that valuable town lots, offered at about $3 apiece, went begging; currency disappeared altogether. In February, 1864, the sun still shone clearly, and the temperatures stayed high. Then some clouds covered the sun briefly, sailed away, and then returned, and on February 11 opened up. But these rains barely slaked the thirst of animals or soil—March, and still no grass! May saw summer-like heat, although a few late storms delivered moisture and put the grass "in a fair condition." Drought continued afterward. Only in 1865 did rain and grass cover return to nearly normal.[35]

This erratic wet-dry cycle was accompanied by yet another natural catastophe, a smallpox epidemic which took an especially heavy toll among the Spanish-speaking of Los Angeles. In February, 1863, physicians counted 276 cases and scores of deaths. Almost the entire settlement of Mexicans and Indians from the plaza north to the mill died. Smallpox, like tuberculosis in recent times, was a disease of the poor and disaffected, since most of the citizens who were better off under-

[34] William H. Brewer, *Up and Down California in 1860–1864*, ed. by Francis P. Farquhar (Berkeley, 1949), pp. 243–244.
[35] James M. Guinn, *A History of California and an Extended History of Los Angeles and Environs* (Los Angeles, 1915), I, 290; Robert Glass Cleland, *The Cattle on a Thousand Hills* (San Marino, Calif., 1951), pp. 125–137.

stood effective preventive medicine. Indians and lower-class Mexicans and Californians either had not been taught the remedy of vaccine or refused to apply it. Instead, they went from house to house administering folk medicine to the sick and dying, thereby furthering the contagion, until the hamlet had more corpses than gravediggers.[36]

A quarter of the state's wealth crumbled from 1862 to 1864, including as much as 40 per cent of its livestock, with the main devastation occurring in the south. In Los Angeles County seven of ten animals rotted on the open range by the end of 1863, possibly 3 million by 1864. The county's assessed valuation fell from about $3,650,000 to $1,622,000. Santa Barbara had 200,000 head of cattle in 1862, a mere 5,000 in 1865. Ranchers there auctioned 50,000 animals at 37½ cents a head in April, 1864, the lowest price ever; even in the Mexican days hide and carcass each had brought a dollar. Five years later epidemic disease ravished more of the remaining longhorns, and on the centennial of the introduction of the first 200 head into California, 1769, the total cattle population in the south stood at 13,000. Southern California's reputation among Yankees as a natural desert and a cultural backwash could scarcely improve after this. Nor had the abajeños experienced anything so devastating since they had begun breeding cattle.[37]

Only sheep survived the drought with ease. Since a desperate "wooly" would eat the plentiful *gayeta* weed and get by on little water, he could outdo even the hardiest longhorn. The sheep census of 1865 stood high at 282,000; wool prices also ran high, especially in 1872. By 1876, sheep were the only economically important remnants of the pastoral era.[38]

For many ranching families, 1864 meant the end of solvency; their names generally went on the delinquent tax list and stayed there until they had sold their property. Horace Bell, returning from Civil War duty, noted that the Californios displayed fewer velvets, sported less gold braid and fewer silver buttons, and wore more cast-off gar-

[36] Hayes, *op. cit.*, p. 283.
[37] Juan José Warner, Benjamin Hayes, and J. P. Widney, *A Historical Sketch of Los Angeles County, California* . . . *September 8, 1771 to July 4, 1876* . . . (Los Angeles, 1936), p. 121.
[38] Cleland, *op. cit.*, pp. 186–192.

ments.[39] Before the catastrophe, practically all land parcels worth more than $10,000 had still been in the hands of old families; by 1870, these families held barely one-quarter. A mean and brassy sky thus eventually did in the south of California what lawyers and squatters had accomplished in the north—the forced breakup of baronial holdings, their transfer to new owners, and the rise of a way of life other than ranching.

[39] *Op. cit.*, p. 83.

XV

The Second Generation,
1865-1890

WHEN the first railroad started running in southern California in November, 1869, shuttling back and forth from Los Angeles to San Pedro, vaqueros would gleefully race their horses against the locomotive. They won the short sprint, but of course lost in the long haul.[1] The results were symbolically quite meaningful, for the civilization represented by the locomotive was bearing down on them slowly but with irresistible force. In September, 1870, the Southern Pacific arrived from the north and in March, 1887, the first Santa Fe Railroad train snaked through the San Bernardino Mountains into Los Angeles. Thereafter, as many as three and four coach trains descended on the city each day, depositing in 1887 alone more than 120,000 tourists, health seekers, farmers, artisans, and businessmen.

These developments inaugurated southern California's first major land boom—"the most extravagant in American frontier experience"[2] —which sealed the coffin of the old California culture. Until the advent of the boom of the eighties, the embattled Californios were still fighting a desperate holding action in the south—forty years after the Mexican War, a generation removed from the gold rush, fifteen years beyond the Civil War and the great drought of the 1860's. Spanish conversation, adobe architecture, and traditional clothing, manners, and recreations had told the newest or most refractory gringo that, like it or

---

[1] Remi Nadeau, *The City Makers* (New York, 1948), p. 30.
[2] Blake McKelvey, *The Urbanization of America, 1860–1915* (New Brunswick, 1963), p. 28. This chapter relies considerably on Glenn S. Dumke, *The Boom of the 'Eighties in Southern California* (San Marino, Calif., 1944).

not, he was in "foreign" territory and could not completely brush the "natives" aside. To all this the boom put an effective end.

Between 1865 and 1890 the second generation of Californios came to maturity: those persons who were only vaguely aware of the Arcadian period and the revolutions and wars that had engrossed their parents, but acutely conscious of the consolidation of the new order. The well-being of this generation greatly depended on the amount of land it might inherit. In the north, where the original estates had been checkered with settlers, alienated from their owners, or greatly reduced in size, the transmission of a viable rancho holding from father to son was a rare event indeed. And yet in the south, islands of rancho land remained intact, at least until the 1870's. They were sometimes large and contiguous, creating the effect of a vast chain or archipelago of rangeland stretching from the Tehachapis to the Mexican border.

By 1875, however, the southern rancho islands had shrunk and had lost their common boundaries. Family farms increased noticeably in their midst, and rails were approaching them from the north with the promise of commercial and real estate developments that would interfere with rancho supremacy.

From 1865 to 1885, miscellaneous ills beset the southern rancheros. At Santa Barbara their vaqueros had to crash through fences to secure access to grazing land, in a struggle reminiscent of the nester-cattleman conflict on the Great Plains.[3] In the San Fernando Valley, a ferocious Basque squatter, Miguel Leonis, armed a hundred fellow countrymen and Mexicans at Calabasas and clung to land by brute force, staving off both Yankees and Californians with better claims than his.[4] At Stockton, Major José Pico was arrested for alleged land-sale fraud concerning property in Baja California.[5] But the most chronic and incurable ills still concerned finances—high mortgage interest, costly litigation, low beef prices, and out-of-state competition for stockmen—and were compounded by the high living expenses of the more aristocratic rancheros. The financial troubles were severe enough to ruin Yankees,

---

[3] Annie L. Morrison and John H. Haydon, *History of San Luis Obispo County and Environs* . . . (Los Angeles, 1917), pp. 81–85.

[4] Horace Bell, *On the Old West Coast: Being Further Reminiscences of a Ranger* (New York, 1930), p. 181 ff.

[5] San Jose *Pioneer and Historical Review*, Dec. 1, 1877.

too—men with lower expenses, more flexible social values, and a keener sense of business tactics than the Californios'. For example, Abel Stearns, the south's wealthiest landowner, whose personal empire had incorporated the defunct Bandini estate, in turn was unable to prevent creditors from eating up his property after the drought.[6]

Three examples drawn from Los Angeles County show the various economic patterns in the breakup of the ranchos. The most benign example of deterioration occurred at Rancho Camulos, in the mountains north of San Fernando Mission, near Newhall. Although in 1861 he left his plaza home and moved to Camulos with his family in order to cover his losses, Ygnacio del Valle had to whittle the property down from 48,000 acres to about 1,500. Furthermore, in 1879 he mortgaged Camulos to moneylender Newhall for $15,776. A gracious and charitable neighbor, Newhall never pressed the bill, which grew enormously each year. Ygnacio died in 1880 at the age of seventy-two, without having paid off the debt, and stipulated in his will that the place be divided among his six children at his wife's death. The early 1880's found the family still living in comfortable circumstances, at least superficially, and the rancho more or less intact, with young Reginaldo del Valle acting as overseer.[7]

Vicente Lugo's rancho property declined more precipitously than that of Don Ygnacio, and he ended up giving his sons much less of it. As a youth Vicente had once branded 48,000 head of cattle on his father's vast holdings, and as recently as 1850 he had owned a 2-league rancho fully stocked with cattle. After the drought, however, he found himself without a single steer, whereupon he leased some land to Yankee sheepmen and started over again modestly, with cows and chickens, saving his profits until he had recovered control of 800 acres around the old casa. Half of these acres he sold in 1869 and 1870 at $8 to $10 an acre; in addition, he gave 40 acres to his son Blas.[8]

Don Julio Verdugo's situation was the most disheartening of all.

[6] John C. Hough, "Abel Stearns, 1848–1871," unpublished MS, ed. by John Caughey, p. 450.

[7] Ruth Waldo Newhall, *The Newhall Ranch: The Story of the Newhall Land and Farming Company* (San Marino, Calif., 1958), p. 48.

[8] Unsigned letter to N. J. Stone, Dec. 18, 1888, in Bancroft, Reference Notes, spring binder, "Biography and Reference," No. 55532, MS, Bancroft Library (Berkeley, Calif.).

Feeling in a bullish mood in 1861, Don Julio decided to mortgage Rancho San Rafael (today's Glendale and part of Burbank) and use the money for sprucing up his casa, buying provisions, and paying taxes. He signed for a $3,445.37 loan at 3 percent monthly interest, which by 1870 had ballooned into a debt of $58,750 and ended in foreclosure, sheriff's sale, and ruination. At the public auction Verdugo's lawyers bought the 36,000-acre San Rafael for themselves, and under court restraint Verdugo also had to yield Rancho La Cañada to other gringos. In the settlement of other debts and taxes, Don Julio traded his remaining land for neighboring Rancho Los Feliz and began deeding 100 acres of it here and 200 acres there, until twenty or so gringo creditors and lawyers owned undivided slices of it. He was still not solvent when a court divided the 6,600-acre Los Feliz in 1871, leaving the former land baron with 200 acres, a gift from one Yankee purchaser who took pity on him. Verdugo thus deserved the penalty for the worst real estate deal of the decade, and his children inherited very little.

Even when the ranchos went into economic decline, the traditional rancho culture persisted stubbornly, in between mortgage payments, and afforded the children a glimpse of life in "antedeluvian" times. Even the miserably dry years did not completely preclude fiestas on the grand scale. When the rains returned, or when the owners received patents, took out new loans, or leased land to gringos and pocketed some cash, they had all the more reason to celebrate. In months when work was slack during the 1870's, the Pico, Arellanes, and Moraga families of the San Fernando Valley would entertain one another in round-robin fashion, feasting for a day and a night, going home for a rest, and ten days later showing up at the next casa for more of the same. Eugenio R. Plummer names at least sixty-eight families or branches of families which mingled at "fiestas large and small all over the county [of Los Angeles] and up Ventura and Santa Barbara way." Men, women, and children danced in traditional finery—rebozos, lace gowns, and slippers for women and straight-brimmed sombreros, ruffled shirts, velvet suits, and soft boots for men. Chaperons still protected the young people on social occasions and, in a sense, the adults too, for the women generally accompanied their men when they traveled to keep them out of mischief. To the bitter end the rancheros clung to their old ways; even when all talk centered on the coming of the railroad, Eugenio Plummer eschewed any means of Sunday driving faster than the careta.[9]

Rancho Camulos in particular, exuded a deceptive air of well-being in the 1880's, considering its financial condition. The del Valles' annual July Fourth fiesta, a four-day affair, brought together as many as seventy-five invited guests, each of whom was personally welcomed by Señora del Valle and conducted to a comfortable room. A servant summoned the guests to the first day's lunch, served at a shaded garden table with Ygnacio's eldest son, Reginaldo, presiding as host. The menu featured roast pig, pickled olives, chilis, claret and white wine, and black coffee. The afternoon enjoyments included riding, singing, reading, conversation, mountain climbing—whatever pleased the guests on a summer afternoon; watermelon and other refreshments were available on call. At seven the visitors reassembled for dinner at a table lighted by lanterns dangling from grape clusters; the main course was roast kid. Then followed an hour's stroll and return for more entertainment—piano, organ, and guitar music, singing, and fireworks. On Sunday morning the widow del Valle attended chapel with her Catholic guests; a Sabbath meal followed.[10]

This latter-day effort to retain the opulent form of the fiesta left a great deal to the imagination, however, since the grounds were filled predominantly with gringos. The cockfights, bull baiting, and horse races of former days were missing, as were the patriotic Mexican and French songs such as had enlivened the memorable San Pedro celebration of July 4, 1853. But the gringos generally enjoyed the festivities at Camulos, and at least one delighted guest was to immortalize the rancho as it then stood; Helen Hunt Jackson used Camulos as the setting for *Ramona,* published in 1883.

The post–Civil War Yankee immigrants who acquired the subdivided ranchos from the Verdugos, the Lugos, and the del Valles significantly altered the uses of the soil. For one thing, they introduced sheep in a big way, generally renting vacant rancho land for grazing

[9] John Preston Buschlen, *Señor* [Eugenio] *Plummer: The Life and Laughter of an Old Californian* (Los Angeles, 1942), pp. 84–87.
[10] Walter Lindley and J. P. Widney, *California of the South* (New York, 1896), pp. 205–206.

purposes and simultaneously managing the ranchero's own stock; some land they bought outright. While the sheep craze lasted, it helped the Californios recoup their cattle losses.

The Americans also promoted agriculture, particularly wheat farming. Rancheros irrevocably wedded to pastoral agriculture could scarcely comprehend, much less use, the new farm techniques and never got into the swim of things. When Antonio María Lugo first saw a mowing machine, he lifted a bony finger and exclaimed in Spanish: "The Yankee is but one finger shy of the devil!" [11] The rancheros' sons and grandsons, however, did wield the devil's instruments. José M. Ramirez experimented with wheat as early as 1872; Rómulo Pico raised a crop near former Mission San Fernando in 1880; and in the same year C. Castro of Santa Clara shipped to San Francisco 400 tons of hay which he had grown on his 250-acre farm. Two years later Señores Olivera, Machado, Higuera, and M. Coronel planted the grain near La Ballona. Truck gardening also increased among the Spanish-speaking.[12] At Los Nietos, east of Los Angeles, more than 120 men ran farms in 1880, including scores of men with Spanish surnames who called themselves "farmer," "small farmer," or "farm laborer," depending on whether they had sons as helpers, worked for a Yankee, or worked for themselves. Few of the 120 owned much land, and several rented parcels or sharecropped on plots of from 15 to 75 acres.[13]

Rancheros and vaqueros uprooted by the drought or by poor finances had to take work they would ordinarily disdain. Able-bodied gentry of the lower and middle ranks went on a sheep-shearing circuit in the 1870's. Fifty or sixty strong—with silver-trimmed bridles and stirrups, tooled leather saddles, broadcloth suits, ruffled shirts, dark sombreros—they rode from one sheep ranch to another looking for work. When hired, these original migratory laborers put away their finery and reappeared in brown overalls and red bandanas, ready for

---

[11] Henry D. Barrows, "Don Antonio María Lugo: A Picturesque Character of California," Historical Society of Southern California *Annual Publications,* III (1893–1896), 32.

[12] *El Demócrata* (Los Angeles), Oct., 1882; H. S. Foote, *Pen Pictures from the Garden of the World, or, Santa Clara County, California* (Chicago, 1888), pp. 350, 488–489; *La Crónica* (Los Angeles), May 25, 1872.

[13] United States Bureau of the Census, Tenth Census, 1880, Enumerator's Roll Book, Los Angeles County (microfilm).

action. They supplied their own bedding and meals and stayed for a month or so at each stop.

The conversion to sheep provided only seasonal labor, however, lasting three to eight months in the year, and it generally made the vaquero a supernumerary. Majordomo Juan Canedo of Rancho Los Cerritos, a dignified person who understood but never deigned to speak English, grew melancholy as the cattle died and the place changed hands and became a sheep pasture. Yet he claimed that he "belonged" to the property when Jonathan Bixby bought it, and refused to leave. To Bixby's daughter he "looked like a bronze statue, with brown face, brown clothes, brown horse and infinite repose." Bixby's son comforted Juan on his deathbed and supported Juan's widow —to repay the old man, as the boy said, for having taught him horsemanship.[14]

Apart from agricultural work, California's Spanish-speaking lower class performed only one other main semiskilled job, mining. "By far the larger portion of work-people in California mines are Mexicans," an expert observed in 1867.[15] Several hundred Mexican gold miners worked in Soledad Canyon in 1880. More important, until 1887 more than half of the world's mercury supply came from California, the greater proportion from the New Almadén Quicksilver Mine near Santa Clara. For this tedious and deadly work, employers rated the Mexicans "more adventurous than Cornishmen," who were generally reputed to be the world's best miners. Using techniques reminiscent of their ancestors three hundred years earlier, the 1,500 Mexicans at New Almadén clambered upward hundreds of feet, on groaning ladders, supporting 200-pound sacks of ore strapped to their foreheads and resting precariously on their backs. Above ground the smelters were often exposed to the fatal mercury fumes and died violently from it. Drinking, gambling, whoring, and murderous brawls erupted every payday, because, as one lady observer explained, New Almadén had "no advantages of church or school." A paternalistic management later organized a model company town, lining the streets with flowers and

[14] Sarah Bixby-Smith, *Adobe Days* . . . (Cedar Rapids, Iowa, 1926), pp. 113–114, 126–127.
[15] J. Ross Browne, "Down in the Cinnabar Mines: A Visit to New Almaden in 1865," *Harper's Magazine*, XXI (Oct., 1865), 549.

whitewashing the miners' cottages, until it became a sightseer's "must." [16] For some unaccountable reason, fashionably attired wedding parties came from San Jose to gape at the men emerging from the pit-head.

The Spanish-speaking did not readily gravitate into newer industries. The oil refinery at Newhall had not a single Mexican hand in 1880. By then, Chinese hands harvested the fruit crops and did other menial jobs the Spanish-speaking might have hired out for previously. Southern California's most important new employer, the Southern Pacific Railroad, used Chinese gangs to bore the mammoth tunnel through the mountains and into the San Fernando Valley in 1875. Only on the last leg of the construction, from the valley to Los Angeles, did Mexicans and Indians join the work gangs, but the hundred railroad hands permanently employed at the downtown switching yard, a stone's throw from Sonoratown, came mainly from the eastern United States, not from Mexico or California. [17]

For many Spanish-American youths, California represented a place that had robbed them of their birthright, but had meanwhile provided innumerable opportunities to steal back parts of it. In any event, many of the disaffected still turned badmen. From 16 to 20 percent of San Quentin inmates from 1854 to 1865 were Mexicans or Californians [18] —a high figure in view of the relative numerical decline of the Spanish-speaking, even when correcting for Yankee prejudice in law enforcement. Mexicans engaged in numerous and brutal individual crimes, but their forte was highway robbery, stage holdups, and rustling, activities in which they continued to surpass all other nationalities, even after the gold rush. As late as 1875 the most notorious characters in the state still wore sombreros.

Spanish surnames headed every sheriff's wanted list, as a new bumper crop of badmen emerged in the 1860's to replace the old ones who were either locked up or had been lynched or chased back into

[16] Carrie Stevens Walter, quoted in Eugene T. Sawyer, *History of Santa Clara County, California* . . . (Los Angeles, 1922), pp. 86–87.
[17] U.S. Bureau of the Census, *op. cit.*
[18] California State Prison Directors, "Annual Report," in California Legislature, *Journals of 1860 Assembly* (Sacramento, 1861), App. 13, pp. 18–19; *1865–1866 Senate and Assembly* (Sacramento, 1866), App., p. 66

Mexico. Many were immigrants, like the Mexican, Narciso Bojorques, for example, wanted for wiping out a family of three Yankees in 1863 and then hanging the family's vaquero and burning its cabin, and for killing one of his own confederates in a cattle-rustling operation. Bojorques narrowly escaped capture for years but finally died at the hands of an American badman. Jesús Tejada, also a Mexican, and Norrato Ponce, a Chilean, were sought for wanton murder and rustling, as was Tomasio Redundo, alias "Procopio" or "Murieta's Cousin," a horse thief, stage-holdup man, and San Quentin escapee.[19] Aside from the immigrants, a good many headliner criminals came from renowned local families and caused immeasurable grief to their more upstanding relatives. Among the native-born badmen were Reyes Duarte, Andrés and Agustín Castro, José and Nicolás Sepúlveda, Pedro Vallejo, Ramón Amador, and Chico Lugo, who never went straight after the Lugo incident of 1851 and was sent away to San Quentin, from which he eventually escaped. Others such as Tiburcio Vasquez and Juan Soto came from lesser clans. The press had two standard comments on the Californio badmen: either that they were besmirching illustrious families, or that they were following the footsteps of their evil fathers. Soto, with a huge frame, long black hair, dark complexion, thick black beard, heavy brows, and cross-eyes, had the reputation of the "most fearsome figure of an outlaw that ever roamed California hills." Mestizoid, ugly, and homicidal, he stood as low as was possible in the social hierarchy and cast fear even among the Spanish-speaking. Vasquez was equally dangerous but less gruesome and became the most famous hero-villain of his day.[20]

The operations of Spanish-American badmen still begat the familiar response of lynching. Sometimes an individual crime touched off a hanging, as when the aged José Claudio Alvitre murdered his wife and was lynched at El Monte in April, 1861,[21] the second person of that surname so executed in Los Angeles County. More often, it was the organized crime that provoked the vigilantes. One classic hanging epi-

[19] See, for example, San Francisco *Call*, May 14, 1882, and Charles Howard Shinn, *Graphic Description of Pacific Coast Outlaws* (Los Angeles, 1958), p. 57 ff.
[20] Joseph Henry Jackson, *Bad Company* (New York, 1949), *passim.*
[21] Harris Newmark, *Sixty Years in Southern California, 1853–1913* . . . (New York, 1916), p. 147.

sode began with the murder of John Rains, prominent rancher of San Bernardino in November, 1862, and the arrest of José Ramón Carrillo and Manuel Cerrada as suspects. A Los Angeles judge released the first for insufficient evidence and sentenced the second to ten years in San Quentin. Thereupon, the Los Angeles vigilantes came aboard the vessel bearing Manuel to jail, overpowered the sheriff, and hanged him from the yardarm. Two years later, a person or persons unknown ambushed and killed Carrillo.[22]

The renewed clashes between bandidos and vigilantes in the cow counties had most of the familiar old ingredients: unsolved murders, night riders, incendiary accusations against "evil Spaniards," moribund law courts, and recriminations from the Spanish Americans about prejudiced enforcers. The only factor lately missing was a mass meeting to dignify and sanctify the work of the vigilantes—now precluded by Civil War disunity in Los Angeles. The "struggle for law and order" resumed in the months following November, 1863, with the discovery of unexplained but seemingly interconnected murders in Los Angeles, Santa Barbara, and Las Cruces. A gang of Los Angeles thieves using a Las Cruces hideout seemed at fault in these crimes, and the vigilantes of El Monte, Los Angeles, Santa Barbara, and San Bernardino were determined to annihilate its members. The enforcers had no luck capturing the three Californians who had robbed and murdered a Los Angeles Yankee on January 5, 1864. When, however, the bodies of Mr. and Mrs. Corliss of Las Cruces were found on January 17, the vigilantes seized three Californios, Quatez, Ruiz, and Santiago Olvera, all in their twenties. Ruiz was "a short, yellow, half-Indian looking fellow, and has a hard name in the lower country." [23] Nonetheless, the Santa Barbara vigilantes could not pin the Corliss murder on the trio and let them off; the crime was later traced to a Mexican shepherd.

Meantime, desperado Jesús Arellanes was detained at San Pedro for a Santa Barbara murder committed months earlier. Jesús was a native of Santa Barbara, a four-time escapee from the law, and a killer of a fellow thief. Hearing of his capture, the still frustrated Los Angeles vigilantes went down to San Pedro and hanged him on February 18,

[22] Los Angeles *Star*, May 28, Aug. 20, 1864; Shinn, *op. cit.*, pp. 63–64.
[23] San Francisco *Bulletin*, Feb. 24, 1864. See also Monterey *Gazette*, Dec. 18, 1863.

before he could be sent to his home town. Unaware of this event, the Santa Barbara Californios, expecting Arellanes to disembark from a steamer when it dropped anchor in the channel, had conspired to rescue him from the town authorities. The news of Arellanes' death evoked a "very bitter state of feeling" among the "natives," who accused the Yankees of consistently executing "Spanish culprits, and letting off Americans." Eventually the bandidos, characterized as "half or quarter-Indian bloods of Mexico and California . . . the creatures and tools of the American gamblers and villains who have so long cursed the Southern mines and the cow counties," fled the country, presumably to "rob and eat up" the poor rancheros of Baja California.[24] Premonitions of trouble in Baja California came true in May, as a matter of fact, when a Yankee sheriff went there to find stolen cattle, tangled with bandido Andronico Sepúlveda, and was killed.[25]

Northern communities resembling Los Angeles and Santa Barbara in ethnic and economic makeup also had to endure the familiar "struggle for justice." One man who escaped the grasp of the Los Angeles vigilantes, the deranged neophyte Indian Gregorio Orosco, nevertheless ended up in a noose in Monterey in January, 1864. He had shot a white man without provocation—"thirsting, apparently for blood," according to one learned diagnosis. The Yankees of Monterey called for his life, but some Californios, "armed and excited, opposed the proposition to hang," and provoked a melee in which several persons were injured. This venture did Orosco little good, however, since the gringos felt convinced that he was one of the "incarnate devils who place themselves—morally—without the pale of law." Explained the Monterey *Gazette:* "We are not disposed to question the mode or manner of punishment, provided it be effectual." Thus, Orosco got the rope treatment, "without expense to the county." [26]

The next month vigilantes took prisoners in the murder of a Chileño at nearby Natividad, quickly fixed the blame on Patricino Lopez, and dispatched him. A year later "a party of citizens" seized bandidos Francisco Alviso and Juan Igera. The first escaped, but the second, "an

[24] San Francisco *Daily Alta California,* n.d., quoted in Bancroft, Reference Notes, spring binder no. 16, MS, Bancroft Library.
[25] Los Angeles *Star,* June 4, 11, 18, 1864.
[26] Jan. 8, 15, 1864.

abandoned wretch only twenty years of age but old in crime," did not. Juan's father had been lynched for murder a decade earlier, and Juan died accused of killing a Santa Clara deputy some months before his capture.[27]

Probably the last old-fashioned mob lynching in California of a person of Spanish-American background occurred in San Jose in 1877, when a pair of confessed murderers and robbers were snatched from the jail and strung from the Upper San Lorenzo Bridge.[28] As popular tribunals gave way to regular law enforcement, banditry in the old manner also declined; gold and livestock were now shipped more securely by railroad, and sheriffs' telegrams flashing up and down the state made a badman's escape more difficult.

A sheriff now could succeed without vigilante aid, particularly if, like Alameda Sheriff Harry Morse, archenemy of bandidos, he possessed perseverance to match their bravado. So closely did Morse hound bandidos that they took him for a demon. Between 1864 and 1874 he trailed Borjorques mercilessly (but never laid eyes on him); killed Norrate Ponce (although killing was not his specialty); captured Tejada; and simply strode up to Procopio in a San Francisco dance hall, laid a hand on the bandido's shoulder, calmly declared, "Procopio, you're my man," and took him to jail.[29] For sheer drama nothing surpassed his single-handed showdown with Juan Soto, whom he began tracking after the badman had robbed and killed a Suñol shopkeeper in January, 1871. With customary aplomb Morse hiked directly into Soto's mountain fastness south of Gilroy, masquerading as a weary and lost traveler. His disguise gained Morse easy entry into Soto's casa for "a rest." When the bandit and his crew discovered the ruse, they began shooting it out with the Sheriff. A Mexican amazon momentarily pinioned Morse's arms, but he broke her grip and got safely outside. Finally the wounded Soto burst from the shack, "bareheaded, his long black hair streaming behind him, a cocked revolver in each hand," and flying suicidally at Morse. At this, the sheriff raised his rifle and shot Soto in the head.[30]

[27] Ibid., May 19, 1865.
[28] Pioneer and Historical Review, May 5, 1877.
[29] Shinn, op. cit., p. 64.
[30] Jackson, op. cit., pp. 264–267.

Although brazenly admitting many evil deeds, the Spanish-speaking still claimed—and with good cause—that the guardians of Yankee justice discriminated against them. The native Californian Ramón Amador, imprisoned in 1871 for murdering an American, made this point to a newspaper reporter:

I have no show. There is no course at all for a poor man. They are down on Spaniards. There are hundreds of cold murderers, but they don't hang them. There was Bill Powers, he killed a man while they played cards. Look at that other man that killed a man and brought him in a wagon. He got off because he had thirty one thousand dollars. Now because I got no friends they going to hang me . . . by J—— C——! Others go to State Prison only, and are pardoned out. Now, sir, the first time they hang, they hang me. I seen other men, they do lots of murders; they rob, they burn the house down, and they would shoot men, not hang me. . . . Well, if the Bible is no more true than the newspapers I no believe it.

Ramón's self-pity—"I wish I was outside now; oh I wish I was outside. . . . I wish I kill him and they never find me"[31]—violated the heroic tradition of the badman, but his indictment of the judicial process would have brought hearty approval not only from his compatriots but also from many Yankees.

"It is almost a disgrace," a Yankee editor complained, "to hang a [poor] man for what rich men and women can escape from by the judicious use of money. The justice that is being administered in California law is a mockery." He was talking about Francisco García, tried in San Jose in 1872 for horse rustling, robbery, and murder committed in 1855, seventeen years earlier. At sixty years of age García naïvely thought it safe to return from Mexico to his native soil, only to find a zealous Los Angeles policeman waiting to haul him away to San Jose to stand trial for the misdeeds of his youth. There the prosecutor dredged up one of García's former confederates in crime who had meanwhile turned state's evidence. Guilty or innocent, the accused had evidently gone straight for seventeen years and lived an industrious life—so argued the editor. Besides, the trial of the "well connected" García would torment "a circle of relatives who are among the respected of Santa Clara," would probably result in acquittal and thus in needless expense to the county. The increasing professionalism of the law en-

[31] *Call*, Sept. 23, 1871.

forcers, therefore, did not automatically guarantee the Spanish-speaking criminals a better break; the case of García and others created in embryo the issue of "police brutality." [32]

After Juan Soto's death, only one important bandido remained at large—Tiburcio Vasquez, a Californio. A long and checkered career as cattle rustler, stage robber, and jailbird lay behind him when he engineered his final spree against the shopkeepers of Tres Pinos. A wanton killing aroused the authorities of several counties to weave a net around him. In a scenario-like episode appropriately played out near present-day Hollywood, a brigade of sheriffs and deputies tightened the net and caught Vasquez. Bound in irons, he seemed at close range as vicious and gallant as the Yankees had expected. When asked for the motives for his crimes, he recalled a boyhood scene in which he bade his mother good-bye and set out to avenge Yankee injustice—a touching and believable explanation, but altogether irrelevant to the judge and the jury that had him executed.[33] Bandido depredations soon subsided in California, partly as a function of Mexico's subsiding political turmoil. The archetypal California badman of the 1880's, Black Bart, wore a dark bowler instead of a sombrero.

Bandido Vasquez personified a major motif among the Spanish Americans in California—alienation of the second generation. Nevertheless, a good many of his contemporaries responded altogether differently to recent events by picking themselves up, resettling in the towns, and making a new life for themselves. In the town environment, the younger generation came in contact with new cultural influences and adjusted accordingly. Submergence of the Spanish-speaking thus entailed various possibilities: for some, an irrational armed resistance through crime; for a few, assimilation into the mainstream of Yankee culture; and for still others, assimilation into the Mexican community.

In the rural hamlets of Los Angeles County, a quarter of the inhabitants had Spanish surnames as late as 1880. Of course, in some townships Yankees reigned supreme. At Pasadena not one of the 392 occupants was Spanish American (the Chinese did all the menial labor); at

[32] Redwood City *Gazette*, Oct. 27, 1872.
[33] Ernest May, "Tiburcio Vasquez," Historical Society of Southern California *Quarterly*, XXIX (1947), 123–134.

Santa Ana only 4 of the 714 were Spanish-speaking; and at the beach suburb of Santa Monica, 7 of the 418. Elsewhere, on the other hand, Spanish Americans clustered so thickly as to alienate gringos. New Mexicans were still entrenched at isolated, self-contained, culturally preserved San Jose township. Also, near former mission San Juan Capistrano, there were 345 Spanish-speaking residents, as indigenous as the famous sparrows, born in California of California parents (some perhaps of neophyte Indian background); the remaining 31 residents were Europeans.

Most communities in Los Angeles County in 1880 came nearer the average of 25 percent Spanish-speaking. At the Texas stronghold of El Monte lived about 390 persons with Spanish surnames among a total of 1,300 residents; the new railroad town of San Fernando had about 460 of a total of 1,120, and kept nearly that ratio in the twentieth century. At the sheep ranches and farms of La Ballona (now Culver City), about 660 of 2,075 had Spanish surnames; at Azusa, 165 of 640; in the predominantly German community of Anaheim, 180 of 1,440; around Soledad, 200 of 350 miners and farmers hailed from California and Mexico.[34]

Within the confines of the town of Los Angeles, Spanish-American influence also proved durable. Spectators of the centennial parade of September 5, 1881, marveled at a careta bearing the sole surviving "founding fathers," two neophyte Indian women aged 102 and 117 years, respectively, both older than the town itself—a tribute to the hardiness of the stock. The view from Fort Hill still revealed the wide use of adobe brick, the prevalance of businesses dealing in pastoral goods such as wool and hides. The old vineyards still flourished within city limits, east of Main Street, from Macy Street south, near the tracks. An occasional careta creaked by; somewhere a vendor shouted, "Tamales, calientes, aguí!"[35] The total population in the town reached 10,000 in 1870 and surpassed 11,000 in 1880, of which the largest minority, 21 percent, had Spanish surnames.

Of course, on the newer Los Angeles streets stretching away to the

[34] U.S. Bureau of the Census, *op. cit.*
[35] Edwin Baxter, "Leaves from the History of the Last Decade—1880–90," Historical Society of Southern California *Annual Publications,* III (1893–1896), 74–79.

west the faces and the homes looked Anglo-Saxon for blocks on end. Only the middle-class Spanish Americans could afford to live there: the Spanish physician Fernandez, a Mexican jeweler, a store clerk (living in his employer's shop), attorney Estudillo, farmer Joaquín Sepúlveda, a harness-maker, *La Crónica* editor de Celis, livery operator Covarrubias, and the Californio women married to Yankees. All these Spanish Americans could maintain their children at boarding school and employ domestic servants (Sonorans, never Chinese). In the midst of three or four hundred residents on fashionable Main Street lived only a handful of Spanish Americans. On the more mixed streets, amid French, German, Chinese, Irish, Bohemian, and Yankee immigrants, dwelled the Spanish Americans of more modest circumstances. On such a street lived the forty-one-year-old widow Ignacia Alvarado with her five children, ranging in age from twelve to twenty years and supported by her earnings as a seamstress and by those of her eldest boys who were barbers. Judge Ygnacio Sepúlveda (living alone and boarding several Germans) and Pio Pico lived nearby.[36]

When a hamlet acquires a railroad, cheap labor, and slums, it is well launched toward cityhood. These requisites for maturity Los Angeles had attained by 1876. Nigger Alley, north of the plaza, had undergone the most striking change since epidemic smallpox had killed off so many Spanish Americans a decade earlier; excepting some French traders, every inhabitant was Chinese. This area was one of two slums. As the town updated itself, the neighborhood east and south of the plaza, as far east as the river and as far south as the railroad, remained a Mexican village and thus, by comparison, a slum. There the shops, saloons, brothels, and gambling dens crowded one another in overwhelming disarray. "Sonoratown" provided all the amusements, comforts, and vices of a ghetto except work, which lay in the better parts of town. The underworld of all nationalities gravitated to Sonoratown, and axe murders, shootings, beatings, and knifings commonly occurred there. Should the police seek an out-of-town villain, they knew where to look, perhaps at Francisco Carmona's disorderly house on Buena Vista Street. Gringo citizens once tried to close the place, but a judge dismissed their case as legally weak although morally sound.[37] Sud-

[36] U.S. Bureau of the Census, *op. cit.*
[37] Los Angeles *Times*, March 6, 10, 25, 1883. See also W. W. Robinson, *Los Angeles, from the Days of the Pueblo* . . . (San Francisco, 1959), pp. 63–64.

denly, about the time of the boom, Sonoratown became Chinatown and the Spanish-speaking went to live in other neighborhoods.

The Spanish-American town dwellers made a living chiefly as laborers, but also as farmers, broom makers, barbers, gamblers, butchers, *zanjeros*, miners, and shepherds. Women, too, worked. Those from better families often had had girlhood training in sewing and thus became seamstresses; others became domestics; and some, prostitutes. Brothels sprang up even outside Sonoratown, as at the docks at Wilmington, where the Mexican-born Señora Paredez lived with two children and three women of Baja California and California; the census taker jotted her down as "Keeping House," and as an afterthought wryly added "of Ill Fame." [38] Indeed, the Spanish-speaking worked at anything to bring in "poco dinero"; they rated higher wages than the Chinese but lower than the Anglos.

The relative impersonality of town life was partly offset by the enveloping warmth of the family. The older the family and the longer its stay in California, the larger it was apt to be; small households denoted recent arrivals, sometimes of single Mexican men living in boarding houses. Californio families ran large in both town and country. Fifty-four-year-old Joaquín Sepúlveda and his wife had nine children, ranging in age from twenty to five years. Tomás Palomares, also in his fifties, lived at suburban San Jose township with his wife and ten children, the eldest twenty-two years and the youngest six months. Dwellings tended to be overcrowded with aged parents, grown and infant children, grandchildren, in-laws, nieces and nephews, boarders, and adopted orphans—all living under one roof, or next door, or down the street. Fifteen Reyeses stuck close together in two Main Street homes. In the household of Mr. and Mrs. Mott and their five children (a branch of the Sepúlveda family), eleven people lived under one roof, including Mrs. Mott's septuagenarian mother, a California-born servant, two sisters-in-law, and Mott's sister.

Since private casas managed somehow to sustain the orphaned or infirm, few of the Spanish-speaking enrolled at charity institutions. The Sisters of Charity had twenty-nine nuns to serve the community in an orphanage and hospital; yet in 1880 only fourteen of their seventy-six steady wards and only two hospital patients of a total of fifty-four had

[38] U.S. Bureau of the Census, *op. cit.*

Spanish surnames.[39] Although familial warmth obviously had its satis-
fying aspects for a sick person; the universal practice of home nursing
cost lives in time of epidemic, until doctors prevailed on the Spanish-
speaking to isolate victims of disease at a makeshift hospital in Chavez
Ravine, called the "Pest house." [40]

As Californio influence waned in Los Angeles, immigrant Mexicans
assured the continuance of Spanish-American culture, which therefore
never died. In San Francisco and other northern localities the Mexican
community evolved independently of the native-born, but in Los Angeles it merged gradually and imperceptibly with them. The number of
Mexicans slowly increased until they were ready to overtake the Californios, probably by the turn of the century. The Mexican community,
moreover, attained a sense of respectability it formerly had lacked. As
the memories of Manifest Destiny waned, Yankees thought better of
Mexico and, at least for the record, had some good words for the sister
republic—perhaps that it was finally "waking up" and "uniting with
our country [in] the spread of civilization in the West." [41] Respectable
Mexican patriotic organizations formed, disbanded, and re-formed,
such as the Hispano-Americano Society of Los Angeles, dedicated to
combating the "decadent" state of the community, the Mexican Progressive Society; the Juarez Patriotic Society (with a branch in San
Juan Capistrano in 1872); and Botello's Cavalry and the Mexican
Lancers, which appeared on festive occasions.[42]

Mexican nationalism provided an ideological solvent for the entire
community. Commemorations of Mexican independence during the
1880's grew increasingly elaborate in scope and spirit until the floats
and pretty girls, the ringing speeches, the band music, and the tramp-
ing feet rivaled the displays on July Fourth. Californians, Yankees, and
Mexicans usually teamed up to organize them. The independence festivities of 1883 illustrate the extent of organization and planning. The
town's mounted police led the parade, followed by Grand Marshal
Eulogio F. de Celis and his aides, then J. D. and Alacala Machado, and

---

[39] *Loc. cit.*

[40] Boyle Workman, *The City That Grew* [Los Angeles] . . . (Los Angeles,
1935) p. 239.

[41] Los Angeles *Times*, Sept. 18, 1883.

[42] Broadside in Coronel Collection, items 1563, 1568F, PC9, Los Angeles County
Museum; *La Crónica* (Los Angeles), June 10, Nov. 2, 1872; Aug. 23, 1873.

Chief of Staff Bernardo Yorba and his aides. Next came a marching band. The president of the Juarez Society was flanked by flag bearers and followed by a carriage bearing Senator Reginaldo del Valle, poet Gregorio Gonzales, and speakers F. H. Howard and J. M. Obando. The Mexican Progressive Society preceded the triumphal car displaying three señoritas bedecked as "America," "Liberty," and "Justice." Judge Sepúlveda had a car to himself. Then came a float of cheerfully waving maidens representing Mexico's twenty-seven states and territories; and finally another carriage conveying the mayor and the French consul. The Vigilance Hook and Ladder Company turned out in full; a float representing "Progress" followed; then Botello's Cavalry and the Mexican Lancers; and, finally, ordinary citizens marching or riding. The celebrants started too late to reach the "American part of town" but wandered through the old town and halted to hear the Mexican national anthem, poet Gonzales' ode, and spontaneous comments from the crowd.[43]

Newspapers tried to serve the new and enlarged Hispanic community. *La Unión* succeeded *La Voz de Méjico* in San Francisco in 1873; *La Crónica* in 1872 took over in Los Angeles the role vacated by *El Clamor Público;* and for each election campaign, the Los Angeles *Times* and the San Francisco *Herald* printed ephemeral Spanish-language sheets to galvanize the Spanish vote. In Monterey, the Mexican editor José Arzaga teamed up with J. M. Soto in establishing the bilingual *New Republic Journal,* which ran only seventeen issues (June to August, 1872) and then had to cease publication for lack of readership.[44] These examples of journalistic demise again indicate the persistence of illiteracy and indifference to contemporary affairs among the Spanish-speaking.

As part of the old-line community blended imperceptibly with the Mexicans, however, another merged into the dominant gringo culture. Thus, in a sense, the Californios were ground down between the upper and nether millstones of two immigrant groups.

The old upper class, particularly the Californios of Caucasian origin, continued to mingle with the new. After Abel Stearns died his widow,

---

[43] Los Angeles *Times,* Sept. 15, 16, 17, 1882. For later celebrations, see also in *ibid.,* Sept. 17, 18, 1883; Sept. 16, 17, 1885.
[44] *La Crónica* (Los Angeles), Aug. 31, 1872.

Arcadia (Bandini), married the prosperous Rhode Islander, Robert S. Baker; James Winston, M.D., wed Arcadia's sister Margarita; jailer James Thompson of Kentucky married Francisca Sepúlveda; and Henry V. Lindsey married Judge Sepúlveda's daughter in Mexico in 1890.

Marriages between Yankee men and mestizo women, although rare, did occur. For example, George Carson married Victoria Dominguez in 1857 and in 1864 moved to her father-in-law's rancho to manage the old man's tangled affairs. More commonly in this generation than in earlier ones, a Californio male might take a gringo bride, as when Ramón Sepúlveda married a girl of Irish background and Blas Lugo married Sophie Charles in 1885.[45] Two of Mariano Vallejo's daughters married Yankees, the Frisbie brothers, and his son Platón returned from a New York medical school with a bride born in Syracuse. For fifty-five years Dr. Vallejo practiced near Sonoma and acquired the storybook reputation of a physician who healed but never rendered bills.[46] These and many other second-generation Californios made the grade in Yankee society, for their faces peer out stolidly from the fashionable "mug books" of the 1870's, the status symbols of the Gilded Age.

Contrary to expectation, old and young Californios alike tried their hand at business and the professions. Jeronimo Lopez and his wife, former students of Mexican teacher Ygnacio Coronel, opened a boarding school in the San Fernando Valley which existed for thirty years, and simultaneously ran an inn at "Lopez Station," to catch the north–south traffic in the valley. On the east–west valley route, the Osos of Encino also converted their casa into an inn. Andrés Pico promoted a scheme to build a road from San Fernando Pass to Los Angeles. The grocery of Juan J. Carrillo was a familiar landmark in the Los Angeles of the 1870's. Emile Ortega opened a chili-packing plant in town in 1898. In 1873 Miguel de Pedrorena, José G. Estudillo, and Chico Foster of San Diego pooled their resources to exploit a gravel vein. Blas Lugo tried his hand at law and business but, failing at both, eventually turned to farming 70 acres given him by his father.[47] As ranchos became towns,

---

[45] Unsigned letter to N. J. Stone, Dec. 18, 1888, op. cit.
[46] Gertrude Atherton, Golden Gate Country (New York, 1945), pp. 117–118.
[47] Daughters of the American Revolution, The Valley of San Fernando (n.p., 1924), p. 39; Los Angeles Star, Jan. 29, 1859; La Crónica (Los Angeles), May 4, 1872; Aug. 20, 1873; H. Newmark, op. cit., p. 87.

some of the young gentry found themselves in the realty business. Two
Sepúlveda brothers owned 4,000 acres of the most salable San Pedro
land, worth $500 to $2,000 an acre. They successfully resisted encroach-
ing monopolists who wanted to purchase it and thus control access to
the town. In 1887 Ramón Sepúlveda sold $75,000 worth of land, re-
paired the roads and built a reservoir, and moved into the finest residence in San Pedro. Among his accomplishments was becoming Master
Workman in the I.O.U.W. and Select King of the A.O.W.[48]

If in olden days the dominant Mexican culture had transformed
some Yankees into "Mexicanized gringos," now the new culture created
a class of "gringoized Mexicans." This did not, however, represent a
true blending of two cultures, but rather a triumph of the most aggressive and a defeat of the most recessive cultural characteristics. The socially prominent del Valle family of Los Angeles aspired toward, and
in most respects attained, the status of the new "better classes." For all
their old-fashioned fiestas at Camulos, their values looked to the
present. Their personal mementos give this impression unmistakably.
The family photograph album captures handsome dark faces, racially
indistinguishable from most Anglo-Saxon ones. The album also con-
tains the ordinary minutiae of the Gilded Age—society column notices,
dance invitations, travel brochures, pressed flowers, flowered station-
ery, wedding and funeral notices, calling cards, school graduation
programs, and illustrations of home furnishings and women's fashions.
Except that many of the items relate to church or parochial-school
functions, one can find scarcely any attributes of the older culture.[49]

Of all the battlefields on which the Spanish Americans fought a holding action to preserve their influence, they succeeded best on the political one. A prestigious Spanish surname (especially when combined
with a Caucasian face) remained a good entreé into public office, and
many Spanish Americans used it successfully. Estevan Castro became a
Monterey constable and later an assemblyman, although Don José
Castro's other sons remained "without social standing"; Martin Aguirre
became Los Angeles sheriff in 1885; Andrés Pico's son Ramón ran for
state treasurer in 1875 (but lost); Andronico Sepúlveda served as Los
Angeles county treasurer in 1873; Andrés Castillero sat in Congress in

[48] Ramón D. Sepúlveda, "Dictation," MS, Bancroft Library
[49] Del Valle Collection, Los Angeles County Museum.

1880; José G. Estudillo was state treasurer from 1875 to 1880; Santa Barbara's Angel G. Escandon served in the legislature from 1869 to 1874; and, following in the footsteps of his father, Manuel Coronel entered politics and served one term in the state legislature.[50]

Of all Spanish-speaking Californians, Romualdo Pacheco accomplished the most brilliant and unusual political stroke, by seating himself in the governor's chair. Born the son of a Santa Barbara army officer in 1831, young Romualdo received a superior Yankee schooling in the Sandwich Islands and came back with a head for figures; then he hired out as a supercargo on various trading vessels plying the California coast. After the Mexican War he managed his mother's rancho in San Luis Obispo and at the age of twenty-two (1853) won an assembly seat. He became state senator as a Democrat in 1858, and as a Union Democrat in 1862. After a stint in the Union Army in 1863, he changed party affiliation and gained election as Republican state treasurer, serving four years (and yielding that post to his kinsman, Ramón Pacheco). Except for Unionism, no particular political views clung to Romualdo's name, but his background made good press notices—he was an aristocratic native son, a ranchero, a bear fighter, a vigilante, a soldier, a sometime stockbroker, and the husband of an Anglo-Saxon woman. His popularity, the modest importance of the "Spanish" vote, and a desire to balance the ticket between two rival factions encouraged the Republican Party to nominate him for lieutenant governor in 1871. He came in during the Republican sweep of that year, serving routinely until 1875. In February, Governor Booth took an interim seat in the United States Senate and handed Pacheco the governorship for the balance of that year. Pacheco was little more than a figurehead in a caretaker government, but even so it gave the Spanish-speaking particular satisfaction to see their man in so exalted a position. The party managers thought better of renominating Pacheco, however, and upon leaving office he turned to selling stocks in San Francisco. Meanwhile, from 1878 to 1882, he served two terms in Washington as Santa Clara's congressman, and spent some of his declining years in Mexico and Texas.[51]

---

[50] *La Crónica* (Los Angeles), March 12, 1873; *El Demócrata* (Los Angeles), Nov. 1, 1882.

[51] Hubert Howe Bancroft, "Pioneer Register and Index," in *History of California* (San Francisco, 1886), IV, 764.

That the Republican Party allowed Pacheco to go as far as he did, but no farther, suggests that they had respect for, but not an abject fear of, the "Spanish vote." A Castroville newspaper argued in 1871 for putting a Californian on every slate, since the Californios are "as ever alert, vigilant, powerful," and the party ignoring them would court "inevitable disaster and overthrow." This defensive compliment greatly overstated the case, except when applied selectively, as in Los Angeles where 22 percent of the registered voters in 1873 were Californians and Mexicans, in a total of more than 5,600 registrants. They helped elect Cristóbal Aguilar mayor in 1872 and helped reelect Ygnacio Sepúlveda county judge. Also, they implanted two Spanish-speaking members on the Common Council (which had nine seats), three on the city Democratic Committee, and four on the delegation to the state Democratic convention—much as they had done decades earlier. At the 1873 election, Aguilar's opponent attacked his faulty English and defeated him, 715 to 358. The gringo mayor succeeded in blocking an ordinance to restore the bilingual printing of laws—also a familiar story.[52]

The current crop of native-born politicos consisted of Aguilar, Sepúlveda, Antonio Coronel, Prudencio Yorba, F. Palomares, E. Pollorena, E. F. de Celis, J. Valdez, M. Requeña, representatives of both the new and the old generations. Ignacio Sepúlveda in particular had remarkable staying power. Born in Los Angeles in 1842, educated in Eastern schools, and admitted to the bar in 1863, he was elected assemblyman in 1864, then stepped from the position of county judge (1870 to 1873) to district judge (1874 to 1879), and, finally, to superior judge (1879 to 1884). After fourteen years on the bench he resigned and went to live in Mexico City with his children, serving as Wells Fargo agent and United States chargé d'affaires. Thirty years of exile did not altogether estrange him from California, for upon his return to Los Angeles friends greeted him warmly.[53]

Since the political decline of Andrés Pico and Tomás Sanchez, the "man to see" in the Los Angeles community was Antonio Coronel. Here was one Californio (technically, a Mexican-American) who adapted to the new environment so well as to defy every generalization about the decline of the Spanish Americans. By some ingenious means he had

[52] *La Crónica* (Los Angeles), May 11, June 8, Oct. 19, Nov. 30, 1872; June 14, 21, 28, Aug. 23, Sept. 3, 1873.
[53] Bancroft, *op. cit.*, V, 716.

escaped the economic consequences of the drought, so that his solvent real estate, moneylending, and grape-growing activities could finance his other interests. Antonio's solvency encouraged the Democratic state organization to assess him $500 in 1867 and $750 in 1871; in 1874 Francisco Arguëllo touched him for $12 to pay a doctor's bill; in 1875 José Sepúlveda asked him for $25; in 1887 the Mexican consul requested a donation for a monument to Juárez in Mexico; and in 1881 a biographical publisher solicited $250 for a spread in Antonio's honor. Antonio served four terms on the Los Angeles Common Council during the Civil War and became state treasurer in 1867. This position made him a patronage boss, but the language difficulties involved prevented his running for a second term.[54]

Antonio Coronel himself never sought any political office, leaving that activity to younger men trained in English. But he did make speeches, donate money, and offer advice on the "native vote"; even the German-Americans came to him for help in organizing their minority. He served innumerable civic causes, as a railroad booster (together with Andrés Pico, F. Machado, and Tomás Sanchez), as director of the Spanish-American Mutual Benefit Society (1879), and as advisor to the Los Angeles Centennial Committee (1881). In 1873 he bought into the weekly La Crónica and remained active in its affairs until 1877. At the September Sixteenth celebration of 1880, the Juarez Society featured him as speaker. He served two terms on a state horticulture board, from 1883 to 1885, and on a water commission, fighting the cause of the right of appropriation in water rights against established riparian law. Helen Hunt Jackson sought him out on Indian lore, and he became one of her best informants on the Indian problem. One of his last public appearances was at the California Admission Day festivities in 1890.[55]

Reginaldo del Valle succeeded to Coronel's chair as "boss" of the "Spanish vote." Born in 1854 and thus even more strictly an American than Pacheco, Sepúlveda, or Coronel, "The Little One," as he was called, studied law and passed the bar in 1877. The voters made him

[54] See, for example, José Sepúlveda to Coronel, Oct., 1875; Francisco Arguëllo to Coronel, Dec. 5, 1874; Mexican Consul to Coronel, Jan. 1, 1887, MSS, Coronel Collection, Los Angeles County Museum.
[55] Coronel Collection, passim; Bancroft, op. cit., II, 768.

assemblyman in 1880 (he was president of the house in 1881) and state senator in 1882.[56] Although he failed at reelection in the state, he ran for Congress as a Cleveland Democrat against a Yankee in 1884. Few could match del Valle's ability to arouse a crowd in the Spanish precincts, and his freewheeling style of speaking prompted the opposition newspaper, La Crónica, to charge him with ungentlemanly conduct. The pro-Republican Los Angeles Times accused him of un-Americanism, not for supporting Mexico, but for boosting "free trade and other English ideas." The Times tweaked his nose by observing that he dressed his "guards" like Redcoats.[57] Since del Valle (and R. Sepúlveda, running for county auditor) carried only the Spanish-American precincts, a Democratic stronghold, he lost. The most important political role he could later find consisted of the chairmanship of the 1888 state Democratic convention. Still, he shared with Coronel the honorary leadership of the Spanish-speaking community and served on countless government boards and civic committees until his death in 1938.

The Spanish-speaking leaders staved off complete annihilation for a remarkably long time, considering their early economic and numerical losses. Perhaps they could have accomplished more had they not isolated themselves from their own people as they entered "society" and abandoned their traditional ways. Perhaps, too, the ethos of the Gilded Age, which resisted social reform and encouraged political cynicism, prevented them from coping with the real social ills that beset the Spanish Americans. The greatest problem of the Spanish-speaking stemmed, however, from their loss of numbers, for which none of their leaders could provide a remedy. Although about 12,000 strong in Los Angeles by 1887, the Spanish-speaking constituted less than 10 percent of the total population, and too many of them were newcomers —ignorant, indifferent, or hostile to Yankee politics.

More or less suddenly, in the 1880's the Californians' political holding action ceased. When Ignacio Sepúlveda retired from the bench, Romualdo Pacheco from Congress, and Antonio Coronel and Regi-

---

[56] Marco ·R. Newmark, Jottings in Southern California History (Los Angeles, 1955), pp. 75–76.

[57] Nov. 2, 1884. See also in ibid., Oct. 31, Nov. 1, 4, 6, 8, 1884; Los Angeles Democrat, Aug. 16, 23, Sept. 13, Oct. 4, 1884.

naldo del Valle from active local politics, gringos replaced them. No younger brothers or sons duplicated the old Californios' prestige. The native-born leaders were left holding honorary chairmanships in this or that committee, but little else, and their community went leaderless.

In 1885 Los Angeles awaited the railroad spike-driving ceremony at Cajon Pass, promised for November, which would greatly promote the direct rail linkup with the East. The completion on September 16 of an intermediary rail hookup with Pasadena created only minor excitement; yet, because it coincided with Mexican Independence Day, it had symbolic meaning and called for a speech by a Spanish-American orator.[58] Not a Mexican, however, but Reginaldo del Valle, was given the honor. In his own and his father's time, the San Gabriel Valley had burgeoned from an Indian hunting ground to a mission pasturage, then to a rancho empire, and was now sprouting farms, orchards, and towns. It turned out to be a notable September Sixteenth, although symbolically confusing; a Californian born in the American period paid tribute to Mexican liberty by speaking in English to a gringo crowd about Yankee progress. As expected, "The Little One" peppered his remarks with humorous anecdotes of the past thirty years, but the unfunny fact was that the same railroad he was commemorating would soon obliterate practically everything connected with the pastoral era, even his own political career.

The boom of the eighties contributed vastly to the ongoing process of "Americanization." The sheer volume of immigration brought to southern California the very transformations the northerners had witnessed a generation earlier. In two years or so the population of Los Angeles jumped 500 percent, automatically transforming the electorate into an Anglo-American one. The mores changed equally radically. The type of consumer goods advertised for sale, the tastes in food and dress, the prevalence of English over Spanish in daily and official conversation, the Gilded Age recreations, and the style of commerce—all changed rapidly and irreversibly. While describing the changing ethos of real estate promotion and commerce, Professor Glenn S. Dumke notes that "from 1888 onward, the southern counties were imbued with Anglo-American aggressiveness." [59] What started out as a "semi-

[58] Los Angeles *Times*, Sept. 17, 1885.
[59] *Op. cit.*, p. 226.

gringo" town and a cultural backwash became practically overnight a booming Yankee commercial center and the best-known place in the entire West.

From the vantage point of the Californios, the most elemental change lay in the chopping up of the ranchos into farms and towns, a process long under way but now dramatically speeded up. Although the economic boom converged on the city of Los Angeles, the chief activity concerned the rancho-blanketed suburbs. In 1887 Los Angeles real estate men and buyers daily engaged in thirty to seventy transactions and exchanged as much as $100,000. The evolution of the ranchos involved a variety of legal and business transformations, all of them well tested in California in previous years. Among the most common were forfeiture of loans, conveyance of mortgages to new owners, tax delinquency, family litigation, legitimate sales, division of undivided interest by court order, and bankruptcy proceedings or sheriff's sales. No set pattern emerges in these transformations, but the eroded claims of the original claimants washed away steadily and flowed into the hands of the newcomers—financiers, railroad developers, town promoters, cooperative colonizers, and irrigation companies.

Some of the larger southern California ranchos, it is true, seemingly impervious to the usual ravages of death and taxes, acquired a kind of immortality of their own. The Irvine Ranch and Dominguez Estates are two venerable properties whose twentieth-century boundaries correspond closely to those of the original Spanish and Mexican grants. More than 24,000 acres remained with Don Manuel Dominguez at his death in 1882, and his will divided them up among his six daughters in 1885.[60] In turn, Dominguez' grandchildren also kept a good hold on their property and were able to lease and develop the estates without selling outright. These durable properties have, however, changed internally with the times. Recent aerial photographs show the sprawling Dominguez properties dotted with oil fields, airports, factories, freeways, shopping centers, and suburban homes, as the city now totally surrounds the rancho that once was set apart by 20 miles of open range. The Yankee-owned Irvine Ranch was operated as a cattle ranch

[60] Robert Cameron Gillingham, *The Rancho San Pedro* (Los Angeles, 1961), p. 271. See also Robert Glass Cleland, *The Irvine Ranch of Orange County, 1810–1950* (San Marino, Calif., 1952), pp. 148–150.

until a decade ago and is only now slowly being urbanized, through carefully controlled regional planning.

More than a hundred towns and thousands of orchards and farms were platted out in southern California before the boom of the eighties collapsed in 1888. But even those evanescent communities, which disappeared as quickly as they arose, had gone through financial and legal gyrations which permanently disrupted the legal basis of most ranchos, much as the drought of the sixties had disrupted the way of life and the economy of those same estates.

XVI

Schizoid Heritage

WHEN Benjamin Hayes reflected that the Lugo family of southern California had possessed $150,000 in 1852 but had practically no wealth by 1865, he concluded that "the finger of Providence seems to mark the decay of the old Californian families." Why God's wrath? "We must not judge," Hayes answered. "But the Indians have suffered great crimes and injustices from the later Mexican governors and people."[1] In explaining the fall of the Californians, Hayes thus supplied the "unrequited toil" theory which Abraham Lincoln suggested in his second inaugural as an explanation of the Civil War. Since by Hayes's own reckoning the Yankees, too, should have felt the Lord's wrath for abusing Indians, the theory sounds smug and lacking in substance. Yet the question of the fall was a good one and perplexed both contemporary and later students of the California scene.

In Hayes's time the Yankee still felt sufficiently free of guilt to regard the Californians' defeat as self-inflicted. The oldest and perhaps most highly respected Yankee pioneer in the state, Alfred Robinson, in a late postscript to his famous *Life in California*, described the downfall as inevitable and regrettable, but as altogether the product of the Californios passivity. His argument supposes a belief in the idea of progress:

The early Californians, having lived a life of indolence without any aspiration beyond the immediate requirement of the day, naturally fell behind their more energetic successors, and became impoverished and gradually dispossessed of their fortunes as they idly stood by, lookers-on upon the bustle and enterprise of the new world before them, with its go-aheadativeness and push-on keep-moving celebrity.[2]

[1] Benjamin D. Hayes, *Pioneer Notes . . . 1849–1875*, ed. by Marjorie Tisdale Wolcott (Los Angeles, 1929), p. 280.
[2] *Life in California during a Residence of Several Years in That Territory . . .* (San Francisco, 1891), p. 254.

277

These words by Robinson, and also those of Hayes, are faintly colored by remorse, but not by guilt or romance; these came later.

The Californians also spoke of a mysterious Providence guiding their lives, but they added a human factor—the malevolence of gringos and Mexicans. Themselves they rarely blamed, except for tactical errors such as a failure to break completely with Mexico when it lay within their grasp to do so in the 1840's, which would have enabled them to appear before their Yankee conquerors as their own masters and to demand genuine Yankee guarantees of ownership of their ranchos. That the conqueror "seeks his own good fortune, not ours," Mariano Vallejo considered "very natural in individuals, but I denounce it on the part of a government [the United States] that promised to respect our rights and to treat us as its own sons."[3] The Californios perceived themselves not merely as the victims of annexation or assimilation, but of deliberate betrayal and bone-crushing repression. By dint of strenuous effort, a few of them had managed to retain enough of their birthright to hand it on to their heirs; but few had held property as confidently as the conqueror had promised. Of the forty-five Californios representing the twenty-five families whom Thomas Oliver Larkin had enumerated in 1846 as the "principal men" of the old régime, the vast majority went to their graves embittered. Indeed, the gentry had experienced what might be called California's only true social revolution: they were a ruling class militarily conquered, bereft of national sovereignty and a constitutional framework, and alienated from their land, homes, civil rights, and honor. They had retained little else besides their religion and a thin residue of honorary political influence.

As to progress in their lives, most professed seeing little of it. With a unique mental genuflection to progress, Vicente Perfecto Gomez insisted that the Californians had definitely improved their morality and intelligence under the new order; he debunked as false their pretensions to high morality and humanitarianism. If they were so virtuous, he asked, why had they so frequently tortured animals? Why had they sliced the hind-leg tendons of old horses and maliciously castrated bulls?[4] But one may discount his recrimination, for Gomez speaks as a

---

[3] "Recuerdos históricos y personales tocante a la Alta California ... 1769–1849," 1875, MS, Bancroft Library (Berkeley, Calif.), V, 229.
[4] "Lo que sabe sobre cosas de California," 1876, MS, Bancroft Library, pp. 40–

Mexican. The native son Salvador Vallejo admitted that lower-class males had "gained to a certain extent" in the new era, but at the expense of upper-class women, who had lost all. Mariano Vallejo thought that the Americanization of California redounded generally to the benefit of agriculture and commerce "but to the moral detriment of the [original] inhabitants . . . demoralized by daily contact with so many immoral persons . . . and a large part of the blame and responsibility may be rightfully attributed to the national and state government. I ask you what has the state government done for the Californians since the victory over Mexico? But, what good will it do us to complain? The evil is done and there is now [1875] no remedy for it." [5] His more mystically inclined brother, Salvador, added: "I abstain from repining [about our losses], for it is useless for mankind to protest against the decree of a wise Providence, whose deep mysteries we mortals are not allowed to fathom or interpret." [6]

Given the irreversible political and diplomatic complications of 1845, few Californians regretted having become Yankees. Had he caviled over his new citizenship, a Salvador Vallejo would not later have joined the Union Army. But all wondered what they had accomplished in the transformation. Don Salvador thought that the old domestic amenities far surpassed anything he had since seen. Californios had bred their children well, he believed, having taught their sons the arts of ranching and their daughters housekeeping. Even the women who were bolstered by an army of Indian servants made good housewives in their own right. This resulted in "cleanliness, good living and economy." Moreover, none of the women formerly wasted money on cosmetics, high-heeled shoes, cotton bosoms, whalebone corsets ("veritable instruments of torture"). All these novelties compared unfavorably with the "simple yet becoming" feminine garments of the "happy days"— and they were happy days, when people of all ages and both sexes roamed free of cost and free of worry "through the hills and plains, through meadows and ravines, with no critics' eyes to fear, no scandal mongers to dread, no loquacious servants to bribe." [7] José Eusebio

41; Hubert Howe Bancroft, *History of California* (San Francisco, 1887), III, 759.
[5] *Op. cit.*, V, 240.
[6] "Notas históricas sobre California," 1874, MS, Bancroft Library, p. 100.
[7] *Ibid.*, pp. 98–100.

Galindo developed the Arcadian image one step further and said that olden California had been a "true paradise." [8]

Not to romanticize but to debunk Yankee myths and lies became the task of the moment. Mariano Vallejo and others had bristled at reading Robinson's *Life;* they could not fathom how a man could love his Californio wife and in-laws as fully as Robinson apparently did and yet write so condescendingly.[9] Mariano started writing a multivolume history—"a true history of the country"—to tell the Americans that the early Californians "were not indigents or a band of beasts," but an "illustrious" race of people. Admittedly the scholarly project he had taken on surpassed the energies of one man, but duty drove Vallejo to work at it, lest "we . . . disappear, ignored of the whole world." [10] In his usual luckless way Mariano lost 900 manuscript pages when fire ravaged his home in 1867, but in his equally persevering way he began again from scratch in 1873.

One Yankee, Hubert Howe Bancroft, a San Francisco businessman, showed equal academic interest in the Californios, for he was writing a "true history." He willingly offered money for the Californios' memoirs and documents. As one of his aides, Thomas Savage, toured the state from 1876 to 1878 to ferret out material, Bancroft, in effect, acquired the last inventory of the old ruling class, catching glimpses of them in various stages of decline. Señor Botello, a prominent public figure in 1859, had meanwhile sunk into dire poverty and loneliness. The seventy-seven-year-old Señor Amador also lived in squalor, but his children nursed him and he maintained both his dignity and a clear memory of events and customs long past. He added a bit of Spanish doggerel with a sad personal twist:

> When I was but a little boy I drained the chocolate pot,
> But now I am a poor man and am condemned to slop.[11]

Ygnacio del Valle enjoyed sumptuous Rancho Camulos, yet could not help Savage because of a "feeble" memory. Don Manuel Dominguez

[8] "Apuntes para la historia de California," 1877, MS, Bancroft Library, p. 70.
[9] Teresa de la Guerra Hartnell, "Narración," in *Pioneer Sketches,* no. 2, 1875, MS, Bancroft Library, pp. 22–23.
[10] To Anastacio Carrillo, Dec. 19, 1865, MS, de la Guerra Collection, Owen Coy Room, University of Southern California (Los Angeles, Calif.).
[11] José María Amador, "Memorias sobre la historia de California," 1877, MS, Bancroft Library, p. 122.

affably refused on the same ground, but Señor Aguilar rebuffed the Yankee with the declaration that he had "no time to spare"[12] for Mr. Bancroft's history. The widows of the Carrillo brothers stiffly refused any recollections, and Señora José Castro bristled at the merest suggestion that she contribute information to clear her husband's clouded reputation. José del Carmen Lugo received some Bancroft money for his time, but in exchange was able to give only a discursive and empty *relación* because of his illiteracy and poor memory. Pio Pico introduced Savage to several informants in Los Angeles, for which the Yankee felt grateful, but the Governor's own testimony lacked merit altogether; Savage considered him a "champion liar."[13]

Bancroft garnered vast amounts of useful data from the Californians, despite their illiteracy and advanced age. Unfortunately, his assistants too often slighted the details of their informants' current condition and missed a valuable opportunity to preserve the Californios' observations on the Yankee era. Antonio Coronel, however, contributed a long and detailed relación which covered the entire span of time since the 1830's and became one of Bancroft's most prized possessions. After years of cajolery, the historian prevailed on Mariano Vallejo to open for investigation his huge collection of documents and his five-volume history. Vallejo finally gave the documents to Bancroft outright—"one of the biggest coups in Bancroft's whole experience as a collector."[14] Juan Bautista Alvarado also wrote a mammoth recollection which founds its way into the Bancroft library, when the former governor grew convinced that the Yankee was doing "great work."[15] The Californios' memoirs perpetrated falsehoods of their own, but they suffered more from inconsistency than dishonesty, from a polemical tone rather than deliberate distortion, and simply from hurt feelings. These personal touches provided, however, an indispensable seasoning ingredient for Bancroft.

In death, the Californios began to assume heroic importance. Grieving at the funeral invitations that came steadily in the 1870's and

[12] Thomas Savage, "Report of Labors on Archives and Procuring Materials for History of California," 1876–1879, MS, Bancroft Library, p. 30.
[13] *Ibid.*, p. 29.
[14] John W. Caughey, *Hubert Howe Bancroft, Historian of the West* (Berkeley, 1946), p. 111.
[15] "Historia de California," 1876, MS, Bancroft Library, V, 276.

1880's, old-time Yankee friends, themselves a dying breed, served as pallbearers to their dead compadres. The press showed belated sympathy, at least to the extent of giving the Californios favorable obituaries:

[He] . . . was one of the best known and most highly respected of our Mexican citizens, and at one time was one of the wealthiest men in this portion of the State. . . . [He saw] the few Mexican huts give way to the march of civilization and improvement, until it became to him a fairy dream. He was an honest, free hearted man. He leaves a long line of friends to mourn his taking away.[16]

This notice of Juan Bernal's death in Santa Clara, September 23, 1878, could substitute for the obituary of any of a hundred rancheros. When Salvedor Vallejo was laid to rest in February, 1876, Sonoma's flags hung at half-mast for the former Union Army officer. He lived his last days with his brother after going bankrupt in the panic of 1873, passing his time reading, painting, fishing, playing the guitar for his nieces, and drowning his bitterness in whiskey. His obituary included the observation that he was "a man of very strong prejudices, and never . . . reconciled to the American occupation." San Francisco's Spanish-language weekly came to Salvador's defense by countering that he was, in fact, reconciled and had left the "wrong doers to God's mercy." [17] The death of Salvador's brother Mariano in 1890 made banner headlines throughout the state.

Even with the aid of hindsight and detailed empirical research, the "final cause" of the Californio's pitiful collapse escapes the scholar. It remains a difficult exercise in historical causation to unravel the complex factors and extract the immediate from the remote causes, the human from the impersonal, the economic from the cultural or social; each contributed in its way.

Clearly, the land problem stands at dead center of the matter, but even on this question there is still no consensus. Professor Paul W. Gates recently revived the "pro-squatter" argument and exonerated the settlers and the Land Law from major blame, while criticizing the original claimants for exaggerating their difficulties.[18] Perhaps the proper

---

[16] San Jose *Pioneer and Historical Review,* Oct. 26, 1878.

[17] Napa *Register,* Feb. 17, 1876; San Francisco *Daily Alta California,* Feb. 20, 1876.

[18] "Adjudication of Spanish-Mexican Land Claims in California," *Huntington Library Quarterly,* XXI (May, 1958), 213 ff.; "California's Embattled Settlers," California Historical Society *Quarterly,* XLI (June, 1962), 99 ff.

response is that, except for a few scheming Yankee spe
Land Law injured all parties irrespective of nationality, and meanw..
prevented the Yankee in general from coming to grips with the legal
and moral responsibility toward the rancheros which he had contracted
for in 1848 but soon afterward had conveniently forgotten.

Culture conflict explains a great deal. Quite plainly, the Californian's
economic naïveté and his penchant for conspicuous consumption led
him to the brink of disaster. California after 1848 provides a classic instance of what David Riesman describes in another connection as the
"inner-directed" society superimposing itself on one that is "tradition-
directed." In this connection, Margaret Mead's anthropological observations about the present-day New Mexican shed clear light on the
Californians of the ninteenth century: "It is still the present, the known
and the sure, which has meaning. . . . [He] wants things as they are,
not as they were or as they should be. . . . The persistence of this
orientation to the present time in the face of equally persistent future
orientation of Anglos is central to the whole process of Spanish American acculturation." [19] There is, however, no theory that easily explains
the *degree* of violence or the *magnitude* of personal trauma among
Californios, compared with similar instances in, say, New Mexico.

Aside from the question as to why the Californios declined, the problem is why their decline took the worst possible form. Perhaps it did
not have to do so. Subsequent generations forgot what Professor C.
Van Woodward, in regard to Southern "Jim Crow," called the "forgotten alternatives." Nothing should blot out the accomplishments in California of the seafarers who readily became "Mexicanized," the army
officers who protected the rights of the native-born and the gringo lawyers who defended them in court, the Yankee politicians who cultivated
the "Spanish vote," and the Californios' Yankee friends who remained
humane and loyal to their dying day. What was possible for some
Yankees should have been possible for most. The experience of the
Latin Americans who survived a less brutal assault on their culture in
New Mexico also suggests better possibilities.

By emphasizing injustice, violence, and broken promises in their
memoirs, the Californians came closer to a meaningful truth than the
Yankees who spoke of Providence. The gringo behaved more violently,

[19] *Cultural Patterns and Technical Change* (New York, 1855), p. 175.

maliciously, and immorally than he thought: it was he who first guaranteed the Californians full citizenship; he who agreed to treat them as equals and not as conquered people; he who broke his word by declaring open season on the rancheros. Many Yankees have variously said that "progress has its price," that "the Californians were culturally unsuited to the new order," that "they brought it on themselves," that "the American yeoman had genuine troubles too in California," or that, "in any case, the race goes to the strong." Perhaps; but then the Yankee's pretense at ethics appears all the more reprehensible. The unalloyed Yankee bigots who took what they wanted and kept still about it appear in retrospect in a better light than those who prated about democracy. One is reminded of Josiah Royce's wish, after reflecting on the conquest of California, that "when our nation is another time about to serve the devil, it will do so more with frankness, and will deceive itself less by half-unconscious cant." [20] [See also note 20a on page 296.]

Californios did not "disappear, ignored of the world," however, as Mariano Vallejo had feared—far from it. No sooner had they died than the gringo practically immolated himself upon their graves. The "Spaniards" went into apotheosis; "Spanish California" became a cult.

Until the 1880's, Americans had "deified" only Joaquin Murietta among the Spanish Americans. When John Rollin Ridge published his potboiler in 1853, it flopped, and he returned east to work for the betterment of his people, the Cherokees. Several years later, in 1859, the California Police Gazette pirated his story and gave it new currency. The ugly memories of the "real" Joaquin had grown fuzzy, while innumerable embellishments of the original Joaquin legend appeared —tales, poems, romances, boyhood adventures, and even "verbatim" conversations with the bandido. A minor San Francisco poet, Cincinnatus Heine Miller, adopted the pen name of "Joaquin Miller." The bandit appeared in fiction as a Mexican or a Spaniard, light-skinned or dark, brave and cruel, romantic and picaresque, foppish and manly. His fame spread to Latin America and Spain, where he melted into older traditions of the heroic bandit. In one slightly anachronistic South American version, Joaquin went to Washington to visit with President Thomas Jefferson.[21]

[20] California from the Conquest in 1846 to the Second Vigilance Committee in San Francisco . . . (New York, 1948), p. 156.
[21] Joseph Henry Jackson, Bad Company . . . (New York, 1949), passim, deals

By worshiping a Joaquin motivated by revenge at Yankee injustices, the Yankees admitted at least partial responsibility for the early struggles with the Spanish-American miners. Even the most circumspect writers such as Bancroft and Theodore H. Hittell accepted Joaquin as real, without possessing more proof than Ridge's story. Twentieth-century authors also accepted Joaquin on that basis, making him the subject of new novels, a play, a motion picture, television horse operas, and a comic strip.

Other Spanish Americans provided leaner pickings for literature, except as objects of ridicule. The real-life villain of Bret Harte's *Story of a Mine*, which reconstructs the conflict over the claim to the New Idria quicksilver mine, was Vicente Perfecto Gomez, the unsuccessful Mexican claimant. No heroics surrounded the mission fathers, either, in the 1870's. Junípero Serra's name probably was unknown even to most Californios; certainly none showed the slightest inclination to romanticize him. With anti-Catholicism in vogue (even President Rutherford B. Hayes lent his name to the nativist movement), Harte wrote an irreverent story about a padre. When an itinerant Mexican friar named Osuna wandered up from Baja California in 1870, his sandals and robe so startled San Diego that the marshal jailed him on a charge of "lunacy" and had him extradited—a perfect illustration of the Yankee's total lack of understanding of or empathy for the era of the missions.

The missions themselves lingered on in the last stages of rigor mortis. As part of President Grant's peace policy toward the Plains Indians, the Catholic church tried to rectify the lot of its scattered mission Indians everywhere, and in 1874 institutionalized its efforts by founding the Bureau of Catholic Indian Missions. On a pilgrimage to southern California to alleviate the plight of an estimated 20,000 former mission Indians, the bureau's head, Bishop François Blanchet, sought $2,000 as a working fund, but got practically no response when he solicited a donation of $20 from each of the more wealthy Californians. Archbishop Joseph S. Alemany also drew a blank when he tried forming a speakers' bureau to publicize the problem, since he could not locate "good speakers who were both available and acquainted" with the missions. The Episcopalians put the Catholics to shame by raising a whopping

with the Murieta myth; Luis Monguio, "*Lust for Riches: A Spanish Nineteenth Century Novel of the Gold Rush and Its Sources*," California Historical Society *Quarterly*, XXVII (Sept., 1948), 237–248.

$50,000 in the 1870's to implement a similar policy throughout the West.[22]

The Church found further retrenchment necessary in California. The chapel of former San Fernando Mission, for example, still served a handful of neighboring Indians. A priest came regularly from Los Angeles to administer the sacraments to them; the chapel altar remained intact; three pleasant-sounding bells still pealed from the roof; and the zanja still brought water from the hillside. For the last thirty years or so, Andrés Pico had been the great eminence there, living in the former *convento*, one of the most ample dwellings in the state—a two-storied, 300-foot oblong, one side graced by arches and columns running the entire length of the building. His 32-acre garden to the south and that of Eulogio de Celis to the north embraced hundreds of olive trees and thousands of vines and assorted fruit trees. Pico had custody of trunks full of memorabilia, including the tallow candles used at the first Mass, seventy-five years earlier.

As time went by, the Indians of the former mission were dying out, and the Southern Pacific Railroad was working its way through the mountains, aiming to emerge in the San Fernando Valley and to slice across the former mission pasturage, to stop at a town to be called San Fernando, and to make its way into Los Angeles. In 1874 the priest held his last Mass and the Indians celebrated their last fiesta—a slightly pagan affair, in which they danced to their native music and burnt the clothes of their dead according to ancient ritual. In 1875 workmen removed the bells from the tower and packed them off for the Los Angeles church, as a crying Indian woman watched. The Indians pressed their last grapes that year. According to one informant, they seized the image of their patron saint to punish him for failing to bring rain, and "baptized" him in the zanja ditch while cursing him. According to tradition, rain then fell. Rómulo Pico, who inherited the convento property from his father, cut the olive trees for firewood and grew wheat there in 1880.[23]

Almost single-handedly a New England novelist—a Protestant—

---

[22] Peter J. Rahill, *The Catholic Indian Missions and Grant's Peace Policy: 1870–1884* (Washington, 1953), pp. 19, 120, 142 ff.

[23] Daughters of the American Revolution, *The Valley of San Fernando* (n.p., 1924), pp. 55–57; Ben C. Truman, *Semi-Tropical California* (San Francisco, 1874), pp. 189–191.

altered California's old "bad image." Helen Hunt Jackson's literary career began in 1881 with *A Century of Dishonor*, a reformist tract, which expostulated with a cynical generation about the condition of the Plains Indians. Its message penetrated and made her an overnight sensation. She toured southern California for five weeks that year, examining other aspects of the Indian problem, and in the course of her travels visited ranchos, missions, pueblos, and rancherías and conversed with old settlers. At San Fernando, Rómulo Pico guided her on a tour of the mission premises and offered her religious relics. (Although intending to accept, she politely asked, "Do you not rather prefer to keep them for the Church?" This seeming reproach caused him quietly to withdraw his offer. Later she asked her friend Antonio Coronel to help her make amends to Rómulo; she wished to accept any relic he would offer.) A visit to nearby Camulos gave her a specific visual picture of a rancho.[24] These impressions and experiences began to churn in her head as the beginnings of a novel, particularly when she mused on the tale Coronel told her of the hardships of the girl born to Hugo Reid's Indian wife. Mrs. Jackson envisaged the girl as the child of two cultures and made her the heroine of *Ramona*.

Among the countless romances of old California, the first remains the most important. Unlike the others, *Ramona* (1884) offers insights into a real historical predicament and is still readable. This novel depicts American immigrants, Franciscan missionaries, and Mexican dons in their decline and the lower classes and Indians in a state verging on despair and degeneracy. The author's hatred of the white man's oppressions and her knowledge of the southern California of her day gave her story an immediacy which, unhappily, the works of her followers and imitators lacked.

A year later, Mrs. Jackson produced *Glimpses of California and the Missions*, the first popular appreciation of the work of the Catholic fathers. George Wharton James followed with a more extended work, *In and Out of the Old Missions*, the classic of that genre. In the next half-century not a year passed without the publication of at least one more book of this kind. Meanwhile, throughout the Southwest a similar phe-

---

[24] To Antonio Coronel, Jan. 30, 1882, in Walter Lindley and J. P. Widney, *California of the South* (New York, 1896), pp. 193–195. See also Ruth Odell, *Helen Hunt Jackson* (New York, 1939).

on occurred: ethnologists, poets, novelists, health seekers, and refugees from Eastern urban turmoil sought the solace of unspoiled wastes, discovered the pre-Yankee culture of the Southwest, and immersed themselves in it. Adolph Bandolier showed the way in New Mexico and Arizona by also delving into Indian culture and the Spanish culture that overwhelmed it.

To this romantic revival historians supplied raw data, narrative accounts, and philosophical speculations on the clash of civilizations. Bancroft alone (backed by a mountain of documentary evidence and a corps of helpers) produced four detailed volumes on California's pre-Yankee era.[25] If anyone could satisfy Vallejo's craving for a "true history" of the early era, Bancroft was the man. He did applaud the destruction of the old order as a necessary stage in mankind's upward march, yet he emphasized the Spanish American's virtues and deplored the Yankee's aggressiveness after 1846. When particular figures such as Pio Pico or José Castro had been unfairly maligned, he went out of his way to set the record straight.[26] Unevenly written, pontifical in manner, and undigested in content, Bancroft's extended treatment of Spanish and Mexican California nonetheless remains the best of its kind. In addition, his library supplied background material which the romantic authors were the first to exploit.

The modish romantic historians of the 1880's did not always intend to compliment the Spanish-speaking. To Charles Howard Shinn, whose *Mining Camps* was the first major history of the gold rush, California supplied an example of the glorious victory of the Anglo-Saxon over the Latin "race." He saw in the Spaniards a mixture of admirable and loathsome traits: the utmost in valor, cruelty, indolence, and fanaticism. "The first Spanish colonists [in America] were lazy and lustful, reckless and turbulent," he insisted in one context, yet added in another that their life "in its freedom from care and in its glorious physical healthfulness, was simple perfection." [27] Moreover, unlike Bancroft, Shinn exonerated the Anglo-Saxons of any guilt in tormenting foreign-

[25] Vol. I, to 1800; II, 1801–1824; III, 1825–1840; IV, 1841–1845; and the miscellany, *California Pastoral* (San Francisco, 1888).
[26] *History of California*, II, 752.
[27] *Mining Camps: A Study in American Frontier Government* (1st ed.; New York, 1885), pp. 47, 61. See also Frank Blackmar, *Spanish Colonization in the Southwest* (Baltimore, 1890).

ers in the mines and traced the troubles to the foreigners themselves, including "Spaniards" actuated by "a sort of distorted patriotism." [28] The most sophisticated historical treatise was Josiah Royce's *California,* sympathetic to the Spanish Americans, although altogether condescending. In that work Royce excoriated the Yankees for heaping abuse on the "amoral" Spanish Americans—a people too weak and innocuous to inaugurate or resist trouble. The Downieville lynching, the foreign miner's tax, and other repressions represented the epitome of Anglo-Saxon evil; the retribution of the "Spaniards" was quite justifiable, he thought.[29]

Despite its Anglo-Saxon cast, the new romantic literature on California represented a sharp departure from earlier accounts. Whereas the original Yankee travelers had carped on the retrograde tendencies of the old order, the new writers vaunted its solid virtues. If the early visitors had glowered at California's wasted resources, the later ones sang the praises of pastoral labor. Whereas fur trapper Jim Pattie and stevedore Richard Henry Dana, Jr., had spoken of tyranny, historian Nellie Van de Grift Sanchez contemplated the benefits of paternalism, the joys of the caballeros, the piety of the Indians.[30] Although eyewitnesses had criticized the Mexican's injustices to the Indians, the new writers pointed to the mutual devotion of missionaries and Indians.

In the year of Helen Hunt Jackson's death, 1884, another New Englander, Charles Fletcher Lummis, came to California and brought to the local-color movement a genius for organization. The Southwest's combination of "sun, silence and adobe" made an impact on him "in many respects as potent as a religious conversion." [31] As editor of the magazine *Land of Sunshine* and author of *Land of Poco Tiempo* and *The Spanish Pioneers* (1893), he established himself as the leading regional interpreter and sought to share the area's beauties with the nation at large. Dedicated followers of his in 1888 organized the Association for the Preservation of the Missions, which in 1895 became the Land Marks Club, working to preserve all manner of old relics, espe-

[28] *Graphic Description of Pacific Coast Outlaws* (Los Angeles, 1958), p. 78.
[29] *Op. cit.,* pp. 25–28, 281–289.
[30] *Spanish Arcadia* (Los Angeles, 1929), *passim.*
[31] Edwin R. Bingham, *Charles Fletcher Lummis: Editor of the Southwest* (San Marino, Calif., 1955), p. 9.

cially adobes, place names, and the Camino Real. Later came the Sequoia League, the Native Sons of the Golden West, and the Southwest Museum to advance the study, preservation, and restoration of the Spanish heritage. The sons and daughters of pioneer Yankee and Californio families gave money to the movement and wrote filiopietistic history.

The "Spanish" heritage enjoyed its greatest vogue, however, when hucksters discovered its salability. The Lummis-planned fiesta of 1895 in Los Angeles, the first to use the tableau idea, was a smash hit and the idea caught on. Throughout southern California, real estate operators, local tradesmen, and the manipulators of the tourist trade began organizing their own fiestas. The Southern Pacific Railroad purchased *Sunset Magazine* and devoted it to local color, the more readily to lure Easterners to the Far West. As a result, within two decades after *Ramona,* materialism had routed the original aestheticism of the local-color movement.

The local-color writers did well to remind the Yankee that he was treading rudely in Indian and Spanish-Mexican footsteps, but those authors also stand accused of distorting the past. Some did so candidly. In the name of literary license they rounded off the rough spots of the Spanish heritage, gave it more lustrous color than it deserved, and imagined conflicts that never had existed or ignored others that had. Practically all minimized the Mexican influences. To this day, the dons' descendants refuse to acknowledge their mestizo ancestry or to recognize that their grandfathers acquired Mexican, not Spanish, land grants. The literature of local color glorified the heroic at the expense of the mundane. The Victorian morality of the feminine pseudohistorians suppressed the "vulgar" aspects of life. The fact that the Franciscans buried nearly as many Indians as they converted lay beyond the mythmakers' comprehension.

The "Spanish" cult was thus comprised of one part aestheticism, one part history, and one part ballyhoo. So popular was this cult by 1890 that one could scarcely recall how recently the Spanish Americans had been in disfavor, or that the real, live ones still were. For only after they had reduced the real-life Spanish-speaking to the status of a foreign minority did the Yankees feel any deep compassion toward Spanish-American culture.

Any effort to assess the impact of the Spanish-Mexican tradition on present-day California is complicated by the lingering romantic tradition. Yet historians now generally agree that the most important pre-Yankee influences consist of innumerable Spanish words, place-names, legal arrangements (as in water rights), architectural forms, and holiday pageantry. Some of these influences have survived easily, others only through deliberate effort. Andrew F. Rolle summarizes current thinking on this matter:

It is, of course, possible to exaggerate California's Hispanic inheritance. This cultural background has largely been submerged by the advance of the Anglo-American frontier, yet one cannot deny the heritage. For example, in this age of the television western one should not forget that the cowboy inherited his know-how, horse, outfit (including reata, spurs, chaps and lasso), and lingo largely from the Spanish era. Lingering aspects of the Hispanic past are also to be found in the very faces of Californians of Spanish background, in their names, customs, and local ordinances—as well as in the colorful, if overly romanticized, exploitation of Spanish colonial history by sentimental antiquarians, genealogists, artists, architects, historical societies, tourist promoters, museum specialists, and countless other persons infatuated by the Spanish past. In short, this seemingly Arcadian past could not be, and has not been, forgotten.[32]

California today sees the Spanish-speaking as living at once in two disharmonious worlds, one mythic, the other real. The mythic world emphasizes the "Spanish" past—carefree, unchanging, and enveloped in a religious aura; the other is a "Mexican" world—disagreeable, mundane, potentially violent. The twain rarely meet, except on public occasions such as the commemoration of Cinco de Mayo and September Sixteenth or of the founding of the city of Los Angeles. Then the "Spaniards" mount white horses to lead the "Mexicans." On one ludicrous occasion, the Olvera Street fiesta committee selected a descendant of Cortés to serve as the Mexicans' *padrino*, or parade marshal— like choosing a descendant of King George III to lead a Fourth of July celebration, mused one wry Mexican-American.[33] From this sort of event strangers sometimes mistakenly conclude that today's aristocratic Californios are the true spokesmen of the Mexican-American community, which is far from the truth.

[32] *California: A History* (New York, 1963), pp. 124–125.
[33] Los Angeles *Times*, Feb. 24, 1963.

One August week in 1963 the Los Angeles *Times* gave a particularly good display of what may be called the "schizoid heritage." Luckily, the editor segregated the items concerned into the news columns and the society section, or they might have been doubly hard to reconcile. A headline on August 5, 1963, blazed that "LATINS HERE . . . PROTEST BRACERO LAW"; that is, that Mexican-Americans denounced the importation of Mexican nationals in a system that "takes advantage of hunger and hardship in Mexico to provide for recruitment of a captive, docile and exploitable foreign farm labor force." That same issue also noted that a Mexican-American "CROWD FORCES DEPUTIES TO FREE PRISONERS"; that is, that a crowd twice attacked sheriff's deputies attempting to arrest juveniles in a gang fracas, whereupon assailants beat one deputy and freed his prisoners, and later were arrested for resisting an officer and violating the antilynch law. Vice President "JOHNSON URGES LATIN CITIZENS TO REPORT BIAS," the *Times* noted three days later. Johnson suggested to 1,000 leading Mexican-Americans that "perhaps you have not been successful in making your needs known," and should report cases of discrimination more urgently—"I mean facts, not mere grumblings."

On August 7, on the other hand, a mere two days later, readers of the society section of the *Times* learned of the opening of the "OLD SPANISH DAYS FIESTA" at Santa Barbara. The five-day annual festivities, timed to meet the August moon, included parades, speeches, and tableaux commemorating the 250th anniversary of the birth of Father Serra, as well as a costume breakfast, a "cocktail fiesta," garden tours, performances of the Mexican Folklorica Ballet, and the opening of a "Spanish market place." The event represented the "apogee of the summer social season" in Santa Barbara and was attended by tens of thousands, including the lieutenant governor of the state.

The romantic heritage gives every indication of continuing indefinitely, despite an unprecedented debunking from sociologists, schoolteachers, and historians and a decimation in the ranks of the romantics. Leo Carrillo personified the romantic tradition until a few years ago, and with valid license, having been born into a venerable local family at the Los Angeles Plaza in 1880. He spoke Spanish well, played the guitar, rode horseback, took part in fiestas and rodeos, listened carefully to the conversation of his elders and transmitted their oral tradition masterfully, read a good deal of local history, and wrote his autobiography with a deep sense of ancestral pride.[34] The smiling, waving Carrillo perched on a lavishly bridled horse was an inevitable part of any southern California parade for two decades. But Carrillo was the last figure who could legitimately personify the Spanish past—although many considered him a mere creation of Hollywood—and his death in 1961 left a gap in the front ranks of many Los Angeles parades.

Mexican-Americans cannot lightly accept or dismiss this "fantasy heritage," for it seems to reproach them for failing to meet impossibly high standards. (Thus it was probably the sight of Carrillo in a parade that prompted a Mexican-American labor leader to swear that if he met the horse-and-rider combination again, he would spit in the horse's eye.[35]) The Mexican-American discovers that "Anglos" are far less kindly disposed toward the living Mexican-Americans than toward the imaginary Californios, and he claims that Yankees fawn over the clay caballeros sold in Olvera Street but tend to show contempt for the people who sell them. Live people constitute a forgotten minority, while the mythical ones are remembered only too well.

After 1900 the living bearers of Spanish-American culture, the Mexicans, created a new stir in the Southwest. They supplied an important source of agricultural and industrial labor, more important than that of the 1850's. Those Americans who had mistaken the rancheros' demise by about 1885 for the extinction of an entire people had to review their thinking. Droves of wetbacks flocked across the border to work in fields and orchards and on the railroads. In both world wars growers imported tens of thousands of *braceros* yearly to work in the Imperial and San Joaquin valleys of California, and as far east as the Mississippi River and as far north as the Dakotas. Mexican-Americans served in the armed forces, sometimes with distinction. Despite ugly wartime incidents such as the Sleepy Lagoon case and the Pachuco Riots in Los Angeles, that city acquired so many Spanish-speaking residents as to qualify for a time as the second-largest Latin-American city (next to Mexico City) in the Western Hemisphere.

By 1964 the Spanish-speaking in California numbered close to

[34] Leo Carrillo, *The California I Love* (Englewood Cliffs, N.J., 1961), *passim*.
[35] Carey McWilliams, *North From Mexico: The Spanish-Speaking People of the United States* (Philadelphia, 1949), p. 38.

2,000,000 (1,426,538 by the 1960 census). They were the state's largest and most rapidly growing minority and about 80 percent urbanized and native born.[36] Even immigration figures reached astonishing levels: 5,400 Mexicans came to the United States monthly in the 1950's, 58,000 residents had been waiting for years to obtain permanent visas, 350,000 have entered legally from 1953 to 1959, and untold thousands have done so illegally. Most of the immigrants came to the Los Angeles area; some 260,000 Mexican-Americans lived within the city limits, 577,000 in the county, more than 700,000 in the metropolitan area. In San Fernando, 28 percent of the population in 1960 or 4,400, had Spanish surnames,[37] which compared very favorably with the percentage in 1880.

The Mexican-American of today [38] finds himself in some situations altogether new and different from those known to his ancestors a century ago. The "patina of romantic mis-information" which surrounds his culture is a major factor unknown a hundred years ago. The frontier is gone, of course, along with the lynchings, although the ritualistic aspects of the Sleepy Lagoon trial and the Pachuco riots during World War II (and the more recent booking of a Mexican-American for violating the antilynch law) strike some familiar notes. The land problem has subsided (although the instance of a Yankee who gained possession of Señor Arguëllo's valid claim to all of downtown Tiajuana, Mexico, is a bizarre reminder of things long past).

Unhappily, the closing of the frontier has also obliterated the "Mexicanized gringo," the Californios' sometime friend and mentor, who had eased their acculturation. The twentieth-century gringo sees fewer and more sordid glimpses of Spanish-American culture than his forefathers did in the 1850's. In the pathetic border towns he visits he sees few amenities comparable to the rancho fiesta. In most of Los Angeles he lives worlds apart from the town's "Serape Belt" and can spend his entire lifetime seeing few Mexican-Americans other than Olvera Street vendors and the occasional Spanish-speaking gardener or delivery boy.

---

[36] State of California, Department of Industrial Relations, Division of Fair Employment Practices, *Californians of Spanish Surnames: Population, Employment, Income, Education* (San Francisco, 1964), p. 5.

[37] *Media Agencies Clients* (Los Angeles), April 2, 1962.

[38] See, for example, a series of articles by Ruben Salazar in the Los Angeles *Times,* Feb. 24 ff., 1963.

At the same time, Yankee hatred has diminished and grown less overt. As one Anglo observed, the Mexican-American of California lives in "a kind of limbo; neither accepted nor rejected." [39] The Americano finds the Mexican-American amiable and anxious to please, but does not understand him in his "displaced status." Some Anglo-Saxons at least experience a sense of guilt toward the Negro for past oppressions; toward the Spanish-speaking, few feel any similar sentiments or any vivid emotion at all.

The Spanish-speaking find themselves, however, in the presence of astonishing continuities and depressing parallels with the past. Francisco P. Ramirez, Reginaldo del Valle, and Antonio Coronel would find their community in 1964 in an all too deplorable condition. The lack of a local Spanish-language newspaper for a vast Spanish-speaking audience would give Ramirez an unhappy reminder of the day he closed up *El Clamor Público* in 1859. Lack of education among Mexican-American youths weighs down upon most of them like an incubus and prevents them from competing for decent jobs.[40] Three-quarters of the youths dropped out of high school in 1950, and the same number in 1960; in short, there has been no progress in that respect. Serious crime and law enforcement problems still strain the mutually exclusive patience of youth and of officers of the law. Young men and women still feel displaced, resentful at the dominant group and thus inclined toward occasional irrational outbursts.

The Spanish-speaking community continues to reinforce itself numerically from the old country. And the newcomers still fan out into the ghettos, which still run in the same general direction as before, east of Olvera Street. The braceros of the 1960's remind one of the Mexican miners of the 1850's. Moreover, the linkup between the Negro problem and the Mexican problem in 1964 is partly a reversion to an earlier time, when the dominant race first debated the fate of dark-skinned laborers of all nations.

Numerically, the Mexican-Americans today have regained the losses

[39] Neil Morgan, *Westward Tilt: The American West Today* (New York, 1963), p. 65.
[40] Southwest Conference on Educational and Social Problems of Rural and Urban Mexican-American Youth, *Summary of Proceedings of the Twelfth Annual Conference* (Los Angeles, 1963), pp. 33–44.

of the Californios; the relative strength of the Spanish-speaking presently exceeds that of the 1880's. But lack of an effective political leadership still hobbles the community much as it did then. Mexican-American leaders could not "deliver the vote" in 1960 as well as they did in 1870.

Because the modern predicament of the Mexican-American jelled a century ago, from 1849 to 1885, and not after the turn of the century, as some suppose, the resolution of these problems looks all the more difficult. Problems ten decades old will not respond quickly to reform; urban and industrial life confound simple problems; a great city will find it hard to shake off the troubles it bypassed as a village. But there is a final hopeful note: If the 1960's find the legendary Spanish heritage in a virile condition, so do they witness a new stirring among those who prefer to cope with the real, though less pleasant, heritage of the past hundred years.

Bibliography

MANUSCRIPT MATERIALS AND DOCUMENTS
(IN THE BANCROFT LIBRARY, UNIVERSITY OF
CALIFORNIA, BERKELEY, UNLESS OTHERWISE
NOTED)

Alvarado, Juan Bautista. "Historia de California." 1876. Vol. V.
———. "History of California: California before '48." Vol. V.
Amador, José María. "Memorias sobre la historia de California." 1877. Translated.
Avila, Miguel. "Documentos históricos de California."
Bancroft, Hubert Howe. Reference Notes (springbinders): "Education: Colleges and Universities, 1849–1886"; "California Land, 1851–1860"; "From History of California, Vol. V"; "Crime, Criminals and Administration of Justice"; "Biography and Reference."
Bandini, Juan. "Historia de la Alta California, 1796–1845." 1874.
Bernal, Juan. "Memoria." 1877.
Berreyesa, Antonio. "Relación. ..." 1877.
Castro, Manuel J. "Relación sobre acontecimientos de la Alta California." 1876.
Coronel, Antonio Franco. "Cosas de California. ..." 1877.
Coronel Collection. Los Angeles County Museum.
Cowan Collection. Special Collections, University of California, Los Angeles.
De la Guerra Collection. Owen Coy Room, University of Southern California, Los Angeles. Translated.
Del Valle Collection. Los Angeles County Museum.
Fernandez, José. "Cosas de California [1817–1850]." 1874.
Galindo, José Eusebio. "Apuntes para la historia de California." 1877.
Gomez, Vincente P. "Lo que sabe sobre cosas de California." 1876.
Hartnell, Teresa de la Guerra. "Narracion," in Pioneer Sketches, no. 2. 1875.
Hayes, Benjamin. "Criminal Trials at Los Angeles: Blotter Notes of Honorable Ben Hayes." 1877.
———. Scrapbooks: "Southern California: Los Angeles County," Vols. I, II, IV; "Mining," Vols. I, II.
Hough, John C. "Abel Stearns, 1848–1871." Unpublished MS, in possession of and edited by John W. Caughey.
Ide, William Brown. "Proclamation to the People of California." [June

1846]. MS, HM 4116, Huntington Library, San Marino, California.

Jewett, George. ". . . Journal, 1849 [–1850]."

Lugo, José del Carmen. "Vida de un Ranchero ... se incluye una narración de la batalla llamada del 'Rancho del Chino.'" 1877.

Pico, José de Jesús. "Acontecimientos en California de que hace memoria." 1878.

Pico, Pio. "Documentos para la historia de California. Archiro de la familia Pico." 1877.

Rico, Francisco. "Memorias históricas sobre California." 1877.

Savage, Thomas. "Report of Labors on Archives and Procuring Material for History of California." 1876–1879.

———. "Documentos para la historia de California." 1877. Vol. I.

Sepúlveda, Ramón D. "Dictation." Dec. 12, 1888.

Serrano, Florencio. "Recuerdos históricos," in *Pioneer Sketches*, nos. 4, 5. 1875.

Sloat, John Drake. "Proclamation to the Inhabitants of California." [July 6, 1846]. MS, FAC 101, Huntington Library.

Soberanes, Clodomiro. "Documentos para la historia de California." 1874.

Stearns, Abel. MSS Collection. Huntington Library, San Marino, Calif.

Torres, Manuel. "Peripecias de la vida California." 1876.

Vallejo, Mariano Guadalupe. "Documentos para la historia de California." 1874. Vol. XIII.

———. "Recuerdos históricos y personales tocante a la Alta California: historia politica del pais, 1769–1849." 1875. Translated as "History of California" by Earl R. Hewitt.

Vallejo, [José Manuel] Salvador. "Notas históricas sobre California." 1874.

PUBLISHED DIARIES, JOURNALS, LETTERS, AND PERSONAL REMINISCENCES

Ayers, James J. *Gold and Sunshine: Reminiscences of Early California.* 1st ed., 1896. Boston: Richard G. Badger, 1922.

Bachman, Jacob Henry. "The Diary of a 'Used-up' Miner . . . ," edited by Jeanne Skinner Von Nostrand. California Historical Society *Quarterly*, XXII (March, 1943), 67–83.

Bari, Valeska, ed. *The Course of Empire: First Hand Accounts of California in the Days of the Gold Rush of '49.* New York: Coward-McCann, 1931.

Bell, Horace. *Reminiscences of a Ranger, or, Early Times in Southern California.* 1st ed., 1881. Santa Barbara, Calif.: Wallace Hebberd, 1927.

———. *On the Old West Coast: Being Further Reminiscences of a Ranger.* New York: William Morrow and Co., 1930.

Borthwick, J. D. *Three Years in California* [1851–1854]. Edinburgh and London: W. Blackwood and Sons, 1857.

Brent, Joseph Lancaster. *The Lugo Case: A Personal Reminiscence.* New Orleans: Searcy and Pfaff, 1926.

Brewer, William Henry. *Up and Down California in 1860–1864: The Journal of William H. Brewer.* Edited by Francis P. Farquhar. 1st ed., 1930. Berkeley: University of California Press, 1949.

Buffum, Edward Gould. *Six Months in the Gold Mines: From a Journal of*

Three Years' Residence in Upper and Lower California, 1847–8–9. Philadelphia: Lea and Blanchard, 1859.

Bynam, Lindley, ed. "Los Angeles in 1854–1855: The Diary of Reverend James Woods," Historical Society of Southern California *Quarterly,* XXIII (June, 1941), 65–86.

Camp, Charles, ed. *James Clyman: American Frontiersman, 1792–1881, the Adventures of a Trapper and Covered Wagon Emigrant as Told in his Own Reminiscences and Diaries.* San Francisco: California Historical Society, 1928.

Carrillo, Leo. *The California I Love.* Englewood Cliffs, N. J.: Prentice-Hall, 1961.

Christman, Enos. *One Man's Gold: The Letters and Journals of a Forty-Niner.* New York: Whittlesey House, 1930.

Clappe, Louise Amelia Knapp Smith [Dame Shirley, pseud.]. *The Shirley Letters from the California Mines, 1851–52.* Edited by Carl T. Wheat. 1st ed., 1854. New York: Alfred Knopf, 1949.

Colton, Walter. *Three Years in California . . . and a Selection of . . . Letters from Monterey.* Edited by Marguerita Wilbur. 1st ed., 1850 Stanford: Stanford University Press, 1949.

Corney, Peter. *Voyages in the Northern Pacific: Narrative of Several Trading Voyages from 1813 to 1818. . . .* Honolulu: Thomas G. Thurm, 1896.

Couts, J. Cave. *From San Diego to the Colorado in 1849 . . . Journal and Maps. . . .* Los Angeles: Arthur M. Ellis, 1932.

Crosby, Elisha Oscar. *Memoirs of Elisha Oscar Crosby: Reminiscences of California and Guatemala from 1849 to 1864.* Edited by Charles Albro Barker. San Marino, Calif.: Huntington Library, 1945.

Dana, Richard Henry, Jr. *Two Years before the Mast: A Personal Narrative of Life at Sea.* 1st ed., 1840. Boston: Bates and Lauriat, 1895.

Frémont, John Charles. *Memoirs of My Life: Including the Narrative Five Journies of Western Exploration, during the Years 1842, 1843–4, 1845–6–7, 1848–9, 1853–4. . . .* Chicago and New York: Belford, Clark and Co., 1887.

Gerstäcker, Friedrich. *Scenes of Life in California.* Translated by George Cosgrave. 1st ed., 1856. San Francisco: John Howell, 1942.

Green, Thomas Jefferson. *Journal of the Expedition against Mier: . . . with Reflections upon the Present Political and Probable Future Relations of Texas, Mexico and the United States.* New York: Harper and Brothers, 1845.

Hayes, Benjamin D. *Pioneer Notes from the Diaries of Benjamin Hayes, 1849–1875.* Edited by Marjorie Tisdale Wolcott. Los Angeles: Marjorie Tisdale Wolcott, 1929.

Ide, Simon. *A Biographical Sketch of the Life of William B. Ide.* N.p., 1880.

Janssens, Agustín. *The Life and Adventures in California of Don Agustín Janssens: 1834–1856.* Edited by William H. Ellison, and Francis Price. San Marino, Calif.: Huntington Library, 1953.

Kip, William Ingraham. *The Early Days of My Episcopate.* New York: Thomas Whittaker, 1892.

Larkin, Thomas Oliver. *The Larkin Papers: Personal, Business, and Official*

Correspondence of Thomas Oliver Larkin, Merchant and United States Consul in California. Berkeley and Los Angeles: University of California Press, 1951–1955. Vols. III–V.

Lugo, José del Carmen. "Life of a Rancher," Historical Society of Southern California *Quarterly,* XXXII (Sept. 1950), 185–236.

Ord, Angustias de la Guerra. *Occurrences in Hispanic California.* Edited by William Ellison; [translated by Francisco Price]. Washington, Academy of Franciscan History, 1956.

Pattie, James Ohio. *The Personal Narrative . . . during Journeyings of Six Years . . . ,* in Reubin Gold Thwaites, ed., *Early Western Travels, 1748–1846: A Series of Annotated Reprints. . . .* Cleveland, Ohio: Arthur H. Clark Co., 1905. Vol. XVIII.

Pérez Rosales, Vicente. *California Adventure.* Translated by Edwin S. Morby, and Arturo Torres-Rioseco. San Francisco: Book Club of California, 1947.

Robinson, Alfred. *Life in California during a Residence of Several Years in That Territory. . . .* 1st ed., 1846. San Francisco: William Doxey, 1891.

Ryan, William Redmond. *Personal Adventures in Upper and Lower California, 1848–9. . . .* London: William Shoberl, 1850. 2 vols.

Sawyer, Eugene T. *History of Santa Clara County, California, . . . with Biographical Sketches of the Leading Men and Women. . . .* Los Angeles: Historical Records, 1922.

Shaw, William. *Golden Dreams and Waking Realities: Being the Adventures of a Gold-Seeker in California. . . .* London: Smith, Elder and Co. 1851.

Sherman, Edwin A. "Sherman was There: The Recollections of Major Edwin A. Sherman," California Historical Society *Quarterly,* XXIII (Dec., 1944), 349–377.

Simpson, George. *Narrative of a Voyage to California Ports in 1841–42.* San Francisco: T. C. Russell, 1930.

Taylor, Bayard. *Eldorado, or, Adventures in the Path of Empire.* 1st ed., 1850. New York: Alfred A. Knopf, 1949.

Woods, Daniel B. *Sixteen Months at the Gold Diggings.* New York: Harper and Brothers, 1851.

GOVERNMENT DOCUMENTS

Browne, J. Ross. *Report of the Debates in the Convention of California, on The Formation of the State Constitution, in September and October, 1849.* Washington, 1850.

California. Department of Industrial Relations. Division of Fair Employment Practices. *Californians of Spanish Surnames: Population, Employment, Income, Education.* San Francisco, 1964.

———. Legislature. *The Statutes of California, Passed at the First Session of the Legislature . . . at the City of Pueblo de San Jose.* San Jose: J. Winchester, 1850.

———. ———. *Journals of the State and Assembly.* San Jose and Sacramento, 1850–1872.

———. ———. *The Statutes of the Sixth Session, 1855.* Sacramento: B. B. Redding, 1855.

Hammond, George P., ed. *The Treaty of Guadalupe Hidalgo, February Second, 1848.* Berkeley: Friends of the Bancroft Library, 1949.

Hoffman, Ogden. *Reports of Land Cases Determined in the United States District Court for the Northern District of California* . . . [1853–1858]. San Francisco: Numa Hubert, 1862. Vol. I.

Manning, William R., ed. *Diplomatic Correspondence of the United States: Inter-American Affairs, 1831–1860.* Washington: Carnegie Endowment for International Peace, 1937.

Miller, Hunter, ed. *Treaties and Other International Acts of the United States of America.* Washington, 1937. Vol. V.

United States. Bureau of the Census. Tenth Census, 1880. Enumerator's Rollbook, Los Angeles County (microfilm).

———. Circuit Court. *Antonio María Peralta, et al., Complainants, v. United States of America, et al.* . . . *March 30, 1910.*

———. President. *California and New Mexico.* 31st Cong., 1st sess., H. Ex. Doc. 17. Washington, 1850.

BOOKS

[Angel, Myron]. *History of Placer County.* . . . Oakland, Calif.: Thompson and West, 1882.

———. *History of San Luis Obispo County.* . . . Oakland, Calif.: Thompson and West, 1883.

Atherton, Gertrude. *Golden Gate Country.* New York: Duell, Sloan and Pearce, 1945.

———. *The Splendid Idle Forties: Stories of Old California.* New York: Macmillan, 1902.

Bancroft, Hubert Howe. *History of California.* San Francisco: A. L. Bancroft, 1884–1890. 7 vols.

———. *Popular Tribunals.* San Francisco: The History Company, 1887. Vol. II.

———. *California Pastoral, 1796–1848.* San Francisco: A. L. Bancroft, 1888.

Bell, Katherine M. *Swinging the Censer: Reminiscences of Old Santa Barbara.* Santa Barbara, Calif.: Katherine Bell Cheney, 1931.

Berthold, Victor M. *The Pioneer Steamer California: 1848–1849.* Boston and New York: Houghton Mifflin, 1932.

Bingham, Edwin R. *Charles Fletcher Lummis: Editor of the Southwest.* San Marino, Calif.: Huntington Library, 1955.

Bixby-Smith, Sarah. *Adobe Days:* . . . *Life* . . . *on a Sheep Ranch in El Pueblo de Nuestra Señora de los Angeles* . . . Cedar Rapids, Iowa: Torch Press, 1926.

Buckbee, Edna. *The Saga of Old Tuolumne.* New York: Press of the Pioneers, 1935.

Burma, John H. *Spanish Speaking Groups in the United States.* Durham, N.C.: Duke University Press, 1954.

Burns, Walter Noble. *The Robin Hood of El Dorado: The Saga of Joaquin Murietta.* . . . New York: Coward-McCann, 1932.

Buschlen, John Preston. *Señor* [Eugenio] *Plummer: The Life and Laughter of an Old Californian.* Los Angeles: Times-Mirror Press, 1942.

Burton, George Ward. *Men of Achievement in the Great Southwest . . . Pioneer Struggles during Early Days in Los Angeles and Southern California.* Los Angeles: Los Angeles Times, 1904.

Caughey, John Walton. *Hubert Howe Bancroft, A Historian of the West.* Berkeley and Los Angeles: University of California Press, 1946.

————. *Gold is the Cornerstone.* Berkeley and Los Angeles: University of California Press, 1948.

————. *California.* 2d ed. New York: Prentice Hall, 1953.

————. *Their Majesties the Mob.* Chicago: University of Chicago Press, 1960.

Caughey, John. Walton, and Laree Caughey. *California Heritage: An Anthology of History and Literature.* Los Angeles: Ward Ritchie Press, 1962.

Cleland, Robert Glass. *The Cattle on a Thousand Hills: Southern California, 1850–1880.* San Marino, Calif.: Huntington Library, 1951.

————. *The Irvine Ranch of Orange County, 1810–1850.* San Marino, Calif.: Huntington Library, 1952.

Cornejo, Roberto Hernandez. *Los Chileños en San Francisco de California.* Valparaiso, Chile, 1930. 2 vols.

Dakin, Susana Bryant. *A Scotch Paisano: Hugo Reid's Life in California, 1832–1852.* Berkeley: University of California Press, 1939.

Daughters of the American Revolution. *The Valley of San Fernando.* N.p., 1924.

De Voto, Bernard. *The Year of Decision, 1846.* 1st ed., 1942. Boston: Houghton Mifflin, 1961.

Dumke, Glenn S. *The Boom of the 'Eighties in Southern California.* San Marino, Calif.: Huntington Library, 1944.

Ellison, William Henry. *A Self-Governing Dominion: California, 1849–1860.* Berkeley and Los Angeles: University of California Press, 1950.

Engelhardt, Fray Zephyrin. *San Gabriel Mission and the Beginnings of Los Angeles.* San Gabriel: Franciscan Herald Press, 1927.

Farquhar, Frances P., ed. *Joaquin Murieta, the Brigand Chief of California. . . .* 1st ed., 1859. San Francisco: Grabhorn Press, 1932.

Fisher, Anne B. *The Salinas: Upside-down River.* New York: Farrar and Rhinehart, 1945.

Foote, H. S. *Pen Pictures from the Garden of the World, or, Santa Clara County, California.* Chicago: Lewis Publishing Co., 1888.

Gamio, Manuel. *Mexican Immigration to the United States: A Study of Human Migration and Adjustment.* Chicago: University of Chicago Press, 1930.

Ganaway, Loomis Morton. *New Mexico and the Sectional Controversy, 1846–1861.* Albuquerque: University of New Mexico Press, 1944.

Gillingham, Robert C. *The Rancho San Pedro: The Story of a Famous Rancho in Los Angeles County and of Its Owners, the Dominguez Family.* Los Angeles: Dominguez Estate Co., 1961.

Goodwin, Cardinal Leonidas. *The Establishment of State Government in California, 1846–1850.* New York: Macmillan, 1914.

Grivas, Theodore. *Military Government in California, 1846–1850, with a Chapter on the Prior Use in Louisiana, Florida, and New Mexico* (Glendale, Calif., 1963), p. 154.

Guinn, James M. *A History of California and an Extended History of Los Angeles and Environs.* . . . Los Angeles: Historical Record Co., 1915. 3 vols.

Hinkel, Edgar J., and William E. McCann. *Oakland, 1852–1938: Some Phases of the Social, Political and Economic History.* . . . Oakland, Calif.: Oakland Public Library, 1939.

Hubbard, Harry P. *Vallejo.* Boston: Meador Publishing Co., 1941.

Jackson, Joseph Henry. *Anybody's Gold: The Story of California's Mining Towns.* New York: D. Appleton–Century, 1941.

———. *Bad Company: The Story of California's Legendary and Actual Stage-Robbers, Bandits, Highwaymen and Outlaws.* . . . New York: Harcourt, Brace and Co., 1949.

Keffer, Frank M. *History of San Fernando Valley.* Glendale, Calif.: Stillman Printing Co., 1934.

Kluckhohn, Florence, Florence Rockwood, and Fred L. Strodtbeck. *Variations in Value Orientations.* Evanston, Ill.: Row, Peterson, 1961.

[Lang, Herbert O.]. *A History of Tuolumne County, California.* San Francisco: B. F. Alley, 1882.

Layne, Gregg. *Annals of Los Angeles . . . 1769–1861.* San Francisco: California Historical Society, 1935.

Lindley, Walter, and J. P. Widney. *California of the South.* 1st ed., 1888. New York: Appleton, 1896.

Loyola, Sister Mary. *The American Occupation of New Mexico, 1821–1852.* Albuquerque: University of New Mexico Press, 1939.

McKinney, William M., ed. *California Jurisprudence: . . . the Law and Practice of the State of California.* San Francisco: Bancroft-Whitney Co., 1921. Vols. I, XVII.

McKittrick. Myrtle M. *Vallejo, Son of California.* Portland, Ore: Binfords and Mort, 1944.

McWilliams, Carey. *North from Mexico: The Spanish-Speaking People of the United States.* Philadelphia: J. B. Lippincott, 1949.

———. *Southern California Country: An Island on the Land.* New York: Duell, Sloan and Pearce, 1946.

Mead, Margaret. *Cultural Patterns and Technical Change.* New York: New American Library, 1955.

Mora. Jo. *Californios: The Saga of the Hard-Riding Vaqueros.* . . . Garden City, N.Y.: Doubleday and Co., 1949.

Morgan, Neil. *Westward Tilt: The American West Today.* New York: Random House, Inc., 1963.

Morrison, Annie L., and John Haydon. *History of San Luis Obispo County and Environs.* . . . Los Angeles, 1907.

Newhall, Ruth Waldo. *The Newhall Ranch: The Story of the Newhall Land*

and Farming Company. San Marino, Calif.: Huntington Library. 1958.
Newmark, Harris. *Sixty Years in Southern California, 1853–1913 . . . the Reminiscences of Harris Newmark.* New York: Knickerbocker Press, 1916.
Newmark, Marco R. *Jottings in Southern California History.* Los Angeles: Ward Ritchie Press, 1955.
Paul, Rodman Wilson. *California Gold: The Beginning of Mining in the Far West.* Cambridge: Harvard University Press, 1947.
Rahill, Peter J. *The Catholic Indian Missions and Grant's Peace Policy: 1870–1874.* Washington: Catholic University of America Press, 1953.
Rice, William B. *The Los Angeles Star, 1851–1864.* Berkeley: University of California Press, 1947.
——. *William Money: A Southern California Savant.* Los Angeles, 1943
Richman, Irving Berdine. *California under Spain and Mexico, 1535–1847. . . .* Boston: Houghton Mifflin Co., 1911.
Robinson, W. W. *Land in California: The Story of Mission Lands, Ranchos, Squatters, Mining Claims, Railroad Grants, Land Scrip, Homesteads.* Berkeley and Los Angeles: University of California Press, 1948.
——. *Los Angeles from the Days of the Pueblo, Together with a Guide to the Historic Old Plaza Area, Including the Pueblo de los Angeles State Historical Monument.* San Francisco: California Historical Society, 1959.
Rolle, Andrew F. *California: A History.* New York: Thomas Y. Crowell Co., 1963.
——. *An American in California: The Biography of William Heath Davis, 1822–1909.* San Marino, Calif.: Huntington Library, 1956.
Royce, Josiah. *California from the Conquest in 1846 to the Second Vigilance Committee in San Francisco: A Study of American Character.* 1st ed.. 1887. New York: Alfred A. Knopf, 1948.
Sanchez, Nellie Van de Grift. *Spanish Arcadia.* Los Angeles: Powell Publishing Co., 1929.
Shinn, Charles Howard. *Graphic Description of Pacific Coast Outlaws: Thrilling Exploits of their Arch-Enemy, Sheriff Harry N. Morse. . . .* 1st ed., 1890. Los Angeles: Westernlore Press, 1958.
——. *Mining Camps: A Study in American Frontier Government.* 1st ed., 1885. New York: Alfred A. Knopf, 1948.
Shuck, Oscar T. *History of the Bench and Bar of California.* Los Angeles: The Commercial Printing House, 1901.
Singletary, Otis A. *The Mexican War.* Chicago: University of Chicago Press 1960.
Southwest Conference on Educational and Social Problems of Rural and Urban Mexican-American Youth. *Summary of Proceedings of the Twelfth Annual Conference.* Los Angeles: Occidental College, 1963.
Taylor, Paul S. *Mexican Labor in the United States.* Berkeley: University of California Press, 1928. 6 vols.
Thompkins, Walter A. *Santa Barbara's Royal Rancho: The Fabulous History of Los Dos Pueblos.* Berkeley: Howell-North, 1960.
Treadwell, Edward F. *The Cattle King* [Henry Miller]: *A Dramatized Biography.* New York: Macmillan, 1931.

Truman, Ben C. *Semi-Tropical California.* San Francisco: A. L. Bancroft, 1874.

Velasco, José Francisco. *Noticias estadísticas del estado de Sonora, accompañadas de ligeras reflecsíones, deducidas de algunos documentos y conocimientos práticos adquiridos en mucho años.* ... Mexico, D.F., 1850.

Walker, Franklin. *A Literary History of Southern California.* Berkeley and Los Angeles: University of California Press, 1950.

Warner, Juan José, Benjamin Hayes, and J. P. Widney. *A Historical Sketch of Los Angeles County, California . . . September 8, 1771 to July 4, 1876.* . . . 1st ed., 1876. Los Angeles: O. W. Smith, 1936.

Williams, Stanley Thomas. *The Spanish Background of American Literature.* New Haven: Yale University Press, 1955. 2 vols.

Workman, Boyle. *The City That Grew* [Los Angeles] *As Told to Caroline Walker.* Los Angeles: Southland Publishing Co., 1935.

Works Project Administration. Writers Program. *Los Angeles: A Guide to the City and its Environs.* New York: Hastings House, 1941.

Yellow Bird, *pseud.* [John Rollins Ridge]. *The Life and Adventures of Joaquin Murieta.* 1st ed., 1854. Norman: University of Oklahoma Press, 1955.

ARTICLES

Adam, V. G. "The Pious Fund," *Historical Society of Southern California Annual Publications,* IV (1899), 228–233.

Bacon, Walter R. "Pioneer Courts and Lawyers of Los Angeles," *ibid.,* VI (1903–1906), 211–222.

Baker, Charles C. "Mexican Land Grants in California," *ibid.,* IX (1914), 236–244.

Barker, Charles A. "Elisha Oscar Crosby: A California Lawyer in the Eighteen-Fifties," *California Historical Society Quarterly,* XXVII (June, 1948), 133–140.

Barrows, Henry D. "Don Antonio María Lugo: A Picturesque Character of California," *Historical Society of Southern California Annual Publications,* III (1893–1896), 28–34.

———. "Reminiscences of Los Angeles in the Fifties and Early Sixties," *ibid.,* III (1893–1896), 55–62.

———. "Pio Pico: A Biographical and Character Sketch of the Last Mexican Governor of Alto California," *ibid.,* III (1893–1896), 74–79.

———. "Don W. Alexander," *ibid.,* IV (1897), 43–45.

———. "Don Ygnacio Del Valle," *ibid.,* IV (1897–1899), 213–215.

———. "The Story of a Native Californian [Ramón Valenzuela]," *ibid.,* IV (1897–1899), 114–118.

———. "Pioneer Schools of Los Angeles," *ibid.,* VIII (1909), 61–66.

Baxter, Edwin. "Leaves from the History of the Last Decade—1880-'90," *ibid.,* III (1893–1896), 74–79.

Browne, J. Ross. "Down in the Cinnabar Mines: A Visit to New Almaden in 1865," *Harper's Magazine,* XXI (Oct., 1865), 545–560.

Cooney, Percival J. "Southern California in Civil War Days," *Historical*

Society of Southern California *Annual Publications*, XIII (1924), 54–68.

Cosgrave, George, ed. "A Diplomatic Incident on the Little Mariposa," California Historical Society *Quarterly*, XXI (Dec., 1942), 358–362.

Dahlke, H. Otto. "Race and Minority Riots—A Study in the Typology of Violence," *Social Forces*, XXX (May, 1952), 419–425.

Dawson, Muir. "Southern California Newspapers, 1851–1876: A Short History and a Census," Historical Society of Southern California *Quarterly*, XXXII (March, June, 1950), 5–44, 139–174.

De Packman, Ana Begue. "Landmarks and Pioneers of Los Angeles in 1853," *ibid.*, XXVI (June–Sept., 1944), 56–95.

Dickson, Edward A. "How the Republican Party Was Organized in California," *ibid.*, XXX (Sept., 1948), 197–212.

Gates, Paul W. "Adjudication of Spanish-Mexican Land Claims in California," *Huntington Library Quarterly*, XXI (May, 1958), 213–236.

———. "California's Embattled Settlers," California Historical Society *Quarterly*, XLI (June, 1962), 99–129.

Guinn, James M. "Exceptional Years: A History of California Floods and Droughts," Historical Society of Southern California *Annual Publications*, I (1890), 33–39.

———. "The Plan of Old Los Angeles, and the Story of Its Highways and Byways," *ibid.*, III (1893–1896), 40–50.

———. "Siege and Capture of Los Angeles, September, 1846," *ibid.*, III (1893–1896), 47–54.

———. "Los Angeles in the Later Sixties and Early Seventies," *ibid.*, III (1893–1896), 63–68.

———. "The Sonoran Migration," *ibid.*, VIII (1909–1911), 31–36.

———. "The Passing of the Cattle Barons of California," *ibid.*, VIII (1909–1911), 50–60.

———. "The Romance of Rancho Realty," *ibid.*, VIII (1909–1911), 234–242.

Hargis, Donald E. "Native Californians in the Constitutional Convention of 1849," Historical Society of Southern California *Quarterly*, XXVI (March, 1954), 3–13.

Hawgood, John A. "The Pattern of Yankee Infiltration in Mexican Alto California, 1821–1846," *Pacific Historical Review*, XXVII (Feb., 1958), 27–37.

Hittell, John S. "Mexican Land-Claims in California," *Hutchings' Illustrated California Magazine*, II (July, 1857), 442–448.

Hunt, Aurora. "California Volunteers on Border Patrol, Texas and Mexico, 1862–1866," Historical Society of Southern California *Quarterly*, XXX (Dec., 1948), 265–275.

Hurt, Peyton. "The Rise and Fall of the 'Know-Nothing' Party in California," California Historical Society *Quarterly*, IX (March, 1930), 16–49.

McGloin, Bernard John, S.J. "The California Catholic Church in Transition, 1846–1850," California Historical Society *Quarterly*, XLII (March, 1963), 39–48.

McKain, Walter C., Jr., and Sarah Miles. "Santa Barbara County between Two Social Orders," *ibid.*, XXV (Dec., 1946), 311–318.

May, Ernest. "Tiburcio Vasquez," Historical Society of Southern California *Quarterly*, XXIX (1947), 123–134.

Newmark, Marco R. "The Story of Religion in Los Angeles, 1781–1900," Historical Society of Southern California *Quarterly*, XXVIII (March, 1946), 35–50.

Parker, Paul P. "The Roach-Belcher Feud," California Historical Society *Quarterly*, XXIX (March, 1950), 19–28.

Parks, Marion. "In Pursuit of Vanished Days: Visits to the Extant Historic Adobe Houses of Los Angeles County," Historical Society of Southern California *Annual Publications*, XIV (1928–1929), 7–64.

Pitt, Leonard. "The Beginnings of Nativism in California," *Pacific Historical Review*, XXX (Feb., 1961), 23–38.

Powell, Emily Browne. "A Modern Knight: Reminiscences of General M. G. Vallejo," *Harper's New Monthly Magazine*, LXXXVI (Dec., 1892–May, 1893), 786–789.

Rice, William B. "Southern California's First Newspaper: The Founding of the *Los Angeles Star*," Historical Society of Southern California *Quarterly*, XXIII (March, June, Sept.–Dec., 1941), 28–53, 87–99, 177–193.

Ripley, Vernette Snyder. "The San Fernando Pass and the Pioneer Traffic that Went Over It." *ibid.*, XXIX (March, Sept.–Dec., 1947), 9–48, 137–142; XXX (March, June, 1948), 43–64, 111–160.

Robinson, W. W. "Myth Making in the Los Angeles Area," *Southern California Quarterly*, XLV (March, 1963), 83–94.

Splitter, Henry Winfield. "Quicksilver at New Almaden," *Pacific Historical Review*, XXVI (Feb., 1957), 22–49.

Taylor, Paul S. "Foundations of California Rural Society," California Historical Society *Quarterly*, XXIX (Sept., 1945), 193–228.

Wright, Doris Marion. "The Making of Cosmopolitan California: An Analysis of Immigration, 1848–1870," *ibid.*, XIX (Dec., 1940), 323–343; XX (March, 1941), 65–79.

UNPUBLISHED THESES AND DISSERTATIONS

Henniker, Helen Blom. "The Beginnings of Nativism in California, 1848–1852." M.A. thesis, University of California, Berkeley, 1948.

Morefield, Richard Henry. "The Mexican Adaptation in American California, 1846–1875." M.A. thesis, University of California, Berkeley, 1955.

Pitt, Leonard. "The Foreign Miners' Tax of 1850: A Study of Nativism and Antinativism in Gold Rush California." M.A. thesis, University of California, Los Angeles, 1955.

Tays, George. "Revolutionary California: The Political History of California from 1820 to 1848," Ph.D. dissertation, University of California, Berkeley, 1932; rev. ed., 1934.

NEWSPAPERS

El Clamor Público (Los Angeles). 1855–1859
La Crónica (Los Angeles). 1872.

Los Angeles *Star* and *La Estrella de Los Angeles.* 1852–1859.
Los Angeles *Times.* 1882–1884.
Marysville *Herald.* 1850–1860.
Monterey *Gazette.* 1856–1869.
Sacramento *Daily Union.* 1855–1856.
Sacramento *Transcript.* 1850.
San Francisco *Call.* 1871–1878.
San Francisco *Daily Alta California.* 1850–1854.
San Francisco *Herald.* 1850–1852.
San Jose *Pioneer* and *Historical Review.* 1877–1879.
Santa Barbara *Gazette* and *La Gaceta.* 1855.
Sonora *Herald.* 1850–1855.
Stockton *Times.* 1850–1851.

Glossary of Ethnic Terms

Anglo: short for "Anglo-Saxon." New Mexican in origin, it was unknown in nineteenth-century California, but is coming into use now. Not at all used in the early part of this text.

Californio: "native-born Californian of Spanish-speaking parents." Yet, Glenn Dumke in *The Boom of the 'Eighties* applies it to all who owned land before the great Yankee migration of 1888, even Anglo-Saxons. Was in widespread use from the 1830's to the 1880's, and therefore is doubly applicable to this study. Rarely, *Californiano.*

cholo: "scoundrel," "half-breed," "servant." In California, after about 1830, the word actually meant "Mexican scoundrel," "Mexican half-breed," and so on.

gachupín: "Spaniard," "Spanish settler." In California this word had a slight connotation of "monarchist."

greaser: epithet for "mestizo," "Mexican," or "Spanish-speaking." It is as abusive a term as "nigger." Probably derives from U.S. Army camps in the Mexican War, but native-born Californians and neophyte Indians turned it around and applied it to disheveled-looking Yankee forty-niners.

gringo: "foreigner," "greenhorn," especially applied to Anglo-Saxons. Derisive but not nearly so abusive as "greaser." *Webster's New International Dictionary* (2d ed., unabridged) links it to "gibberish." Some suppose a connection with the song sung by the U.S. Army in Mexico, "Green Grow the Violets." Seldom capitalized.

hidalgo: "illustrious one," "nobleman." It has sometimes been loosely applied to the California scene (see Franklin Walker's *Literary History of Southern California*) to draw attention to the aristocratic, Old World culture of the early inhabitants, but it has never gained favor among California specialists.

Hispano: short for the awkward "Hispano-American," which parallels "Anglo-American." The word comes from New Mexico or Texas and is scarcely ever used in California, even to this day.

Latin American: practically interchangeable in this study with "Spanish American" (although technically more inclusive, embracing also persons of Portuguese and French ancestry).

Mexican: should be reserved strictly for Mexican nationals. Often misapplied to United States citizens of Mexican background, it thus takes on a slightly derogatory connotation.

Mexican-American: a valuable twentieth-century term, although cumbersome. It parallels "Irish-American," "German-American," and so on. It is more precise than "Mexican" when applied to Mexicans having United States citizenship, but is somewhat illogical in that Mexico *is* in America.

mestizo: "person of mixed Indian and Spanish background." A proper racial term.

native Californian: for present uses, "one who is born in California of Spanish-speaking parents," or, "one who is born in Mexico but is a long-term California resident." Synonymous with *Californio,* and sometimes expanded into "native-born Californian." Was used from about 1846 on, but gradually lost meaning as more and more Anglo-Saxons could claim to be "natives." Strictly speaking, the term should be applied only to Indians.

Norte Americano: "One who comes from the United States."

Spaniard: "one who is born in Spain." Widely misused by Anglo-Saxons as a catchall which (sometimes deliberately) obliterates all sense of nationality. The native-born used it (or, the Spanish term *Españole*) for themselves, yet *they* always remained conscious of national differences and gave it the connotation of "Spanish-speaking." When the native-born Californians meant to say "one who is born in Spain" they frequently said, *gachupin.*

Spanish American: a useful term, used by contemporaries and widely used in this study. Practically interchangeable with Latin American (although actually slightly narrower).

Spanish-speaking: a most apt term, because it draws attention to the lowest common denominator—language, though it was never used in the nineteenth century. It gained official status in the U.S. Census of 1950. It does, however, embrace many who speak Spanish and yet are peripheral to this study, such as Chileans and neophyte Indians.

Yankee: refers to immigrants from the United States or Britain who are of Anglo-Saxon background. The disadvantage of its use is that it negates the more customary regional meaning elsewhere in the United States. Universally used in California from about 1846 on, but never spelled *Yanqui* there.

Index

Abarca, Luis, 122
Adams, Edson, 97
Agriculture: in Mexican California, 12; cattle, 76, 244, 245–246, 247; Midwestern ideal of, 87–88; sheep, 247, 253–254, 254–255; developments in south, 254
Agua Mansa, 245
Aguilar, Blas, 123
Aguilar, Cristóbal: on Board of Supervisors, 134, 137; as mayor of Los Angeles, 271; and Bancroft, 281
Aguirro, José Antonio, 220–221
Aguirre, Martin, 269
Alameda County, 118
Alemany, Bishop Joseph S.: arrives in California, 214; on anti-Catholicism, 215, 216; as leader, 217; and imposition of tithe, 219; on language issue, 226; and aid to Indians, 285
Alexander, D. W., 134, 139
Alexander, H. N., 164
Alvarado, Ignacia, 264
Alvarado, Joaquina, 93
Alvarado, Juan Bautista, 7, 182; as radical, 3, 4; and secularization, 9; and patriotism, 13; overthrows Gutiériez, 19; and American conquest of California, 20, 23, 24–25; and military government, 35; as bankrupt, 36; retires from politics, 43, 138–139; on David Jacks, 101; and Badillo lynching, 179; as president of Islas' junta, 211; recollections of, 281
Alviso, Francisco, 259
Alvitre, Félix, 160–161
Alvitre, José Claudio, 257
Amador, José María, 280
Amador, Ramón, 257, 261

Amador County, 78, 80, 81
Amat, Bishop Tadeo: replaces Alemany, 217; petition of Los Angeles to, 220; and anti-Catholicism, 223; and Los Angeles orphanage, 224, 225; moves to Los Angeles, 227
American Party. See Know-Nothings
Anaheim: Californio population of, 263
Arao, Jacinto, 71
Ardillero, Guerro, 169
Arellanes, Jesús, 258–259
Argüello, Francisco, 272
Argüello, Luis, 113–114, 115
Argüello, Santiago, 3
Arizona, 45, 230
Arrelanes, Teodoro, 93
Arzaga, José, 267
Asistencia of Our Lady of Angels, 218
Association for the Preservation of the Missions. See Land Marks Club
Australians: in mines, 56, 57; as criminals, 76
Avila, Enrique, 184
Avila, Juan, 196
Avila, Susan, 225
Ayalya, Francisco, 237
Azusa: Californio population of, 263

Badillo, Felipe, 180
Badillo, Francisco, 179
Baja California, 285; proposed annexation of, 206; William Walker in, 207; Pico property in, 250; California bandits in, 259
Baker, Robert S., 268
Bancroft, Hubert Howe: on Bear Flag Rebellion, 26; on vigilantes, 70; on José Castro, 138; memoirs of, 280–281; accepts Joaquin legend, 285

Tirado, Ramón, 223
Torres, Manuel, 240
Trade, 12
Tuolumne County, 61, 71
Twist, W. W., 123, 136, 171
Twist's Southern Rifles, 218

Union City, 83
Utah, 45, 230

Valenzuela, Joaquín, 80
Valenzuela, Joaquín (alias Joaquín Ocomorenia), 176, 178
Valenzuela, Juan (of Flores' gang), 169
Valenzuela, Juan (rancher), 170
Vallejo, Mariano, 55, 111, 182, 284; as radical, 2–3; on family life, 12; and Americans, 23, 278, 279; and Bear Flag Rebellion, 27–30; situation of, after war, 36, 37; as agent for Indian affairs, 38; at constitutional convention, 43, 44, 45; on forty-niners, 52; land troubles of, 97, 118; in state office, 139, 140; retires from politics, 141; and Pablo de la Guerra, 146–147; on San Francisco vigilantes, 193; on Frémont, 198–199; and Islas, 211; and church, 215; and Juárez, 243; daughters of, 268; writes history, 280; and Bancroft, 281; death of, 282
Vallejo, Pedro, 257
Vallejo, Platon, 240, 242, 268
Vallejo, Salvador, 146; and Bear Flag Rebellion, 27; situation of, after war, 36; and land law of 1851, 80, 96; and Frémont, 140; commands Native Cavalry, 230, 233, 242; in politics, 239–240; on conquest, 279; death of, 282
Vallejo, Udislao, 242
Varela ("El Chino"), 172
Varela, Servulio, 33, 233, 244
Vasquez, Tiburcio, 75, 257, 262
Vega, Placidio, 242–244
Vejar, Ricardo, 110
Verdugo, Julio, 133, 251–252
Victoria, Manuel, 4, 139
Vigilance Committee of 1849, San Francisco, 64, 178
Vigilance Committee of 1856, San Francisco, 193

Vigilantes, 198, 207; in San Francisco, 64, 178, 193; and lynching of Juanita, 73; in 1850's, 76, 77, 82; in Los Angeles race conflict, 154–159, 164–166; opposition to, 165, 178; against southern bandidos, 169–180; in Santa Clara, 172; in Santa Barbara, 174; Ramirez on, 192–193; in 1860's, 257–260
Vignes, Luis, 224, 227

Walker, William: in Baja California, 207–208; in Nicaragua, 209
Wall, Isaac, 99
Warner, J. J., 140
Warner, John, 19
Weller, John, 202
Wetbacks, 67, 293
Whaling, Marshal, 159
Whigs, 202; in 1850's, 135; and Know-Nothings, 137; seek Mexican vote, 139; lose power, 142, 199; in coalition, 203
Wilkes, Charles, 15, 16
Wilson, B. D., 109, 166, 224
Wilson, Benito, 124
Winston, James, 268
Wolfskill, William, 124, 204
Women (American California): in mining communities, 72; in Los Angeles, 124; dress of, 128, 252; education of, 187; and travel, 252; in courts, 261; working, 265; mestizo, 268; effect of conquest on, 279
Women (Mexican California): attendance of, at Mass, 4, 215; Dana on, 15; and Yankees, 23
Woods, James, 222
Workman, Rowland, and Temple, 106, 107
Workman, William, 204

Yorba, Bernardo, 110, 156, 267
Yorba, José Antonio, 156
Yuba River, 58, 60
Yuma, 232, 235

Zavaleta, Doroteo, 156, 192
Zurita, Manuel, 179